My Bombay Kitchen

TRADITIONAL AND MODERN PARSI HOME COOKING

NILOUFER ICHAPORIA KING

Foreword by Alice Waters

UNIVERSITY OF CALIFORNIA PRESS
BERKELEY LOS ANGELES LONDON

THE PUBLISHER GRATEFULLY ACKNOWLEDGES THE
GENEROUS CONTRIBUTION TO THIS BOOK PROVIDED
BY THE ASIAN STUDIES ENDOWMENT FUND OF THE
UNIVERSITY OF CALIFORNIA PRESS FOUNDATION

University of California Press, one of the most distinguished university presses in the United States, enriches lives around the world by advancing scholarship in the humanities, social sciences, and natural sciences. Its activities are supported by the UC Press Foundation and by philanthropic contributions from individuals and institutions. For more information, visit www.ucpress.edu.

University of California Press
Berkeley and Los Angeles, California

University of California Press, Ltd.
London, England

© 2007 by The Regents of the University of California

All line illustrations are by David Shaw King.

Library of Congress Cataloging-in-Publication Data

King, Niloufer Ichaporia, 1943–
    My Bombay kitchen : traditional and modern Parsi home cooking /
Niloufer Ichaporia King.
        p. cm.
    Includes bibliographical references and index.
    ISBN-13: 978-0-520-24960-8 (cloth : alk. paper).
    1. Cookery, Indic—Southern style.   2. Cookery—India—Bombay.
    I. Title.
TX724.5.I4K54 2007
641.5954—dc22   2006037040

Manufactured in the United States of America

15 14 13 12 11 10 09 08 07
10 9 8 7 6 5 4 3 2 1

To my mother and her mother

CONTENTS

FOREWORD | *Alice Waters*

Niloufer Ichaporia King is one of the great cooks I know. Her food is so unexpected, and at the same time so exactly what I want to eat, that since I know I can't reasonably expect an invitation to dine at her house as often as I want, it is profoundly frustrating to me that she has never opened a restaurant. Whenever I *do* have the privilege of sharing her table, I'm as speechless with delight as when I first walked into her house and kitchen more than twenty years ago.

Dinner with Niloufer and her husband, David King, is wonderful in ways beyond my powers of description. Before you even turn the handle of the period doorbell of their modest stick-style San Francisco Victorian and hear its vintage bicycle-bell "brring," you know something special is up. Your nostrils will have been beguiled by the jasmine blooming in the dooryard, and your eyes will have been drawn to some mysterious temporary adornment of the porch—various objects, mineral, vegetable, or manmade, arranged with the sensibility of an Andy Goldsworthy. Time will be slowing down. You will have a perfect threshold moment.

Once indoors, you will hear the raucous squawk of Niloufer and David's irascible, iridescent pet parrot, Ordle; the noble strains of Niloufer's grand piano from upstairs and her equally musical contralto laughter; and, as you look around, your own little gasps of wonder at the sight of more curiosities than you could possibly take in—from Niloufer's coconut-grater collection to the gorgeous seashells that David began to amass as a boy scientist. Both David and Niloufer are travelers, scholars, and connoisseur polymaths with long family histories; and libraries, collections, and heirlooms—which include that grand piano as well as such things as an African ceremonial bowl the size of a small canoe—fill their narrow house to overflowing. Every object in the house has a story, and all the stories are fascinating. The effect of it all is overwhelming and soothing at the same time. You can't help but feel a little like a kid in a treasure house with the wisest, most charming curators.

Their house itself was built as stacked railroad flats and retains its original floor plan, so there is a crowded kitchen on every floor, where—to use a silly catchphrase without irony for once—the magic happens. Niloufer's home cooking is exotic in the best, uncondescending sense: it is intriguing, unusual, and unforgettable. The last time I ate at Niloufer and David's there were roasted cashews with *ajwain* in the kitchen, and then we sat down to sweet potatoes with chile and lime, a vindaloo with flavor as deep as the Marianas Trench, a perfectly dressed salad, and, for dessert, the lushest California mangoes I've had so far this season. Every dish was something I would want to prepare myself.

Built on the culinary foundation of the Parsi cuisine of her native Bombay, Niloufer's cooking is rooted in traditions of hospitality thousands of years old—one of which is an ancient tradition of culinary appropriation, which Niloufer cheerfully maintains today. With negligible religious prohibitions to restrict their diet, Parsis have enthusiastically adopted and adapted whatever recipe took their fancy, in the process creating what Niloufer calls "magpie cuisine" (magpies, of course, being notoriously larcenous scavenger birds).

When Niloufer's Parsi ancestors migrated to southern India from Persia, they were perfectly situated to develop a memorable fusion of Persian, Indian, and, eventually, European foodways. The Parsification process continues in California. See, for example, Niloufer's mouthwatering menus, so many of which include salads of garden-fresh lettuces, herbs, and other greens. I would flatter myself that I was an influence on Niloufer's cooking if I didn't know that, long before we met, she was already as crazy about salad as I am.

After leaving India at age nineteen, Niloufer migrated to California via Baltimore and Madison, Wisconsin, with her notebook of family recipes (dictated by her mother's cook) and a Bombay women's club cookbook ever at her side. She had always been keenly interested in food, and as a graduate student in anthropology at the University of California, she cooked her way through school, catering various sorts of gatherings and later assisting and cooking for visiting celebrity chefs at the Great Chefs of France cooking school at the Mondavi Winery. From the moment we were introduced by Marion Cunningham, we became fast friends. Her influence on the Chez Panisse family of cooks, waiters, and customers has been manifold. Thanks to Niloufer's omnivorous enthusiasm and expertise, many of us learned first from her about tropical and subtropical ingredients and techniques from all over Central and South America, Asia, Africa, and the Pacific. (Long before anyone else in America was paying attention to the worldwide phenomenon of street foods, for example, she was doing field research, taking notes, sharing information, and, as early as the 1980s, cooking street foods for us—memorably for Chez Panisse's twentieth birthday in 1991.) She wears her erudition like one of her saris: gracefully. (For proof, browse through the indispensable glossary she has provided for this book.)

Niloufer's most notable gift to Chez Panisse has been a new holiday for us to celebrate. Thanks to her, every year for almost twenty years, on or near the date of the vernal equinox, the restaurant has observed the Parsi new year with a feast that Niloufer graciously oversees. The menu invariably incorporates traditional Parsi dishes such as *faluda,* the New Year's milk shake, and the festivities include stenciling beautiful Parsi designs in colored chalk on the restaurant's threshold, steps, and courtyard. Now we can't imagine the restaurant's festal year (which also includes the restaurant's birthday, the café's birthday on April Fools' Day, and a garlic festival on Bastille Day) without Parsi New Year.

Although I've never been able to persuade Niloufer to start a restaurant (preferably open twenty-four hours a day, with savory breakfasts a specialty), she has now given us a remarkable cookbook. Not only is it that almost unheard-of thing, an accurate record of the way a wonderful home cook actually cooks, it is also an accurate record of a largely unknown, but thoroughly accessible, authentic, and coherent cuisine—one that deserves recognition for its sheer deliciousness. Now that Parsi cooking is disappearing, falling victim to modernity and population decline, it is especially fitting that this cuisine reach the broader audience who will be enchanted by this book: culinary historians, professional cooks, home cooks, weekend dabblers, and nightstand fantasy cooks alike. The recipes work, too.

ACKNOWLEDGMENTS

Apart from my immediate family—my parents and my auxiliary mother, my maternal aunt Mani Masi—there are four friends who are responsible for this book. Almost twenty years ago, Alice Waters, who loves all new years, suggested we celebrate my favorite of the three observed by Parsis, Jamshedji Navroz, at Chez Panisse. There she has given me carte blanche, year after year, to play with ideas about Parsi food. Ten years after our first Navroz dinner at Chez Panisse, Catherine Brandel and Fran McCullough suggested that, since my wide-ranging interests clearly sprang from a polyglot Parsi approach, it would be a good idea to begin right there and write a book about how Parsis eat. Two years later, Alta Tingle gave me the keys to her Healdsburg house so that I could work on an unwieldy investigation of tropical food plants, but at the end of a week in isolation, I came back with the nucleus of this book instead. Thank you, Alice, for your friendship and generous-hearted support. Thank you, Catherine, sister of my heart and colleague for close to thirty years. Thank you, Alta, for the ongoing gift of solitude in beauty, and thanks to Fran for being coach and midwife to this book throughout its long and sometimes impossibly difficult gestation, and for never being too busy to talk.

In the Parsi sphere, my family and my parents' friends taught me that good food can indeed be taken for granted. On my mother's side, thanks to my cousin Nazneen Dubash, and on my father's side, thanks to my cousins Lyla Bavadam (my favorite prowling companion), Roshan Bavadam, Jeroo and Kurus Coyaji, Katy and Pheroze Dalal, and Bomi and Rati Ichaporia. Affectionate thanks to Parsi friends Dhun Bana, Myrna and Sam Dalal, Katy Doctor, Piloo Ginwalla, Rustom Jeejeebhoy, Firoza Kanga, who appears throughout this book, Amy Nicholls, Shirin and Jehangir Sabavala, Shirin and Noshir Sethna, Gool Vakharia, and Statira and Farrokh Wadia. Mehlli Gobhai, the older brother I never had, enfolded me into his household, where Irene and Manoj

Suryavanshi and Dharamraj Madai took tender care of me. Ardeshir Khambata stayed up all night to read and comment upon the manuscript. To Jamini Ahluwalia, Vanraj Bhatia, Esther and Raju Daswani, Meera and Bhawat Devidayal, Malu Divecha, Chandu Morarji, Salome and Pranav Parikh, Rajni and Shirish Patel, Neeta and Sushil Premchand, Asha Sheth, and Nanda and Birendra Singh, my thanks for their generous hospitality and for many wondrous food adventures in non-Parsi Bombay kitchens.

At the University of California, Berkeley, thanks to Frank Norick of the Phoebe Apperson Hearst Museum (then the Lowie Museum), who earmarked funds for me to make a field collection of Parsi ethnographic material. I am forever grateful to Nelson Graburn, my adviser in the Department of Anthropology, for encouraging my research, which at the time was not regarded as being within the purview of anthropology. Thanks, too, to colleagues in anthropology for conversations and explorations, particularly Winifred Dahl, Barbara and Eberhard Fischer, Donna Garaventa, Pamela Johnson, Melissa and Julius Kassovic, Kirin Narayan, and Juree Vichit-Vadakan.

John Harris of Aris Books offered me his test kitchen to give a series of classes in which to explore ideas in tropical cuisines; Sue Conley and Peggy Smith of Cowgirl Creamery, then at Bette's Oceanview Diner, sponsored another series on rice and coconut; Alta Tingle again provided a venue for more explorations; James David and Gary Pease arranged a class at the Word of Mouth kitchen in Austin; and, most recently, Amaryll Schwertner and Lori Regis of Boulette's Larder have allowed me to improvise with ideas from this book. Thank you to all of them.

Katherine Cowles got the book off the ground, and Lizbeth Hasse and Jan Constantine moved it forward when it was badly stuck. Fritz Streiff and I sat side by side for countless hours, physically and in cyberspace, through the first four versions of the manuscript. My thanks to him for conversation and debate, for his help in turning wayward, eccentric narratives and recipes into cookbook form, and for introducing the book to my present publishers. Rita Fabrizio, Norman Smith, and Praveen Raj Kumar have all helped with my endless computer crises.

At the University of California Press, my thanks to Hannah Love for her whole-hearted sponsorship of the project; to my editor, Dore Brown, for her intellectual rigor cushioned with patience, good humor, and enthusiasm; to Chalon Emmons for her meticulous reading of the manuscript; to Thérèse Shere for her legendary capabilities as an indexer; and to Nola Burger for turning the manuscript into a beautiful book.

At Chez Panisse, Mary Canales, Patricia Curtan, Phillip Dedlow, Kelsie Kerr, Jean-Pierre Moullé, Lindsey Shere, Alan Tangren, and my kitchen hero, David Tanis, are among the brilliant cooks who have worked on the Parsi New Year dinners that end up involving the office, dining room, and flower people as well as the kitchen. I thank all of you, named and unnamed, for the deep satisfaction of working with you year after year. In the food and cooking sphere, along with those mentioned earlier, I thank Eleanor Bertino, Randal Breski, Cecilia Chiang, Gary Danko, Janet Fletcher, Christopher Hirsheimer, Nancy Jenkins, Diana Kennedy, Roberta Klugman, Peggy Knickerbocker, Sibella Krauss, Sue Moore, Davia Nelson, Gilbert Pilgram, Gayle Pirie and John Clark, Judy Rodgers, Stephen Singer (my wine guru) and Michel Boynton, Patricia Unterman (my food-prowling companion) and Tim Savinar, and Paula Wolfert for friendship and enthusiastic encouragement throughout the long gestation of this book.

Recipes need testers. Thanks to all of the friends who have been pressed into service. Caroline Adams, Christopher and Jane Adams, Bob Carrau and Tony Oltranti (my breakfast guinea pigs), Ben Davidson and Gregory Riley, and Julie Steinberg and David Abel were my principal testers. Among the many friends who've cheered the project along, sometimes summoned to eat at very short notice, I thank Bill Brown, Ethan Chorin, Mary Clemmey, Chuck Cody, Usha Cunningham, Alice Erb, Denise Fiedler, Richard Gilbert, the Graburn family, the Gray family, Shireen Kanga, Christina Kim, Yogini and Raj Kumar, Andrea Lewin, Denise Moullé, Valerie Reichert and Ira Schrank (who photographed the stencils for this book), Richard Schoenbrun, David Strada, Malgosia Szemberg, Yoko Tahara, Vimal and Jag Talwar, Ellen and Bill Taubman, and Alice Zacca.

Cooks need markets. It's also helpful to remind ourselves that there was a time when curry leaves couldn't be found in U.S. grocery stores. The Fujimoto family of Berkeley's Monterey Market have my enduring gratitude for being far ahead of others, for taking risks, and for absorbing the financial loss of unsold bins of unfamiliar fruits and vegetables, which they continued to put before the public until finally there was a market for them. The Monterey Market, the Berkeley Bowl, and the burgeoning farmers' markets all over the United States have contributed to a global cuisine that might not have been possible anywhere else in the world. My particular thanks go to the many vendors at San Francisco's greatest unsung cultural pageant, our nearby Alemany Market, source of both comfort and inspiration.

For conversations about plants, thanks go to Scot Medbury of the Brooklyn Botanical Gardens, Bian Tan of Botanical Gardens Conservancy International, Dr. Chin See Chung of the Singapore Botanic Garden, and Herbert Philips of the University of California, Berkeley. For questions about fish, thanks to Paul Johnson and Monterey Fish and William N. Eschmeyer of the Steinhart Aquarium. For correspondence on Persian matters, thanks to Touraj Douryaee of California State University, Fullerton. Neeta Premchand came to my aid with Gujarati translation, and I received later help from David Nelson, Babu Suthar, and Aditya Behl of the University of Pennsylvania. I owe special thanks to Panna Naik, poet and former lecturer in Gujarati at the University of Pennsylvania, who reviewed all the Gujarati equivalents for the title and for chapter headings.

Thanks to Alicia Baccay for taking care of my mother, thereby allowing me to work on the book.

Most of all, thanks to my husband, David King, partner in countless market and kitchen adventures, illustrator of this book, honorary Parsi.

INTRODUCING BOMBAY, PARSIS, AND THE AUTHOR

A Bombay kitchen can be anywhere in the world. All you need is an insatiable curiosity about food and a love for sharing it. Over the past forty or so years since I first left India, my Bombay kitchen, a Parsi one, has moved across the United States from the East Coast to the Midwest and now finds itself settled in San Francisco, where I've lived for twenty-five years with the illustrator of this book, my husband, David King; my mother, Shireen Ichaporia; and an eccentric Amazon parrot who rules over us all.

A freewheeling approach to food isn't unique to this house, of course; it's characteristic of open-minded port cities like San Francisco and Bombay (which Mumbai will always be to those of us who grew up there before the name changed). It is especially characteristic of Bombay's Parsis, who carry on an ancient tradition of xenophilia wherever we find ourselves on the globe—and Parsis are now sprinkled everywhere. Generous estimates have our current worldwide population at about seventy-five thousand, concentrated in Bombay with large clumps in North America and Australia. The prediction that by 2020 our numbers will have dropped to twenty-five thousand startled Parsis into paying attention to what was disappearing fast. Under the aegis of UNESCO's PARZOR (Parsi Zoroastrian) project, there's a tardy but earnest effort at the ethnographic salvage of the remains of a culture UNESCO declared to be three thousand years old in 2004.

When I began writing this book in 2000, I didn't yet know about the UNESCO project. It was the year of my mother's ninetieth birthday. I thought of this account of Parsi food transmitted from grandmother to mother to me not as salvage ethnogastronomy but as a way to acknowledge this milestone in both our lives. Transcribing notes and mining my memories brought on an awareness of the persistence of my sense of Parsiness, far away in time and space from my origins in Bombay, and of how much of that Parsiness is wrapped up in thinking about food, past, present, and to come. I'd always taken my Parsiness for granted as a comfortable cloak, worn with unquestioning ignorance in my parents' household and my own, even more secular than theirs. In common with many other Parsis who have gone through similar educations, for whom English is the only language in which we're literate, the truest, most unself-conscious expression of my Parsi self has been through simple everyday things, mainly cooking. It's a style of cooking that's rare because there aren't many of us, and there are very few restaurants that serve it. Parsi food flourishes best in a private world of households, clubs, and sumptuous ceremonial feasts. *My Bombay Kitchen* invites you into that world by leading you through one family's story as it relates to food. To put that story into context, we need to take some long leaps through Parsi history and the story of Bombay, the city that has become our cultural matrix.

First, here's a brief introduction to Parsis. Our story begins in Persia with the birth of the prophet Zoroaster in the seventh century B.C.E.—a hotly disputed date, with many claiming that Zoroaster was born far earlier, about 6000 B.C.E. Zoroaster started a religion based on divine revelation. This religion influenced a civilization that at its height stretched from Greece to Hindustan, central Asia to Egypt. Although the three great Persian empires—Achaemenid, Arsacid or Parthian, and Sassanian— stretched their boundaries as far as they could go in all directions, it was never their express mission to ordain or enforce mass conversions on conquered soil. Subject people such as the Jews were allowed to go on as before, but their Persian rulers' beliefs had an impact on Judaism that eventually carried over into Christianity in the concepts of a supreme deity, heaven, hell, the coming of a messiah, and a final day of judgment, to name a few. (The three wise men of Christian lore bearing gifts from afar were possibly magi, Zoroastrian priests, bearing the most precious substances known to them.)

Then and now, the essence of Zoroastrianism is the belief in an ongoing struggle between light and dark forces within each human being. Popular imagination has us classified as fire worshippers because the forces of light embodied in the ultimate godhead, Ahura Mazda, are symbolized by the sacred fires kept burning in the inner sanctums of our temples. To defeat the forces of darkness, personified by Angra Mainyu, followers of Zoroaster are urged to concentrate on "good thoughts, good words, good deeds," a mantra easily rattled off but harder to act on. As embodied in the Avesta, our holy book, which contains the teachings of Zoroaster in his words, ours is a religion of responsibility in the personal and public spheres; and indeed, this is how I see my Parsiness, a religion of conduct rather than of piety. In an ideal state, all nations and peoples are equal, as are men and women; harmonious coexistence is one of life's goals, and that includes stewardship of the land and water. Striving for the greater good against the darker forces does not mean hair shirts, stern faces, and forced attendance at religious services. To the contrary, a full, hedonistic enjoyment of the physical and material worlds fortifies us all against the malign forces ever lurking about. One way of keeping them at bay is to take joy in good food and drink in happy company, and to share good fortune with the less favored among us.

Herodotus, describing in the fifth century B.C.E. the material splendor of Persian life, commented on the delicacies placed before Persian generals—perhaps the first and last good review ever given to army food. Two hundred years later, Alexander the Great defeated the Persians under Darius, sacked their capital, Persepolis, and destroyed their libraries, but was seduced by their food and culture, which he took with him onward to India and then back to the Mediterranean. Over time the Persian Empire revived, casting off the Hellenic influences that followed Alexander during the Seleucid period in favor of a more fervid Zoroastrianism, which eventually reached its peak during the four centuries of Sassanian rule. It was in this last period that Zoroaster's teachings, thus far committed to memory for centuries by generation after generation of hereditary priests, were finally put in writing in a specially devised alphabet. Under the Sassanians, an already rich civilization grew even more elaborate, its priesthood more powerful than ever before. Although there's less archaeological material from the Sassanian period than from earlier ones, the ruins of their capital, Ctesiphon (Tisphoon), still tell of the magnificence of their court.

It was possibly the top-heavy complacency that goes with long-entrenched luxury that gave the desert-hardened Arab invaders their advantage in 641 C.E., when the last Zoroastrian dynasty finally gave way under Yazdegard III to Islamic rule. Once more, though, the victors were seduced by the vanquished. Although Islam replaced Zoroastrianism as the state religion, Persian culture continued, shifting its center from Ctesiphon to a nearby settlement, Baghdad ("garden of Dad," a revered dervish of the time), and Zoroastrian priestly scholars continued to produce works on religion, customs and manners, and cosmology several hundred years into the Arab occupation.

While the Arabs were spreading the good news about Persian food in their westward expansion across the Mediterranean, a small, stubborn band of diehard Zoroastrians resisted conversion to Islam, holding fast to the old faith, carrying its symbolic flame, the Iranshah, with them in their wanderings. These were the ancestors of people who would later be called *Pars-i,* "people of Pars," or Persia. In the absence of solid evidence, dates are vague and controversial, but there's general agreement that it took about a century and a half after the Arab conquest for this band to reach the port of Hormuz, where they prepared to set sail for India in seven ships. According to the most reliable sources, it was about 936 C.E., another disputed date, that they reached landfall at Diu, a barren island off the Gujarat coast of western India. Nineteen years later, in response to signs and portents, they set sail again, this time landing on the Gujarat coast itself, at a place they named Sanjan after their town in the province of Khorasan.

India was not unknown to the Persians of that time. There were long-established trade routes linking the two civilizations by land and sea. The *Qissa-i Sanjan,* a narrative poem written much later, in 1600 C.E., suggests that it may have been the awareness of previous Persian settlers in India and the country's reputation for tolerance that prompted the exiles to head toward India. All Parsi children are told various versions of the legend of how our ancestors were allowed to settle in India. The priestly

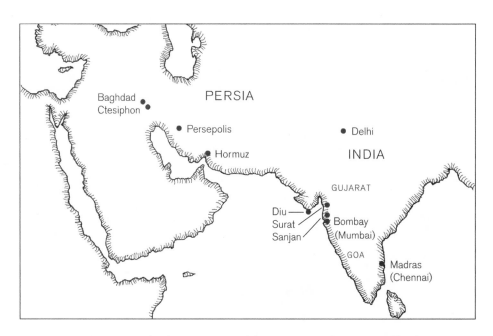

Ancient Persia and India. Parsis migrated from Hormuz on the Persian Gulf to the Gujarat coast of western India. (Modern cities are included for context.)

leaders were brought before the local ruler, Jadi or Jadhav Rana, who presented them with a vessel brim-full of milk to signify that the surrounding lands could not possibly accommodate any more people. The Parsi head priest responded by slipping some sugar into the milk (or as another version has it, a coin; yet others, a coin followed by sugar) to signify how the strangers would enrich the local community without displacing anyone. Whether it was the coin in the milk or the *Qissa-i Sanjan*'s more factual account of the Parsi priest's eloquence in pleading his case, Jadi Rana granted the exiles lands to cultivate and gave them permission to continue practicing their religion unhindered if they would observe certain conditions. They were to lay down their arms, adopt local dress, respect local customs, conduct weddings and other ceremonies involving processions only at night, and learn the local language, Gujarati, which became our mother tongue. Farsi, the Persian word for the language of modern Iran, is in large part the ancient Pahlavi language our exiled ancestors agreed to stop using in favor of Gujarati. Modern Parsi Gujarati, a creole language, still uses many Persian words, along with liberal helpings of English and any other handy language as it fits the circumstance. Hindu speakers of Gujarati find our spoken version of the language hysterically funny.

For the next five hundred years or so, Parsis spread out along the coastal plains of Gujarat, some engaged in agriculture and trade, some in weaving and shipbuilding, others in their hereditary priestly profession, and all slowly forging a tradition of adapting, adopting, and enriching. In the fourteenth century, the Muslim occupation of Gujarat resulted in turmoil and tragedy shared with the local Hindus, but at no point then or in the following centuries of Mughal rule was there the drive to convert all nonbelievers to Islam that forced our ancestors out of Persia. Under the sixteenth-century Mughal emperor Akbar's ecumenical rule, Dastur Meherji Rana, a venerated priest, was summoned to court to explain the religion and customs of the Parsis, receiving land and honors in exchange. It was the arrival of the Portuguese and the British that brought the most dramatic changes to the placid, pastoral rhythm of Parsi life in Gujarat.

Vasco da Gama sailed around the Cape of Good Hope and landed on the western coast of India in 1498, establishing the first European colonial presence on the subcontinent. The Portuguese based themselves in Goa, but pushed farther north into Gujarat to establish fortifications and gather not only riches but also converts. The seven islands known then as Mumbai were not considered to be as important as the ancient mainland ports of Cheul and Bassein. Mumbai was then populated by the Koli fishing community, who had been joined over the centuries by farmers and toddy tappers (hereditary collectors of palm sap) from the mainland. Arab pirates trolled the seas. Garcia da Orta, a Portuguese physician and botanist, established a finca there, which would be transformed into the citadel of the British East India Company and later into a vast, crowded metropolis that hasn't stopped expanding. The fiercely proud indigenous Kolis have never given up their claim to ownership, continuing to mend their nets and dry their fish out in the streets, right in the midst of skyscrapers and traffic, heedless of blaring horns and glaring drivers.

Wanting a chunk of the spice trade so lucrative for the Dutch, the British East India Company arrived in Gujarat in 1608 bearing a charter granted by Elizabeth I. In 1615, with the Mughal emperor Jehangir's approval, the British established a factory (or trading post) in the Gujarati town of Surat, which soon became an important entrepôt thronged by Dutch, French, and Portuguese traders, all seeking the treasures of the Indies. Unhampered by rules of caste or food taboos, Parsis got along with both local suppliers and foreign buyers, acting as brokers and interpreters.

In 1641, the Portuguese princess Catherine of Braganza married Charles II of England. As part of her dowry, the Portuguese king carelessly gave away the seven islands of Bom Bahia, as Mumbai was now known. A year later, the English Crown leased them for a pittance to the British East India Company, which wasted no time in transforming a few fishing villages into a thriving commercial center, taking full advantage of the deep natural harbor. Bom Bahia ("beautiful bay" in Portuguese) became Bombay, the new headquarters of the East India Company. In the late seventeenth century, Sir Gerald Aungier, the progressive second governor, encouraged a diverse population of Europeans and Indians who could tap the vast resources of the mainland. Once more the ideal mediators and brokers, Parsis flocked to the growing city and, as an inducement, were granted land, now the primest of real estate, for the disposal of Parsi dead by exposure to birds of prey and the elements.

Bombay and Parsis were made for each other. In no time at all, Parsis became the architects of the spreading metropolis and the roads that crossed it, as well as the builders of the ships that sailed out of it. (Francis Scott Key wrote "The Star Spangled Banner" on a Parsi-built ship, H.M.S. *Minden.*) They became bankers, importers and exporters, business magnates, interpreters, and clerks; they started presses, hospitals, schools, and charitable institutions; they became liquor merchants and tavern keepers, doctors, lawyers, and accountants, actors and entertainers. There seemed to be no area of Bombay life that didn't involve Parsis.

Within a hundred years, though the great Parsi temple towns of Navsari and Udwada continued as spiritual centers, the commercial and cultural life of the community passed from rural Gujarat to urban Bombay, and the history of the city and Parsis became inextricably fused. The opening of the Suez Canal in 1858 and the arrival of steam navigation started a new chapter in Bombay's history. Before long, Bombay became the commercial hub for all of India, its busy harbor a point of convergence for rail and sea routes. The "urbs prima in Indis," or India's greatest city, as the British were to name it, soon became the gateway to India, and not only to India but to all of the East beyond.

Parsis continued to play an active part in every type of venture, in commerce, industry, education, and the arts, in a city that seemed to embrace every current of change or diversity. By the mid-nineteenth century, Parsi merchants were already trading with the United States, East Africa, China, and Japan. Sons of the well-to-do were sent to school and university in Europe, and a sojourn in Europe became part of the well-to-do Parsi's education in life. Parsi girls were educated and given far more freedom of movement than their Hindu and Muslim counterparts. Parsi domestic style gradually swung away from the Hindu patterns adopted for hundreds of years and began to follow the European model, though women still wore saris. During this period Parsis acquired official surnames stemming from occupation or place of origin, where till then, children had acquired the first name of their father as their second name, and women had adopted their husband's names at marriage. (For instance, my mother's maiden name, Dubash, came from Do-bhasha, literally [speaker of] "two languages," or interpreter. My father's family name, Ichaporia, means "person from Ichapur.") Men and women ate together at meals again, just as they had in Persian times, and these meals grew to be the perfect reflection of the exuberant eclecticism of Bombay. There were some gains, but also some major losses. In the embrace of a Victorian ideal of modernity, many of our forebears flung aside their Indianness in favor of things from anywhere but India. Western music, Western food, westernized dress, Western education all helped to produce people who became the darlings of the Raj, who could move fluidly anywhere in the world but eventually grew to feel disconnected from the country they'd lived in for almost a thousand years. Although many Parsis believed in and supported Indian Independence, a great many of my parents' generation felt disoriented by the departure of the British in 1947.

· · ·

But to get back to our main topic, food: By the twentieth century, Parsi cuisine had acquired many layers on top of the meat- and dairy-centered diet of the Persian plateau. To begin with, the tropical bounty of the coastal plains of Gujarat must have been a source of great excitement to Parsis after years of wandering through the Arabian Desert and two decades on barren Diu. They had brought with them memories of the rich food traditions of ancient Persia, still seen in the cooking of Iran's Zoroastrians—an enduring love for saffron and rice; for meat cooked with fruit and vegetables; for fruit and nuts, even coconut, which was known in Persia as the Indian nut; for eggs cooked with vegetables; for herby lentil stews; for milk, cheese, and cream; for sweetmeats and wine and the taste of sweet-and-sour. On the west coast of India, Parsis came to the source of the spices and coconuts they'd enjoyed in their Iranian homeland, to abundant seafood, and, to top it all off, to mangoes and other tropical fruit. Parsi cooking absorbed Hindu influences, and in time, those of the Muslim conquerors of India, who themselves came bearing post-Islamic Persian food traditions. Chiles— or chillies, as they've come to be called in India—tomatoes, potatoes, cashews, and other New World food trophies followed in the wake of the Portuguese who arrived at the end of the fifteenth century. Exposure to the West through travel or constant mingling with Europeans brought in custards, gratins, soufflés, patties, cakes, and a love for pastry, cheese, and chocolate. (Never wonder what treat to take a Parsi friend in India. Cheese or chocolate or both will do.)

By the latter part of the twentieth century, all this adopting and adapting and enriching had led to an urban Parsi cuisine with an immense range of tastes and techniques, a real magpie cuisine. At one end of the continuum, you find a simple dish of pureed lentils with little more than salt and cumin; at the other, the potage of five different kinds of lentils, eight vegetables, and twenty-something spices that's our emblematic dish, *dhansak* (page 178), which is descended from a simpler Persian version. My mother's Wobbly Cauliflower is gentle enough to feed to a sick child, whereas a Goa curry can be hot beyond imagination. There's the technical simplicity of a stew gently seasoned with ginger, garlic, onions, and a lone chile contrasting with the rewarding labor entailed in producing Mother's Favorite Chicken (*chicken maivahlans,* page 144), a European-inspired extravaganza of a gratin that contains all the major favorite Parsi foods—poultry, cream, eggs, onions, garlic, dried fruit, and nuts. To this day, Parsi food is characterized by our ability to size up the offerings of another tradition and make them our own, adapting and transforming whatever we've taken a fancy to. Irish stew and custards came into Parsi kitchens in the nineteenth century; now we have pizza and burgers and salads.

This rich and inventive cuisine comes out of a long tradition of gleeful borrowing. Herodotus was correct when he observed that the Persians were ever alert to foreign influences and seized on whatever took their fancy. Achaemenid rulers employed vast corps of people to scout out novel food and drink for their kitchens. Later, in Sassanian times, a Pahlavi or Middle Persian text, *Husrav al Redag* ("King Khosro and his page"), recounts the exchange between a young man of noble birth and the ruler who questions him on the most important aspects of his education. Food and wine, music, pleasure—all these come first.

Herodotus also commented that he never knew people to make such a fuss about birthdays as the Persians. That's still true. Modern Parsis have two birthdays each, one according to the old Parsi calendar, and another according to the Gregorian. Both are acknowledged, perhaps with a Parsi breakfast for the birthday according to the Parsi calendar and a cake for the other, a few days apart. Thanks to discrepancies in the two calendars, we end up with three New Year's Days: the old one, March 21; another one with a movable date that now falls around mid-August; and, of course, January 1, which is a general public holiday all over India. Whether the new year should be celebrated in March or August became one of the divisions within the community. There are those who hold out for March 21—the Cadmis—and all the rest—the Shehenshais. Both days are celebrated with food, domestic ritual, and visits to the fire temple to make offerings of sandalwood and frankincense, the smell of which for me is the very essence of being Parsi.

One very important occasion in every Parsi child's life is the Navjot, an initiation ceremony before puberty that invests us with the external symbols of the religion, a fine muslin undershirt, the *sadra,* and the *kasti,* a lamb's-wool cincture of seventy-two threads wound thrice around the waist. All devout Parsis are supposed to wear both of them forever. The Navjot is celebrated at home or in enclosures festooned with tuberoses, spider lilies, and other scented flowers, with all the fanfare a family can muster. Parents then have at least a decade to recover before the next big event, the wedding, is celebrated with even greater elaboration. Food is central to both events, and the menus are identical. Navjot and wedding feasts are handled by established caterers who manage to serve thousands of guests in three seatings with a dozen or more lavish, freshly prepared dishes served on banana leaves, each dish offered twice.

My grandmother's cousin's Navjot, ca. 1910.

My grandmother's cousin's wedding, ca. 1920.

Then there are auspicious days according to the Parsi calendar, festivals or other periods of religious observance, and many personal ones besides birthdays, such as examinations passed, ships or careers launched, travelers setting out or returning. All of these days are acknowledged in some way with food, each family putting its own stamp on custom.

Because food and the arts of everyday life have traditionally been regarded as women's concerns, ephemeral and therefore trivial, passed down through oral tradition or private notebooks, the literature we have on Parsi food is relatively scant. I know of nothing published before the first part of the twentieth century. One book of that period, *Vividh Vani* (1915), is enchanting in its vigorous Parsi eclecticism, an eclecticism carried even further by *Manpasand Mishtaan* (1958), which offers us

Chicken Mousse with Bunny Salad, Flan à Cervelle, Pizza, Tamil Curry Pepper Water, Cottage-Cheese Clown Salad, Gâteau Mille-Feuilles, and Strawberry Valentine Pie, along with all the Parsi standards. Recipes from that period, published or in manuscript, presume a still, calm, unchanging life with lots of household help, for whose benefit the recipes seem to have been written down. Instructions use language like "send for 2-pice worth of cloves from the bazaar" and specify such measurements as "as much as will fit on a 2-anna coin."

Food was always important in my grandmother's household and my mother's. My grandmother, Meherbai Khan, came from a family who'd made their fortune in gemstones. At the age of sixteen she was introduced to my grandfather, Noshirwan Peerozeshaw Dubash, who came from a family of ship chandlers in Karachi, then part of Bombay Presidency. My grandfather had been packed off to school in England by his older brothers, staying on to study law. Shy and forever a little stern, Meher fell in love with the handsome young solicitor. After all those years abroad, Noshirwan had progressive ideas about the place of women in his household. In keeping with his wish to lead a modern life with a modern wife, my grandfather forbade his new bride to cover her hair with the white cotton kerchief required of all married women. (Later, he forbade her and their daughters to continue the ancient custom of isolating menstruating women.) He wanted her to travel with him at his side, to entertain his colleagues and their friends together, to bring up their children with every opportunity a liberal education and bank balance could provide. What he didn't expect was that all of his children would be girls, the last two my mother and her twin, born in 1910.

"We had such a happy childhood," my mother says. "Everything was so easy, and we had so much fun." Though observant of Parsi religious and social customs, my grandfather ordained a pretty secular household. All his daughters were educated in English-speaking schools, while my grandmother made sure they could read and write Gujarati. My grandmother, Nana as I was to call her, led a leisurely life on the surface, but running a large household with her sister's family tacked on to hers must have been like running a small army, especially when they traveled on family holidays such as visits en masse to the Karachi branch of the family or to Calcutta for my oldest aunt's wedding.

My mother and aunts all remember the most delicious food being served in their mother's house, and much care and ceremony at the dining table, where children weren't allowed until they could behave well enough not to annoy the grown-ups. My

A page from the table of contents of Manpasand Mishtaan, *a 1958 Parsi cookbook.*

My maternal grandmother, Meherbai Khan, on her father's knee, ca. 1885.

grandmother rarely entered the kitchen, then the province of the cook and his helper, but she had a strong sense of how things should look and taste. In the early part of the twentieth century, cookbooks in Gujarati began to appear, with recipes for not only traditional Parsi food but also all the European exotics that had been absorbed and, in some cases, unrecognizably transformed. These were intended to be manuals for instructing the household cook. My grandmother bought everything that came out, and I still have some of her books. Although good food continued to be part of family life after my grandfather's sudden death at fifty-five, my grandmother retreated into her inherent austerity. Her beloved Noshirwan, whose word was law, brought out a tenderness in her that her children never really felt or ever saw again after their father died. They all remember him as a doting husband and father, broad-minded and fair, committed to letting his daughters do whatever they needed to do to be happy, even when it meant going along with my oldest aunt's divorce from a suitable but

*My mother, Shireen Dubash (left), on the running board of her paternal
uncle's Daimler in Karachi. The other people include her five sisters, her parents,
and her Karachi uncle, aunt, and family, 1925.*

nasty husband. My mother and her twin got the short end of the stick, since their widowed mother was not at all inclined to let them go off wherever they liked. So my mother, Shireen, remained at home, unmarried, until she was thirty, a worry to her mother and a cause for all her sisters, who were charged with putting eligible bachelors in her path. My favorite aunt, Mani, took this mission seriously. She met my father on one of his trips to Bombay from Cochin, where he was posted, and immediately got to work.

Like my maternal grandfather, my father, Minocher Ichaporia, had recently returned from England, where he'd gone to pursue his studies in chemistry. He was the first person in his family with an interest in science rather than humanities. His father, Bomonji Shapoorji Ichaporia, was from Ichapur, near Surat, where his forebears were local priests who tended the small fire temple attached to their house. Priests and priestly families often had more learning than money, and in my grandfather's case,

*My mother (left, seated), with her sisters, parents, and
new brother-in-law in Calcutta, 1918.*

more children than rural life could support, even with the income from acres of rice
and coconuts. My grandfather sold some land and moved to Bombay, where he had
charge of a fire temple. After his first wife died, he married my grandmother, Piroj-
bai Ghadially, and with her he had three sons and three daughters, a total of thirteen
children, including those from his first marriage. Where my maternal grandparents'
household was worldly and pleasure-loving, the Ichaporia household was traditional,
austere, and occupied with learning. My grandfather, a scholar, read and spoke several languages and expected nothing less from his children. My father and his brothers had a Jesuit education through college, St. Xavier's School followed by St. Xavier's
College, the same college my cousins and I went to many years later. Bapaiji ("father's
mother") always seemed ferocious and unapproachable, but I'm told she was an ex-

The ship that carried my father, Minocher (Minoo) Ichaporia, to England in 1935.
His mother and sisters are standing in the foreground.

cellent cook, especially noted for her pickles and preserves, and I now feel regret that we never connected through food, the thing we had in common. To Bapaiji, whose own daughters all had master's degrees, my mother seemed frivolous and pleasure-loving, characteristics guaranteed to entrance my father, who probably longed for the more expansive style of everyday living he saw in my mother's family.

My mother found him awe-inspiringly handsome and brilliant, she says. He found her pretty and modern, and he really liked her family. They were married in 1942 and

The author, age six, dressed by her maternal aunt Mani as a Koli fisher-woman. The tray held marzipan fish.

went straight to Cochin on the Kerala coast, where they spent the next eleven years in what my mother saw as a dreadful exile from civilization. (I, however, loved it.) She came to a household ruled by my father's man, Parmeswaram. Within a month, he offered his resignation on the silver tray required by my mother. It began, "Dear Master, due to the attitude of utmost rigour and suspicion to which I have been subjected since the arrival of Madam . . ." Without Parmeswaram, "Madam" suddenly realized that she was now in for it. Apart from a recreational cooking class her mother had sent her to, she didn't have any idea how to make breakfast, lunch, tea, and dinner happen in, quite literally, the alien backwater they inhabited. (The large, airy house they lived in was right on one of Cochin's palm-fringed backwaters.) Luckily, she met an older Parsi woman who taught her what she needed to know, simple everyday Parsi food. Letters from Bombay in my grandmother's delicate Gujarati script filled in the blanks. In due course, another cook came along, one who was under Madam's thumb from the

start. Aiyyapan was then in his fifties, a treasure of treasures. He could produce magically varied and polished meals of newly learned Parsi food along with his large existing repertoire of "European" fancy dishes, working in a smoke-filled kitchen where the stove was earthworks on a cement platform. I can remember a guest asking for lemon meringue pie as a challenge to the cook who could make anything. He did.

In 1943 my mother returned to Bombay, following the custom of returning to one's mother for the birth of a child. A year or so later, my grandmother left Bombay to accompany my aunt Mani to Ootacamund in the Nilgiri hills of South India. I don't know how she managed it, but my Mani Masi (*masi* meaning "mother's sister") persuaded my parents that Ooty's cool climate was far more suitable for a young child than the mosquito-ridden backwaters of Cochin. So my early childhood until the age of six was spent in her sprawling, well-ordered house, with its doting adults and dogs. My earliest memories and the happiest ones all come from that house, and, not surprisingly, they are of food, often something I couldn't have, like mushrooms. There was never any trouble getting me to eat anything: I had only to be told that the thing in question was for grown-ups only. Parents of fussy feeders should take note of this ploy.

Following their mother's example, my mother and aunt went over the day's menus at the breakfast table, with the cook at their elbow to make suggestions and to go over the previous day's reckonings. The cook then went off to the bazaar to fetch fresh meat, fish, and vegetables, and on his return he would be given the necessary ingredients from the household stores. Refrigerators were just beginning to be a standard household item, but even then, fresh food was bought and cooked every day. Leftovers weren't in the picture. It's ironic that in those days, imported, tinned, and packaged food had such cachet. Fruit cocktail and peaches from California, Spam, Tasmanian jams made by IXL, Kraft cheese in tins from Australia, biscuits from England, canned frankfurters and cocktail sausages from Denmark, tinned asparagus and mushrooms, and the pantropical favorite, sweetened condensed milk—these were our exotics. My mother and people of her generation drew on travel and foreign magazines for new recipes and menu ideas. From our present point of view, menus of that day would seem spectacularly odd. My favorite lunch at a school friend's house was chicken vol-au-vent followed by prawn curry and rice, finished off with homemade ice cream with chocolate sauce and more chocolates afterward.

At a fairly early age, I started going to a convent boarding school, first in Ooty, during the week, and later, at the age of six, in Kodaikanal, where we came home once a year from November to February. During my last Cochin holiday, at the age of nine, I had my Navjot, performed by a priest imported from Calicut under the stern eye of Roda Fui (*fui* means "father's sister"), who came to see that things were done correctly and that I had properly memorized the long string of prayers drilled into me by an older Parsi schoolmate. No cast-of-thousands Navjot feast for me, because there were no Parsi caterers in that part of South India and just a few Parsi families, all of whom used to show up by car or launch for one another's functions.

When my mother's exile in Kerala ended with my father's transfer back to Bombay in 1953, she had one regret—the loss of Aiyyapan, whom she mourned through a succession of Goan cooks and Lalya (Gujarati) bearers. For me, coming to Bombay for the holidays opened up a dazzling new world of food. In addition to my mother's Parsi-plus repertoire, there were Navjots and wedding feasts I'd never experienced before, there were restaurants of all sorts, and there was even a brand-new espresso bar. In addition to the restaurants, clubs served a wonderful range of food. It was at a club that I tasted my first steak, my first plain green salad straight from the garden, my first sole Véronique (only it was pomfret) and lobster thermidor, my first waffles, and my first *vacherin*. However, in those days Bombay's beloved snack, *bhel puri,* could be found only on the streets or beaches or in tiny stalls, and eating it had the thrill of the forbidden and the dangerous. Now it's tamely available on hotel and club menus, and Indian groceries in the United States offer kits for making it at home. You can, too, with the recipe on page 67.

After some years of watching her go through cooks, a friend sent a young lad to my mother with a note that he knew just one or two things but seemed to be a quick learner. This was Andrew de Souza, and he stayed with my parents for almost twenty years, until the employment boom in the Persian Gulf states lured him and others like him away. By then he had turned into an accomplished, versatile, and curious cook whom my mother's false friends were constantly trying to hire away from her. My mother never got over what she saw as the perfidy of his departure, and to the day she left India for good, in 1998, she thought he would return, contrite and grateful to be back, with lots of new recipes. After Andrew left, there were a few more cooks, none of whom lasted long. My parents resorted to *bahar nu bhonu* (literally, "food from outside"), meals delivered to subscribing households by entrepreneurial Parsi cooks working out of their own home kitchens. When any one person's *bahar nu bhonu* got too monotonous to endure any longer, my mother took on simple Parsi cooking for her household of two until that got to be too much, whereupon the *bahar nu bhonu* started up again. My mother was a self-deprecating cook. I thought she had a delicate touch and great patience, and though she thought her repertoire was limited, everything she made was simply perfect.

When I left India at the end of 1962, newly and rebelliously married to a man from Baltimore, I went straight from pocket money to running a household in a strange country. While I had no clue about how to vacuum or do the laundry, cooking held no terrors, thanks to Andrew's patiently dictated and remarkably accurate recipes plus the Bombay food bible, the first edition of the Time and Talents Club cookbook. Through all its successive editions, the Time and Talents book continues to be the perfect window into Bombay's changing food-of-everywhere culinary culture.

Baltimore in the 1960s was not the place for fresh ginger, coriander, or chiles, some of the staples of Parsi cooking. Supermarkets seemed cold and dreary, but all was not lost because Baltimore had several old-fashioned markets. Lexington Market, which I rushed to every week like a person starved, had a stall selling freshly grated coconut for cake- and pie-makers. With books and notes and letters back and forth, I slowly learned how to cook Parsi food that tasted as I remembered it while expanding my horizons by reading through entire shelves of the food section of the Enoch Pratt library. Ginger, fresh coriander (cilantro), and chiles required expeditions to Washington, D.C., or imploring calls to Mee Jun Low, the one Chinese restaurant in town, which was sometimes willing to part with a sad little handful. Some years later, at the end of marriage number 1, I fetched up in California, drawn to the Bay Area by the eucalyptus-clad hills that still assuage my longing for the South Indian mountains of my youth. California markets were an unexpected bonus. Long before you could occupy yourself going to a different farmers' market every day of the week, Berkeley stores were brimming over with so many ingredients that uncompromising Indian cooking became possible as never before. Finding fresh coriander and ginger and green chiles was no longer an expedition but an errand. I was also lucky enough to fall into a group of friends who loved to cook and eat, all of us self-taught, amateurs in the true sense of the word.

In the early seventies, while I was in graduate school studying design and working at what was then the Lowie, now the Hearst, Museum of Anthropology at Berkeley, great bundles of old Chinese-embroidered Parsi sari borders began appearing at Cost Plus in San Francisco. I wondered whether other precious things were as quickly disappearing from Parsi households. Indeed they were, tossed out without much reflection on the past or the future into the eager hands of the *jharipurana walla,* the man summoned to haul off bottles, papers, and anything else to be discarded. With the perspective that time, distance, and anthropology can bring, I enlisted my father's help and set about trying to salvage everyday household and ceremonial objects for the Lowie Museum—temple vessels, old kitchen utensils, chalk stencils, *sadras, kastis,* prayer caps, saris, on and on. After all those years of a convent education, which left me more familiar with the Gospels than the Gathas, making this collection gave me my path back to where and what I'd come from, and in an unexpected way, it did the same for my father. Later on, in the course of pursuing a doctorate in anthropology at the University of California, Berkeley, I went on exploring various aspects of the expression of ethnic identity; and on a parallel track, I cooked for money, not just Parsi or Indian food but whatever seemed right for the client—anything but quiche, tabbouleh, and carrot cake, the ubiquitous food emblems of Berkeley in the seventies.

Even though household goods and sari borders were being jettisoned, no one in Bombay seemed to be tossing out Parsi food, which was animated by change, not left behind in its wake. Navjots and weddings still followed the old pattern with the same beloved succession of dishes, the main difference being the sad replacement of the two live accordion bands, Goody's and Nellie's, by a deejay. Through collecting specimens and talking to people, I ventured further into Bombay Parsi food and became aware of the rich traditions of Surat, Bharuch, Balsar, and other bastions of Parsi life

Chalk stencil showing a ritual tray of symbolic objects (ses):
(A) holder for vermilion, (B) rose water sprinkler, (C) "Happy New Year,"
(D) betel leaf, (E) rock sugar container, (F) grain of rice, (G) coconut,
(H) almond, (I) fish, (J) ceremonial tray with flowers.

in Gujarat. Unlike massive, carved Parsi furniture, Parsi food is portable across geographical and cultural boundaries, and because of that, it remains our cultural mascot even when other household customs slowly fall away. For instance, my grandmother always followed the daily practice of hanging garlands above the door and making chalk stencils on both sides of the threshold, with more-elaborate garlands and chalk patterns for extra-special days. Morning and evening, a footed German silver vessel of burning sandalwood and frankincense would be carried through the house to purify the air and ward off mosquitoes. My mother hung garlands and "did" chalk, but only on scrupulously observed auspicious days, and she thought Flit was more effective against mosquitoes than frankincense. In my own house in California, patiently threaded garlands are a fond wish since there's no garland maker around the corner; we do chalk occasionally, and burn sandalwood and frankincense from time to time, but like my mother, I'm attentive to food customs and adore celebrating birthdays.

One of these food customs is the celebration of the new year, but since the movable New Year's Day falls in August, at the end of the summer, it seems to make much more sense to celebrate the ancient Persian one, Jamshedji Navroz, on March 21. This has become my favorite day of the year, and I love filling the house with flowers and people and lots of wonderful food. After one such party, my friend Alice Waters, who loves all new years, asked me if I wouldn't consider doing a similar thing at her restaurant. We just celebrated our tenth Parsi New Year's dinner at Chez Panisse, and it has taken on the air of a joyful, rowdy Parsi family party, with chalk patterns at the entrance and scented garlands in all the doorways.

Seeing how happy our friends were when eating Parsi food made me want to sit my mother down and make her tell me everything she knew. In the mid-eighties, my parents paid us two long visits, the first one to inspect the man their daughter had started living with ten years after her divorce from husband number 1. Both times, my mother and I cooked Parsi food every day for several months. I watched, took down, and actually measured her quantities, ranging from "one cigarette-tin full" to the poetic "almost not there." My mother instructed, my father supervised, rocking back and forth on his feet, towering above his tiny wife and medium-size daughter. He and my mother would constantly argue about whose mother's way was better. The ultimate praise from him was, "It tastes correct." At the end of their second visit, there were still things we hadn't worked through. I sat by my mother while she lay back on the sofa in a trance of recollection. "Seven things," she might say, repeating

PARSI NEW YEAR

Tuesday, March 21, 2006

Garlands of marigolds and gardenias will hang
from the rafters, spices will perfume the air, we'll eat,
drink and celebrate Navroz and the arrival of spring.

POMEGRANATE KIR ROYALE

CASHEWS WITH AJWAIN; SRI LANKAN CUCUMBER PICKLES; CRISPY PAPADS

SEARED SPRING PEAS; MORINGA TOASTS

RITUAL DAL

GREEN CHUTNEY FRIED FISH AND OYSTERS

GRILLED GUINEA HEN
CAULIFLOWER WITH CURRY LEAVES; GINGERY GREENS

WILD MUSHROOM BIRYANI

SILVER LIME ICE

FALOODA AND SWEETS
LEMONGRASS AND MINT TISANE

Followers of the ancient religion of Zoroaster, Parsis are descendants of a band
that fled Persia for India in the 7th century. Parsi food today is an ongoing
interplay of Persian heritage with influences from India and Europe. Niloufer Ichaporia,
author of a forthcoming book on Parsi food, traditional and modern, will prepare
favorite festive dishes to celebrate the new year, Navroz, and the arrival of spring.

SEATING IS LIMITED. PLEASE CALL 510.548.5525 FOR RESERVATIONS
$125 PER PERSON

Chez Panisse Restaurant

*The announcement of the Chez Panisse menu for the
2006 Navroz (Parsi New Year's) dinner.*

them so that I could write them down in my ragged red notebook, bought in Delhi's Chandni Chowk. It is still this notebook I go to, along with Andrew's recipes, which are in essence hers, when I want Parsi food to taste correct, no matter who else gets consulted.

A Hindu friend from Bombay who heard that I was doing a book on Parsi food said, "Well, that won't be very big, will it? *Dhansak, patia,* and *akuri!*" Quite the opposite. Even if I included a recipe for only those dishes and their variants that were served in my mother's house, the book would still be twice as long as it is, and it wouldn't take into account the whole sweep of Parsi cooking, urban and provincial, the dishes that I don't yet know about. What you'll find here is a distillation of one family's favorites, in one family's style—for that, too, can vary from household to household or, as in our case, from generation to generation. Some recipes in this book are useful for demonstrating interesting transferable techniques, such as souffléed eggs on a seasoned base or popped seeds in hot oil; others for updating and brightening old favorites, such as the Parsi "ratatouille"; and others for demonstrating the use of some pan-Asian vegetables that deserve more attention.

My hope is that people reading this book will see Parsi food as a living, moving tradition, not as culinary archaeology, and to do as Parsis have done for millennia—mix things up magpie fashion, grab an idea here, an ingredient there, relying always on a personal sense of what tastes good. To that end, I've been deliberately loose with things like time and quantities of things that depend so much on any individual cook's abilities and taste buds or the tremendous variability of ingredients, stoves, and pans. The menu section is full of suggestions, but you should consider them signposts, not blueprints.

Many of the recipes came from a period when time and other people's labor were both plentiful, as in my grandmother's day, when salad meant mayonnaise and plumpness was a charming female attribute. My mother had to learn how to cook, and she ran a household considerably less well staffed than her mother's. In our house, time seems forever short, we're the staff, salad means leaves with vinaigrette, and we don't want to look like bejeweled sofas. Parsi food in our San Francisco household is geared to our times, our tastes, and the great banquet of possibilities that markets in the United States now set before us. It's no less authentically Parsi to explore unfamiliar ingredients or ideas now than it was for Persians in the seventh century to eat peaches from China, or for their descendants several hundred years later, in India, to experiment with potatoes from Peru. Our cuisine has been evolving for a long time, responsive to every interesting current, first in Persia, and for the past thousand years or so in India. With so many Parsis now in North America, it's on the move again, with new ingredients, new circumstances, and a traditionally inventive cook in every household.

My mother is now ninety-six. I'm so glad we had that time of cooking together, because she lost a lot of her zest and her once-keen memory for details after my father died in 1990. But to this day, her Parsi love of food and the company of laughing, singing people continues unabated. She may have had a three-hour screaming fit when I wanted to smoke a Char Minar cigarette at the age of fifteen, but I'm forever grateful that she never stopped me from playing with food.

Note on Transliteration

There are several systems for the transliteration of Indian languages in current popular use, as opposed to scholarly use, where there's perhaps more agreement. Since this is a book to cook from (and take to the market), it might be useful to state that the transliteration of recipe titles and plant names in Gujarati here generally follows the contemporary United Nations system without diacritical marks: words such as *Parsee, Hindoo, jerdaloo* (apricot), *jeera* (cumin), *kheema* (ground meat), *paneer* (soft cheese), *kheer* (a milky sweet), and *oombaryu* (a bean dish) are rendered as *Parsi, Hindu, jardalu, jira, khima, panir, khir,* and *umbaryu,* and so forth, except when the proper noun or word has migrated over to English. For instance, Punjab is now on the map of India, where it should strictly be Panjab; *ghee* should be *ghi;* and *vindaloo* should be *vindalu.* It's an imperfect world, and in the effort to be understood, and for readers to be understood, there'll be the occasional inconsistency.

Readers from India or any other country whose use of English is still shaped by the British will notice that our familiar, indispensable "chilly" and "chillies"—heat-packing members of the nightshade family—are rendered here as "chile" and "chiles," following the University of California Press's orthographic preference for the Nahuatl word romanized by the Spanish.

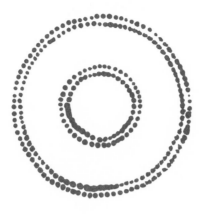

સાધની

———◇———

KITCHENS, EQUIPMENT,
AND THE BASICS

Kitchens in India have changed a lot since my grandparents' generation, when they were smoky places ruled over by the family cook. Even now, the average Indian kitchen would look primitive to American eyes. Yet the quality of the food that comes out of these kitchens on a daily basis is nothing short of astounding. It really doesn't take more than three bricks and a fire to cook a meal, a sobering reminder that it's the individual who makes the food, not the equipment. Indian family cooks I've known have been ingenious in finding ways to meet their needs. Faced with my aunt's shrinking appetite, her cook devised a method for making tiny amounts of food: he used an empty sardine tin with a coat-hanger wire wrapped around it to make a handle. As a spatula and mini-whisk, he used a chicken's wing feather. Young Dharamraj Madai, who watches over my friend Mehlli Gobhai, has the best garlic crusher imaginable, a beautiful rough beach pebble that fits his hand exactly.

That being said, it's not as though well-run households didn't have their kitchen essentials. It's interesting to look at what my grandmother in her day and my mother in hers thought essential for getting food onto the table. For both of them, the key elements were a well-trained kitchen and table staff. They themselves did not go into the kitchen and took care to keep children out of it. Today's kitchens in the United States are well-equipped playpens for friends and family, not places far removed from the goings-on of family life as the kitchens of my childhood used to be.

Three Generations of Kitchen Equipment

This is an approximation of what my grandmother needed to feed her family of five daughters, plus her sister and her three children, not to mention a large household staff.

- A cook, known and addressed as *mistri* (cooks in Parsi households were mostly Goan).
- A cook's helper, sometimes known as the matey, a British nautical term.
- A bearer or butler in a starched white uniform for serving. Extra bearers for large parties.
- A wood- or charcoal-burning cast-iron range with an oven and, later, a gas stove, the gas piped in by the city.
- A *sigri,* a portable cylindrical grill about 18 inches high, for grilling or for an extra heat source.
- A kerosene stove (for emergencies or an extra heat source).
- Tinned copper vessels, deep, with lids like dinner plates to hold water or coals. Tinning was and still is done by wandering *kalai wallas,* tinsmiths, who can set up shop in a three-foot-square space with a fire, bellows, and some tin.
- Straight-sided shallow tinned copper vessels with flat lids, no handles.
- *Khumchas,* circular trays with straight sides for working dough and other uses. Made of tinned copper or German silver.
- Various tongs for lifting lids or turning chapatis; perforated spoons, usually metal.
- A cast-iron *lohri* or *tava,* a lens-shaped griddle about a foot across, for cooking chapatis or dry-roasting anything.
- Frying pans like woks, *karhais,* in sizes geared to the household (made of cast iron, tinned copper, or possibly aluminum, in diameters ranging from 8 to 16 inches).

- A grinding stone, *masala no patthar*—slab and roller, the surface to be roughened from time to time by an itinerant worker, the *tankiwali,* who would go from house to house announcing her presence.

- A large domed aluminum steamer (on the bottom, Queen Mary in profile) for a sweet called *sandhna.*
- A mortar and pestle, made of heavy brass.
- Knives to suit the cooks.
- A rotary eggbeater (although egg whites and cream could be whipped up with a fork in a soup plate, too).
- Miscellaneous work bowls and plates, molds for desserts, baking dishes.
- Large Chinese storage urns for grains; brass canisters and boxes for storing other staples.
- An icebox, later a refrigerator.
- A perforated vessel for cheesemaking.
- Strainers and colanders of various sizes.
- A dal masher made of wood.
- A slender wooden rolling pin and circular board for rolling out chapatis and puris.
- A hand-cranked meat grinder.
- A household balance and various weights and measures for grains and liquids; these would be in various systems, Indian and imperial.

What my mother thought essential for her household of three was most of the above, especially the *tava,* the masala stone, the mortar and pestle, and the rolling pin. In addition to the old tinned copper vessels, there were aluminum and stainless steel pots made in traditional Parsi shapes. The big change came in the 1950s with the pressure cooker, which was supposed to change life completely by saving time and fuel. I don't know a single Indian urban household now that doesn't have a pressure cooker put to constant use. About thirty years ago, the demand for natural gas outstripped the supply, so the city stopped piping it in. Everyone now cooks with propane, the procuring and changing of cylinders a constant bother. Under these circumstances, a pressure cooker makes great sense.

My mother's generation ushered in an era of electrical appliances—refrigerators were a must, as were toasters, mixers, and blenders, most of which were kept off-limits to the kitchen staff and as a result often rusted from disuse. In the sixties, a new kitchen essential came to the fore, the mixer-grinder, which could do the job of a masala stone, something the Western blender failed to do. The first and best of these was invented by a devoted engineering genius so that his wife could continue making first-rate Indian food in Germany, where they happened to be posted. Known as mixies, these grinders have now become standard equipment in urban Indian kitchens, where the roar of electric motors is now replacing the music of the masala stone.

What do I consider essential for Parsi food and Indian food in general? Kitchen supply stores make fortunes on our current love for specialized equipment, but you can open your Bombay kitchen with pretty much what you have on hand plus a visit to a supermarket, an Indian grocery, or the Internet.

For the recipes that require the prepared pastes known as masalas, it helps to have a food processor or, even better, an electric wet-dry grinder such as the Sumeet Multigrinder (see Sources). Before the Sumeet I used a food processor, but the results were not the same. Blenders and food processors cut food up into ever-smaller pieces suspended in liquid, and hard ingredients like coconut can never be ground to a fine paste. The Sumeet and its equivalents have blades designed to grind wet and dry ingredients together as would happen on a stone. This was its test: I made a coconut-based green chutney (*lili chatni,* page 227) in the newly unpacked Sumeet and presented it to my mother in a perfect ball on a plate. She looked admiringly at it, tasted it, and asked when I'd become so handy with a masala stone. A food-processor coconut chutney can't be formed into a ball because too much water needs to be added to keep the mixture moving.

I love my Parsi utensils, the tinned vessels, the trays, tongs, slabs, and rollers, most of them from my grandmother's kitchen, and I enjoy their beauty and the sense of continuity; but cast-iron skillets and heavy stainless steel–lined pans such as All-Clad are my kitchen mainstays. For frying, I have a range of *karhais,* the round-bottomed Indian frying pans, but I also use a wok. I use an electric coffee mill to grind dry whole spices and nothing else, and I have many more devices for grating coconut than I need.

Before You Begin

The recipes in this book have been tested in a variety of kitchens by a variety of cooks, some with a lot of experience, some with none. Our own kitchen is bursting with ingredients, but the stove and refrigerator are at least twenty years old and nothing extraordinary. Most important in cooking is reliance on one's senses, all seven—touch, taste, smell, sight, hearing, sixth, and common. Granted, some of that comes with time and practice. For that reason, experienced cooks might think there's too much elementary detail in the recipes here, while neophytes might feel there's not enough. Since the intention of this book is to open up a different perspective on food rather than to instruct in basic kitchen tactics, I'm assuming that most readers already have a general cookbook to rely on.

NUMBER OF SERVINGS

These are given with the proviso that how many people a dish serves depends on the appetite of the eaters and what else gets offered at the same time. Two enthusiastic people can demolish a pound of cashews in five minutes or less; at other times, one has leftovers after eight people have helped themselves. The same is true with Mother's "Italian" Eggs (page 58). Some things beget wild greed. Plan accordingly. As a Parsi, I tend to overprovide.

INGREDIENT QUANTITIES

With the exception of cake and cookie ingredients, you should see these as approximations geared to the taste of one household. Most of the dishes in this book are forgiving: it really doesn't matter if there's a little more or a little less. Fresh coriander (cilantro), for instance, is very much a matter of personal taste. Some people love it; others don't. Half a cup of chopped fresh coriander is an uncompressed handful.

TIMING AND TEMPERATURE

How long things take to prepare or to cook is again a matter of approximation. I'm a fast worker and cook on a natural-gas stove. Some of the variables are type of stove— gas, electric, or other; type of gas—propane or regular; material and gauge of pots and pans; distance from the flame; ambient temperature; temperature and moisture content of the food itself; type of oil used in frying; variable ovens and oven temperatures. My scientist husband says that it might be possible to work out a complex equation that takes care of the variables. My suggestion is that there's nothing like working out a harmonious connection between you and your stove and pans (which don't need to be expensive). I have a horror of electric stoves and always hate having to cook on one, but even there, you can manage. For instance, if you have to start a dish at high heat and then simmer it, have another burner set to low at the ready and switch the pan over to it.

RESULTS

Get to know a dish, and yank it around to suit you. There will be times when things burn or scorch and you have to start again or salvage what's left. Remember, it's just dinner, not Judgment Day. If you burn something on the bottom of a pan, plunging the bottom into cold water at once allows you to rescue some of the contents before they get a scorched taste.

Basic Techniques

There's nothing frighteningly unfamiliar about the basic methods of Parsi cooking. Except for the first technique—popping or sizzling of aromatics to start or finish a dish—those discussed below—browning onions or aromatics, and shallow-, deep-, and dry-frying—are all pretty standard approaches to transforming raw to cooked.

FINAL SEASONING

Vaghar in Gujarati, *tadka* in Hindi: this is a technique often called tempering, in which a dish is seasoned at the last minute with spices or other aromatics sizzled briefly in hot oil or ghee in a very small pan. (Sometimes a savory dish will start with the sizzling of whole spices before the onions go into the pan.) I use our smallest cast-iron skillet or a small, battered aluminum frying pan bought at a garage sale in Madison, its handle repaired with a wooden spool.

BROWNING ONIONS

Kando ne lal karvanu (literally "making the onion red"): When you work with the drier pink onions in India, the term makes more sense. Here, we brown onions. Most meat dishes of the wet type start with browning onions, sometimes sliced, sometimes chopped. To some cooks, like my epicurean friend Eddie Khambata, it makes a huge difference whether they're chopped or sliced to begin a dish; to other Parsi cooks, it might be a case of angels on a pin. Whether you're turning your onions red or brown, a chopped or sliced onion should have the merest tracery of brown on its edges. At times, you want the onion to soften without browning. This should never take more than a few minutes unless you're scaling up the quantities, and your sense of smell and the way the onion looks tell you the right time to stop.

Browning the onion is often followed by frying a masala paste for a few minutes. This takes care and attention because it can catch on the bottom, scorch, and ruin your dish. Vigilance, stirring, and adding a splash of water as you go keep this from happening. In Hindi and Hinglish this is known as *bhunao-ing.* The pans I use for this kind of cooking are usually aluminum or copper, lined with stainless steel. My mother and grandmother managed very well with tinned copper and, later, aluminum, not particularly heavy. I often start the browning in a cast-iron skillet and transfer the contents to a deeper pot if necessary.

FRYING

There is one rule for all frying: don't wander off. A thermometer may be handy but in most cases it is not essential. Again, sight and smell and testing a small piece can give you the answer. Use the oil you like best for frying. I use peanut or grapeseed oil. For shallow- and deep-frying, please let me be nannyish once in this book and ask you not to use wads of paper towels for draining, but to line a baking sheet or tray with layers of brown paper (supermarket bags, for instance) and put a layer or two of paper towels right on top. It's absolutely true that we shall never see a poem lovely as a tree.

Dry-frying. Here you use the merest film of oil on a heavy skillet or griddle, preferably cast iron like the Indian *tava* or the classic skillet, but not nonstick. I use both *tavas* and skillets, depending on what's closest at hand.

Shallow-frying. How much oil you use depends on how wide and deep the pan is. Here's where you can use an ordinary frying pan, cast iron or your preferred metal, because the oil needs to be about one inch deep. Pans with curved bottoms give you greater depth with less oil, but please make sure they don't wobble on the stove. A skillet is fine for shallow-frying.

Deep-frying. Again, the size of the pan determines the amount of oil you'll need. The oil should be hot but not smoking—about 360 to 370 degrees Fahrenheit if you want a measurement, but the best test is the ingredient you're frying. It should cook through and get golden brown at the same time. My grandmother's emphatic rule for deep-frying was that things always look paler in the oil than they do out of it. For deep-frying, I use a large wok when I'm frying for a crowd; otherwise, for six or eight people, any pan that allows you to pour in oil to a minimum depth of three inches will do the trick. A pan that's about eight to ten inches across will allow you to handle four to six pieces of fried food, depending on their size. That's why I like the Indian *karhai;* you get maximum depth with minimum oil.

FRYING PAN

Basic Ingredients

SALT

Everything depends on salt. With Indian food particularly, judicious salting can make the dish, giving it its meaning and its anchor. Without the right amount of salt, spices float around in search of a leader. To ensure depth of flavor and seasoning, we add a small amount of salt at the start of a dish as well as at the end, tasting as we go.

For cooking, my mother and grandmother used coarse salt from the salt pans around Bombay or from the coastal areas of Maharashtra and Gujarat. This is a wet, gray salt sold in gunnysacks at traditional groceries. For the table, there was a saltcellar or a shaker with fine salt that never poured because of Bombay's humidity. I use coarse sea salt for most cooking, but play with many other salts for finishing a dish. When we travel, I always look for the local salt. It's the basic *goût de terroir.* We all need to do this to keep these small saltworks from being squeezed out of existence by commercial salt conglomerates trying to make cooks in the developing world feel that their indigenous salt is inferior.

SUGAR

Parsi cooking uses white sugar and *gor,* or jaggery—solid unrefined cane or palm sugar—depending on the dish. One of the characteristics of Parsi cooking is a touch of sweetness in savory dishes, a taste that must have come with us from Persia.

Indian white sugar has large crystals and a pronounced taste of sugarcane. American standard white sugar is excellent for baking, but unwashed and turbinado sugars have much more of the good taste of cane and are now easy to find, even in supermarkets.

GHEE AND OIL

Ghee is usually described as clarified butter, but it goes a step beyond. In clarified butter, the milk solids have separated but they're still white. Given more cooking time, they turn a toasty brown and sink to the bottom of the pan. The golden liquid floating on top is ghee. It's as different from clarified butter as a freshly cut slice of bread is from a piece of toast. You absolutely must have ghee to make the taste of some of the dishes in this book ring true. Most Indian groceries sell ghee, but I really want you to make your own for three reasons: it's not much bother, you don't have to buy more than you can use, and your house will smell heavenly.

To my grandmother's generation of cooks, ghee was the all-purpose cooking fat. A prodigal use of ghee indicated prosperity and generosity. Times changed, and by the middle of the twentieth century, Parsi kitchens used both ghee and a modern newcomer, hydrogenated oil, often represented as vegetable ghee. By the 1960s, hard fats were under attack and all over India these shortenings were edged out by polyunsaturated oils such as peanut, sesame, safflower, and corn. Ghee, however, held on to its ancient place in Indian life and cooking. Most Parsi kitchens today use vegetable oil for most things, and ghee where nothing else will do. Lard, suet, chicken fat, bacon grease, and the like don't figure at all in Parsi cooking.

GHEE
CONTAINER

When my parents lived in Cochin, my mother often had ghee made from white buffalo's-milk butter, sold by wandering vendors and weighed out on their portable balances lined with dark green banana leaves. I still remember its slightly cheesy smell. Later, in Bombay, ghee was made from the accumulated cream skimmed off the daily milk that was brought to the door in enormous vessels carried around on their heads by the milkmen, *dudhwallas,* usually from the Parsi Dairy Farm, whose logo is a fat black buffalo. I use up ends of butter to make ghee, but often start with freshly bought unsalted butter. Cow's and buffalo's milk each make a distinctly flavored ghee. Many Indians have a strong preference for one or the other. I rather like buffalo's-milk ghee, but my husband prefers cow's-milk, which is lucky for him because we haven't got a choice.

The rule of thumb with ghee is that you end up with a little more than half the volume you start with, depending on how much water the butter contains. I like to use unsalted butter because a scoop of the toasty residue can then be stirred into rice or a scrambled egg. (This doesn't work with salted butter, because although the ghee turns out okay, the residue burns more easily and is intensely salty.)

To make about 12 ounces of ghee: Put 1 pound unsalted butter in a sturdy pan over moderate heat. Let it melt completely, then turn down the heat to very low. The ghee will be ready when the solids sink to the bottom and turn a toasty color. If they turn dark brown, the flavor, smell, and color of the ghee will be affected: You'll get something brownish-gray instead of a golden ivory. The timing depends on the thickness of the pan and your heat source. Until you're familiar with both, don't wander too far away. Set a timer to remind yourself to check every 15 minutes. This amount of butter should be done in about an hour at absolutely the lowest heat and about 45 minutes at a higher, but still low, setting.

Let the ghee cool a little before straining it into a heatproof jar. Tradition suggests straining the warm ghee through cheesecloth or muslin, but a very fine-meshed strainer does the job. Let the ghee cool completely before capping the jar. Discard the residue or save it to flavor other dishes. Ghee can be stored at room temperature in a cool, dark place for up to six weeks; for long-term storage, put it in the refrigerator.

Ginger-Garlic Paste | ADU LASAN

Every Parsi household must have its supply of this paste. In households where there is a grinding stone and a person to do the work, it is prepared every morning, along with the other pastes needed for the day's menus. The preparation of pastes is now more often done in an electric wet-dry grinder, which can almost duplicate the smooth texture produced on a stone. Fortunately, Ginger-Garlic Paste can also be easily prepared in a food processor. It keeps well for up to two weeks refrigerated, and even longer in a freezer. Or if you're in a rush, you can combine equal quantities of very finely chopped or grated peeled fresh ginger and garlic, just as much as you need for the recipe. *Makes about 1 cup.*

> *About ½ cup roughly chopped peeled fresh ginger (about 4 ounces)*
> *About ½ cup roughly chopped peeled cloves garlic*
> *About ½ teaspoon salt (optional)*
> *Vegetable oil*

- In a wet-dry grinder or food processor, grind the ginger and garlic to a smooth paste, using as little water as possible. Add the salt if you plan on storing the paste. Pack it into a small, tightly covered jar with a nonreactive lining to the lid. Pour a thin film of oil on top of the paste. Store in the refrigerator.

. . .

Note: Ginger-garlic paste is now commercially available, both in India and in the United States. It's a good idea to look at the ingredients before you buy any. I like Poonjiaji's for emergencies because it is preserved with small amounts of vinegar and salt rather than additives with a metallic aftertaste. Of course, nothing is as good as a paste ground at home.

THE BIG THREE SPICE MIXTURES

These are the spice mixtures, or masalas, you need to have for many Parsi recipes to taste correct. Not many urban Parsi households make their own dry spice mixtures anymore, since even with a grinding stone it would be hard to pound them by hand in the quantity generally needed. With an electric coffee grinder kept just for spices, making the big three isn't that hard, but if this seems like too much to take on, the Sources section offers some excellent, tested alternatives.

Parsi Garam Masala

Of the big three, this is the simplest. *Garam masala* literally means "warm spices," but the warmth here refers not to their taste but to their properties. The customary ingredients—cardamom, cinnamon, cloves, nutmeg, and pepper—are regarded as "warming" to the body in those medical systems (Parsi, Hindu, Arab, Chinese) that divide edibles according to whether they cool or heat. Garam masala is usually added toward the end of cooking to finish a dish.

It's commercially available, but anything you buy is likely to have a larger proportion of the cheaper spices like cumin or pepper, and just a whiff of the more expensive ones like cardamom. Black cumin seeds *(kala jira)* can be found at Indian groceries.

The recipe is for a small amount because that is all you should have on hand; the flavor gradually fades if kept for a long time. *Makes about ½ cup.*

2 tablespoons cardamom pods
2 (2-inch-long) sticks cinnamon or cassia
1 teaspoon black cumin seeds or regular cumin seeds
1 teaspoon whole cloves
1 teaspoon black peppercorns
¼ teaspoon nutmeg

- Grind all ingredients together in a coffee mill reserved for grinding spices. Store tightly capped in a cool, dark place.

Sambhar Masala

This recipe is a combination of Bhicoo Manekshaw's, from *Parsi Food and Customs,* and Sarla Sanghvi's, from the original 1959 edition of the Time and Talents Club cookbook. This is the only use of asafetida I know of in Parsi cooking. Use it in its natural resinous form if you can find it, in powder if you can't. Sesame oil, called *til* or gingelly oil, is available at Indian groceries and in many natural foods stores. The dark amber Chinese or Japanese variety made from toasted sesame seeds is not a substitute. *Makes about 2 cups.*

¾ cup cayenne pepper or Indian chilly powder
2 tablespoons salt
1 tablespoon ground turmeric
1 ½ teaspoons crushed asafetida resin or 2 teaspoons powdered asafetida

½ cup fenugreek seeds
2 tablespoons brown mustard seeds
1 teaspoon black peppercorns
1 teaspoon broken-up star anise pod
1 teaspoon whole cloves
1 (3-inch-long) stick cinnamon or cassia, broken up
1 tablespoon untoasted sesame oil or peanut oil

- Measure the cayenne, salt, turmeric, and asafetida into a bowl. Grind the fenugreek and mustard seeds, peppercorns, star anise, cloves, and cinnamon to a fine powder in a coffee mill reserved for grinding spices. You may need to do this in two batches. Add to the cayenne mixture.

- In a small pan, heat the oil until it starts to shimmer. Make a well in the middle of the spice mixture and pour in the hot oil. Keep mixing with a spoon until the oil is completely incorporated and the mixture loses its powdery look.

- Bottle and store in a cool, dark place.

Dhana Jiru or Dhansak Masala

In essence, this is an elaborate garam masala. Literally translated, *dhana jiru* means "coriander and cumin," but you can see that this is only the beginning. There's also some terminological confusion. Some people see *dhansak masala* as synonymous with *dhana jiru;* others see the former as a combination of *dhana jiru* and *sambhar.* I prefer to keep them separate and combine them as necessary. Use this recipe when either *dhansak masala* or *dhana jiru* is called for.

Recipes for these mixtures often call for the most esoteric ingredients, such as *duggar ka phul,* a lichen, and for tiny amounts of hard-to-find spices like *nag kesar,* or snake saffron—often mistranslated as "saffron," but a totally different thing, resembling a peppercorn with a tail. I have left them out here because they are not generally available in the United States. I've eaten great wads of lichen to determine what its effect is and still don't know. Should you be determined, and should you be able to find them, add one teaspoon of the *duggar ka phul* and half a teaspoon of *nag kesar.* Your best strategy for making this masala is to shop where you can buy spices in small amounts. Refer to the Glossary and the Sources section for more details on identifying and locating these ingredients. To avoid fits of sneezing while you're grinding, sifting, and bottling, wear an ordinary hardware store dust mask. *Makes more than 1 pint.*

1 cup coriander seeds

½ cup dried cassia leaves or ¼ cup Turkish bay leaves

¼ cup cumin seeds

¼ cup dried red chiles

1 tablespoon white poppy seeds

2 tablespoons broken-up stick cinnamon or cassia

2 tablespoons black peppercorns

1 tablespoon whole cloves

1 tablespoon cardamom pods

4 black cardamom pods

1 teaspoon caraway seeds

1 teaspoon black cumin seeds

1 teaspoon fenugreek seeds

½ teaspoon ground turmeric

Pinch of saffron threads

1 nutmeg

1 strand mace

- In a large heavy skillet, dry-roast the coriander, cassia, cumin, peppers, poppy seeds, cinnamon, peppercorns, cloves, cardamom, black cardamom, caraway, black cumin, and fenugreek just enough for them to start smelling toasty but not to color. Let them cool down for a few minutes before you go on to the next step.

- In a coffee mill reserved for grinding spices, pulverize the toasted spices with the turmeric, saffron, nutmeg, and mace. Sift them into a bowl, pressing through the sieve rather than shaking, which raises too much nose-tickling powder. Pour the mixture into a jar; cap it tightly and store in a cool, dark place.

COCONUT

Dealing with coconut is an everyday operation in Parsi kitchens. In earlier days, there was no other way of getting coconut milk except by cracking one open. Now there are options. Throughout the book, I will let you know when a substitute is acceptable and when nothing but the freshly prepared ingredient will do.

An exotic in ancient Persia, coconut has become an important part of Parsi ceremonial life and food alike. Our ritual array of symbolic objects, the *ses,* always has a coconut on it. Coconuts figure as a symbol of fertility and bounty in just about every important ceremony throughout the life cycle, as they do for a large part of India.

One of the characteristic morning sounds in Parsi households is (or was) the thump-thump-thump of a stone roller against a granite slab as it crushes pieces of coconut to be ground into smooth pastes, masalas, for the day's cooking. Coconut is used in so many Parsi dishes that it's important to talk about some fundamentals. We'll deal first with fresh coconuts and then with the alternatives.

Buying coconuts. For those who don't live in the palm belt, buying a coconut is a gamble. I could tell you to choose a coconut that's heavy, to listen for a dull sloshing sound as you shake it, to make sure there are no cracks and nothing growing out of the eyes. You could bring home a coconut that met all these requirements and still end up with a dud. The important thing, then, is to buy coconuts where there's a brisk turnover or responsible selling policies. When you bring a coconut home, plan to use it soon. Nowadays, you can buy coconuts described as young; but for making coconut milk, you want mature ones. Young coconuts have a delicious leathery texture that's wonderful in salads, and their water is sweet and refreshing, but they're not the right ones for coconut milk.

Cracking the coconut and dealing with it. There's a really easy way to get into a coconut. First strip off any extra fiber. Then hold the coconut over a bowl to catch the water. Using a standard hammer—no dainty tools here—give the coconut several sharp whacks around its equator, where it will generally crack in two. Inspect the flesh and taste it. There should be no trace of mold, and the smell and taste should be fresh and sweet. Sometimes, with mature nuts, the juice—known as coconut water—can taste a little sour but the flesh will be absolutely sound. If the water tastes good, drink it as the cook's bonus. You can also use it in the making of coconut milk or for cooking rice.

The next step is determined by what you want to do with the coconut. If you're making a masala paste and you have a wet-dry grinder, you can pry the coconut away from its shell in pieces. If you want to grate the coconut for making coconut milk, you can hand-grate the pieces you pry out, or throw them into a food processor or powerful blender with some coconut water or tap water. (If you want pristine white coconut milk, you need to peel off the tough brown skin first.) Or you can do what's done in India, Sri Lanka, and points eastward, all the way to the Philippines: Use a rotary coconut reamer-grater or a coconut grating stool. The rotary graters are usually mounted or clamped to a

ROTARY COCONUT
GRATER AND A COCONUT
GRATING STOOL

table. The business end is a hemispherical grater on a shaft that gets turned with a hand crank while the halved coconut is pressed against the blades with the other hand. With a grating stool, you sit or kneel on it and rotate the coconut around a fixed rasp. Coconut grated in either of these ways yields more and better milk. Sometimes when you need grated coconut for a dish, a good way to get a small amount is to use an old-fashioned crinkly-edged bottle cap, the kind known as a crown cap or crown cork, and scrape it against the inside of the coconut.

Making coconut milk. An average mature coconut will yield about 4 cups of grated meat. Barely cover the grated coconut with boiling water, using the coconut water for part of the liquid. Let it stand for at least 30 minutes. The simplest way to squeeze the milk out of the coconut is to put a couple of handfuls at a time into a good-size piece of dampened cloth. Gather up the ends and squeeze very hard over a bowl until the grated coconut is dry. Repeat with the rest of the coconut. The milk is now ready to be used and the wrung-out coconut either discarded or used for making sweets. For curries, let this milk stand for 2 to 3 hours until the cream rises to the top. The thinner part is used in the cooking of the dish; the cream gets saved as a finishing touch, added just before serving. In India, the squeezed coconut is moistened and squeezed yet again. This is known as the second milk, also used in cooking.

Lazy coconut. Sometimes, time and the coconut odds are against us. There are options: these are desiccated or frozen grated coconut; and frozen, canned, or spray-dried coconut milk. Let's dispense with desiccated coconut straight away, especially the sweetened supermarket kind.

Frozen grated coconut comes sweetened and unsweetened. Stick with the unsweetened. You can get it grated in 1-pound bags in the frozen foods section of Southeast Asian markets. This is really decent stuff for making chutney, masala, or coconut milk to be used in cooking.

My first choice in prepared coconut milk, the kind that is closest to fresh, is the frozen variety that comes from Thailand, usually in flat plastic packets. My second choice is coconut milk in tetrapacks (like the packages of juice that children take to school). The best brands are made in Malaysia, Singapore, and India, but may be difficult to find except on the Internet, so consider bringing some back with you if you travel. Some brands of canned coconut milk, such as Chao Koh, are consistently more reliable than others and do well for most dishes.

Spray-dried coconut milk is a product that is a little misunderstood. It is simply coconut milk that has been spray-dried (like powdered cow's milk). There are no noxious additives, apart from maltodextrin or sugar, and it's easy to find brands that are less sweet. I was first told about it by Sri Lankan cooks almost twenty years ago. In our house, we use it from time to time in emergencies. It works perfectly well for curries, for anything that's cooked, and for some sweets.

TAMARIND

The English word comes from the Arabic *tamar-i-hind,* "date of India." For information on the plant itself, see the Glossary. In U.S. markets, tamarind sometimes comes in its original package, a brown beanlike pod with a brittle skin containing several seeds encased in a fibrous sweet-sour pulp. The more mature the tamarind, the darker and sweeter the pulp. It is also sold in blocks of compressed pulp, the Indian version very dark and dry, the Thai, moister and lighter. A third option is the commercial tamarind extract from Thailand and India. The Thai varieties, which I prefer, are thinner and fresher-tasting; the Indian ones are darker, thicker, and sometimes almost tarry.

To extract tamarind pulp from whole fruit, break the brittle covering off the whole seedpods and tear off the fibrous net around the pulp. (If you're using compressed tamarind, simply break off the amount called for by the particular recipe.) Cover the tamarind with boiling water and let it steep for at least 30 minutes and up to a few hours. Or put it in a nonreactive pan, cover with water, and simmer over low heat for 15 to 20 minutes; then let it steep until it's cool enough to handle. Break up the tamarind with your fingers and rub it through a stainless steel or nylon strainer into a bowl, scraping the bottom of the strainer to collect the pulp as you go. Moisten the residue with a little warm water and rub and push it through the strainer again.

Freshly extracted tamarind pulp keeps for at least a week in the refrigerator. Tamarind residue is used in many Indian households to clean brass and copper. Coarse salt and tamarind residue are particularly successful with copper.

BREADS

For us, there are two kinds of bread: leavened bread and *rotlis,* the Gujarati word for the almost universal Indian flat bread, the chapati. In some households, the family expects to see both types at every meal. In my mother's house, *rotlis* appeared almost every night, but rarely in the afternoon; in her mother's house, I suppose they must have appeared on demand. *Rotlis* can be made with a variety of flours—rice, millet, whole wheat—but the only ones I ever saw in my mother's house were made of whole wheat; many Parsis dismiss robust grains such as millet and barley as being too coarse or heavy.

There was usually a loaf of white or brown bread for breakfast toast and teatime sandwiches. India is one of those countries where you can still find good, common white bread available to everyone. The modern presliced loaves in their plastic wrappings are now considered more desirable in that backwards way that thinks it is progress to rush from anything preindustrial. Nevertheless, it's still possible to get energetic, yeasty white bread in loaf or roll form.

In Bombay, you can have bread brought to your door every morning even if all you buy is one roll a day. Before eight, a man arrives at your house on a bicycle weighed down with two large canvas bags of crusty rolls *(gotli pao)* and soft rolls *(naram pao)*, regular loaves like good *pain de mie,* and for those who've forgotten to buy them elsewhere, a few eggs, butter, and the processed cheese spreads so popular in India. Once a month, a bill is presented on a scrap of paper with a precise, scribbled accounting, and on every festive occasion, regardless of religion, the householder is expected to remember the rain-or-shine diligence of the *pao walla* (bread man). For me, this wonderful daily bread, sometimes still breathing warmth, is one of the food highlights of being in India. It's one of the rarer experiences of something that's unassumingly taken for granted and utterly luxurious at the same time.

I like to alternate *gotli pao* with *naram pao,* hard pressed to say which is better. With the bread, I love dark, medicinal *jambul* honey from Mahableshwar near Poona, or sticky guava jelly that fights the spoon, or one of the peerless jams from WIT, a Bombay women's collective, either the grapefruit marmalade or a Cape gooseberry jam. If the timing is lucky, the *panir walla* will have shown up in time for breakfast, in which case, there are soft fresh cheeses floating in their whey.

People say that San Francisco sourdough can't be duplicated anywhere else. Perhaps the same is true of the yeasty breads of Bombay's small bakeries, though I'd love to see someone give it a try in the way that so many Americans have re-created here the breads they fell in love with in France and Italy. There are some Parsi dishes that demand *gotli pao* or its equivalent, a first-rate crusty baguette. These are lentil stews like *masur* and *channa ni dar,* as well as *kharia,* the slow-cooked unctuous union of black-eyed peas and goat's feet. With any dish not accompanied by rice, *rotlis* are expected in a Parsi household.

Chapatis | ROTLIS

Chapatis, flat breads, can be found anywhere in India now, even in the south, but each community or area has its own approach and its own idea of perfection. Chapatis can be dry, strong, and forceful or pliant and silky like the ones in this recipe, where the addition of ghee to the dough makes the difference, so that they can be kept for more than a day without stiffening. (There are special metal boxes for storing cooked chapatis, but any container with a tight lid will do, for instance a round metal cookie tin.)

As a child, I loathed dolls but loved the small board and rolling pin a family friend of my parents had made for me. I spent endless hours playing with dough, rolling it out in odd maplike shapes. I confess to being an unpracticed *rotli* maker—unlike my mother, whose *rotlis* were superb, perfect rounds, patiently baked over medium heat on her *tava,* the lens-shaped cast-iron griddle that now lives in our house. My *rotlis* aren't always round and I have to fight a tendency to turn up the heat too high, which makes them stiff. Practiced *rotli* makers roll and bake as they go, unconscious of the extraordinary beauty and grace of their actions.

Here is the traditional method, followed by a food-processor alternative. For optimal success, buy chapati flour at an Indian market. *Makes 8 to 10.*

1 to 2 teaspoons ghee
½ teaspoon salt
1 cup whole wheat flour, plus extra for adjustments and rolling
⅓ cup (or more) boiling water

- Rub the ghee and salt into the flour on a *thali,* a round tray with straight, 1- to 2-inch-deep sides, or on a rimmed baking sheet, adding enough boiling water to turn the flour into a soft, elastic dough that doesn't stick. Add small amounts of flour or water as needed to firm up or relax the mixture. Knead the dough for a few minutes, cover it with a bowl, and leave it to rest in a warm place for at least an hour.

- Form the dough into a log and divide it into 8 to 10 pieces. On a lightly floured surface, roll out each piece about ⅛ inch thick. It should be thin but not transparent or it will tear.

- Heat a *tava* or cast-iron griddle until a drop of water dances on its surface. Turn the heat down to moderate. Lightly coat the griddle with oil or ghee, wiping up the excess with a paper towel, and start baking the *rotlis* one at a time. As soon as the *rotli* begins to look dry and blistery, flip it over and smear a minute amount of ghee over its surface, using the back of a spoon; keep pressing down on it with the flat side of a pancake turner until it puffs up. Remove at once and repeat until all the *rotlis* are baked, keeping the stack covered as you go. If you like, you can fold them as they come off the fire. Eat them as soon as possible.

- There's a deluxe version in which you divide each of the pieces into two flattened balls. Smear one with ghee and press both balls together, pinching the edges, before rolling out. You get an extra-puffy *rotli* this way.

• • •

Food Processor Method: You can use a food processor for mixing the dough, but turn it out onto a board and knead it briefly by hand before letting it rest. Put the flour and salt in the food processor bowl. Melt the ghee in a small amount of boiling water and sprinkle it over the flour. Then start the machine and add more boiling water through the funnel until the dough pulls away from the sides of the bowl. Let it thump against the bowl thirty times before removing it and letting it rest.

Tortilla Press Method: You can also use a tortilla press for making chapatis if you find you don't get the hang of rolling them out perfectly. Indian groceries now sell them as chapati presses, a perfect example of successfully transferred technology. A further technological development is the electric tortilla/chapati press, which flattens and bakes in one operation.

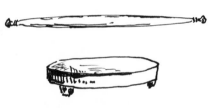

If all this still seems like too much work, do what a lot of U.S.-based Indians do: Buy the darkest whole wheat tortillas you can find. Many supermarkets carry them. Also, most Indian groceries now have an array of close-to-homemade chapatis/*rotlis* for sale.

ROLLING PIN AND BOARD FOR
ROLLING CHAPATIS AND PURIS

Puris

Few things in cooking are as dramatic as slipping a small, flat disk into hot oil and watching it puff up into a perfect sphere. In India, when you're lucky enough to be invited to lunch or dinner in a Gujarati household, the puris keep coming out, wave after wave. The way they're offered is irresistible. "Just one?" And so they keep adding up.

Although people take cold puris on train journeys and picnics, if you're going to all the trouble, they should be hot, hot, hot. Someone has to be on puri duty if you're doing this for more than two or three people. It goes against the American grain to see someone slaving away while others eat, but you have to believe that this is the only way, and that it does give the maker some degree of pleasure to turn out puffy puris *à la minute.* When I was really little, my mother sometimes made puris and let me make my own beside her, practicing with my own child-size board and rolling pin. She used to fry my overworked gray efforts for me while she cooked cleaner ones for consumption by family and friends. This was one of the few kitchen things she did herself from time to time, perhaps just to entertain me. Unlike in Gujarati house-holds where they can appear at every meal, we usually had puris with *papeta nu sakh* (page 202), named Parsi hash yellows by our friend Bob Carrau. My mother's for-mula for puris is the same as for chapatis. *Makes about 12.*

1 to 2 teaspoons ghee
1 cup whole wheat flour (preferably chapati flour), plus extra for
   adjustments and rolling
¼ teaspoon salt
⅓ cup (or more) warm water
Peanut or grapeseed oil, for deep-frying

- Rub the ghee into the flour and salt on a *thali,* a round tray with straight sides, or on a rimmed baking sheet. Add ⅓ cup warm water, or more as needed to make a soft, elastic dough that doesn't stick. Knead by hand for a minute or so, even if you've used a food processor for the mixing as in the previous recipe. Cover with a bowl and let rest at room temperature for at least an hour.

- Roll the dough out ¼ inch thick. Using a cookie cutter or a glass with a good strong edge, cut out puris to the size you want them. My mother's puris were about 3 inches across. The usual Indian way is to divide the dough into lots of little pieces and roll out each puri individually, frying as you go. It drives Americans crazy to see such apparent inefficiency, but a skilled puri or chapati roller can turn them out at a brisk clip and not miss a beat. In the end it's more efficient than constantly gathering the trimmings and rerolling them.

- Heat about 3 inches' worth of peanut oil to 370 degrees in a large, deep frying pan or wok. Deep-fry the puris 2 to 3 at a time in the oil. Push the puris below the surface to make them puff up. They're done as soon as they puff and look golden brown. Remove, drain on absorbent paper and eat while still hot.

Papads

Call them *papads* or *papadams,* or *appalams* in the south—these are the universally popular flat breads of India. Papads are usually, though not invariably, made of the flour of various dals, sometimes plain, sometimes highly seasoned. (A friend recently gave me fabulous potato papads from Benares with coriander leaves embedded in them.) Making papads requires the kind of time, space, and labor that most urban households lack. The dough has to be rolled paper-thin and the parchmentlike disks laid out to dry in the sun. In some rural communities, papads are made by cooperatives of women who take the dough home from a central mixing station and bring it back rolled, dried, and stacked, ready to be packed up and sent to cities in India and all over the world.

Papads vary in size and seasoning from region to region. South Indian ones are usually small, thin, plain, and at their best when fried. Papads from the rest of India are often seasoned with cumin, garlic, chiles, or black pepper. Sizes range from very small (potato-chip size, known as cocktail papads) to 15 inches or more in diameter.

Indian groceries in the United States sell papads of all sorts. Experiment until you find the ones you like the most. My favorites are plain or black pepper- or cumin-flavored, and I like to buy papads made by women's cooperatives.

There are three ways of dealing with papads: frying, toasting, and the microwave (with which I have no experience). Parsi households tend to fry small, plain papads. There's no argument that a billowy, well-fried, well-drained papad is a delicious thing to eat, but it's impossible to stop with one. If you don't want to be like the universe, forever expanding, a toasted papad is equally delicious. It's also a little sturdier and more versatile as a predinner nibble and as a vehicle for spreads. Here are the basic guidelines for both frying and toasting.

To fry papads. Heat oil in a wok or frying pan with a curved bottom to ensure maximum depth for the amount of oil used. You'll probably need about 2 cups. Slip a papad into the hot oil, turning it quickly and removing it as soon as it's puffed, in the case of the South Indian ones, or blistered and opaque, if it's one of the thicker kind. Remove at once and drain on paper towels. Serve immediately. Keep eaters waiting if necessary.

To toast papads over a gas or charcoal flame. You will need to work out a rhythm with your heat source and remember that you can't look away for a second. Turn on a gas burner to medium-high, or find a place on your charcoal grill that doesn't incinerate the papad as soon as you set it down. Using tongs, keep repositioning the papad nimbly until it changes from smooth translucence to blistery opacity. Little dark spots are all right; huge burnt ones are not. Neither are unblistered, raw patches. You will have to sacrifice one or two victims until you work out your papad choreography. Once you get good at it, you can keep two going at the same time. Stack them as you go. Papads can be done ahead and kept warm in an oven with a pilot light or reheated briefly in a low oven before serving as part of the introduction to the meal or as an accompaniment to a rice dish.

ફરસાણ

—◦◆◦—

BEGINNINGS

Before dinner, along with drinks, my grandmother might set out bowls of nuts, usually fried cashews or peanuts, salted and sometimes sprinkled with Indian chilly powder (much like American cayenne pepper). Other favorites would have been *chura* (an addictive mixture of fried pressed rice, nuts, and seasonings, usually scooped with a little teaspoon, put onto the palm, and quickly gobbled up) or *sev-gantia,* an umbrella term to describe the infinite forms that seasoned chickpea flour batter can take when extruded through a special press (see page 71) into hot oil. For something more substantial, my grandmother might have offered crisp little triangular "mutton" samosas with a chutney, but not often. This was not yet the cocktail-party generation.

My mother, on the other hand, used to serve all sorts of things before dinner, things considered the height of luxury: perhaps tinned pineapple on cheese, olives, little asparagus rolls, Vienna sausages or Danish minifrankfurters on toothpicks, tiny "cocktail" *kavabs* of meat or shrimp (referred to as prawns in India), *patrel* (taro-leaf rolls), slices of panir and various cheese and meat mixtures on Monaco biscuits (Indian Ritz crackers). Nowadays, a Parsi hostess might offer crostini and dips of various sorts, like guacamole, or little puff-pastry numbers filled with creamed mushrooms in addition to the perennial favorites, potato chips (which we call wafers), *sarias* (fried sago crackers, recalling the Indonesian *krupuk*), and little "cocktail" papads.

In our house, we're almost required to serve roasted cashews to placate Ordle, our parrot, but predinner nibbles vary from very lean to very indulgent depending on what's to follow. And we love potato chips, too, especially with Champagne.

There's another kind of beginning, the meal that starts the day. Starting in the nineteenth century, urban Parsi breakfasts followed the British pattern of porridge followed by eggs and ham, bacon or kidneys, toast and jam or marmalade, and tea or coffee. My parents dropped the porridge but stuck to the eggs and toast. In our house, breakfast gets reinvented constantly. This section of the book offers you two of our household favorites; others can be found in the eggs chapter and in the sweets section (the two birthday breakfasts).

Roasted Cashews with Ajwain | MASALA KAJU

Among the treasures of the New World brought to India by the Portuguese, cashews are at the top of the list. The usual Indian way with cashews is to fry them, as my mother and grandmother always did, but I prefer roasting them to a pale gold before tossing them with a very small amount of ghee, butter, or olive oil as stickum for pounded *ajwain* seeds and salt. *Ajwain*, or *ajowan*, with its heady oregano-like scent, is my favorite cashew-spicing option. *Serves 2 to 10.*

> *1 pound raw cashews*
> *1 tablespoon ghee, butter, or olive oil*
> *2 teaspoons (or more) salt*
> *About 1 tablespoon ajwain seeds, coarsely pounded to release the aromatic oils*
> *1 teaspoon cayenne pepper or Indian chilly powder (optional)*
> *Freshly ground black pepper (optional)*

· Heat the oven to 325 degrees.

· Tip the nuts onto a baking sheet big enough to hold them in a single layer. Roast for 7 minutes and then start checking every 2 minutes, roasting for another 4 to 8 minutes and moving the nuts around if your oven has hot spots. The cashews should be golden, not brown, although a few brown flecks are all right. Coppertone tan is too brown. If you want to make a smaller quantity of nuts, a toaster oven works well, but you need to be extra-vigilant with cashews.

· After the nuts are out of the oven, let them sit until they're cool enough to handle, but still warm. Add the ghee, following it immediately with salt, *ajwain,* and the cayenne, if you like. Alternatively, give the cashews at least forty twists of a pepper mill, set for a coarse grind. For best results, mix thoroughly with your hands.

· Serve when the nuts have cooled down to the point that they become crisp again. This takes about 15 to 20 minutes.

· · ·

Note: To avoid wasting what's left of the buttery *ajwain* in the bowl after the cashews are gobbled up, use it as a seasoning for boiled or steamed corn on the cob.

BRASS MORTAR
AND PESTLE

Cheese and Almond Crisps

For most Parsis of my generation, *cheese* generally means processed cheddar, the kind that for many years was imported in blue tins from Australia and is now replicated in India. Anything with a cheese flavor attracts Parsis like ants to sugar. Cheese straws, cheese biscuits, little cheese-flavored crackers, cheese sandwiches, all of these are popular nibbles before or between meals. These buttery cheese crisps are a nostalgic evocation of the addictive cheese oat biscuits from Bombay's hidden treasure, the Paris Bakery. The added crunch of sliced almonds comes courtesy of Simon Hopkinson, whom both David and I admire fervently as a chef and a writer about food. Serve the crisps before lunch or dinner. They're in the category of clean, dry nibbles, useful when people are standing around in dressy clothes juggling food and drink. The drink here can be anything from mineral water to a martini, though I think Cheese and Almond Crisps go particularly well with red wine or sherry.

If you've got odd bits of dry cheese, here's where you can use them up. It's worth the extra bother to grate the cheese yourself, and far more accurate to go by weight than by volume, since different graters produce varying volumes. The suggested weight yields about 2 cups grated on a Microplane. Use whatever you find easy, a hand grater or a food processor. The *ajwain,* cumin, and freshly ground pepper are all optional. Feel free to leave them out or increase the amounts. *Makes 50 to 60 or more.*

1 cup regular rolled oats

1 cup flour

1 cup flaked almonds or chopped walnuts

3 to 4 ounces Parmesan or other hard dry cheese, finely grated

½ to 1 teaspoon cayenne pepper or Indian chilly powder

1 teaspoon Colman's dry mustard

1 to 2 teaspoons ajwain or cumin seeds, lightly bruised, or 1 to 2 teaspoons coarsely ground black pepper (optional)

1 teaspoon (about) salt (depending on the cheese used)

1 large egg, lightly beaten

½ pound (2 sticks) butter, melted

· Give the rolled oats a few pulses in a food processor to break them up. Combine them with the flour, nuts, cheese, cayenne, mustard, *ajwain* (if you like), and salt.

· Add the egg and stir well. Follow with the butter and work the mixture until it clumps. Use your hands to press the mixture into a cohesive mass. Divide it into three or four pieces and form logs or loaves about 2 inches in diameter, though there's no reason not to make them narrower and longer to increase the yield. Press in any crumbs or bits of nut that fall off. Wrap tightly in plastic and refrigerate until thoroughly chilled, a few days or even longer, or freeze the logs.

· Heat the oven to 350 degrees. Using a heavy knife, cut into slices no more than ⅛ inch thick. If the logs seem too hard, let them rest at room temperature for a few minutes until they cut more easily. Since these crisps don't spread, set them out fairly close together on ungreased baking sheets. I like parchment paper or Silpat liners, but they're not crucial here. Depending on your oven and your baking sheets, you might need to bake the crisps in two batches.

· Bake for 12 to 15 minutes or until pale gold. Start checking after about 10 minutes and move the trays back to front or swap levels for even cooking. Try not to let the crisps get brown or they'll taste burnt.

· You can serve these crisps while they're still a little warm, but they're equally good at room temperature. They are best baked on the day you plan to serve them, though you can store them in an airtight container for a few days. In that case, warm the crisps slightly before serving.

Parsi Crudités | KACHI TARKARI

A dish of sliced cucumbers or green mango crescents or pineapple chunks or sticks of jicama accompanied by little bowls of salt and cayenne pepper and some lime wedges is sometimes is all you need to begin a meal.

Just before you want to eat them, cut up the fruit or vegetables into handy pieces. Cucumbers, peeled or unpeeled, can be cut into sticks or on the diagonal into long ovals. Hard green mangoes are easily dealt with: remove the "cheeks" by cutting parallel to the seed, peel each one, put it flat on a cutting board, and cut it into crescents.

Serve with a small bowl of cayenne or Sambhar Masala (page 37) and one or more interesting salts. Have a lime wedge or two handy. Eaters dip their chosen piece of fruit or vegetable into the salt and the spices and add a squeeze of lime.

You can also make a quick pickle with lime juice and salt on lotus-root slices cooked until barely tender, or sliced daikon or watermelon radish. You'll need enough lime juice to wet the slices thoroughly. Allow to sit no more than an hour before serving.

Seared Peas | TAVA PEAS

Thousands of flower-crowned pilgrims make their way to the basilica of Chalma, near Malinalco in Mexico, an ancient pre-Conquest shrine now dedicated to Our Lord of Chalma. Chalma will forever be a pilgrimage spot for me, too, though I'm drawn by greed, not piety. My pilgrimage will be to Our Lady of Heavenly Peas, who sits in a small plaza leading to the basilica. From this food vendor I learned this ravishing, drop-dead-simple thing to do with peas. She sits there, pushing the rather warty pea pods back and forth on a dry iron *comal,* chatting with her neighbors as she hands you a bright plastic plate of peas still in their pods, blistered and smoky and sprinkled with coarse salt. The idea is to pull the peas out of the pod with your teeth, just like eating an artichoke leaf.

We hardly bother doing anything else with peas now. No one ever seems to get tired of them, including my friends in Bombay, who named them *tava* peas. Be sure to buy pea pods that have not been sprayed with pesticides. *Serves 2 to 6.*

> *1 pound pesticide-free peas in their pods*
> *Maldon salt or any other coarse flaky salt*

TAVA

- Coat a cast-iron skillet with the merest film of oil and wipe it out with a paper towel. Heat the skillet over a high flame. When it's hot, add the peas in one layer, pushing and turning them until the skins go from brilliant green to a blistery black-flecked olive. If the skillet isn't big enough, you might have to do the peas in two or three batches. Be careful not to overcook the peas.

- Sprinkle with the salt and serve at once. You might have to do an eating demo, but you won't have to do it twice.

. . .

Bean Variations: Try green soybeans, *edamame,* this way, or even fresh chickpeas still in their skins. Fava beans can be done this way, too, out of their pods but still in their skins, according to restaurateurs Walter and Teresa Gonzalez of Los Placeres in Malinalco.

Note: Any good salt will do, including kosher salt. Maldon salt from England just happens to be my favorite for these peas. It's not impossible to find. *Fleur de sel* is equally good.

Taro-Leaf Rolls | PATREL

If there were a top five of favorite Parsi snack foods, *patrel* would be on everyone's list. It's one of those dishes with Hindu Gujarati origins now completely absorbed into our cuisine and transformed by it. *Patrel* is definitely exotic and requires some effort, but it is worth all the time you put into it because there is no other taste quite like it. This recipe, which produces *patrel* of the highest order, was adapted from the one in the 1975 edition of the Time and Talents Club cookbook; its contributor, the late Mary Jamsetjee, my friend Firoza's aunt, was a respected authority on Parsi food.

Patrel for Parsis, *patra* for Gujaratis, consists of taro *(Colocasia esculentum)* leaves spread with a sweet, sour, hot paste and then stacked, rolled, tied, and fried, following the traditional approach, or simply steamed, which I prefer. To finish the dish, the rolls are sliced after they cool and then lightly sautéed or grilled. For Parsis, *patrel* is a finger-food snack or appetizer, although Gujarati cuisine has recipes for *patrel* in coconut milk or other sauces.

Having made *patrel* for almost thirty years, I just recently discovered that large uncrinkly chard leaves make an entirely satisfactory substitute for the taro leaves. The size of the leaves determines the yield. You'll get from four to eight rolls and at least forty to fifty slices of *patrel* from this recipe—enough for a gathering. *Serves a crowd.*

MASALA

About 4 green chiles, depending on heat

About 4 dried red chiles, depending on heat

1 (1-inch-long) piece peeled fresh ginger

3 cloves garlic

½ teaspoon cumin seeds

½ teaspoon ground turmeric

1 tablespoon vegetable oil

1 egg-size piece compressed tamarind or 1 cup Thai prepared tamarind pulp

1 ½ cups chickpea flour (besan)

¼ cup rice flour

¼ cup whole wheat flour

1 medium-size very ripe banana (best if too mushy to eat)

2 to 3 tablespoons jaggery or brown sugar

Salt to taste

12 large untorn taro or chard leaves (15 inches long from base to tip, not including the stem), or more smaller leaves

About 1 cup vegetable oil for shallow-frying

Lime wedges

- For the masala: grind the chiles, ginger, garlic, cumin, and turmeric to a paste in a food processor. Heat the oil in a small skillet over medium heat. Add the paste and fry for 3 to 5 minutes, until the aroma rises.

- Place the compressed tamarind in a bowl. Pour in enough boiling water to cover the tamarind generously and soak about 15 minutes. Rub the softened pulp through a strainer. Measure 1 cup of pulp into the bowl of a food processor and add the fried masala paste, all the flour, the banana, and the jaggery. Pulse to a smooth, thick paste. Season the filling with salt to taste.

- Wash the taro leaves gently, and trim off the stems. Using a knife or vegetable peeler, carefully shave down the midribs. If leaves tear in handling, save them for the inner layers, where you can also use smaller leaves or make a patchwork. Make piles of 3 to 4 leaves, keeping the strongest ones for the outermost layer.

- Put a leaf in front of you, dull side up, pointed end facing away. Using your hands or a rubber or wood spatula (you don't want to tear the leaves with something metal), spread thinly with the filling. The filling should be thin enough for you to see bits of leaf through it. Stack another leaf on top and spread with filling, then repeat the operation with 1 or 2 more leaves, making a stack of 3 to 4 leaves. Fold the 2 bottom lobes away from you. Fold in the sides and crease slightly. Then roll up away from you as tightly as you can, easing over the hump where the stem joins the leaf. Tie with cooking twine in three places so that you have a neat cylinder. Repeat until you use up the filling and leaves.

- It's best to cook the rolls right away. Place in a single layer in a bamboo or metal steamer and steam for 25 to 30 minutes. You know *patrel* is cooked when a thin sharp knife slips easily through the thickest part of the roll without any resistance. Even though *patrel* is fully cooked at this stage, it will not be firm enough to slice until it is thoroughly cold. At this point, the rolls can be held, refrigerated, for a few days.

- When ready to serve the *patrel,* cut the cooled roll into ½-inch-thick slices and shallow-fry them (the usual Parsi method), grill them briefly, or dry-fry them in about 1 tablespoon oil in a hot cast-iron skillet, the type with ridges if you want a striped effect.

- Serve hot or warm with a squeeze of lime.

. . .

Patrel Fritters: An alternative approach to serving *patrel* is to dip the slices in a batter (such as the one in the recipe for Fritters, below) and fry them. This is really de luxe.

Notes: Do not undercook the taro leaves. All parts of the taro plant contain minute crystals of oxalic acid that need to be cooked out. Some individuals are genetically more predisposed to react to the crystals (nothing more serious than an itchy mouth). I am one.

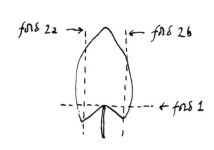

Look for taro leaves at farmers' markets catering to a pan-Asian clientele, Southeast Asian groceries, and West Indian shops. If you're faced with a choice between large torn leaves and small sound ones, go for the sound ones.

If you're substituting chard for taro, use the largest, flattest green leaves you can find. For gardening cooks, this is an ideal way to use those really enormous leaves. Trim the stems off and reserve them for other dishes. Pare the midribs carefully if they seem too stiff, then proceed as with taro leaves. Use extra bits of leaf to make patches. I am astonished at how authentic a chard *patrel* tastes.

FOLDING TARO LEAVES

Fritters | BHAJJIAS

Whether you call them *bhajjias,* the western Indian term, or *pakoras,* more common in the north, Indian fritters tend to be bits of vegetable dunked in a simple chickpea-flour batter and fried. The idea is to cook the vegetable in the time it takes to get the coating as crisp as possible, which depends on correctly gauging the thickness of the pieces of vegetable to be fried. *Bhajjias* are one of Bombay's favorite snack foods, at home or on the streets.

The recipe works perfectly well with ordinary water but is even better if you use soda water instead of tap water. Nalini Swali of Bombay gave me this surprising tip, specifying a brand of local soda water that has finer, denser bubbles than others. Make sure that what you're planning to fry is very dry before you dip it into the batter; this is especially important for leafy vegetables. *Serves about 6 to 8.*

1 cup rice flour
1 cup chickpea flour (besan)
¼ teaspoon baking soda
¼ to ½ teaspoon salt
1 to 2 cups fizzy mineral water or club soda
Vegetable oil, for deep-frying
Any combination of the following, in quantities sufficient for 6 to 8 fritters
per person: well-dried spinach or amaranth leaves; Chinese or
Japanese eggplant, cut into ¼-inch-thick ovals; onion rings; potatoes
or sweet potatoes in ¼-inch-thick slices; summer squash or pumpkin,
sliced no thicker than ¼ inch; lotus root, cut into ¼-inch-thick slices and
blanched; Cuban oregano; cauliflower, cut into ¼-inch-thick slices

· Sift together all the flour, the baking soda, and the salt. Mix with enough mineral water to make a batter the consistency of heavy cream. Leave it on the thick side until you test-fry a piece or two of vegetable.

· Pour enough oil into a deep saucepan, wok, or *karhai* to reach a depth of 3 inches. Heat the oil over medium heat until it is hot but not smoking, 360 to 370 degrees. Dip 1 trial piece into the batter, shaking off the excess, and drop into the hot oil. Repeat. Do not crowd the pan; fry in batches as necessary, turning once. Cooking times will vary depending on the main ingredient; test-fry one or two until you get a feel for the technique. Transfer to paper towels to drain, and serve hot.

· · ·

Cheese Fritters: A great nonvegetable thing to fry is soft cheese like Bellwether Farms ricotta, *ricotta salata*, Manouri, or your own homemade panir (page 63) left to firm up and dry out in the fridge for a couple of days.

Mother's "Italian" Eggs

Italian eggs are as Italian as the French dressing you buy in supermarkets is French. Throughout my early childhood, though, this is how I imagined Italian food might taste. I wonder if there's some equally improbable counterpart in Italian cuisine, something *all'indiana.* My mother dates Italian eggs—no Gujarati name for them—back to her own childhood, a recipe from a family friend, Tehmina Lalkaka. In an early-twentieth-century Parsi cookbook written in Gujarati there's a recipe for Italian eggs, but it is for hard-boiled eggs in a tomato sauce, not the provocative sweet, sour, and hot mayonnaise mixture in this version of deviled eggs. I never make fewer than six to eight eggs at a time because they vanish more quickly than you can imagine. My food-writer friend Patty Unterman found these eggs ravishing and wrote about them, and later Fran McCullough picked them up from Patty's column for her *Best American Recipes of 1999.* My mother was delighted, but rather matter-of-fact: "Well, they are very good." *Serves 4 to 12.*

> *6 large eggs*
> *2 tablespoons mayonnaise*
> *2 tablespoons butter, room temperature*
> *2 (or more) green chiles, finely chopped*
> *1 tablespoon (or more) lime juice, preferably from a Mexican or Key lime*
> *½ cup chopped fresh coriander (cilantro) leaves*
> *1 tablespoon (or more) honey*
> *Salt to taste*
> *Whole small coriander leaves or diagonally cut slivers of fresh red or*
>   *green chile, for garnish*

- Place the eggs in a saucepan of cold water and heat to a boil. Turn the heat to a simmer and cook for 12 minutes. The yolks need to be firm. Plunge the eggs into cold water until cool enough to handle, and peel. Halve them lengthwise. If you see any thin spots in the white, cut the egg so that the thin spot is on the bottom. You can reinforce it with a shaved patch from the thicker half.

- Scoop out the yolks and set aside the whites. Mash and cream the yolks with the mayonnaise, butter, chiles, lime juice, chopped coriander leaves, and the surprise ingredient, honey—at least 1 tablespoon, but possibly more. Add salt to taste. You want the mixture to be assertive, so don't be timid with the sweet, the sour, or the salt.

- Mound the yolk mixture into the egg white halves. Leave the surface rough, gently cross-hatched with the tines of a fork. Chill until the filling firms up, about 1 to 2 hours. Remove from the refrigerator about half an hour before serving. At serving time, garnish each half with a single perfect coriander leaflet or a diagonally cut sliver of fresh green or red chile.

· · ·

"Italian" Egg Salad: Chop the hard-boiled eggs. Toss with all the ingredients except the butter; compensate with a little extra mayonnaise. Serve on a bed of lettuce and cucumber or as a first-rate egg-salad sandwich with lots of lettuce and cucumber on whole wheat bread. To make a sturdy filling for thin, crustless sandwiches, leave in the butter and refrigerate the mixture until it's firm.

Notes: The quantities are a starting point. Please use your judgment when it comes to heat. If you don't like the filling hot, start with half a chile and take the seeds out before you chop it. Do suspend any disbelief about the honey. Its presence is magical. You don't want to use a dark, medicinal honey. Stick with one in the light-to-medium floral range.

If you can get tiny pullet eggs, use them and make a whole dozen at a time. But don't even think of making this recipe with quail eggs.

For scaling up the recipe, if you're not comfortable with a grab-and-fling approach to cooking, the easiest way is to measure the egg yolks. For each generous cup of cooked yolks measured without packing (about 8 eggs), add 3 to 4 tablespoons each butter and mayonnaise, 1½ cups coriander leaves, 3 to 4 hot green chiles, 2 tablespoons or more honey, and lime and salt to taste. You can put the ingredients in a food processor and blend them until the filling is creamy but still has texture from the coriander leaves and chiles.

Smoked Fish Spread

You can make any smoked fish taste like Bombay by giving it this treatment. Serve this spread as an hors d'oeuvre in a crock with toast or sliced cucumbers, or make little canapés or even crustless sandwiches out of it. *Serves 4 to 6.*

8 to 12 ounces smoked trout, whitefish, or sablefish (black cod)
½ to 1 cup Yogurt Cheese (page 62), prepared without the cumin, or mild goat cheese
2 (or more) tablespoons olive oil
2 to 3 green chiles
2 to 3 tablespoons finely chopped shallots or 1 to 2 green onions, finely chopped
Freshly ground black pepper to taste
Salt to taste
Lime or lemon juice to taste
Chives or chive blossoms, for garnish

- The lazy way is to whomp it all up in a food processor. I like to process just the trout, yogurt, and oil until they're well mixed but not the texture of toothpaste. Transfer to a bowl and add the chiles, shallots, and a few twists of the pepper mill. Salt to taste.

- Let stand for about an hour before serving. Just before spreading on toast or mounding into a crock, add a healthy squeeze of lime juice. Garnish with chives or, better yet, purple chive blossoms.

. . .

Smoked Fish Sandwiches: For sandwiches, add ½ cup (1 stick) room-temperature butter to the recipe. Use a sturdy white bread or *pain de mie* that you can slice yourself. The slices of bread should be half the thickness of the average piece of commercially sliced bread.

Parsi Pâté | KALEJI NO PATE

Parsi hostesses love morsels of brightly spiced chicken liver served on toast (page 151). This pâté gives you the same effect with no last-minute fuss. The technique may be French in origin, but the taste is authentically Indian. The pâté can be spread on toast or on oven-crisped whole wheat tortilla or pita triangles. If it's a do-it-yourself arrangement, set out a bowl of Allium Confit (page 186) warmed with a touch of cayenne pepper. If you're preparing a tray of canapés, put a small dab of chutney on each one.

Besides making a first-rate hors d'oeuvre, this terrine can be served as the main course of a light lunch for six to eight people, accompanied by crusty bread, some Parsi Tomato Chutney (page 231), and perhaps a salad of rocket or curly endive with fresh figs and chopped toasted almonds or hazelnuts.

The recipe makes enough to fill a 3- to 4-cup terrine. This pâté tastes better if prepared at least a day ahead of time, so that the flavors can develop. In fact, it keeps for a week, getting better every day. *Serves 10 to 12.*

1 pound chicken livers, trimmed, each lobe halved
¼ cup ghee or clarified butter
⅓ cup chopped shallots
1 teaspoon Parsi Garam Masala (page 37)
½ to 1 teaspoon cayenne pepper or Indian chilly powder
1 teaspoon salt
¼ cup Madeira, medium-bodied sherry (such as amontillado), or cognac
3 large eggs
1 cup heavy cream

· Heat the oven to 350 degrees. Very lightly butter a 4-cup terrine or soufflé dish and find an ovenproof pan you can set it in with high enough sides that you can add water to come halfway up the sides of the terrine.

· Pat the livers dry with paper towels. Heat half the ghee in a sturdy skillet over medium-high heat. Add the shallots and let them barely brown. This won't take long. Remove the shallots from the pan and set aside. Add the remaining ghee to the pan, bring the heat up to high, add the chicken livers, and brown them quickly. Remove the livers while they're still pink inside. Set aside. Reduce the heat to medium-low and add the garam masala, cayenne, and salt to the pan. Stir for a minute until the aroma rises. Add the Madeira, and stir for a few moments to deglaze the pan. Combine the livers, shallots, cooking juices, eggs, and cream in a food processor and pulse until smooth. Adjust the salt.

· Pour the mixture into the prepared terrine. Give it a little thump on the counter to settle the contents. Set the terrine in a pan of hot water and put it in the center of the oven. Let the terrine cook for about 45 to 50 minutes, checking it after about 35 minutes. You'll know the terrine is done when it doesn't tremble. It will have puffed up a little and have a slightly cracked surface. Be careful not to overbake or overbrown.

- Remove the terrine from the hot water bath. Let it stand until cool enough to refrigerate. Serve cool, not cold, or at room temperature.

Yogurt Cheese | MATTH

Parsis use yogurt cheese to make creamy sauces that won't break as they might with undripped yogurt. They also make a delectable spread out of it with nothing more than some pounded cumin seed.

For an easy hors d'oeuvre, try it on toast or crisped whole wheat tortillas, with some walnuts and mint, Persian style. To make enough for a party, simply increase the amount of yogurt and add pounded cumin and salt gradually until you get the taste you want. *Serves 6 to 8.*

> *Salt*
> *1 pint cow's- or goat's-milk yogurt (nonfat is all right if it doesn't have stabilizers)*
> *1 to 2 teaspoons cumin seeds*

- Very lightly salt the yogurt. Dampen a generous piece of cheesecloth or muslin. Pour in the yogurt. Bring the ends of the cloth together and tie them over your kitchen tap, with a bowl underneath to catch the dripping whey, which you can save to drink or use as a cooking liquid. The thickness and closeness of the weave influences how fast the dripping goes. Allow a couple of hours at least.

- When the yogurt is reduced to almost half its original volume, you're left with yogurt cheese. If you've used goat's milk yogurt, you have a nice little fresh goat cheese.

- Bruise the cumin seeds in a mortar. Gradually stir the cumin into the yogurt, adding enough to please your own taste. Remember that the flavor will develop on standing. Add a bit more salt, if needed.

• • •

Green Peppercorn Cheese: Chopped green peppercorns, fresh or brined, 1 teaspoon or so, make a good alternative to cumin.

Note: Yogurt cheese is sold at Middle Eastern groceries as *labneh* or kefir cheese. Some people add the cumin seeds to the yogurt before dripping. Your choice.

Creamy Panir

For Parsis, panir is fresh cheese made from the milk of cows or buffaloes—yes, the kind that plough fields and give you mozzarella. (In Bombay, most of our milk comes from buffaloes, and so does a lot of our "beef.") There are two general types of panir. One is the Punjabi variety: resilient, dryish, destined for cooking because it holds its shape. The other is panir that is meant to be eaten fresh. There's a lot of unnecessary mystery associated with making good panir, which is why many people in India buy it, but it's easy to make at home.

There's yet another kind of panir I need to tell you about, though I can't tell you how to make it well, because all of my attempts have failed. It's one of India's disappearing food treasures, *topli nu panir,* or "basket panir," made by dripping milk coagulated with rennet derived from dried chicken gizzard through individual flowerpot-shaped baskets. The result is a wobbly basket-marked cylinder of custardy consistency, slightly tart and ravishingly delicious.

In Bombay, about the only way you can now get *topli nu panir* is to have it brought to the door. A *panir walla*'s phone number is as prized as that of a good pedicurist, haircutter, or electrician. Until fairly recently, panir used to be taken around in earthen pots, floating in its whey, but the current vessels are aluminum or stainless steel—lighter for hauling around, if less picturesque. My mother's old *panir walla* went back to his *muluk* (village of origin) long ago, and in his place we have Salim, a young man who'd very much like to come to the United States and take panir around from door to door.

Two Parsi women I know of in Bombay make *topli nu panir.* One of them is Dhun Bana, who kindly gave me two lessons from start to finish, which I documented with notes and pictures. Both times, the moment I returned to San Francisco I tried in vain to duplicate her efforts using the correct baskets my dear father had made for me by the basket-making family near the bottom of Princess Street. It's yet another lesson in never underestimating the art of repeated actions.

VESSEL FOR MAKING
PANIR AND A PAN FOR
BOILING MILK

My mother seldom made panir, though, because the very best was just a phone call away, made by a woman who spent her evenings dressed in beautiful antique saris, playing cards for high stakes at the Willingdon Club. My first attempts at panir were unsuccessful, mediocre at best, even following my aunt Mani's advice and direction, until I found a recipe in a long-out-of-print book by the mother of one of my parents' friends. Sehra Albless's 1956 cookbook, *My Favourite Recipes,* is a good example of the diet of her contemporaries. It's full of Parsi classics plus lobster bisque, rose-petal fritters, artichoke savory, asparagus shortcake, and the like. (The foreword, by one of the writer's cronies, takes a square potshot at "that pathetic obsession of the century—the need for streamlining the female form.") Her recipe, adapted here, makes a perfect creamy panir.

If you want your panir on the acid side, let the yogurt stand at room temperature overnight or until it is quite sour before you use it. For this recipe, you will need a nonreactive mesh strainer and some fine cheesecloth or muslin. Average supermarket cheesecloth is useless. You will also need a perforated panir-making utensil or a device improvised from your strainer, a plate, and a one-pound weight, or three 1-pint strawberry baskets. Panir vessels are available in Bombay at traditional utensil shops or at the Sahakari Bhandar, a large buy-everything-here kind of place right in the middle of town near the Taj Mahal Hotel. *Serves 2 to 6.*

1 cup cow's- or goat's-milk yogurt
2 teaspoons sea salt
½ cup heavy cream
4 cups whole cow's or goat's milk (unpasteurized if possible)

- Stir together the yogurt, salt, and cream. Set aside. Put the milk in a pan roomy enough to allow it to climb up as it boils without overflowing. Set the saucepan over moderately high heat. When the milk comes to a boil, let it come all the way up to the top of the pan. Lift the pan off the burner while the milk subsides. Do this four more times. Don't ask why. Just do it. It's magic. After the fifth boil subsides, add the reserved yogurt-cream mixture and quickly whisk it into the milk until it just begins to separate. It should look like a cloudy sky breaking up, not a solid overcast.

- Pour into a nonreactive mesh strainer lined with fine cheesecloth or muslin and placed over a large bowl. After most of the whey has dripped through into the bowl, about 15 to 30 minutes, fold the cloth over the curds, transfer the bundle to a perforated metal panir-making utensil, and put a weight on the lid. A weight of about 1 pound should do. Alternatively, fold the cloth over the top of the panir, leave it in the strainer, put a small plate over it, and stand a weight on the plate. Or transfer the cloth-wrapped curds into two nested 1-pint strawberry baskets, fold the cloth over the top, and press it down with another strawberry basket holding a 1-pound weight. Save the whey and use it for making dal (page 176) or for cooking beans or lentils.

- Stand this device on a plate, to catch stray drips, and refrigerate the panir for 4 to 5 hours, or even overnight, until it is firm and the cloth peels back easily. Remove from the refrigerator, peel off the cloth, and if you're not ready to serve, wrap it in plastic wrap and refrigerate again. Serve at room temperature, perhaps on a leaf-lined plate.

. . .

Notes: Sometimes it seems as though the panir will never form curds. In these cases, no need to fret; a few drops of lemon juice and a little more stirring over moderate heat usually get things going. Goat's milk is especially recalcitrant, so if you use it, be prepared to stir for a few minutes before getting anxious or going for the lemon juice.

The beauty of this formula is its balance of creaminess and solidity, but you may be tempted, as I have been, to make the panir extra-rich by using half-and-half instead of milk or adding a lot more cream. If you intend to fry the panir, as we sometimes do, resist the temptation, but if you want it soft and voluptuous and damn the consequences, go ahead, see how you like it.

Krishna's Breakfast

The Krishna in question is not the Hindu deity but Krishna Riboud, a brilliant epicurean friend who put this breakfast together after inspecting the possibilities in my tiny Berkeley kitchen one morning. We had some apricot jam and fresh panir I'd made for her, which I thought we'd be eating with freshly warmed whole wheat tortillas and some strong Darjeeling tea—a perfect Parsi breakfast—but her eye fell on the fresh turmeric pickle from the night before.

Twenty-five years later, Krishna's breakfast is still one of the most exciting things to eat that I know. Think of it as something to eat throughout the day, not just for breakfast. We usually serve it as an intriguing hors d'oeuvre, and always, there's a gasp of delight when people realize they're not eating chopped carrots. If you can't make your own cheese, serve a fresh goat cheese or Manouri, a sheep cheese from Greece, or even a not-too-salty feta, say Bulgarian. If you don't want to make your own chapatis, whole wheat tortillas are in many supermarkets—my favorite brand is El Grano de Oro. If you do, it's not hard (see page 44).

This is what you do to put together Krishna's breakfast. You need Creamy Panir (page 63), Yogurt Cheese (page 62), or any fresh goat or sheep cheese; the ultra-simple Fresh Turmeric and Ginger Pickle (page 234); and chapatis or whole wheat tortillas, heated over an open flame so that they're blistered and flecked with dark brown. Organize a tray with a leaf-lined plate of fresh cheese, a thick napkin wrapped around the chapatis or tortillas, and a bowl of the pickle. If you're serving Krishna's breakfast as plateless finger-food, be sure to have napkins handy.

This is how you eat Krishna's breakfast: Each person takes a chapati or half of one. Break off a small piece, enough to make a mouthful. Smear it with some cheese. Put a small amount of the turmeric pickle on the cheese, wrap the chapati or tortilla around it, and pop it into your mouth. It's like eating sparklers.

Mehlli's Orchard Breakfast | POHUA

Part of the fun of going to our local farmers' market with our neighbor pals, Bob and Tony, is having breakfast afterward, surrounded by the morning's spoils. It's the perfect time for one of my favorite Indian breakfasts, such as *pohua*. *Pohua* is the Gujarati word for rice flakes, or rice that has been steamed, pressed, and dried. It's sold at Indian markets as pohua or poha; select the finer flake variety. It forms the basis for India's universal junk food, *chivda,* which is somewhat like salty Rice Krispies with various additions such as peanuts, coconut, and curry leaves. Parsis also use *pohua* in a milky dessert or simply soaked and cooked with potatoes as a light savory dish.

In my dear friend Mehlli Gobhai's *chiku* (sapodilla) orchard house three hours north of Bombay, his brilliant young cook, Dharamraj, produces this *pohua* for breakfast in a matter of minutes. My mother used to serve it for lunch occasionally, but I never realized how easy it was until I watched Dharamraj. All you need to do ahead of time is boil the potatoes. This is my reconstruction of Dharamraj's *pohua.* The chiles can be chopped if everyone likes their food hot; otherwise leave them whole for flavor without heat.

For breakfast, serve this *pohua* with a poached egg or two. The eggs can be poaching while the *pohua*'s cooking right next to it. For a light lunch, serve *pohua* with a dollop of yogurt, some Eggplant Pickle (page 235), and a cucumber salad. You could also serve *pohua* as a starchy accompaniment to simply cooked fish, meat, or chicken. *Serves 4 to 6.*

2 cups fine pohua (often labeled "poha")
2 tablespoons vegetable oil
4 coin-size slices peeled fresh ginger, finely chopped or julienned
10 to 12 curry leaves

2 to 3 green chiles, left whole or finely chopped

1 scant teaspoon brown mustard seeds

1 small or ½ medium onion, very finely chopped

½ teaspoon ground turmeric

2 to 3 medium waxy potatoes (such as Yukon Gold), boiled, peeled,
    and cut into small cubes

½ to 1 teaspoon (or more) salt

½ to 1 cup chopped fresh coriander (cilantro) leaves and stems to taste,
    some reserved for garnish

Freshly grated coconut (optional)

Lime wedges

- Put the *pohua* in a strainer and run cold water over it, wetting it thoroughly. Set it aside.

- In a wok or skillet, heat the oil over moderately high heat. Add the ginger, curry leaves, and chiles. When the chiles look blistered and the ginger toasty, add the mustard seeds. When the seeds begin to crackle and pop, immediately add the onion. Let the onion soften and brown, keeping the contents of the pan moving, about 3 minutes. Then add the turmeric, give things another stir, and add the potatoes. Toss the potatoes in the onion base for 2 to 3 minutes and let them take on a good yellow color. Add about ½ to 1 teaspoon salt. Stir to combine well. Add the *pohua*. Toss very gently, shaking the pan back and forth to get the contents of the pan mixed without handling the rice any more than you have to. If the rice does get mashed a bit, it's really all right. Taste for salt again.

- Stir in the coriander leaves just before serving, and sprinkle some over the top, along with some grated fresh coconut, should you happen to have it. Serve with a squeeze of lime.

Bhel Puri

Bombay's claim to street food fame. No one has yet come up with a reliable answer to where and when *bhel* originated. I know it was well entrenched in my grandparents' time, when it probably had more of the allure of the forbidden than it has today. *Bhel* has now become almost pan-Indian, and for both good and bad has gone beyond its street and beach origins. You can now be served *bhel* in the luxurious surroundings of India's poshest clubs and hotels, and you can get it in more humble, yet air-conditioned places with names like Hot and Love Fast Food and Dreamland Snack Home. But nowhere is it as good as it is on a street corner or on a beach by the light of a kerosene lamp, with the salt breeze blowing in from the Arabian Sea and a thousand other scents and sounds, your portion handed to you on what could very well be someone's recycled algebra exam.

There is nothing else like it in the world, and it's impossible to describe easily. In Bombay, *bhel* is the umbrella term to cover two preparations, one more expensive and elaborate than the other. Basic *bhel* consists of crumbled crisp puris mixed with *sev* (fine chickpea flour strands), chopped onions, chopped boiled potato, chopped fresh coriander (cilantro), perhaps some chopped green mangoes if they're in season, puffed rice, and a bit of each of two chutneys, one sweet, the other killingly hot. All this is tipped onto a square of newspaper or school exam paper with a squeeze of lime to finish it and extra salt or chutney if you want. You scoop it up with a puri. *Sev batata puri* is the dress version. On your square of paper, you get usually six puris per portion, potatoes, onions, coriander, mangoes, the two chutneys, and a sprinkling of *sev* on top before the squeeze of lime. The puris act as a conveyance for what rests on them. A generous *bhel puri walla* (vendor) will often give you a small mound of bland puffed rice mixed with *sev* on another piece of paper to clean off your fingertips and restore your tongue to consciousness if you've done what most Bombay folk do—eaten your *bhel* so hot that you don't know whether you're dying of pain or ecstasy. Off to the side there's generally a pail of water and a lad to pour it over your hands if you get them really messy. In fancy places, everything comes on a plate with a spoon. In less-fancy places, you get two spoons.

If you follow my recipes, you will get *bhel* that has brought expressions of sick nostalgia to expatriate Bombaywallas. "The ultimate fantasy," said one, "*bhel* without amoebas!" Allow half a day to get everything together and have about six people to share it with. The puris are the most fiddly part of the operation; everything else is easy.

Puris (see recipe below)
4 to 6 waxy potatoes (such as Yukon Gold), boiled with 1 teaspoon turmeric,
*   peeled, and roughly diced*
2 to 4 medium-size red onions, the sweetest possible (or a combination of onions
*   and shallots), finely chopped*
Puffed rice, for simple bhel
Salt to taste

Sweet Tamarind Chutney (see recipe below)
Hot Green Chutney (see recipe below)
Sev (see recipe below)
2 to 3 cups coarsely chopped fresh coriander (cilantro) leaves and stems
Finely chopped hard green mangoes
Lime wedges

- *Bhel puri wallas* are masters of unstudied artistry. For *sev batata puri,* arrange everything within easy reach. Make each portion separately: start with a puri, top with potatoes and onions and a sprinkling of salt; then add a drizzle (to the individual's taste) of each chutney; then the *sev* and coriander, green mango, and a squeeze of lime. Eat immediately so the crisp elements don't get soggy.

- For a simple *bhel,* crumble puris into a bowl, add a small handful of potatoes, crushed with your hands, a sprinkling of onion, puffed rice, *sev,* and coriander and barely moisten with the two chutneys and squeezes of lime. Salt to taste. Mix just before serving. Scoop up with a whole puri.

- I have known people to use crumbled chapati chips (whole wheat tortilla triangles oven-toasted until crisp) and commercial *sev* to make *bhel.* It's lower in both labor and calories. Commercial *sev,* available at Indian groceries, is not at all bad, but packing and handling reduce the long, airy strands to near crumbs. The finest *sev* is sometimes labeled as "nylon," which has nothing to do with its contents; this is what you should buy.

- Make the service as no-nonsense as possible. Use your old blue books or cut-up *National Enquirers* or the tabloid of your choice. Do this outside if you can or in a setting where the tablecloth is not important.

- In Bombay, you're likely to find a coconut vendor close by to quench the flames. If not, drink water or lemonade.

• • •

Bhel-Style Potato Salad: Quartered and sliced boiled potatoes laid out on a serving dish can be topped with all the *bhel* fixings, like finely chopped onion, green mango, and several squeezes of lime. Blanket the potatoes with a lightly whisked yogurt. Drizzle the yogurt with streaks of Date and Tamarind Chutney (page 230), and sprinkle with fresh coriander and optional *sev.* This makes a first-rate potato salad, using most of the addictive elements of *bhel* without the calories in fried puris.

Flat Puris

These are the opposite of conventional, inflated puris. They are flat, hard, and crisp. While the puri dough is resting, you can (1) make the *sev* mixture; (2) boil 4 to 6 waxy potatoes (reds or Yellow Finns) in salted water with 1 teaspoon turmeric, which will make them an attractive yellow; and (3) make the two chutneys.

1 ⅔ cups all purpose whole wheat flour or Indian chapati flour
⅓ cup fine semolina (suji) for crispness
½ teaspoon salt
2 tablespoons oil, plus more for deep-frying
½ cup (or more) water

- Combine the flour, semolina, and salt. Add 2 tablespoons of the oil and enough water to make a stiff dough. Start with ½ cup water and increase if necessary. Knead until smooth by hand or in the food processor. Let the dough rest, covered but not refrigerated, for about an hour.

- Divide into four portions. Roll out each portion until it is as thin as possible short of transparency. (When turning puris out in volume, I once used a pasta machine to get even sheets of dough.) Cut out 1½-inch-diameter rounds. Score the surface of each puri lightly to discourage puffing. Combine scraps, press them together, and reroll, continuing to cut out rounds until the dough is used up. If you're lucky enough to have help, one can roll while the other fries. It's not a good idea to let the puris stand, and on no account let them touch each other before frying, because they have a way of gluing themselves together.

- To fry, heat oil to a depth of at least 2 inches in an Indian *karhai,* a wok, or anything else you like to fry in. When the oil reaches 375 degrees, fry the puris, four to six at a time, until crisp and golden brown. Drain on paper towels. While the oil is hot, proceed with the next step.

Sev

For making *sev* you need a special gadget, something like a cookie press. It's available at most Indian groceries that sell kitchen equipment. A chickpea-flour paste extruded into hot oil, *sev* can be thick and twiggy or fly-away thin, a variety often described as "nylon" *sev.* This is the kind you need for *bhel.*

1 cup chickpea flour (besan), thoroughly sifted
½ teaspoon salt
½ teaspoon ground turmeric
Oil, for deep-frying

- Sift the flour, salt, and turmeric together thrice to be sure there are no lumps to clog the holes of the *sev* maker. Mix with just enough warm water to form a heavy paste.

- To fry the *sev,* heat a minimum of 3 inches of oil to about 370 degrees in a deep heavy pan (you can also use the hot oil from making the puris). Fill the cavity of the *sev* maker and press the mixture through the plate with the finest holes into the oil, drawing the strands in a straight line across the surface to avoid criss-crossing and clumping. Set the gadget aside for the few seconds it will take to flip the mat of strands over to fry the other side. Do not brown. *Sev* crisps as it cools.

- Lift out the fried *sev,* drain on paper towels, and repeat the procedure until all the mixture is used. What doesn't get used for *bhel* keeps well in an airtight tin.

· · ·

Sev-Gantia: Our household name for these is *squiggles.* Add ½ teaspoon chile powder and ½ teaspoon or more lightly pounded *ajwain* to the *sev* mixture. Taste for salt and add more if you like. Press the mixture into the hot oil through any of the plates with larger openings—a star, slits, or circles. Again, take out the *sev* (fine round holes) or the *gantia* (slits or stars) before it gets dark brown. Drain on paper, let cool to room temperature, and break up to serve. You can serve it in a tall mound of strands, or squiggles, and let your guests break off as much as they want.

Sweet Tamarind Chutney

1 walnut-size piece dried tamarind
½ to ¾ cup (or more) boiling water
25 pitted dates (for fancy chutney), or ¾ cup jaggery
½ teaspoon ground turmeric
½ cup fresh coriander (cilantro) leaves and stems
2 to 3 green chiles
Salt to taste

PRESS FOR EXTRUDING
SEV AND GANTIA

- To extract the tamarind pulp, cover the piece of dried tamarind with the boiling water and leave for at least an hour. Rub the softened tamarind through a sieve, covering the residue with more boiling water and pressing it through again, and perhaps even a third time.

- Mix the strained tamarind pulp with the dates, turmeric, fresh coriander, chiles, and salt in a blender or food processor until completely smooth (no chunks of chile or coriander). Strain if you sense little bits of date skin on your tongue. Adjust the balance of sweet and salt and sour and hot. This chutney should be a little hot but not very. Its consistency should be about that of slightly thin ketchup.

Hot Green Chutney

This chutney must be ferociously hot; it's raucous, not refined.

½ cup roasted small chickpeas (channa), preferably husked
1 cup (or more) water
10 to 15 hot green chiles
1 cup fresh coriander (cilantro) leaves and stems
Salt to taste

- Put the roasted chickpeas in the food processor with 1 cup water and reduce them to a fine paste. Then add the chiles, fresh coriander, and salt and process to a slightly rough-textured, soupy state, adding more water if necessary. The consistency should be sloppy without being watery.

· · ·

Notes: When I wrote this recipe in 1984, the only shortcut available was commercial *sev. Bhel* has become so popular as a do-it-yourself fool-around food that many Indian groceries sell kits of very decent commercial puris, *sev,* and bottled chutneys. I buy the commercial puris and *sev* but wouldn't compromise on the chutneys. It's not hard to make them while you're waiting for potatoes to boil. Another acceptable shortcut is the excellent bottled tamarind extract from Thailand, which I keep on hand for emergencies.

Bhel puri wallas have to think of the bottom line, so they often make the sweet chutney with inexpensive jaggery instead of expensive imported dates. We don't need to cut corners at home, but it's good to keep a little jaggery or brown sugar at hand for adjusting the final balance of the chutney.

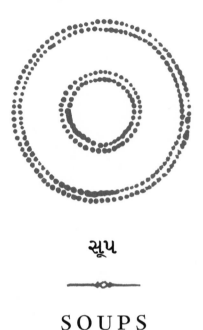

સૂપ

SOUPS

Parsis love soupy food—though soup as a category is a relative newcomer to Parsi cuisine, an appropriation from the Raj. My mother remembers soup appearing regularly on the dinner menu when she was growing up, always as the opening course, never as the center of a meal. Cooks in Parsi households, and other Indian ones for that matter, could take humdrum soups from English cuisine and turn them into delicious hybrids. Tomato and other cream soups were always popular, along with a mulligatawny that bore little resemblance to the Anglo version made with chopped apple and curry powder.

I've sometimes heard thundering from the culinary pulpit that to be any good, all soups have to be made with meat stock. The Parsi approach to soup proves this wrong. The vegetable soups in this section rely on their main ingredient, helped along with adroit finishing touches. They make a sprightly introduction to a complex main course. Some of the other soups here do rely on fish or meat, such as the Parsified Provençal fish soup (page 79) or the Mulligatawny (page 81), and these serve very well as main dishes.

Carrot and Fresh Coriander Soup

Any carrot soup made in my mother's or grandmother's kitchen would have been thoroughly cooked, creamed, and perhaps thickened, with delicious freshly fried croutons floating in it. I prefer vegetable soups with a fresher character and a coarser texture so that you're not full before the meal's under way. This soup can be served cool, at room temperature, or warm, with finely chopped fresh coriander leaves, mint, or chives stirred in just before serving. A little jab from finely chopped green chiles is entirely up to you. A soup like this makes a perfect introduction to a rich or complex main course. *Serves 6.*

2 pounds carrots, peeled and cut into chunks (about 4 cups)
Salt to taste
Sugar (optional)
½ to 1 cup finely chopped fresh coriander (cilantro) leaves and stems to taste
¼ to ½ cup chopped fresh chives or mint, instead of or in addition to the coriander
1 to 2 green chiles, finely chopped (optional)
Juice of 1 lime or small lemon
Yogurt or crème fraîche, for garnish
Chive or borage blossoms, for garnish (optional)

- In a pot of lightly salted water, simmer the carrots until barely tender. Drain the carrots, reserving the cooking water.

- Put the carrots through a food mill or a food processor to produce a coarse-textured puree. Add enough of the reserved cooking water to achieve a soupy consistency. Add salt to taste. You might want to add a couple of pinches of sugar if the carrots don't seem sweet enough. The soup can be prepared to this point hours ahead.

- At serving time, warm the soup if you want it hot. Stir in the chopped coriander leaves and/or the chives or mint, and the chiles if you want an extra kick. Add the juice of a lime or small lemon, tasting as you squeeze. Stop before the acid dominates.

- Serve with a drizzle of beaten yogurt or crème fraîche. Garnish with chive or borage blossoms if you have them in your garden.

• • •

Carrot Soup with Ginger: Garnish the soup with about 2 to 3 tablespoons of finely julienned ginger that has been sizzled in olive oil until it begins to look toasty. Each bowl gets a little sprinkle. This is especially good in winter.

Tomato and Ginger Infusion

This soup was inspired by my aunt Mani's wonderful Tomato and Orange Drink (page 271). Tomato soup in Indian hands takes on a whole new meaning. Like the other single-vegetable soup in this section, this tomato-ginger infusion steps lightly but provocatively into the meal, and like the carrot soup, it lends itself to being served at any temperature the season and menu suggest. At room temperature, all the flavors get equal attention. *Serves 6.*

3 pounds ripe tomatoes of any color
1 cup (about) water
Salt to taste
Sugar (optional)
½ cup grated peeled fresh ginger
Orange juice or tangerine juice to taste (optional)
Lime or lemon wedges, beaten yogurt or crème fraîche, green peas, or purple
  basil leaves, for garnish (optional)

- Cut up the tomatoes roughly and put them in a nonreactive pan with the water. Bring to a boil; reduce the heat and simmer gently about 15 minutes.

- If you use a food processor or blender for pureeing the tomatoes, you will need to strain the tomato mixture. Otherwise, push the mixture through a stainless steel strainer or food mill, saving the residue. Moisten the residue with water and put it through the strainer again to extract every bit of tomato richness. If necessary, thin the puree with more water to the consistency you want. Salt to taste and add sugar in pinches if the tomatoes aren't sweet enough.

- Press the grated ginger through a fine-mesh strainer into a bowl, being sure to get all the juice out of the fiber. Stir the ginger juice into the tomato, taste, and be prepared for a little jolt. This is as it should be. If your taste tells you to, you can even add a little more.

- Let the infusion stand until you're ready to serve it, allowing at least half an hour for the ginger to steep. The soup can be made hours ahead.

- When you're ready to serve, taste the soup. If you like, you can squeeze orange or tangerine juice into it just before you ladle it into cups or bowls or even into something like a martini glass. Serve with wedges of lime or lemon or a drizzle of yogurt or crème fraîche. If you can find a few tiny peas, throw them raw into the bottom of the bowl. Purple basil makes a good color contrast as a leafy garnish.

. . .

Tomato Ice: Be sure the mixture is more highly seasoned. If you have an ice cream maker, follow the instructions that come with it. If not, pour the tomato mixture into a shallow tray. Freeze till almost solid. Whomp it up in a blender or food processor and refreeze to a slush.

Tomato Aspic: For an old-fashioned Parsi favorite, turn this soup into a tomato aspic by dissolving 1½ tablespoons gelatin over low heat in about ½ cup water. Stir a little soup into the gelatin before stirring the gelatin into the rest of the soup. Pour into an oiled mold or an attractive bowl or bowls and allow to set, refrigerated, until firm. Tomato aspic was one of my mother's big favorites for a first course at lunch.

Note: Someone asked me why the tomato and ginger can't be cooked together. They can, and I've done it myself, but I've come to the conclusion that the fresh ginger juice gives you an almost electric charge of excitement, a wonderful way to begin a meal.

Mother's Get-Well Soup

I loved the vegetable soup my mother made for me when I was under the weather. It was a broth of meat and vegetables, with onions, ginger, garlic, turmeric, cloves, and peppercorns for their taste and healing properties. Sometimes there would be barley, sometimes steamed basmati rice. Lamb riblets are ideal for this soup, though chicken and turkey work well, too. *Serves 2 to 4.*

½ pound lamb or kid riblets, or ½ pound turkey or chicken legs, backs, or wings
1 ½ teaspoons Ginger-Garlic Paste (page 36)
1 onion, finely chopped
3 whole cloves
6 black peppercorns
¼ teaspoon ground turmeric
6 cups (about) water
1 teaspoon (or more) salt
¼ cup barley or 1 cup cooked barley (optional)
¼ to ½ cup diced carrots
¼ to ½ cup green beans, cut into pea-size sections

- Cut the meat into small pieces or cubes, being sure to trim off all visible fat. Uneven pieces of meat won't matter. Combine the meat, paste, onion, cloves, peppercorns, and turmeric in a pan with the water and 1 teaspoon salt. If using barley, add now.

- Bring to a boil; reduce the heat and simmer until the broth tastes rich and the meat is completely tender and falling apart and the barley is completely soft, about 45 minutes. Taste and add more salt if you like. Add the carrots and beans and cook till tender, about 10 minutes. This is not a time for challenging texture. Taste for salt again.

My Get-Well Soup

My mother told me that she once had dreadful bronchitis that went on for weeks, and the thing that finally saved her was a friend bringing her soup made with lots of pepper. This is my interpretation of that friend's soup. In memory of that friend, to spread her good idea, I make this whenever anyone's down with nastiness in the chest, and our pal Alta Tingle swears by its efficacy.

Far from being charming medical folklore, the antibiotic properties of aromatic spices and rhizomes like ginger and turmeric are well established and documented in scientific journals. Any culture that grows ginger, turmeric, and pepper knows their medicinal value.

Add a scoop of cooked rice to each bowl to make the soup more sustaining. *Serves 4 to 6.*

1 small chicken (about 2 pounds), all visible fat removed
6 to 8 slices peeled fresh ginger
6 to 8 slices fresh turmeric
4 cloves garlic, crushed
6 whole cloves
12 (or more) black peppercorns
1 (2-inch-long) stick cinnamon or cassia
1 teaspoon (or more) salt
2 ½ quarts water
Lime or lemon halves
Freshly ground black pepper

LADLE

- Put the chicken in a deep pot with the ginger, turmeric, garlic, cloves, peppercorns, cinnamon, and about 1 teaspoon salt. Cover with the water. Bring to a boil; reduce the heat, cover, and simmer gently until the chicken is falling off the bones. If the water seems to be boiling away too fast, add a little more. Taste and add more salt if you like.

- Skim the fat off the broth by chilling it or by any other means you know. Serve the broth with or without the chicken, depending on the patient. Don't strain out the roots; they're there to be chewed on. For vitamin C, serve with a half lemon or lime to squeeze into the bowl at the time of eating. Grind in as much pepper as you can stand.

Yogurt Soup | DAHI NI KADDHI

Here's a dish borrowed from the Hindu vegetarian cuisine of Gujarat, tweaked to suit Parsi tastes, with cumin seeds rather than the usual Gujarati mustard seeds. Each Parsi family must have its own version. My mother's reflects her loathing for acidity and love for sweetness.

Dahi ni kaddhi is usually served with rice or a dry, fluffy *khichri* such as the version I give on page 166. It also makes a first-rate soup served in small amounts. I use demitasses or Chinese teacups. *Serves 6.*

> *1 tablespoon ghee, clarified butter, or vegetable oil*
> *½ to 1 teaspoon cumin seeds*
> *2 to 3 green chiles, slit to the stem*
> *6 curry leaves, if available*
> *1 medium onion, finely chopped*
> *2 to 3 cups water*
> *¼ teaspoon ground turmeric*
> *2 tablespoons chickpea flour (besan)*
> *2 cups whole or low-fat cow's or goat's milk yogurt*
> *2 teaspoons to 2 tablespoons superfine sugar to taste*
> *2 tablespoons (about) finely chopped fresh coriander (cilantro) leaves*

- Heat the ghee in a medium saucepan over medium-high heat. Add the cumin seeds, chiles, and curry leaves and sizzle for a moment. Follow with the onion and let it brown a little on the edges, stirring occasionally. Add 2 to 3 cups water and the turmeric. Whisk in the chickpea flour. Bring to a boil; reduce the heat and stir constantly for a few minutes while the soup thickens.

• Turn off the heat and whisk in the yogurt. The consistency should be like heavy cream. Sweeten to taste (my mother would add at least 2 tablespoons fine white sugar), and finish with the coriander leaves.

• • •

Note: Slitting chiles almost all the way to the stem gives you flavor without maximum heat. You're not supposed to eat floating chiles or curry leaves unless you really want to.

Fish Soup with Parsi-Style Rouille

During the heyday of the Julia Child cooking shows in the late 1960s, *Gourmet* magazine printed a marvelously simple recipe for a Provençal fish soup, *aïgo sau,* served with a *sauce rouille.* Like other favorites, it became etched in my memory—the idea behind it, if not the exact particulars. *Aïgo sau* inspired the following soup based on the seasonings for *khari machhi,* our mild Parsi fish stew (page 102), considered comfort food suitable for convalescents. You can use thickish white fish fillets that will hold their shape, or you can use whole fish like rock cod, snapper, or true cod cut into steaks or chunks. Oily fish like tuna and mackerel are not what you want here. Crusty bread on the side and a simple salad to follow would make it a complete meal. *Serves 4 to 6.*

PARSI-STYLE ROUILLE

> *2 (or more, for ferocity) dried red chiles*
> *¼ to ½ teaspoon coarse sea salt*
> *2 to 3 cloves garlic*
> *¼ cup (about) bread crumbs*
> *2 tablespoons olive oil*

SOUP

> *1 to 2 teaspoons (or more) salt, plus extra for salting the fish*
> *1 ½ pounds sturdy white fish fillets, or a 2-pound fish cut into steaks or chunks*
> *1 to 1 ½ pounds medium-size waxy potatoes (such as Yukon Gold), unpeeled*
> *2 medium onions, halved and sliced*
> *2 (or more) tomatoes, coarsely chopped*

1 cup fresh coriander (cilantro) stems and leaves, left whole
½ cup chopped tops of celery stalks, stem and leaf
2 to 3 green chiles, slit to the stem
3 to 4 cloves garlic, crushed
6 to 8 black peppercorns
1 bay leaf
2 quarts water

- To make the rouille: Cover the chiles with boiling water and soak until they swell and become soft. Drain and pound them in a mortar along with the salt, garlic, bread crumbs, and olive oil. You can also use a food processor, which will result in an even-textured sauce. Set aside while you make the soup.

- To make the soup: Lightly salt the fish and let it stand while preparing the broth.

- In a large pan, combine the potatoes, onions, tomatoes, fresh coriander, celery, chiles, garlic, peppercorns, and bay leaf with the water and 1 to 2 teaspoons salt. Bring to a boil; reduce the heat to a simmer, cover halfway, and cook until the potatoes are barely tender. This should take about 20 minutes. Taste the soup and add a bit more salt if you need to, remembering that the fish is also salted.

- Add the fish to the soup. Bring to a boil again; reduce the heat and cook for a few minutes until the fish is just tender. The time will vary, so be vigilant after about 3 to 4 minutes. Remove from the heat at once.

- Thin the rouille to a spoonable consistency with a tablespoon or so of the soup broth. Add more salt if needed.

- Serve the broth at once in bowls or soup plates. It's all right if bits of tomato or onion get into the bowls. The fish and potatoes make a second course pointed up by the hot and garlicky version of *sauce rouille.*

· · ·

Shellfish Soup: You can add shrimp, clams, or mussels to the fish, or use any one of these options on its own. Just don't overcook them. Have people waiting at the table.

Mulligatawny

Here's a dish that's done some wandering. The word *mulligatawny* comes from the Tamil *mulluga thanni*, which means, literally, "pepper water." Mulligatawny underwent its first change when made for the British by their Tamil cooks and changed yet again when it came into Parsi hands. You'll also find it made with curry powder, raisins, and apples, but not by any Indian person. In my mother's house, mulligatawny was served for lunch as a main dish with lots of rice or as a dinner-party first course with just a little rice in the center of the soup plate. The essential finishing touch is a squeeze of lime just before you begin to eat. On most Parsi tables, there's usually a little dish of cut-up limes to be used throughout the meal, squeezed over anything you want.

If you can't find white poppy seeds (sold at Indian markets), add five extra almonds. For more on preparing the coconut, see pages 39–42. *Serves 4 to 6.*

MASALA

1 tablespoon white poppy seeds

1 tablespoon uncooked basmati rice

1 tablespoon coriander seeds

1 ½ teaspoons cumin seeds

1 (1 ½-inch-long) stick cinnamon or cassia

4 whole cloves

½ teaspoon black peppercorns

½ teaspoon ground turmeric

1 cup (loosely packed) fresh coriander (cilantro) leaves and stems

5 green chiles

10 almonds

4 cloves garlic

1 (1-inch-long) piece peeled fresh ginger

SOUP

½ coconut, grated, or 1 cup frozen, canned, or reconstituted dried coconut milk

2 tablespoons vegetable oil

1 medium onion, finely chopped

1 pound skinless, boneless chicken (preferably thigh meat), trimmed and cubed

1 ½ quarts (about) water or chicken stock

Salt to taste

4 to 6 cups cooked Perfect Plain Rice (page 162)

Lime wedges

- To make the masala: Toast the poppy seeds, rice, coriander seeds, cumin seeds, cinnamon, cloves, peppercorns, and turmeric in a heavy skillet until the poppy seeds begin to change color. Let cool for a few minutes. If you're using a wet-dry grinder, all masala ingredients can be ground to a paste together. If you're using a food processor, pulverize the dry ingredients in a coffee mill reserved for grinding spices before combining them with the fresh coriander, chiles, almonds, garlic, and ginger for further grinding. In both instances, use as little water as you need to in order to keep the paste as thick as possible.

- To make the soup: If you're using fresh coconut milk, extract it from the grated coconut. Set this milk aside and let the cream float to the top. Make a second extraction from the residue by pouring boiling water over the grated coconut, letting it rest, and squeezing it out. Reserve this liquid for cooking, along with what settles in the bottom of the container in which you've put the milk from the first extraction.

- Heat the oil in a medium pot and sauté the onion until browned. Add the masala and stir for a few minutes, taking care that it does not stick. Add the chicken, water, and reserved coconut liquid (do not add the cream or the frozen, canned, or reconstituted milk yet). Bring to a boil; reduce the heat to a simmer, add a little salt, stir well, cover the pan loosely, and do something else for half an hour or so.

- When the chicken is very tender and the oil floats to the top, add the thick coconut cream or the frozen, canned, or reconstituted coconut milk. Stir well. Serve over the rice with the lime wedges on the side.

· · ·

Fish Mulligatawny: Mulligatawny is delicious made with fish. Use about 1 pound of firm white fish, cut into small pieces. Use water and coconut water or fish stock for the cooking liquid. Add the fish in the last few minutes of cooking or cook it on the side and add it just when you're ready to serve.

Light Mulligatawny: To serve mulligatawny as a lighter soup, leave out the meat altogether and use chicken or vegetable stock instead of water. Serve with just a tablespoon or so of rice.

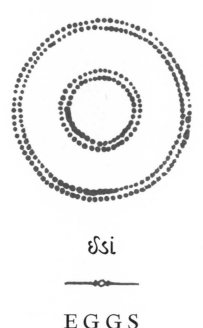

ઈંડા

---◆---

EGGS

The link between Parsi longevity and Parsi egg consumption would make fabulous Egg Board propaganda. We've never needed to be told that eggs are the perfect food, nor have we ever really believed the canard that they weren't.

To give you some idea of the importance of eggs, let's look at an ordinary day's meals in a Parsi household like my mother's. Breakfast usually means eggs. Ever since I can remember, my mother's breakfast has been a restrained soft-boiled egg. My father liked his eggs fried, with bacon. There are tales of heroic trenchermen in my grandparents' generation who ate six-egg omelets cooked in lots of ghee. Lunch can mean more eggs in the form of an egg dish—*kasa par ida,* Eggs on Anything (page 89)—or eggs can appear in Wedding-Style Fish (page 103), or in the coating for some fried thing like potato *pattis,* or in a curry. If it's an occasion, there might be a dessert made with eggs—a Bavarian cream, say. Teatime can mean more things with eggs, perhaps a cake or *ida pak,* a rich Parsi sweet made with dozens of eggs; and then we get around to dinner, which brings us to more visible and invisible eggs, perhaps in the sauce for a gratin like Mother's Wobbly Cauliflower Custard (page 190), or an hors d'oeuvre of "Italian" eggs (page 58), or something like *île flottante.* Our long and lavish wedding dinners feature eggs in two guises, early in the meal on a savory base of onions, and a few courses later as a dense custard, served just before the rice.

Besides being one of the main props of meal planning, eggs play a role in Parsi ritual. On certain important occasions, the *ses,* a silver tray of auspicious substances and objects, will include an egg, along with coconuts, fish, pomegranates, dried fruit, betel nut, and betel leaf. In the *achu michu* ceremony of welcome, the officiating senior woman waves a raw egg seven times clockwise around the head of the person being blessed with symbols of goodness and fruitfulness.

Concrete goodness and fruitfulness, the egg dishes here range from the simple innocence of plain scrambled eggs through a few of my favorite variations on the theme of eggs on anything (including potato chips) to the sophistication of a Franco-Parsi green chutney soufflé. For Parsis, eggs are the ultimate comfort food. We couldn't march without them.

Creamy Scrambled Eggs | CHARVELA IDA

It's not hard to make scrambled eggs voluptuously creamy the French way, with lots of butter, but it's good to know that there's an alternative. You can make equally creamy eggs using a small amount of butter and a little slug of milk, about a tablespoonful per egg.

The high-heat, short-order cook's approach to scrambling eggs doesn't work here because the goal is creamy softness. You'll be surprised how many lovers of firm scrambled eggs are converted by this approach. You need to use a saucepan for the best results. Nonstick pans are fine, although I've seen cooks in Bombay use thin aluminum pans with great success. *Serves 4 generously.*

> *8 large eggs*
> *½ cup milk or half-and-half*
> *1 to 2 tablespoons ghee, clarified butter, or butter*
> *4 pinches (about) salt*

• Whisk the eggs and milk lightly together in a small 1-quart saucepan. Add the ghee and about 4 pinches of salt. Over low heat, stir the eggs constantly with a wooden spatula, keeping contact with the bottom of the pan. In 5 minutes or so, the eggs will be creamy, soft, and ready to serve.

• Best eaten with a spoon.

. . .

Scrambled Eggs with Seafood: Just as the eggs begin to set, try adding a few spoonfuls of crabmeat or diced lobster, some snipped chives or green onion, and perhaps a few flecks of chopped green chile. This makes a wonderful light dinner or late-night supper. Asparagus, green or white, is a harmonious accompaniment. A little toast, of course, is always welcome.

Note: Many Parsis, including my mother, love eating these creamy scrambled eggs with lentil stews such as *masur* (page 180). It's a surprisingly comforting combination.

Parsi Scrambled Eggs | AKURI

Akuri consists of eggs scrambled with onions and other things. There's *akuri* with tomatoes; there's the *akuri* of Bharuch, ancient bastion of Parsi culture and cuisine, rich with onions and raisins deep-fried in ghee; there's *akuri* made with the flowers of the drumstick tree; and on and on. Each Parsi family probably has its rules about the correct way to make *akuri*. When my parents and I were cooking together, I pretended I had no opinions at all and let my mother dictate the quantities and methods. Quite predictably, this no-opinion state lasted two minutes before all three of us, my father included, started having an energetic discussion about the only best way. My mother claimed that my father and I liked too many onions: "You don't taste the eggs that way." Then both parents started arguing about the use of turmeric, where I sided with my mother. In spite of the scuffle, the *akuri* we made together tasted very good. Just remember, you are in charge and your opinion counts. Exact quantities are not important. Note that this version doesn't include tomatoes or turmeric. That's because I'm the boss of this particular recipe. Tomatoes make *akuri* watery, and turmeric adds a color that the eggs don't really need.

Serve this immediately with buttered toast, or with hot chapatis or whole wheat tortillas. Leftover *akuri* makes an excellent filling for sandwiches and turnovers. *Serves 4.*

1 tablespoon (or more) ghee or butter
1 medium-size yellow or red onion, finely chopped, or a large bunch of green onions, chopped with their greens

1 to 2 teaspoons Ginger-Garlic Paste (page 36; optional)
2 green chiles, finely chopped
½ to 1 cup coarsely chopped fresh coriander (cilantro) leaves to taste
½ teaspoon (about) salt
6 large eggs, lightly beaten with 2 tablespoons milk or cream

• In a heavy skillet, melt the ghee over medium heat. Add the onions and brown them slowly, stirring occasionally, until they begin to caramelize. Add the paste if you want it and the chiles. Stir for a minute. Add the fresh coriander and the salt. Check the seasoning. Add the eggs and an indulgent extra dollop of ghee if you want the added richness. Over low heat, scramble to your taste, to barely set creaminess or firm. Check for salt before serving at once.

• • •

Note: When green garlic is in season, it's often used in *akuri*. The green garlic we get in Bombay is sold in bunches with stems as thin as chives and tiny, tender cloves the size of the nail on your little finger. If you have your own garlic patch, do give this a try, even if it seems like infanticide.

Parsi Omelet | PARSI PORA

For thirty-two years now, the same group of friends has been taking the same food to the same beach on the same Sunday in October. Children and new dishes have been added over the years, but the core menu remains untouchable. My contribution has always been Parsi omelets. Here by popular demand is the recipe for my mother's version of *pora,* which started the whole thing. Other mothers have different versions, but the basics are the same. Some people add a bit of cubed boiled potato to the omelet mixture. The ginger-garlic paste and *dhana jiru* give you an authentic Parsi taste, but even if you leave them out, the omelets are completely satisfying.

To serve these *poras,* just plop each omelet on a plate, or put it in a pita pocket or on a chapati or whole wheat tortilla heated over a gas flame, or stick it between two pieces of buttered bread, white or whole wheat. Avocado is a good accompaniment, though not traditionally Parsi. Good tomato or mango chutney goes well served alongside. *Serves 4 to 6.*

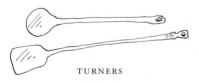

TURNERS

6 large eggs
2 medium onions, very finely chopped
4 to 6 green chiles, finely chopped
1 cup chopped fresh coriander (cilantro) leaves and stems
1 teaspoon Ginger-Garlic Paste (page 36; optional)
½ teaspoon Dhana Jiru (page 38; optional)
Salt to taste
½ onion, for rubbing the pan
Ghee or clarified butter, for frying

- Lightly whisk the eggs to combine yolks and whites. Add the chopped onions, chiles, fresh coriander, and the paste and *dhana jiru,* if you like. Salt to taste.

- The traditional Parsi way to cook *poras* is to shallow-fry them one at a time in oil or ghee, turning once, without folding. This makes an authentically rich, dark brown *pora.* My slightly different way is to cook them in a lightly greased cast-iron skillet or in a nonstick frying pan. Let the skillet get very hot. Rub it with a cut onion (an old South Indian trick to prevent sticking) and add the merest film of ghee. Pour in a ladleful of the omelet mixture. Cover. After a few minutes, when the top looks dryish, flip the omelet and let it cook on the other side. You don't want a runny omelet. Repeat the whole process until the mixture is used up, stirring before dipping the ladle each time so that the solids don't all settle to the bottom of the bowl.

Omelet Soufflé

Parsi omelets are delicious, but when the same ingredients get turned into a soufflé, the results are spectacular. I got the idea from Shirin Sabavala, who's responsible for the fabulous green chutney soufflé that follows. Serve this with chapatis or crusty bread and a salad. *Serves 2 to 4.*

2 tablespoons butter
4 tablespoons all purpose flour
1 cup whole milk
4 large egg yolks
2 cups chopped green onions, tops and all
4 (about) green chiles, finely chopped
1 cup finely chopped fresh coriander (cilantro) leaves and stems
5 large egg whites
Pinch (or more) of salt

- Heat the oven to 375 degrees.
- Make a béchamel sauce by melting the butter in a small heavy saucepan over medium-low heat, and when it starts sizzling, stir in the flour. Stir together for a minute or so, then whisk in the milk. Bring to a boil; reduce the heat and cook for a few minutes, whisking constantly, until the sauce is thick and smooth. Off the heat, whisk the egg yolks into the béchamel one at a time. Add the green onions, chiles, and fresh coriander. Season with salt if you like.
- Beat the egg whites with a pinch of salt to stiff, shiny peaks, being careful not to overbeat. Quickly fold the egg whites into the béchamel mixture. Pour into a 4- to 6-cup ungreased soufflé dish or any baking dish with high straight sides. Bake about 35 to 45 minutes, until well risen and golden brown on top. This is one soufflé you don't want runny in the center.
- Serve at once.

Green Chutney Soufflé

This is one of those brilliant expressions of Parsi innovation, combining tastes and techniques normally worlds apart. This recipe comes from Shirin Sabavala, who—with her husband, Jehangir, a renowned painter—gives some of Bombay's most glamorous and interesting parties. Her chutney soufflé is legendary, so I begged her for the recipe, which she unhesitatingly asked her cook, Mutthu, to relate to me.

This soufflé makes a lovely centerpiece for a lunch for four, accompanied by a salad of cucumber and a crusty baguette. *Serves 4 to 6.*

> *4 tablespoons butter*
> *4 tablespoons all purpose flour*
> *2 cups whole milk*
> *6 large eggs, separated*
> *1 cup Parsi Green Chutney (page 227)*
> *Pinch (or more) of salt*

- Heat the oven to 375 degrees.
- Make a béchamel sauce by melting the butter in a small heavy saucepan over medium-low heat, and when it starts sizzling, stir in the flour. Cook together for a minute or so, then whisk in the milk. Bring to a boil; reduce the heat and cook for a few minutes, whisking constantly, until the sauce is thick and smooth. Off the

heat, whisk the egg yolks into the béchamel one at a time. Stir in the chutney. Check for salt if you like.

- Beat the egg whites with a pinch of salt until stiff. Fold about a quarter of the egg whites into the soufflé base to lighten the mixture. Follow with the rest of the egg whites, folding them in quickly. Pour into an ungreased 6- to 8-cup soufflé dish. Bake for 40 minutes or so, until the soufflé is puffed and golden brown on top. Serve immediately.

Eggs on Anything | KASA PAR IDA

A Hindu friend jokes about our Parsi eggomania, saying, "The only thing you people haven't yet put eggs on is eggs." *Kasa par ida*—eggs on whatever you like—is one of the cornerstones of Parsi food. Sometimes it's a hastily improvised dish that appears as part of the evening meal; there's also a place for it in our long ceremonial banquets. What goes under the eggs is left to imagination or expediency; usually it's a vegetable, sometimes meat. Since these foundations for *kasa par ida* are dishes in their own right, you will find them in the vegetable and meat chapters. I'm giving you a mere sampling of the many possibilities.

There are two approaches to Eggs on Anything. In the first, eggs are broken onto the surface of the mixture and then steamed. This way, you need at least one egg per person, or three quail eggs for an especially playful hors d'oeuvre or first course.

The second approach is a simple steamed soufflé blanket billowing up over the base and then settling into a light, spongy topping. It uses fewer eggs to far greater dramatic effect and has the advantage of not having to be eaten immediately. Both approaches make delectable late breakfasts, light lunches, or light suppers.

- *Method 1.* Have the base mixture (see the variations below) ready in a skillet with a lid handy. Make shallow depressions in the surface of the mixture. Break the eggs, 1 or more per person, into these hollows. Pour a little water around the edge of the mixture. Turn up the heat until steam rises; clap on the lid, reduce the heat to low, and let the eggs cook until the whites are set but the yolks are still runny. Serve at once.
- *Method 2.* Have the base mixture ready in a skillet. Have a high-domed lid handy, or use a suitably sized metal bowl. Three eggs will cover the contents of a 10-inch skillet and serve six, more if it's an hors d'oeuvre, four as a first course. Separate the eggs. Beat the whites stiff with a pinch of salt. Stir the yolks, add a spoonful of the

beaten whites to lighten them, and then quickly fold in the rest of the whites. Pour a drizzle of water around the mixture in the skillet. Cover the surface of the mixture with the egg, going all the way to the edges. Turn up the heat to generate steam. Cover the pan with the high-domed lid. Turn down the heat to low and let the eggs puff up. You know they are done when the surface is dry and slightly springy when touched. The billow of egg will subside almost immediately into a topping with a really lovely texture. Serve at once, or eat later at room temperature. Eggs this way make a good hors d'oeuvre or first course served on small plates.

• • •

Eggs on Onions (tarela kanda): Make the recipe for Allium Confit (page 186).

Eggs on Ridge Gourd Ragout (turia par ida): Make the Ragout of Ridge Gourd recipe (page 193).

Eggs on Okra (bhida par ida): Make the recipe for Sautéed Okra (page 199). Okra haters become surprised okra lovers after eating this dish.

Eggs on Tomatoes (tamota par ida): Make the recipe for Sweet-Sour Tomatoes (page 199).

Eggs on Onions and Potatoes (papeta par ida): Make the recipe for Parsi Hash Yellow Potatoes (page 202).

Eggs on Plantains (kera par ida): Make Fried Plantains (page 204).

Eggs on Parsi Ratatouille: Make Parsi Ratatouille (page 206).

Eggs on Potato Chips | WAFER PAR IDA

For years I thought that putting eggs on wafers, as we call potato chips in India, was a joke recipe, a loony fantasy or a way of lampooning our Parsi love affair with eggs. Then I tried it with Fran McCullough, bosom pal and potato chip expert, egging me on. Guess what! It's not a joke. You will not believe how absolutely delicious this dish can be and how you'll laugh with delight as you eat it, just as we did that first time and every time after that. In an ideal universe, your potato chips are homemade (page 201) or fresh from one of Bombay's several potato-chips works, where a vat of oil is always on the bubble. The idea of making potato chips just to try out this recipe won't appeal to anyone, so instead use the best of the commercial ones available to you. They shouldn't be too brown or the dish will taste burnt. *Serves 2 to 4.*

1 tablespoon ghee, clarified butter, or mixture of vegetable oil and butter
1 small onion, finely chopped
½ teaspoon Ginger-Garlic Paste (page 36; optional)
2 to 3 hot green chiles, finely chopped
½ cup coarsely chopped fresh coriander (cilantro) leaves
4 good handfuls of plain potato chips from a just-opened bag
4 large eggs
1 tablespoon (about) water

- Heat the ghee over medium heat in a sturdy medium skillet, preferably cast iron. Add the onion and let it soften, stirring occasionally, a few minutes. Before it browns, add the paste if you like and the green chiles, and as soon as the mixture looks cooked, add the fresh coriander. Crumble in the potato chips, tossing the contents of the pan to combine them thoroughly. Make nests in the surface of the mixture— they won't be perfect hollows—and crack an egg into each. Pour a tablespoon or so of water around the edges of the pan to generate some steam, cover the skillet tightly, and let the eggs cook just long enough to set the whites without turning the chips soggy.

- Turn out onto waiting plates.

• • •

Note: One of my authorities on Parsi food, Firoza Kanga, says, "Oh, yes, *wafer par ida.* Delicious. Next time, try it with a little bit of cream poured over the chips before the eggs go on."

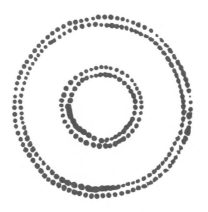

માછલી

FISH AND SEAFOOD

Every auspicious occasion in a Parsi household requires fish, because fish represents fertility, respect for the waters, prosperity. It may be a symbolic representation in chalk stencils on the floor, it may be a silver replica for the ritual tray, it may be a fish-shaped sweetmeat, it may be a pair of beautiful freshly caught pomfret brought to the door as a present, and it must be part of the day's lunch menu, to be eaten with rice and plain dal. One might assume that fish became important in Parsi life and ritual only after the arrival in India. After all, fish were not nearly as abundant on the Iranian plateau as they were in the coastal waters off Gujarat. The archaeological record suggests the opposite: Bas-reliefs from the time of Cyrus (about 500 B.C.E.) at Pasargadae show fish as a motif, and we know that fish—dried, we hope—were considered a highly esteemed offering at many temples of the ancient Near East, because of their scarcity.

Fishmarkets in Bombay are a wild, wet, noisy, colorful scene with dozens of varieties of freshly caught seafood loudly sold by spirited Koli women who don't take any nonsense from anyone. Of the many kinds of fish sold, there are barely six that most Parsis consider good to eat, and of the six, the silver pomfret *(Pampus argenteus)* is the fish of choice. (Pompano is a close match.) Shrimp, swimming crabs (portunids), and spiny and slipper lobsters *(Panulirus* spp. and *Thenus orientalis)* are all cooked in interesting ways. In season, no one can get enough of the Bombay duck

POMFRET

(Harpodon nehereus), a small gelatinous fish, coated in bread crumbs and fried. The only way it's exported is in its dried form, and I have not yet seen it for sale in the United States.

Anyone going to Bombay should make it a point to visit one of the fishmarkets and to go to one of the many fish restaurants around the city. For the very best Parsi fish dishes, though, you'll have to eat at someone's house, or at a wedding, or make your own. Most of the favorites are here. My fish suggestions are based on what's available in Northern California. You might want to consult a good fish reference for your own part of the country (I recommend Paul Johnson's *Fish Forever,* due in mid 2007, because it deals with just about everything commercially available in the Western Hemisphere).

Crab Salad

There's nothing like a good mayonnaise—homemade if possible—to hold crab together in a salad with other ingredients; but I'm always looking for ways to pare down fat without compromising taste, so we tend to have half mayonnaise–half yogurt dressings or sometimes just yogurt with a drizzle of olive oil.

Serve this salad as a first course or light lunch with lightly dressed greens, or as an hors d'oeuvre, with at least two big leaves per person of butter lettuce or another suitable variety, offered separately so that everyone can make their own crab-salad wraps. *Serves 5 to 6.*

> *2 to 3 cups crabmeat (about 1 pound), picked over*
> *1 cup mayonnaise, or ½ cup each mayonnaise and yogurt, or 1 cup yogurt plus*
>   *2 to 3 tablespoons olive oil*
> *2 to 4 fresh green or red chiles, finely chopped*
> *2 to 3 green onions, finely chopped, tops included*
> *½ to 1 cup chopped fresh coriander (cilantro), tender stems and leaves, to taste*
> *Salt to taste*
> *½ to 1 cup finely diced hard ripe mango (optional)*

½ to 1 cup seedless cucumber in small cubes (optional)
Firm but ripe avocado, cubed or sliced, for garnish

- Lightly toss the crab with the mayonnaise, chiles, green onions, fresh coriander, salt to taste, and the mango and cucumber if you like. Serve with a garnish of avocado.

. . .

Note: On the East Coast of the United States, use fresh blue crabmeat. On the West Coast, the best way is to start with live Dungeness crabs right out of the Pacific.

Crab Gratin

When I was growing up in Bombay, we airily requested crab for lunch with no thought of the labor involved for our cook. It was only after I dealt with enough small blue crabs to feed four—it took hours—that I realized what poor Andrew de Souza must have gone through producing enough stuffed crabs for the family and guests as just one part of a meal to be served between the time he got back from the bazaar and half past one.

His version of crabs baked in their shells was based on a béchamel with some egg; I like the West Indian version with bread crumbs soaked in milk from a cow or a coconut. The crabs he bought were palm-size; we in California have jumbo Dungeness crabs a foot across or the luxury of fresh, carefully picked-over eastern crabmeat. My mother liked crabs presented in their shells; I use an oval baking dish. *Serves 4 to 6.*

2 to 3 cups crabmeat (about 1 pound), picked over
1 cup dry crumbs from sturdy white bread, crusts removed, plus more crumbs
  for sprinkling on top
1 ¾ cups (or more) milk, half-and-half, or coconut milk
2 large eggs, lightly beaten
2 to 4 teaspoons finely chopped fresh green or red chiles
3 green onions, finely chopped, tops included
½ cup chopped fresh coriander (cilantro) leaves and stems
Salt to taste
2 tablespoons (about) butter
Sliced almonds (optional)
Lime wedges

- Butter a shallow ovenproof dish that will hold 5 to 6 cups. Go over the crab to check for little bits of shell that escaped the first scrutiny.

- Soak 1 cup of the bread crumbs in the milk until all the liquid is absorbed, about half an hour. Add more milk, if necessary, to achieve the consistency of thick oatmeal. Add the eggs and stir well to combine. Then add the crab, chiles, green onions, fresh coriander, and salt.

- Heat the broiler, or heat the oven to 350 degrees. Transfer the mixture to the prepared baking dish. Sprinkle the top with the additional bread crumbs, dot the surface with tiny bits of butter, and sprinkle a liberal handful of sliced almonds over the top, if you like.

- Put the baking dish under the broiler long enough to brown the top and heat the crab thoroughly, about 5 minutes; or bake until golden, 20 to 25 minutes. If you use almonds, be especially careful to avoid incinerating them under the broiler. Serve at once, accompanied by wedges of lime.

. . .

Note: When my mother and my friends' mothers wanted to make crab very special, they'd add canned pimientos in little dice. We can do this, too, with *piquillo* peppers from Spain. Or better yet, make a salad of roasted peppers, *piquillos* or just market reds and yellows, with a simple dressing of olive oil and lemon juice, to serve with the crab.

Masala Seafood | TARELI ATTVA BHUJELI MACHHI

I'm in love with any easy effect, where simplicity yields results far outweighing the effort. The basic Parsi treatment of fish and seafood is a stellar easy effect. It's an incredibly simple dry rub for fish or seafood you'll be frying, grilling, or even roasting. If you have shrimp, fish sections or fillets, or squid ready to go, the entire process will take no more than five minutes. The quantities are suggestions. You can increase or decrease any of them to your taste.

As a main course, fish or seafood cooked with a spice rub is traditionally served with plain dal and rice (page 176). I love it with Firoza's Khichri (page 166). Try squid or shrimp as an hors d'oeuvre, straight out of the pan or off the grill, with a squeeze of lime and some cubed avocado. *Serves 6 to 8.*

DRY RUB

1 tablespoon cayenne pepper or Indian chilly powder
1 tablespoon ground turmeric
1 tablespoon fine sea salt

Vegetable oil
3 pounds whole fish, fish steaks, or fillets; or shrimp, peeled and deveined; or squid

- Mix the cayenne, turmeric, and sea salt for a truly instant easy effect. This dry rub can be doubled or tripled and stored for months in a cool, dark place.

- *Frying instructions:* Use about 1 tablespoon dry rub for each pound of shrimp, squid, or fish steaks or fillets, and rub it in well. For whole fish, cut three diagonal slits on each side almost down to the bone; rub the spice mixture inside and outside the fish, especially into the slits. Shallow-fry in the smallest amount of oil possible until barely tender. The average Parsi household uses much more oil than we do in our house and the fish is absolutely delicious, but we tend to go for nearly dry fries.

- *Grilling instructions:* Mix the spices into a paste with a little vegetable oil. Use a lot of the rub if you want a hot, intense flavor, less if you want a more subtle effect—Parsoid rather than Parsi. Let sit for about ½ hour. Thread shrimp, squid, or chunks of fish onto skewers. My husband, David, who does our grilling, says, "The coals should be hot and the grill almost on top of them. A good way to tell when something's ready to turn over is when you see an opaque white border. Then flip it and give the other side half or a third as much time as it took to get to the white halo stage. Then off and onto the plate with a big slice of lemon or lime." A ridged cast-iron pan is a decent substitute for a grill. "Grilling whole fish!" says David. "Now, that's a complicated set of variables: surface-to-volume ratio, size, stage of growth, oiliness of the fish itself, and then all the different grills. It's all got to be done by feel." Two fish experts, Paul Johnson of Monterey Fish and Patricia Unterman of the Hayes Street Grill, said similar things. Paul Johnson suggests a range of 5 to 15 minutes a side, more or less. Think of something like a trout at the 5-minute end of things, a 3-pound fish at the higher end. Longer cooking means a more moderate fire. Until you work things out with your own grill, you will have to test the fish. It should be barely opaque at the bone. Turning the fish can be difficult, so if you're anxious, try one of those metal grilling baskets made for just this purpose.

• *Roasting instructions (for fish only):* Position an oven rack in the topmost spot and heat the oven to 500 degrees for a few minutes. Put the fish on an oiled baking sheet, and slide it into the oven; cook for 8 to 15 minutes, depending on the thickness of the fish. This works best with fillets. The top gets kissed with little flecks of brown, and the inside is moist. For a whole fish, cook it in the middle of the oven at 450 degrees, allowing 15 minutes per inch of thickness.

• • •

Masala Vegetables: This same simple spice mixture shows its versatility when rubbed onto vegetables, pumpkin or eggplant in particular. If you're frying the vegetables, all you need to do is rub them with the spices. If you're roasting or grilling, mix the spices in a bowl with just enough oil to make a thin paste.

Irene's Fabulous Fish Cakes

When I spent several months in Bombay a few years ago seeing to family business, my friend Mehlli Gobhai's house was an oasis of calm, order, and entertainment. My mother's kitchen had been dismantled. The hearth was dead. But Mehlli's was very much alive a few doors away, where I was welcome to eat and cook as one of the family. His cook, Irene, calm and shy, has a wonderful touch. No one ever tires of her fish cakes.

Irene likes to use mackerel and its relatives because of the assertive taste. If you prefer milder fish, by all means use snapper, cod, or other flaky white fish. I sometimes like to use salt cod, soaked and then poached in milk.

Form the mixture into eight patties for a main dish, or into sixteen to twenty little balls to make enough appetizers for eight to ten guests. *Serves 4 as a main course.*

1 pound mackerel, snapper, or cod fillets
1 to 1 ½ cups cooked potato, mashed
3 large eggs
1 medium onion, finely chopped
3 to 4 green chiles, finely chopped
1 cup (scant) finely chopped fresh coriander (cilantro) leaves and stems
1 teaspoon Ginger-Garlic Paste (page 36; optional)
Salt to taste
1 to 2 cups fine bread crumbs
Vegetable oil, for frying

- Line a tray or baking sheet with waxed paper or parchment paper and set aside. Poach the fish for a few minutes in lightly salted water until cooked through. Transfer the fish to a plate. When it's cool enough to handle, drain it well and flake it, being sure to remove any little bones. Mix together the fish, potato, 1 of the eggs, onion, chiles, fresh coriander, paste if you like, and salt. Shape into patties 3 inches across and 1 inch thick if they will form part of a main course, or into smaller balls or patties if for hors d'oeuvres.

- Beat the remaining 2 eggs. Dip the patties in the beaten egg and roll in the bread crumbs to coat. Place on the prepared tray and refrigerate until ready to fry.

- Shallow-fry until golden on both sides. Drain on absorbent paper and serve hot or at room temperature.

Shrimp, Squid, or Fish Balls | KOLMI NA KAVAB

Depending on their size, these delectable mouthfuls can appear as hors d'oeuvres with drinks or as part of a meal. Since everything's chopped micro-fine or pulsed in the food processor, it's really better to start with small or medium shrimp. Jumbos (prawns) aren't necessary here. What is necessary is not to be surprised if these *kavabs* fly off the plate before you've counted to ten. Use the *dhana jiru* if you want a true Parsi taste, but the *kavabs* are equally fabulous without. You can make twelve large or many smaller *kavabs. Serves 4 to 8.*

> *1 ½ cups small to medium shrimp (about 1 pound), measured after peeling and deveining, or the equivalent in prepared squid mantles and tentacles, or 12 ounces snapper or cod fillets*
> *1 large egg*
> *½ onion, finely chopped*
> *2 to 3 green chiles, very finely chopped*
> *¼ to ½ cup finely chopped fresh coriander (cilantro) stems and leaves*
> *1 teaspoon Ginger-Garlic Paste (page 36)*
> *½ teaspoon Dhana Jiru (page 38; optional)*
> *¼ teaspoon ground turmeric (optional)*
> *½ to 1 teaspoon salt*
> *2 tablespoons (or more) chickpea flour (besan), or ½ cup grated potato, or ¼ to ½ cup fine bread crumbs*
> *Peanut, grapeseed, or sunflower oil, for frying*
> *Lime wedges*

- Chop the shrimp until they are nearly pureed and then combine with the egg, or buzz the shrimp with the egg in a food processor until they turn into a coarse puree. Add the onion, chiles, fresh coriander, paste, *dhana jiru* and turmeric if you like, salt, and flour. You should have a stiff mixture you can shape into balls with dampened hands. Add more flour if the mixture seems too slack.

- Pour oil into a wok or *karhai* (see page 30) to a depth of at least 1 inch and heat. When it reaches 375 degrees, drop in a trial piece, just ½ teaspoon or so, and fry it until it's brown. Taste it and add more salt if necessary, or more chile if you want things hotter. Then drop balls of the size you want into the hot oil, taking care not to crowd them. When they're golden brown on one side, flip them and cook a little longer, until golden on the other side. Always remember what my grandmother said: Things in oil look misleadingly pale. Cut open the first one to be sure you have your heat and time right. You might want to reduce the heat so that the *kavabs* don't get too brown outside before they're cooked through inside, or even raise the heat a little.

- Drain and serve as soon as possible, accompanied by wedges of lime.

• • •

Note: In Parsi terminology, *kavab* does not necessarily denote something skewered, though it may. It refers to seasoned mixtures baked or grilled or fried in various shapes and guises.

Fish in Banana-Leaf Parcels | PATRA NI MACHHI

If anyone were to ask me what my favorite Parsi dish was, this would be it. Finding a piece of *patra ni machhi* on your plate is like being given a very nice present. You peel off the banana-leaf wrapping, releasing gusts of maddeningly aromatic steam, and then you get to a piece of fish, moist and tender, coated in green chutney. Getting banana leaves in India is not difficult at all. There, as in Mexico and other tropical countries, they're almost to be had for the asking. Now, Asian and Latin American groceries sell frozen one-pound stacks of banana leaves from the Philippines. These aren't as good as fresh ones, which are now beginning to appear, but they do perfectly well. Freezing softens them so they need no further treatment.

GRANDMOTHER'S
STEAMER

Fresh banana leaves need preparation. Pass them over a flame for a moment until they soften. That way, they won't split. Cut large pieces on either side of the midrib. Set aside. In India, cooks use strips peeled off the midrib to make string for tying. You can also use regular kitchen string.

The fish Parsis use most often is pomfret, but pompano will do if you can get it, or salmon fillets, lingcod, tilapia, or sea bass. It's well worth investing in a steamer. Chinese and other Asian markets have a wide range of metal and bamboo steamers in many sizes at very reasonable prices. I use one at almost every meal.

The recipe can be doubled, but make the chutney in small batches. *Serves 6 to 8.*

CHUTNEY
> *½ coconut, peeled and cut up (see page 40), or 2 cups unsweetened frozen grated*
>   *coconut, thawed*
> *6 green chiles*
> *1 cup (packed) fresh coriander (cilantro) leaves and tender stems*
> *½ to ¾ cup fresh mint leaves (optional)*
> *½ teaspoon cumin seeds*
> *2 tablespoons (or more) lime juice*
> *Sugar and salt to taste*

FISH
> *Salt*
> *2 to 2 ½ pounds fish fillets*
> *About ½ pound banana leaves*

- To make the chutney: Grind the coconut, chiles, fresh coriander, mint if using, and cumin. Add enough lime juice to make a smooth paste. Add sugar and salt to taste.

- Lightly salt the fish on both sides. Coat the fish with the chutney. The coating should not be too thick or the fish will be eclipsed. Wrap the fillets in banana leaves and tie. Place the wrapped fish no more than two deep in the top part of a steamer. Cover and steam until tender, about 5 minutes for thinner pieces or 10 minutes for thicker pieces like salmon fillets. Test by unwrapping one of the pieces, or pierce through the banana leaf with a skewer.

     • • •

Jumbo Patra ni Machhi: If you have a whole side of salmon or a large fillet, you can make a giant *patra ni machhi* parcel.

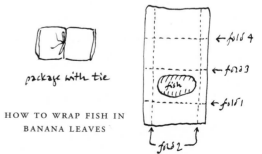

package with tie

HOW TO WRAP FISH IN
BANANA LEAVES

fold 4

fold 3

fold 1

fold 2

Coat the fish on all sides with the chutney, make a big parcel of leaves or parchment, and steam it if your steamer is big enough, or bake it in a 400-degree oven for 15 to 20 minutes, depending on the thickness of the fish.

Note: If neither fresh nor frozen banana leaves can be had, you can use other large edible leaves such as chard, *ti* leaves *(Cordyline terminalis),* ornamental ginger leaves *(Hedychium),* or fig leaves. Parchment will do in a pinch.

Simple Seafood Stew | KHARI MACHHI

Khari machhi, which means "just plain fish," is a dish so basic, so unadorned that Parsis consider it suitable for convalescents. Like so many simple things in Parsi food, its depth of flavor is astonishing. When my mother and I were making this dish together, I asked why we didn't use *adu lasan,* the paste of ginger and garlic with which nearly every Parsi savory dish has to begin. "You don't use ginger with fish," said my mother sternly, but she didn't have an answer to the inevitable "Why?" except to say that her mother said so. If her mother had been Chinese, she would not have been allowed to cook fish *without* ginger.

Use any type of white-fleshed fish you like, such as pompano, cod, snapper, or striped bass. Serve it with steamed basmati rice or another rice of your choice, ladling the poaching liquid over fish and rice alike. *Serves 4 to 6.*

Salt
1 ½ pounds fish steaks, thick fillets, or chunks, or 1 pound shrimp or
    prawns, peeled and deveined
1 tablespoon vegetable oil
½ to ¾ teaspoon cumin seeds, lightly pounded
2 to 3 cloves garlic, very thinly sliced
1 to 4 green chiles, slit to the stem
5 to 6 curry leaves, if available
1 medium-large onion, very thinly sliced
1 medium tomato, chopped or grated
¼ teaspoon ground turmeric
½ cup chopped fresh coriander (cilantro) stems and leaves

- Lightly salt the fish and set aside while preparing the poaching liquid.
- Heat the oil to medium-high in a sauté pan wide enough to hold the fish in a single layer. Add the cumin, garlic, chiles, and curry leaves and let them sizzle a moment

before adding the sliced onion. Cook, stirring occasionally, until the onion is softened without browning at all, a few minutes. Add the tomato and turmeric, letting everything stew together for about a minute before adding the fresh coriander.

- Add enough water to poach the fish without drowning it, say 1 ½ cups, and salt lightly. Let the sauce cook for 5 to 10 minutes to gain some presence. Then lay the fish in the pan. Bring the liquid to a boil; immediately lower the heat, cover, and let cook a few minutes longer, until the fish is done.

- Serve in a deep plate to hold the poaching liquid.

Wedding-Style Fish or Shrimp | LAGAN NO SAHAS

At Parsi wedding banquets, fish is the first thing to be brought around in deep round trays, one man holding, the other serving it onto the waiting banana leaves. It can be *patra ni machhi,* fish wrapped in banana leaves (page 100), but more often it's pieces of pomfret in a sweet-and-sour cream sauce made with eggs and vinegar, barely cooked cherry tomatoes dotting the top. There's no part of a pomfret that isn't good, so the servers seem entitled to mutter about everyone wanting tails and how many tails is a fish supposed to have?

Bhicoo Manekshaw writes that this dish may well have been a nineteenth-century Parsi interpretation of the decidedly uninteresting English-style fish in white sauce. There are other, more elaborate, versions, but I like the relative simplicity of my mother's method. The recipe works with a variety of white-fleshed fish such as pompano, snapper, flounder, cod, sea bass, or the Parsi favorite, pomfret; you can even use shrimp, in which case the dish becomes *kolmi no sahas.*

Serve *lagan no sahas* with homemade Potato Wafers (page 201) or with its traditional accompaniment of *khichri* (page 165)—the dry, fluffy kind, in which case the dish becomes *khichri sahas,* a festive meal. For the sake of color on the plate, accompany *khichri sahas* with a vivid green vegetable like zucchini or spinach, or with a simple lime- and salt-dressed dish of sliced cucumbers and ginger (page 218). *Serves 6.*

FISH

Salt

1 ½ pounds white fish steaks, thick fillets, or chunks, or 1 pound small to medium
   shrimp, peeled and deveined

2 tablespoons vegetable oil

1 teaspoon cumin seeds, lightly pounded
3 cloves garlic, very thinly sliced
6 green chiles, slit to the stem
1 large onion, very thinly sliced
1 medium tomato, chopped or grated (optional; leave out if you want a white sauce)
1 teaspoon cayenne pepper or Indian chilly powder
½ cup chopped fresh coriander (cilantro) stems and leaves
3 cups water

SAUCE

4 large eggs
1 tablespoon granulated sugar
¾ cup cane or rice vinegar
1 cup small cherry tomatoes
6 sprigs fresh coriander (cilantro), for garnish

- To make the fish: Sprinkle salt over the fish and set aside. Heat the oil to medium in a pan large and deep enough to hold the fish and its poaching liquid. Add the cumin seeds, garlic, and chiles and sizzle for a minute. Add the onion and let it soften without browning. The optional tomato goes in now. Add the cayenne and fresh coriander. Stir the mixture before adding the water and a small amount of salt. Bring the poaching liquid to a boil. Reduce the heat and simmer for about 15 minutes. Add the fish and let it poach gently until barely cooked through. Carefully remove it from the cooking liquid and set it on a warm serving dish. Reserve the cooking liquid.

- To make the sauce: Just before serving, whisk together the eggs, sugar, and vinegar. Pour the mixture into the poaching liquid over low to moderate heat without letting it boil. This is very important. Use a whisk to combine the poaching liquid and eggs and cook a few minutes until they thicken into a creamy sauce. Taste for salt and sweetness. Add the cherry tomatoes and barely heat them so that they don't collapse into the sauce before you serve the dish, yet don't squirt rudely when you bite into them.

- Pour the sauce over the fish. Strew a few sprigs of coriander over the top.

Fish in Coconut Milk | FISH MOLI

Now here is an absolutely luxurious, creamy coconut and fish dish. *Fish moli* entered Parsi cooking by way of the Malabar coast, the region now known as Kerala. My mother's version of *fish moli* is delicate, savory, and super-easy if you use lazy coconut milk (see below); it's more laborious if you start with a whole coconut, though it's well worth the effort.

Serve with steamed basmati rice and wedges of lime. Chayote steamed and dressed with lime and salt and a few snips of fresh coriander makes a fabulous accompaniment to *moli*. The color and texture are just right. If you can't find chayote, try winter melon. *Serves 4 to 6.*

1 coconut, or 2 cups canned coconut milk, or 3 cups frozen or reconstituted dried coconut milk
2 tablespoons vegetable oil
3 to 6 green chiles (use just 1 to 2 if you want a very mild dish), slit to the stem
8 to 10 curry leaves
1 medium onion, finely chopped
3 cloves garlic, sliced or finely chopped
½ teaspoon ground turmeric
Salt to taste
1 pound fish fillets, small steaks, or chunks
Lime wedges

- Extract the milk from the coconut in one squeezing (see page 41). Let stand until the thick coconut cream floats to the top, about 2 to 3 hours. Skim off the cream and reserve. See the note at the end of the recipe for instructions on using canned, frozen, or reconstituted dried coconut milk.

- Heat the oil in a large skillet, add the chiles and curry leaves, and sizzle them for a minute or two. Add the onion and garlic and let them soften without browning, stirring occasionally. Add the turmeric. Pour in the thin coconut milk and bring everything to a boil. Add a little salt, reduce the heat, and simmer for a few minutes to make a nice poaching liquid for the fish. Add the thick coconut cream, raise the heat just a bit, and add the fish. Reduce the heat again and simmer, partly covered, until the fish is cooked through, 5 to 10 minutes. Try not to let the liquid boil vigorously or it might curdle. Serve with lime wedges on the side.

• • •

Seafood Moli: You can substitute 2 cups of peeled and deveined shrimp or prawns, or even 2 pounds of scrubbed and debearded mussels or clams, for the fish. If using mussels or clams, discard any that do not open during cooking.

Note: My *moli* is often made the lazy way with shortcut coconut milk, either reconstituted dried or canned. You'll need about 3 to 4 cups of liquid in all, depending on how soupy you want your *moli.* If you're using canned milk, don't shake it up before opening it. Use the thinner part supplemented with about 1½ to 2 cups water for the first stage of cooking, saving the thick coconut cream for finishing the dish. If you're using frozen or reconstituted dried coconut milk, you need about 3 cups. For the first stage, use 2 cups supplemented with a cup of water, and add the last cup with the fish.

Andrew's Goa Curry

Andrew de Souza was my mother's cook for twenty years. For every day of those twenty years, he had just one thing for lunch and dinner: this curry. All sorts of fascinating fishy things went into Andrew's curry that the family never saw. One of them was skate, which I later got my mother to eat in San Francisco by calling it fanfish.

Unlike Indian curries characterized by creaminess, this particular type of Goa curry is very thin, very hot, and very sour. I remember my mother and her friends once having a competition over whose curry was the hottest. I was there the night of the winning entry, watching eight grown-ups weeping in bliss.

Serve this curry with plain or steamed rice. If you have the time, make the curry a day ahead because it really does improve with standing. Accompany with cucumber salad. *Serves 4 to 6.*

MASALA

6 cloves garlic
8 to 10 (or more if you really like heat) dried red chiles
2 teaspoons coriander seeds
1 teaspoon cumin seeds
A few black peppercorns (optional)
½ teaspoon ground turmeric

CURRY

　2 tablespoons vegetable oil

　1 medium onion, finely chopped

　A few curry leaves (optional)

　2 cups coconut milk

　2 to 3 cups water

　½ to 1 cup boiling water

　1 walnut-size ball of compressed tamarind (see page 42)

　Salt to taste

　1 pound fish fillets; or 1 pound shrimp or prawns, peeled and
　　deveined; or 1 pound squid, cleaned

- To make the masala: Grind the garlic, chiles, coriander, cumin, peppercorns if you like, and turmeric together into a stiff paste with a few teaspoons of water. If you don't have an Indian wet-dry grinder like the Sumeet (see page 30), the best approach is to pulverize the chiles and other whole dry spices in your spice grinder, pureeing the garlic separately. Then mix together the spices, garlic, and turmeric powder and add enough water to form a stiff paste.

- For the curry: Heat the oil in a large skillet over medium-high heat. Sauté the onion in the oil, stirring occasionally. Add the masala paste and the curry leaves, if you have them, and stir a few moments. Add the coconut milk and enough water to make about 4 to 5 cups liquid. Bring to a boil; reduce the heat and simmer until the oil rises to the top, about 45 minutes.

- Meanwhile, pour the boiling water over the dried tamarind, let sit for half an hour, and rub the softened tamarind through a strainer. Add the strained pulp to the curry and season with salt to taste. Add the seafood after the curry is finished and cook it for just a few minutes.

· · ·

Goa Curry with Vegetables: Andrew de Souza would sometimes add a vegetable to the curry, usually either okra or tindola (ivy gourd), a gherkinlike member of the squash family (see the Glossary). You can skip the fish altogether and use hard-boiled eggs instead, which I always like in combination with the vegetables. Other vegetable options might be zucchini or winter melon, bottle or sponge gourds, or sections of Chinese or Japanese eggplant.

Kokam Curry: As a souring agent, *kokam (Garcinia indica)* makes an interesting variant on tamarind. It's an intensely sour, blackish-purple relative of the mangosteen. Rinse any sand off 8 to 10 pieces of *kokam* and add them with the cooking liquid. Sometimes *kokam* is used as the only solid ingredient in a curry.

Seafood Ragout | PATIA

Patia, or *patio,* is one of the cornerstones of Parsi menu planning. It's part of the trinity of *dhan dar patio*—white rice, plain yellow dal, and this richly flavored seafood ragout—served on a *saro daro,* auspicious day, or on any day at all.

The traditional Parsi method is to cook the fish or vegetables along with the tomato and onion base for at least a half hour, but we prefer to fry the seafood components separately and add them to the *patia* slightly underdone, finishing the cooking just as it's time to serve the meal.

Patia is usually served with plain dal and boiled rice, or rice and red lentils cooked together as *khichri* (page 165). *Serves 4 to 6.*

MASALA

> *6 dried red chiles*
> *4 cloves garlic*
> *2 teaspoons cumin seeds*
> *½ teaspoon ground turmeric*

RAGOUT

> *1 pound shrimp or prawns, peeled and deveined; or fish fillets or steaks*
> *1 to 2 teaspoons of the dry rub for Masala Seafood (page 97)*
> *2 to 3 tablespoons vegetable oil*
> *2 green chiles, slit to the stem*
> *1 to 2 medium onions, finely chopped*
> *4 to 6 ripe tomatoes, chopped*
> *1 cup (loosely packed) coarsely chopped fresh coriander (cilantro) leaves and stems*
> *Salt to taste*
> *2 tablespoons jaggery or brown sugar*
> *1 to 2 tablespoons prepared tamarind pulp (page 42) or lime juice*

- For the masala: Using a wet-dry grinder, grind the red chiles, garlic, cumin, and turmeric together into a paste (or see the note below).

- To make the ragout: Rub the shrimp or fish with the dry rub. Heat 2 tablespoons of the oil in a heavy sauté pan or skillet over medium-high heat. Add the green chiles, allow to sizzle for a moment, and follow with the onions. Sauté, stirring occasionally, until the onions are golden. Add the masala paste and stir over moderate heat until the aroma rises. Add the tomatoes—skin, seeds, and all—and the fresh coriander. Cook over low heat to the consistency of marmalade. Add salt to taste, the jaggery, and tamarind or lime juice to get a good sweet-sour balance, adjusting to suit your own palate.

- Fry the shrimp or fish separately in as little oil as possible until tender. Add to the onion and tomato mixture. Cook together just enough to heat through and make the seafood part of the composition.

. . .

Squid or Shellfish Patia: Try other seafood options, such as squid, cutting the body into rings or scored squares so that they roll up when cooked. Or use shellfish such as clams or mussels.

Shad Roe Patia (gharab no patio): Shad roe is a seasonal delicacy. Parsis love to turn it into a fiery pickle to be eaten with plain dal, but my favorite way is to have it in a *patia*. Make a *patia* base following the recipe above. While the base is cooking, prepare the roe. Allow 1 lobe per person, 1 pair for two people. Have a skillet or wide-bottomed pan with 2 to 3 inches of boiling salted water at the ready. Prick the roe in several places with a pin or needle. Gently place the roe sacs in the boiling water, reduce the heat, and simmer until the skin turns opaque and appears firm. Don't worry about bits bursting out. Plunge the roe sacs into cold water. If they curl up and that bothers you, flatten them between two plates. Rub them with the dry rub and let rest for 15 to 30 minutes. Lightly brown them in 2 tablespoons oil for a couple of minutes on each side, then place them in the pan of *patia* base. Don't worry if they split and splutter; just dodge flying bits. Cook the roe for a few minutes in the hot *patia*. A handful of small okra cooked to near tenderness in the *patia* base before the shad roe goes in gives you one of the great Parsi favorites, roe and okra *patia (gharab bhida no patio)*.

Vegetable Patia: Add ½ pound of whole tiny okra to the *patia* base along with the fish. Or leave out the seafood altogether and have an okra *patia*. Eggplant, too, makes a succulent addition or substitution. I like to use small, dark Chinese eggplants and leave them whole, especially when I find little ones hardly thicker than a macho Mont Blanc pen. Pumpkin, alone or with eggplant, also makes a *patia* for vegetarians.

First Course Patia: You can serve *patia* as part of a soupy first course by putting a little plop of rice and *patia* in the middle of a wide, shallow soup plate of dal (page 176).

Note: If you haven't got a grinder, you can still make *patia masala* in a food processor or blender. Pound the cumin seeds first in a sturdy mortar or pulverize them in a spice grinder, then add them to the food processor bowl along with the garlic, chopped first to make grinding easier, 1 to 2 teaspoons cayenne pepper, and the turmeric. Dribble in just enough water to turn the mixture into a paste.

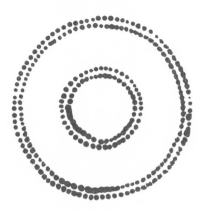

ગોસ્ત અને મરઘી

—•—

MEAT AND POULTRY

Parsis brought a tradition of lavish meat eating to India, and centuries of co-existence with the vegetarian populations around us in Gujarat did not change our omnivorous, carnivorous ways—though we did avoid cows, out of respect for the Hindus, and later pigs, out of respect for the Muslims. No aspect of Parsi cooking reflects the food of pre-Islamic Persia as much as the way we deal with meat and poultry. Modern Iranian cooking also reflects the food of our common Sassanian ancestors, whose traditions were preserved, cultivated, and disseminated by the Arabs who conquered Persia and fell in love with the food. For example, take a stew of lamb or kid with okra or apricots. You can find similar dishes from Bombay to Tangier, taken eastward to India by Parsis, westward by the Arabs as they swept as far as Africa and Spain, each region lending something of its own. India, for instance, adds chiles, warm aromatic spices, and coconut. Other Parsi meat dishes, such as vindaloo and *baffat,* come to us from the Portuguese connection in Goa, and the English influence can be seen in croquettes, cutlets, and mixed grills.

In India generally, and certainly in Bombay, the meat of goats or sheep of any age is known as mutton, which can confuse the traveler. Bombay's "mutton" is usually the meat of young goats, butchered and sold by Muslims, who also deal in "beef," which can be the meat of cows or water buffaloes. Pork is in the hands of Christians. Most Bombay Parsis avail themselves of everything on offer. Tongue to trotters, all parts of the animal are considered delicacies. Modern poultry raising has made chicken an everyday meat where once it was considered special, and the specter of a live chicken's head sticking out of the cook's bazaar bag no longer haunts the dreams of children.

With any kind of meat, though, there's an iron rule: meat is painstakingly trimmed of all fat and sinew, washed, and then rubbed with a paste of ginger and garlic. The reason for this is twofold. First, Parsis do not like the taste of meat untempered by ginger and garlic. Second, in a warm climate, the antibacterial properties of ginger and garlic serve a good purpose. Here in the United States, we do not need to wash our meat, because the conditions under which animals are butchered and sold are very different. In Indian cuisines, meat is never cooked rare, again partly for aesthetics, partly for health. Not only do I violate this rule, but there are times when I skip the ginger and garlic rub, too, especially with quail and other quickly grilled things, where I don't want the taste of uncooked ginger and garlic to dominate.

The selection of meat dishes here is just a snapshot of possibilities and a greatly abridged version of our own household favorites. Traditional techniques have been adjusted to the materials and conditions in the United States. In olden days, not that distant, the liberal use of ghee was considered the mark of a righteously lavish household. Times have changed, so I've made a few alterations in method to satisfy our contemporary preference for dishes with a leaner structure, without any sacrifice in taste.

Savory Braised Lamb | KHARU GOS

In Persia, they call this a *khoresh;* in Morocco, they call it a *tagine;* in France, it might be called a *daube;* but to Parsis in India, it is *kharu gos,* "savory meat," a very prosaic name for something completely delicious. Not only is this style of cooking meat deep and rich, but it's a simple braise that's perfectly satisfying by itself or as a base from which any number of variations spring. This is the food of our long-ago Persian ancestors. Any reader familiar with the cooking styles of the Near East, Turkey, and North Africa will be struck by their common approach to stewing meat, either plain or with fruits, nuts, or vegetables, which originated in ancient Iran.

In India, "meat" usually means kid or goat. While kid and goat are within reach in the United States—the presence of halal butchers sees to that—most of the time, we settle for lamb. An alternative loved by Parsi cooks in the United States is stewing veal, which delivers the melting quality we love in meat. Chicken thigh meat works well, too, or even pork shoulder. Beef couldn't be anything but good cooked this way, but it has entered the Parsi diet only in modern times.

Here is the key recipe for basic *kharu gos,* followed by some of the innumerable variations. This is Parsi family food—meat and vegetables, comforting, satisfying, and surprisingly easy to make. Using lamb shanks instead of cubed meat makes an extra-succulent stew. *Kharu gos* is usually served for dinner with Chapatis (page 44) or crusty bread. In our house, there's usually rice instead. *Serves 6 to 8.*

> *1 ½ to 2 pounds well-trimmed cubed shoulder or leg of lamb; or goat, stewing veal,*
> *   or boneless chicken thigh meat; or 4 to 6 lamb shanks, sawn in halves or thirds*
> *2 teaspoons Ginger-Garlic Paste (page 36)*
> *2 tablespoons vegetable oil*
> *2 to 3 dried red chiles*
> *½ teaspoon cumin seeds (optional)*
> *1 large onion, finely chopped or sliced*
> *Pinch of ground turmeric (optional)*
> *1 teaspoon (or more) salt*

- Rub the lamb with paste and let it sit at room temperature for at least half an hour. Heat the oil in a heavy large skillet or pan over medium-high heat. Add the chiles and the cumin seeds, if using, and let the chiles brown slightly before quickly adding the onion. Let the onion soften and begin to brown, then add the meat, tossing it constantly so that it colors without burning or sticking to the pan. Add splashes of water as necessary to keep things from sticking.

- When the lamb has colored a little, pour in enough water to come up to the top of the lamb without flooding it. Add the turmeric, if using, and about 1 teaspoon of salt for a start. Bring the liquid to a boil; reduce the heat, cover, and let the meat cook until it's tender but not in shreds, which will take at least 45 minutes for lamb, an hour for goat and veal, and less than half an hour for chicken. Lamb shanks take about 1½ hours. Taste for salt. There should be ample gravy, which is what Indians generally call the liquid in any finished dish.

· · ·

Soupy Meat (khara ras chaval): Follow the key recipe, only add more water, enough that the meat is set afloat in it, at least 4 to 5 cups. For Parsis, this is a supercomforting main-dish soup, to be eaten with rice. Green Chutney (page 227) is the preferred accompaniment.

Meat with Plantains (kera ma gos): The platter of meat in its gravy is surrounded by Fried Plantains (page 204), which soak up the juice.

Meat Stewed with Potatoes or Other Vegetables (papeta ma gos, kasa ma gos): Follow the main recipe, adding 6 to 8 medium potatoes, peeled and quartered, halfway through the cooking. To be fancy, fry the potatoes first, just enough to give them a golden skin, before adding them to the stew. This gives them a lovely texture. The efficient way to do this is to fry them when you start the recipe. When golden, remove the potatoes, set them aside, and go ahead with the recipe by frying the chiles and so on, adding a touch more oil if you need to. Some Parsi cooks add one or several tomatoes, quartered, with the water. Other vegetables, such as whole okra (traditionally fried first), tindola (ivy gourd), or summer squashes (either whole or cut up), are added in the last 15 minutes. They should be thoroughly cooked but not mushy.

Meat Braised in Tomato Sauce (tamota ma gos): When tomatoes are plentiful, try this dish. The meat braises in a gently spiced tomato sauce that cooks down to a rich but light gravy with a touch of sweetness. Add two 2-inch-long sticks of cinnamon and 6 whole cloves to the sizzled whole spices. For the cooking liquid, add 8 to 10 tomatoes, grated (about 1 quart of pulp), and then pour in enough water to come up to the top of the meat, as in the main recipe. Finish the dish with a touch of brown sugar. You can use canned or tetrapack chopped tomatoes for this dish. Just be sure to choose a brand with lots of flavor.

Meat Stewed with Cauliflower (cauliflower ma gos): Follow the main recipe. Halfway through the cooking, add about 4 cups of cauliflower florets along with 1 cup of coconut milk. Canned is fine. Allow the cauliflower to soften completely. This dish is a great favorite for regular family dinners. For color, sprinkle a little finely chopped fresh coriander (cilantro) over the top before serving.

Meat Cooked with Greens (bhaji ma gos): Follow the recipe, except substitute 2 to 3 green chiles slit to the stem for the dried red chiles in the initial sizzle of whole spices. Add 4 cups of very thinly julienned or chopped spinach, amaranth, or fenugreek greens halfway through cooking. Add a cup of shelled young peas shortly before the dish is to be served, though the standard method is to cook them for a long time.

Meat Stewed with Peas (green peas ma gos): Follow the main recipe using green chiles instead of red. Add 2 cups of finely chopped fresh coriander (cilantro) with the meat, and add 2 cups of shelled young peas shortly before the dish is to be served, so that the peas are barely cooked. I sometimes use sliced leeks instead of onions. This is a fabulous spring dish.

Note: In my cousin Roshan's house, many of these meat dishes are turned into satisfying vegetable stews simply by leaving out the meat—but not the ginger-garlic paste.

Kid Stewed with Potatoes | KID PAPETA MA GOS

Kid papeta ma gos is a dish for festive occasions like weddings; meat braised with fried potatoes is enriched and thickened with milk from a cow or a coconut. This is a dish to convert people who think that Indian food is not for them. It proves that "spiciness" has little to do with how hot something turns out. It is truly meat and potatoes *in excelsis.* The method is essentially the same as for a simpler braised meat, *kharu gos* (see above). Accompany this with a bright green vegetable. *Serves 6 to 8.*

1½ to 2 pounds well-trimmed cubed shoulder or leg of kid; or lamb, stewing veal,
  or boneless chicken thigh meat; or 4 to 6 lamb shanks, sawn in halves or thirds
2 teaspoons Ginger-Garlic Paste (page 36)
6 tablespoons ghee
6 to 8 medium potatoes, peeled and quartered lengthwise
2 to 3 dried red chiles
2 (2-inch-long) sticks cinnamon or cassia
4 cardamom pods
4 whole cloves
½ teaspoon cumin seeds
1 large onion, finely chopped or sliced
4 to 5 cups rich milk, half-and-half, or coconut milk
1 teaspoon (or more) salt
Sprigs or whole leaves of fresh coriander (cilantro), for garnish

- Rub the meat with the paste and let it sit for at least half an hour.
- Heat half the ghee in a heavy skillet or pan over medium-high heat. Fry the potatoes until they get a golden skin. Remove them from the pan and set aside. In a Dutch oven, heat the remaining ghee. Sizzle the chiles, cinnamon, cardamom, cloves, and

cumin seeds for a minute before quickly adding the onion. Lower the heat and let the onion soften and begin to brown for a few minutes. Add the meat, tossing it constantly so that it colors without burning or sticking to the pan. Add splashes of water as necessary to keep things from sticking.

• Pour in enough milk to come up to the top of the meat without flooding it. Add about 1 teaspoon salt for a start. Bring the liquid to a boil; lower the heat, cover, and let the meat simmer gently until it's tender but not in shreds, which will take at least 45 minutes for kid or lamb, an hour for veal, and less than half an hour for chicken. Lamb shanks will take about 1 ½ hours. Halfway through the cooking, add the fried potatoes. The milk will cook down into a thick, curdy gravy. If you want a smooth sauce, remove the whole cinnamon, cardamom, and cloves before giving the cooking liquid a few pulses in a blender or food processor, then return it to the pan.

• Serve garnished with the fresh coriander.

Cutlets or Meatballs | KATLES KAVAB

Throughout the sphere of Persian Arab influence, including northern India, a kebab or *kofta* can be meat or fish, ground or in chunks, shaped, impaled or not, and either fried, stewed, or grilled. For Parsis, the Gujarati word *kavab* signifies a mixture of meat, fish, or vegetable shaped and then stewed, fried, or cooked on a griddle. In Bombay, the meat of choice is usually lean kid; my preference is for chicken or turkey. Supermarket ground lamb can be too fatty for Parsi tastes, but there's no reason for an American cook not to use the leanest possible hamburger or, for that matter, ground pork.

In traditional Parsi everyday menu planning, there's usually something in a category known as a *sukki vani:* a dry dish, usually ground meat, fried as a *kavab* or as a *katles,* pronounced "cut-lace," a pan-Indian adaptation of British *cutlets.* Like a *kavab,* a *katles* can be a malleable mixture of anything. What distinguishes it is its shape, a flattened oval. This basic recipe can be easily adapted to make cutlets. It is enough for about a dozen small *kavabs* or six to eight *katles.* Cold or room-temperature cutlets make an excellent sandwich filling.

Shaped around skewers and brushed with oil, the *kavabs* can be roasted or grilled, in which case they are called *sikh* (stick or skewer, not to be confused with the religious community) *kavabs. Serves 4 to 6.*

1 pound ground chicken or turkey; or leanest lamb, pork, or beef
1 to 2 boiled potatoes, roughly mashed
1 medium-size red or yellow onion, finely chopped
2 to 3 (or more) green chiles, finely chopped
2 teaspoons Ginger-Garlic Paste (page 36)
½ cup finely chopped fresh coriander (cilantro) stems and leaves
½ teaspoon ground turmeric
1 teaspoon salt
1 large egg; plus 1 to 2 additional eggs, lightly beaten, if coating
1 teaspoon Dhana Jiru (page 38; optional—for kavabs only)
1 cup dry bread crumbs (optional)
Vegetable oil, for frying

- For *kavabs:* Mix together the ground meat, potatoes, onion, chiles, paste, fresh coriander, turmeric, salt, and 1 egg. For a "correct"-tasting *kavab,* add the *dhana jiru* spice mixture. Using damp or oiled hands, shape the mixture into balls or flatten it into small, thick patties. For a predinner nibble, often known as a "cocktail *kavab,*" make them the size of a walnut; for dinner, they should be about 2 to 3 inches across. Some cooks dip *kavabs* in egg and bread crumbs before frying. I don't.

- Shallow-fry dinner *kavabs* or deep-fry smaller ones. A wok or *karhai* gives you greater depth of oil for the amount used. Heat the oil over medium-high heat until hot but not smoking before adding the *kavabs.* It should take about 5 to 10 minutes for a thick dinner *kavab* to get cooked through, 3 to 5 minutes for the little ones. Sometimes small *kavabs* are given a quick pass through oil before being finished in a stew or curry.

- For *katles:* With wet or oiled hands, shape the combined ingredients into 6 to 8 flattened palm-size ovals. Have a shallow bowl with the lightly beaten eggs and a plate with the dry bread crumbs at the ready. Dip each cutlet into the beaten egg, then the crumbs, and shallow-fry in 1 cup oil over medium-high heat until golden on both sides, 5 to 10 minutes. Alternatively, "dry-fry" the cutlets: Heat a heavy skillet or griddle and pour the merest film of oil on it. In this case, they will have a less unctuous character than if they were shallow-fried, but they will have attractive dark brown speckles. This is my preferred way.

Tomato Gravy | TAMOTA NI GRAVY

Cutlets are often served with this tomato gravy, which resembles a sweet-sour cream of tomato soup. They then become *tamota ni gravy na katles.*

1 tablespoon vegetable oil
1 small onion, finely chopped
1 teaspoon Ginger-Garlic Paste (page 36)
¼ to ½ teaspoon cayenne pepper or Indian chilly powder
1 ½ pounds tomatoes, chopped
Good shake of Worcestershire sauce
Jaggery or brown sugar
Salt to taste

· Heat the oil in a 2-quart saucepan over medium heat. Soften the onion without browning, stirring occasionally. Add the paste. Stir for a moment before adding the cayenne, ¼ teaspoon to start. Add the tomatoes and bring to a boil. Reduce the heat and simmer for a few minutes until the gravy is thick and saucy. Add the Worcestershire sauce, jaggery, and salt. Taste and add more of any seasoning if necessary.

• • •

Note: For a smoother sauce, puree and strain the tomatoes before adding them to the onion and spice mixture.

Parsiburgers

There are times when my husband and I both crave this streamlined version of the conventional Parsi *kavabs.* With a baked potato and a salad, perhaps one with avocado, they make a perfect lean, comforting lunch or dinner. If you boil the potatoes or have corn on the cob as a starch, you can get the whole dinner on the table in half an hour. *Serves 4.*

1 pound ground chicken, turkey, or lean pork
1 small red or yellow onion, or 4 green onions, finely chopped
6 slices peeled fresh ginger, finely chopped
2 to 4 green chiles, finely chopped
½ cup (or more) chopped fresh coriander (cilantro) leaves and stems

¼ cup chopped mint leaves (optional)
1 large egg
Salt

- In a bowl, combine the ground chicken, onion, ginger, chiles, fresh coriander, mint if you like, and egg. Season with salt and mix thoroughly. Shape into 4 to 6 flat patties.

- Heat a cast-iron skillet with the merest film of oil. Moderately high heat is better than a blazing-hot pan, which can char the meat before the insides are cooked. Fry the burgers on both sides until brown, about 5 to 10 minutes a side, depending on the thickness.

• • •

Parsi Meat Loaf: Heat the oven to 350 to 375 degrees. Double the recipe above, adding 4 to 6 ounces of grated potato as filler, so that the texture isn't too tight. Shape into a loaf and place in a metal or glass baking pan. Brush with 1 tablespoon of oil mixed with 2 teaspoons of pomegranate molasses. Bake about 45 to 50 minutes, just like any other meat loaf. Even confirmed meat loaf haters come around after tasting this version. Tomato Gravy (page 118) is good with this, but I like it plain with a baked potato, a steamed green vegetable, and a salad.

Khima

One criterion for a great comfort food is that it never get dull. This gentle, savory stew of ground meat meets that test. *Khima* is found in most Indian meat-eating cuisines; the word refers to the main ingredient, ground meat, as well as to the finished dish. Our Parsi version makes a wonderful meal as is, but it lends itself to a great many other good dishes: it goes under poached or puffy Eggs on Anything (page 89); it's a stuffing for vegetables like eggplant, summer squashes, green peppers, or tomatoes; it's an important part of another great Parsi dish, Khima-Stuffed Potato Cakes (page 121); Bombay's shatteringly crisp samosas and curry puffs are filled with it; and it makes a great pizza topping. It wouldn't surprise me if somewhere in the United States, some inventive Parsi cook is adding kidney beans to *khima* to make a chili.

Parsi cooks in India would use lean ground kid or lamb. Here we have a wider choice. My preference is to use ground chicken or turkey. You can make this dish as mild as you want by cutting down on or leaving out the cayenne pepper. The amount of water used in cooking *khima* can vary, too, depending on whether you want it soupy, to serve over rice (the dish then becomes *khima na ras chaval*) or over *khichri* (page 165), or relatively dry, to use under eggs or as a filling (page 121). Like *khari machhi* (page 102), *khima* is regarded as a dish that can be served to invalids, stimulating but easy to digest and full of the natural antibiotic properties of ginger, garlic, and cloves.

Typical Parsi ways to serve *khima* are with Angel-Hair Potatoes (page 200) or Potato Wafers (page 201), or Tomato Rice (page 169). We like boiled or riced potatoes or plain rice, too. *Serves 4 to 6.*

1 to 2 tablespoons vegetable oil

5 to 10 curry leaves

2 to 3 whole cloves

2 green chiles, slit to the stem

1 medium onion, chopped

1 teaspoon Ginger-Garlic Paste (page 36)

1 teaspoon Dhana Jiru (page 38; optional)

1 teaspoon Sambhar Masala (page 37; optional)

½ to 1 teaspoon cayenne pepper or Indian chilly powder

½ teaspoon ground turmeric

½ cup chopped fresh coriander (cilantro) leaves and stems, plus extra for garnish

1 (or more) medium tomato, grated or chopped

1 pound ground chicken, turkey, or leanest lamb, beef, or pork; or
  ½ pound textured soy protein, soaked to soften

1 ½ to 2 cups (or more) water

1 teaspoon (or more) salt

- Heat the oil in a large skillet over medium-high heat. Add the curry leaves, cloves, and green chiles and let them sizzle for a minute or two. Add the onion and cook, stirring occasionally, until it's soft and beginning to turn golden. Add the paste and stir back and forth for another couple of minutes, adding a small splash of water to keep things from sticking. Add the spice mixes, if you have them, along with the cayenne, turmeric, and fresh coriander. The *dhana jiru* and *sambhar masala* are optional, but necessary for an authentic Parsi taste. Add the tomato (more than one can be used, depending on the season and the cook's mood), and let the mixture cook for another minute or two. Add the meat and stir until it loses its raw look. Then add water, 1 ½ to 2 cups or even more if you want to make a really soupy *khima*. Add 1 teaspoon of salt for a start. Bring the mixture to a boil; reduce the heat and simmer, partly covered, until the *khima* is cooked, 30 minutes or less. You will know when the *khima* is done by tasting a little; it should be tender. Another sign is when the oil floats to the top. Check for salt and add more to taste. Garnish with more chopped fresh coriander and serve.

• • •

Sweet-and-Sour Khima: Sometimes *khima* is made *khattu-mitthu,* sweet-and-sour. Right at the end, add 1 to 2 teaspoons jaggery or brown sugar and a couple of teaspoons of cane vinegar. Taste and adjust the balance.

Khima-Stuffed Vegetables: Steam a large halved eggplant until it's soft. Let it cool. Gently scoop out the flesh, leaving a shell to hold the filling. Mix the scooped-out eggplant with the *khima* cooked dry, 2 eggs, and extra chopped fresh coriander. Fill the eggplant halves. Sprinkle with dry bread crumbs and dot with butter. Brush the outside of the shells with a little oil. Put in a baking dish with Tomato Gravy (page 118) and bake for 30 to 40 minutes at 350 degrees, until the top is golden brown. *Khima* is also a good stuffing for cabbage leaves or bell peppers.

Khima Samosas: Samosa strips or *pattis (patti* means strip, not to be confused with the following recipe for *pattis)* are similar to wonton wrappers but are longer, thinner, and crisper when fried. If you're lucky, you can find them in the frozen-food section of well-stocked Indian groceries. Put a teaspoon or two of cooled, cooked-dry *khima* in the bottom corner of the samosa strip, and keep folding tightly, corner to edge, as if folding a flag, tucking in the margin of surplus pastry and sealing it with flour and water paste. Deep-fry in medium-hot oil (about 360 degrees) and serve hot with Homemade Tomato Ketchup (page 232) or Date and Tamarind Chutney (page 230). Serve as an appetizer. (It's all too easy to make a meal of these Bombay favorites.)

Khima-Stuffed Potato Cakes | KHIMA NA PATTIS

This must be a nineteenth-century adaptation of an English original transformed by Indian cooks into something far more delicious than the original patties. *Khima na pattis* was one of my favorite childhood dishes. It consists of flattened patties of ground meat enclosed in mashed potato and fried. It's remarkably hard to execute unless the filling and coating are the right consistency and in the right proportion to each other. For years, until my mother showed me the tricks, my efforts were like potato and *khima* greasy mess. You need to have the *khima* cool enough to handle and some mashed potatoes, egg, bread crumbs or semolina, and oil for frying—simple ingredients with spectacularly rewarding results. It is worth anyone's while to learn how to make *pattis;* they are without a doubt one of the great Parsi dishes.

Serve with Parsi Green Chutney (page 227) or Tomato Gravy (page 118). Cold *pattis* make good picnic food. *Serves 4 to 6.*

About 1 ½ cups Khima (about half the recipe on page 119)
3 large russet potatoes
Salt to taste
1 tablespoon butter
2 large eggs
1 to 2 cups homemade dry bread crumbs
1 to 2 cups vegetable oil, for frying

- While the meat is cooking, prepare the potatoes. Boil them, halved for quicker cooking, in salted water until soft. Peel them and mash with the salt and butter. Don't be tempted to add too much butter. You want potatoes that are firm but pliable. Let the potatoes and *khima* cool before shaping the *pattis.*

- Lightly beat the eggs in a wide, shallow bowl. Have a plate of the bread crumbs ready, plus a tray lightly dusted with crumbs. Keep a bowl of water near you so that you can keep wetting your hands. This is vital to the successful shaping of *pattis.* To shape the *pattis,* grab a handful (½ cup) of potato in a wet hand. Shape it into a ball, and then flatten it to a 4-inch-diameter or palm-size circle. Place 2 to 3 tablespoonfuls of cooled meat filling in the center and enclose it in an even coating of potato. I've found that saving ¼ of the potato ball and using it as a lid makes neater *pattis.* Repair any holes or thin spots with extra potato. All this happens while the *pattis* is still in your hand.

- Coat each *pattis* with egg by either dipping or brushing, then put it in the tray of crumbs and shower it to cover it completely, flattening the *pattis* into a 2-inch-high patty with neat, straight sides. Set aside on the prepared tray until all the *pattis* are shaped. Three large potatoes yield six large *pattis.*

- Heat oil to a depth of 1 inch in a skillet or wok over medium heat. Shallow-fry the patties in two batches, splashing oil on the sides, till barely golden brown. Transfer to paper towels to drain. In response to my wailing about fat-fat-fat and frying-frying-frying, Andrew de Souza, my mother's cook, sometimes baked *pattis* on a lightly greased *tava,* an iron griddle. Fried patties are very good, but the griddle-baked ones have their own charm from the slight charring of the bread crumbs. Serve hot or at room temperature.

• • •

Stuffing Variations: Vary the filling for *pattis* with *akuri* (page 85) or Parsi Green Chutney (page 227).

Parsi Shepherd's Pie: To get the overall effect of *khima*-stuffed potato cakes without all the work, put the *khima* in a baking dish. Cover the surface with seasoned mashed potatoes, using as much butter as you like. Give the top an egg wash and sprinkle with bread crumbs and a few microdots of butter. Bake at 375 degrees until the top is golden brown, at least 30 minutes.

Grilled Lamb "Lollipops"

This is a California Parsi dish; we never had lamb tenderloin in Bombay. Some years ago, we were marinating lamb tenderloins in pomegranate molasses, black pepper, and some garam masala. My mother looked at the tray and beckoned me out of the kitchen with a strange grin on her face. "Niloufer, are these the lambs' . . . lollipops?" she asked. Lollipops they've been since then.

Lamb tenderloins are an unabashed luxury, because each lamb has only two. The recipe is simple. No ginger and garlic, no elaborate ground masala or long marinating here, because the meat is cooked quickly and the spices need to stay on the surface instead of being drawn down into the flesh. Quantities are suggested, not ironclad.

These are very good with grits or polenta and Parsi Ratatouille (page 206). *Serves 6 to 8, with leftovers.*

1 tablespoon olive oil
1 tablespoon pomegranate molasses
½ teaspoon cayenne pepper or Indian chilly powder
¾ teaspoon Parsi Garam Masala (page 37)
Liberal grinding of black pepper
1 teaspoon salt
12 lamb tenderloins (about 1 ½ to 2 pounds)

• To make the marinade, mix together the oil, pomegranate molasses, cayenne, garam masala, pepper, and salt. Taste for salt and cayenne. Rub the marinade into the lamb tenderloins; set aside for 1 to 2 hours, not more.

• Prepare a coal or gas grill. Grill the tenderloins until brown and lightly crusted on the outside but still pink on the inside, about 3 to 5 minutes per side. Press them to check for doneness: they should feel like the fleshy part of your thumb when it's stretched out. For people who don't like rare lamb, cook another minute or so. Alternatively, heat a cast-iron skillet or ridged grill pan over high heat and sear the tenderloins. Serve at once.

· · ·

Note: Lamb tenderloins can vary in size. This quantity assumes they are on the skinny side.

Braised Leg of Lamb or Kid | ROST MATAN

Along with cutlets and breaded chops, a plain roast leg of kid or lamb has its origin in the Raj, but there's nothing English about this succulent Parsi version, marinated in the required paste of ginger and garlic, gently or ferociously spiced with dried red chile, and then slowly cooked in melted onions until the meat almost falls away from the bone but stays firm enough to slice. The smell of it cooking will perk up flagging appetites or drive a hungry person crazy with anticipation. Plan on having enough left over for at least one sandwich. Bombay cooks generally use kid or goat, because that's what we get, but a well-trimmed leg of lamb does perfectly well.

Potatoes are the perfect vegetable accompaniment, mashed or roasted. Parsi cooks would fry half-cooked peeled potatoes, then put them in with the meat to soften and absorb the juices. Another approach is from Nathalie Hambro's cookbook *Particular Delights:* Halve unpeeled raw waxy potatoes such as Yukon Golds. Brush them with oil (if you like), sprinkle with salt, and set them cut side up on a baking sheet in a 350 degree oven until they are cooked through and puff up, about 30 minutes. This sounds unlikely, but it really does happen.

For the vegetable component, think of broccoli or broccoli rabe, chard, kale, spaghetti squash, or Pumpkin Crescents with Curry Leaves (page 197).

My risophilic husband, David, who has no objection to several starches in a meal, suggests cooking equal amounts of rice and quinoa together. They take the same amount of time to cook. Or try the Caramelized Fried Rice on page 168. *Serves 4 to 6.*

1 (4- to 6-pound) leg of lamb or kid

3 to 4 tablespoons Ginger-Garlic Paste (page 36)

2 teaspoons (or more) salt

1 teaspoon (about) cayenne pepper or Indian chilly powder (optional)

½ teaspoon cumin seeds, freshly ground (optional)

2 to 4 tablespoons vegetable oil
2 to 4 dried red chiles
1 teaspoon whole cumin seeds
2 medium onions, sliced

- Trim off as much of the lamb fat as you possibly can. A few little streaks of fat here and there won't matter, but you don't want any visible deposits or layers. Poke the meat all over with a kitchen fork or a narrow-bladed knife. For a gently spiced roast, rub it with the paste mixed with about 2 teaspoons salt. If you want your roast fiery, add the optional cayenne and ground cumin to the mixture, adding just enough water or oil to make a paste. Cover the lamb and leave it to marinate in a cool place for several hours.

- When you're ready to cook the lamb, heat the oven to 350 degrees. Heat 1 to 2 tablespoons oil in a skillet and sizzle the chiles and the whole cumin seeds for a minute or two. Add the onions and cook, stirring occasionally. When they are soft, transfer them to the bottom of a roasting pan. I like those inexpensive blue-enamel covered turkey roasters, but covering a lidless roasting pan with a bonnet of tightly anchored aluminum foil will do in a pinch.

- Heat the remaining 1 to 2 tablespoons oil in a very large skillet over high heat. Quickly brown the lamb all over before transferring it to the roasting pan. Deglaze the skillet with a little water and add the juices to the roasting pan. Add more water so that the onions are covered but not drowning. Put the roaster on the stove top over high heat and let the liquid come to a boil. Before it's too hot, taste for salt. You can always add more later, but you need some to start with for the roast to have its full depth of flavor. Put the lid on the roaster and transfer it to the oven.

- Roast the lamb in the oven for 2 to 3 hours, checking it midway to be sure the cooking liquid hasn't dried up and adding more water if necessary. You will know when the roast is done when the main shank bone seems to spring loose from the flesh. Let the lamb rest on a warm platter while you skim any visible fat off the cooking juices and organize your accompaniments. Taste again for salt. Serve the roast sliced at the table with a bowl of the pan juices to pour over it.

· · ·

Braised Lamb Shanks: You'll need 4 jumbo or 6 small shanks. Trim them well. Cut little slits all over them and rub in the masala. Proceed as for leg of lamb, adjusting the time: lamb shanks are usually meltingly tender in about 1 ½ to 2 hours.

Bombay-Style "Mutton" Sandwich: Spread good white bread with butter. If you can find an English mustard such as Colman's, a whisper of that goes on top of the butter, followed by the meat sliced in proportion to the thickness of the bread. Obviously you don't want a thick piece of meat between two thin slices of bread or a tissue-thin piece of meat between two doorstops. Trim off the crusts or not as you prefer, and cut in half diagonally or into quarters. Go on a picnic.

Twice-Cooked Grilled Lamb or Kid | BHUJELU GOS

We made this fabulous barbecue for a Chez Panisse Parsi New Year's dinner, using kid provided by a wonderful woman near Sacramento who moved to California from Hawaii with a planeload of her animals. You'll be able to find goat's meat at any halal butcher anywhere in the United States; kid is a little harder to find. Lamb is a perfectly good alternative and pork shoulder or butt, though not a Bombay alternative, makes succulent morsels. Ask your butcher to cut the meat into thick, evenly sized generous chunks. In India, meat on the bone is desirable, but it's not vital to the success of the dish, so boneless shoulder will work.

The grill we used in Bombay was a cast-iron cylinder with a grate on top of the chamber for charcoal. Here in San Francisco, we use a hibachi in our tiny fireplace. A Tuscan fireplace grill would be splendid if you have one. Those ridged cast-iron stove-top pans work well, too. Resist the temptation to skip the preliminary braising. Using this marinade on top of meat to be grilled rare doesn't do justice to either meat or marinade, and you'll end up with something that tastes of raw meat and raw spices.

The cooking liquid can be used to make a *pulao* (page 167) to serve alongside. This main-course recipe could also serve a larger group as a nibble. *Serves 4.*

MASALA

> *6 dried red chiles*
> *½ to 1 teaspoon cumin seeds*
> *4 cloves garlic*
> *1 (1-inch-long) piece peeled fresh ginger*
> *1 to 2 tablespoons hoisin sauce*
> *Vegetable oil*

> *2 pounds shoulder of lamb or kid, trimmed of all visible fat and sinew; or*
>> *3 pounds lamb riblets, well trimmed, cut into 2- to 3-rib sections*
> *2 teaspoons Ginger-Garlic Paste (page 36)*
> *1 teaspoon salt*

- To make the masala rub: Grind together the chiles, cumin, garlic, and ginger with the hoisin sauce and enough oil to moisten. Set aside.

- Put the meat in a large saucepan with the ginger-garlic paste and enough water to cover. Add the salt. Bring to a boil; reduce the heat to low, cover, and cook until the meat is almost tender, 45 minutes to 1 hour. A skewer or the tip of a knife should go through the meat with no resistance, but the meat should not be falling off the bone. If you have the time, let the meat cool to room temperature in the broth. Drain the meat thoroughly, reserving the cooking liquid for making an accompanying pulao. Let the meat air-dry before proceeding, or use a hair dryer if you're in a hurry. Refrigerate the cooking liquid so the fat can be skimmed off easily.

- Rub the meat with the reserved masala and let sit at least 2 hours. Grill over moderately hot coals. (In India, we put a bed of hay over the coals to lend an extra-smoky flavor to the grilled meat.) After about 15 minutes, it should have an appealing reddish-black crust and be meltingly tender inside.

PORTABLE
CHARCOAL STOVE

• • •

Parsi Carnitas: Cook chunks of pork or lamb shoulder in enough water to cover, flavored with the *bhujelo gos* masala. Use a wide deep pan that will hold the chunks of meat in a single layer with the water barely covering the surface of the meat. Bring to a boil; reduce the heat and let the water simmer away slowly. This will take about an hour. Continue cooking the meat over a low flame until the chunks are appetizingly brown outside and meltingly tender inside. This is a winner! Serve with a stewy vegetable dish and some rice. These carnitas are good with Simple Onion Kachumbar (page 223) and wrapped in heated lavash or the beautiful bathmat bread from a Middle Eastern grocery.

Goan Meat or Poultry Stew | VINDALOO

My mother had a very good dodge—or if it wasn't a dodge, it was an unconscious way of guaranteeing I'd eat everything put before me. I was told that this or that tantalizing thing was just for grown-ups. One of these things was vindaloo. I still remember my first taste of it—and it was just a taste—and being put to bed very envious of what my parents and their laughing guests were eating.

Vindaloo comes to Parsi households from the Portuguese connection. Its original name was probably *vin d'alho,* literally "wine of garlic," more likely than *vino e alho,* which is proposed by some. Pronounce it "vin-DAH-lu." Traditionally, vindaloo is made with only vinegar as a cooking liquid, which makes it a kind of meat pickle that keeps well. I often use half vinegar and half water or wine for the cooking liquid. Use a good cane or coconut vinegar if you can find one. Philippine groceries usually have both. Otherwise, rice vinegar from Japan or even cider vinegar works well. If you've got odd bits of wine, red or white, this is a good way to use them up, though the taste of the dish then veers away from the truly Indian.

In my mother's house, vindaloo was usually served with fried potatoes or crusty bread. Rice, polenta, or grits are also perfect accompaniments. Steamed root vegetables such as turnips, rutabagas, and carrots or amaranth or bitter greens are welcome on the plate, as they offset the hot-sour richness of the vindaloo.

Vindaloo is one of those stewy dishes that are excellent the day they're made but taste even better the next day or the next, as the flavors settle in. *Serves 6.*

MASALA

10 to 12 dried red chiles

1 teaspoon cumin seeds

1 (2-inch-long) piece peeled fresh ginger

6 to 8 cloves garlic

3 (2-inch-long) sticks cinnamon or cassia

5 whole cloves

10 black peppercorns

½ teaspoon ground turmeric

Pinch of salt

1 teaspoon (or more) cane, coconut, rice, or cider vinegar

MEAT

2 tablespoons vegetable oil

1 large onion, finely chopped

2 to 3 pounds cubed pork, lamb, or kid shoulder; or 8 to 10 duck legs; or 8 chicken thighs; or 2 cut-up squabs

2 to 3 cups cane, coconut, rice, or cider vinegar

2 teaspoons salt

Jaggery or brown sugar (optional)

- To make the masala: If you have a wet-dry grinder, the chiles, cumin, ginger, garlic, cinnamon, cloves, peppercorns, turmeric, and salt can go in all at once with a splash of vinegar. Otherwise, pulverize the dry spices in a coffee mill reserved for grinding spices, then pulse with the ginger and garlic in a food processor, with enough vinegar to create a smooth, thick paste.

- To cook the meat: Heat the oil in a heavy, deep, nonreactive pot over medium heat. Add the onion and cook, stirring occasionally, until softened. Add the masala, and then the meat. Stir well. Add enough vinegar to barely cover the meat, along with the salt. Bring to a boil; reduce the heat and simmer until the meat is tender, about 20 to 25 minutes for chicken, 30 to 40 minutes for duck, and 45 minutes to an hour for lamb, kid, or pork. Skim off any oil that floats to the surface if you don't have time to chill the vindaloo before skimming off the fat. Check the seasoning.

- Some people like a sweet-and-sour vindaloo. If you do, add a little jaggery to offset the acid.

• • •

Note: To cut down on the fat, I often brown the meat or poultry in a dry cast-iron skillet before marinating.

Goan Rich Pork Stew with Vegetables | BAFFAT

Along with vindaloo, *baffat* comes from the Portuguese-influenced cooking of Goa. *Baffat* is a dry, hot-sour dish of meat and vegetables thickened with peanuts and roasted chickpeas and sometimes coconut. This is my mother's version with no changes, except that the meat is treated in a way that renders out as much fat as possible before cooking.

Roasted chickpeas are sold at most health food stores. At Indian groceries, ask for husked channa or gram.

Serve with Chapatis (page 44), or whole wheat tortillas, or crusty bread in the Parsi manner. We always serve greens, too. *Serves 6 to 8.*

MASALA

5 to 6 dried red chiles
1 teaspoon coriander seeds
1 teaspoon cumin seeds
1 (2-inch-long) stick cinnamon or cassia
4 whole cloves

¼ cup unsalted raw peanuts

¼ cup roasted chickpeas (husked channa)

½ cup fresh or frozen grated coconut; or ½ cup canned, frozen, or reconstituted dried coconut milk (if using a food processor)

1 teaspoon (or more) cane, coconut, rice, or cider vinegar

MEAT

2 pounds pork or lamb shoulder; or boneless chicken thigh meat; or 6 to 8 duck legs

2 teaspoons Ginger-Garlic Paste (page 36)

2 tablespoons vegetable oil

1 large onion, finely chopped

1 teaspoon (or more) cane, coconut, rice, or cider vinegar

1 to 2 tomatoes, chopped or grated

1 teaspoon (about) salt

12 small boiling onions, peeled and trimmed

4 to 6 medium potatoes, peeled and halved

2 to 3 carrots, peeled and cut into 2-inch pieces

2 to 3 regular turnips, peeled and cut; or 12 tiny ones

- For the masala: If you have a wet-dry grinder, grind together the chiles, coriander, cumin, cinnamon, cloves, peanuts, chickpeas, and coconut and a splash of vinegar. Otherwise, pulverize the dry spices in a coffee mill reserved for grinding spices and then process them in a food processor with the peanuts, chickpeas, coconut milk, and enough vinegar to create a fine, thick paste.

- For the meat: Cut the meat into generous chunks, 2 to 3 inches across. They seldom turn out perfectly even. Carefully trim off as much fat as possible. Heat a dry cast-iron or other heavy skillet over medium-high heat. Add the meat and sear. Transfer the meat to a bowl, mix in the ginger-garlic paste, and let it sit for half an hour.

- In a sturdy stewing pan or Dutch oven, heat the oil over moderate heat. Add the onion and cook until softened, stirring occasionally. Add the masala and cook 3 to 5 minutes, adding small amounts of vinegar to keep things from sticking and burning. Add the meat and toss to combine thoroughly with the contents of the pan. Add the tomatoes next. Pour in enough water to come to just above the top of the meat. Add the salt and stir well. Bring to a boil; lower the heat, cover the pan, and simmer gently until the meat is tender, between 30 and 90 minutes, depending on the type used. (If you're using boneless chicken, it will be tender after about 30 minutes, before the *baffat* is considered fully cooked. Remove the chicken and return it to the pan when the gravy is thick and the oil floats to the top, about 30 minutes more.)

- Add the onions, potatoes, carrots, and turnips to the stew during the last 15 to 20 minutes of cooking. Let them get thoroughly tender but not too soft. (The vegetables could also be served as a side dish, steamed or boiled.)

Irish Stew

I can imagine the first time some Parsi woman was served an Irish stew in its original form: "Nothing wrong here that a little ginger, garlic, and a few cloves won't fix." That's all it takes to transform something unremarkable into something deliciously savory. My mother's version of Irish stew, I remember, had cloves in it but no other floating spices except sometimes a stray peppercorn. When you want something quiet but comforting and tasty, think of Irish stew. If you like *blanquette de veau,* this is for you.

A little grated lemon peel and finely chopped fresh coriander (cilantro) sprinkled on top just before serving give Irish stew a sprightly touch. Add a clove or two of finely chopped garlic to make a Parsi gremolata. *Serves 4 to 6.*

1 to 1 ½ pounds breast or shoulder of lamb or kid; or stewing veal;
  or boneless chicken thigh meat
1 to 2 teaspoons Ginger-Garlic Paste (page 36)
2 tablespoons vegetable oil
4 whole cloves
1 (2-inch-long) stick cassia or cinnamon
6 black peppercorns
1 green chile (optional)
1 large onion, finely chopped
1 ½ cups milk
1 ½ cups water
1 teaspoon (about) salt

- Cut the meat into 1- to 2-inch pieces, trimming off every bit of visible fat. Rub with the paste and set it aside for half an hour or so.

- Heat the oil in a heavy deep pot or Dutch oven over medium-high heat. Add the cloves, cassia, peppercorns, and chile, if using, and sizzle for a moment. Then add the onion. When the onion is soft and translucent, add the meat. Toss and stir the mixture over moderately high heat until the meat no longer looks raw. Add splashes of water to keep things from sticking and burning. Add the milk and water; the liquids should come to the top of the meat without setting it afloat. Add the salt and bring to a boil; lower heat and simmer, partly covered, until the meat is tender, 45 minutes to an hour for lamb or kid, 40 to 45 minutes for veal, or 20 to 30 minutes for chicken (it should be meltingly tender). If the sauce is still thin and the meat is cooked, remove the meat and boil the sauce, uncovered, to reduce it. The ideal consistency of Parsi Irish stew is that of a thin béchamel. Some people like to add a little flour, but not adding flour to sauces is one of my mother's golden rules. Return the meat to the sauce.

. . .

Irish Stew with Vegetables: Add cubed carrots and potatoes for the last 15 minutes, string beans and lima beans closer to the end of cooking, and peas right at the end, so that nothing overcooks. If you haven't added potatoes to the stew, serve it with mashed potatoes. Or try it with buttered orzo, or wide noodles tossed with a little black poppy seed (instead of the white variety more common in Parsi cooking). You can never go wrong with fluffy steamed basmati rice, either.

Kerala Stew: In this recipe, you can substitute coconut milk for 2 cups of the liquid with great success. Cooks from Kerala, where coconut milk is on a par with mother's, have a similar dish known simply as "stew." Kerala stew comes in a version with mixed vegetables and in a version with meat and some token vegetables; both are delicious.

Bombay Curry

Once you've had or made this characteristic Bombay Parsi curry, you'll understand why Indians tend to think of most curry powder as a joke. Curried this or that, especially with raisins and chopped apple, is planets away from the complex, intense thing we call curry. The list of ingredients may seem dauntingly long, but once the masala is ground, you're making a simple stew.

Roasted chickpeas are sold at health foods stores and Indian groceries (ask for husked *channa* or *gram;* split chickpeas are called *channa dal*). If you can't get either type of chickpea, just double the quantity of peanuts.

All you need to go along with a curry, aside from a drift of fluffy white basmati rice (or Tomato Rice, page 169) on a large platter, are fried or toasted Papads (page 47) on the side, Simple Onion Kachumbar (page 223; the equivalent of a salsa), and wedges of lime to be squeezed over everything. This was my favorite Saturday lunch in Bombay in my mother's house and is an occasional dinner treat in ours. The recipe is exactly as dictated to me in 1962 by my mother's cook, Andrew de Souza.

Curry is perfectly wonderful served immediately, but a day or more in the refrigerator allows the flavors to melt together even more. *Serves 6 to 8.*

> *1 ½ pounds well-trimmed boneless lamb, stewing veal, or boneless chicken thigh meat;*
>   *or 2 pounds chicken legs or thighs*
> *2 teaspoons Ginger-Garlic Paste (page 36)*
> *1 walnut-size ball of compressed tamarind (see page 42); or substitute*
>   *lime juice to taste or 8 pieces of kokam (see page 108)*

MASALA

> *½ coconut (if using a wet-dry grinder; optional)*
> *4 cloves garlic*
> *1 (1-inch-long) piece peeled fresh ginger*
> *6 to 10 dried red chiles*
> *1 tablespoon raw peanuts*
> *1 teaspoon roasted chickpeas (husked channa or gram) or split chickpeas*
>   *(channa dal); or 1 additional tablespoon peanuts*
> *2 teaspoons coriander seeds*
> *1 teaspoon cumin seeds*
> *1 teaspoon white poppy seeds*
> *½ teaspoon ground turmeric*
> *1 (2-inch-long) stick cinnamon or cassia (optional)*
> *4 to 6 whole cloves (optional)*
>
> *2 to 3 tablespoons peanut or sesame oil*
> *1 large onion, chopped*
> *10 to 15 curry leaves*
> *2 cups coconut milk (if not using fresh coconut in the masala)*
> *1 teaspoon (or more) salt*
> *1 to 2 potatoes, each peeled and cut into 8 pieces*

- Cut the meat into 1- to 2-inch pieces; rub it with the paste and let it marinate at least half an hour.

- Soak the tamarind in 1 ½ cups boiling water for at least half an hour. Using your fingers, loosen the pulp from the seeds and press it through a strainer. If there's still a lot of pulp on the seeds, resoak the tamarind in warm water and press it through the strainer again. Reserve the strained pulp and discard the residue.

· To make the masala: If you are using a wet-dry grinder, pry the coconut meat out of the shell. Using a stout knife or a peeler, peel off the tough brown skin. Cut the coconut meat into small pieces. Coarsely chop the garlic and ginger. Pull the stems off the chiles. Grind the coconut, garlic, ginger, and chiles to a paste with the peanuts, chickpeas, coriander, cumin, poppy seeds, turmeric, and cinnamon and cloves, if you like. Add water to make a paste, using as little as possible. If you are working with a food processor or powerful blender: Because coconut never gets ground to a paste in a food processor, omit it and use commercial coconut milk as part of the cooking liquid. Pulverize the dry spices—chiles, coriander, cumin, poppy seeds, turmeric, and cinnamon and cloves, if using—in a coffee grinder before combining them with the garlic, ginger, peanuts, and chickpeas in the food processor or blender. Use just as much water as you need to make a fine, thick paste.

· Once the masala is made, heat the oil in a large skillet over medium-high heat. Add the onion and curry leaves and cook until the onion is browned, stirring occasionally. Add the meat and cook, stirring constantly, until it loses its raw look. Then add the masala paste. Cook over moderate heat for 5 to 10 minutes, stirring so that the masala doesn't stick to the bottom and burn. Add a tablespoon or so of water from time to time, just enough to keep it from sticking and burning.

· Add enough water to cover the meat generously (or water and coconut milk, if you made the masala without fresh coconut), at least 5 cups of liquid in all. Salt, starting with 1 teaspoon. Bring to a boil; reduce the heat to a simmer and cook, partially covered, until the meat is meltingly tender and the oil floats on top. Lamb or veal will take about 45 minutes to an hour, but the chicken will be tender long before the curry gravy is ready. Remove it after about 30 minutes and simmer the curry liquid for at least another 15 to 20 minutes, returning the chicken to the pot when the curry is completely cooked. It should be a thick, spoonable gravy, not at all watery or runny. Add the potatoes halfway through the cooking.

· When the curry is done, add the tamarind bit by bit until the curry is pleasantly acid.

· · ·

Roasted Masala Curry: For a darker, smoky-tasting curry, perfect with lamb, chicken, or game, roast the chiles, coriander seeds, cumin seeds, white poppy seeds, cinnamon, and cloves first in a dry cast-iron skillet or on a cast-iron griddle. Watch the roasting very carefully and stop it the moment the chiles begin to look toasted. The seeds should all look darker but not dark brown. Let cool before grinding.

Egg Curry: Shelled hard-boiled eggs can be substituted for the meat in this recipe. Add them just before serving—either whole, if the eggs are small, or halved, if they're large. One and a half eggs per person is usually enough.

Vegetable Curry: Another meatless alternative is to replace the meat with any vegetable that stands up to long cooking. I like tindola (ivy gourd), whole okra, snake gourd (a particularly succulent curry addition because of its capacity for absorbing surrounding flavors while keeping its own character), chayote or other summer squashes, eggplant, or cauliflower. The vegetables can be used singly or in combination.

Green Curry | LILI KARI

My friend Firoza says that in addition to her ever-ready supply of ginger and garlic paste, she always keeps some green masala handy. The combination of green chiles, fresh coriander (cilantro), ginger, garlic, and cumin is so versatile that it can serve as a coating for brain cutlets (page 152) before they are breaded and fried, as a sauce for chicken livers and simple meat stews, and here, as the masala for a gently spiced curry with a lovely color.

Serve with Perfect Plain Rice (page 162) and Simple Onion Kachumbar (page 223). *Serves 6.*

MEAT

1 pound stewing lamb or veal; or shoulder of kid or goat; or boneless chicken thigh meat

1 teaspoon Ginger-Garlic Paste (page 36)

MASALA

1 cup (lightly packed) fresh coriander (cilantro) leaves and stems

½ cup broken raw cashews or almonds

3 to 6 green chiles

2 teaspoons Ginger-Garlic Paste (page 36)

1 teaspoon cumin seeds

½ teaspoon ground turmeric

CURRY

> *2 tablespoons vegetable oil*
> *8 to 10 curry leaves*
> *2 to 3 whole cloves*
> *1 medium onion, thinly sliced*
> *2 cups coconut milk, fresh (see page 40) or canned, frozen, or reconstituted dried*
> *1 teaspoon (or more) salt*
> *2 medium potatoes, peeled and quartered (optional)*
> *½ lime*

- To prepare the meat: Trim as much fat off the meat as you can. Cut it into 1½-inch pieces. Rub the pieces with the paste and let sit for half an hour.

- To make the masala: While the meat is marinating, grind the fresh coriander, cashews, chiles, paste, cumin, and turmeric to a smooth paste in a wet-dry grinder with the barest minimum of water. Or use a food processor, in which case first pulverize the cumin seeds in a spice grinder.

- For the curry: Heat the oil in a large deep pot or Dutch oven over medium heat. Add the curry leaves and cloves and sizzle just until the leaves curl. Add the onion and cook, stirring occasionally, until softened. Add the meat and stir-fry until the meat loses its raw look and begins to brown. Then add the masala and continue stir-frying over moderate heat for 3 to 5 minutes. Add a little water if things seem to be sticking to the bottom of the pan. Add the coconut milk and enough water to come up to the top of the meat. Add the salt. Bring to a boil; quickly lower the heat and simmer gently until the meat is tender and the gravy thickens, with streaks of oil floating on the top. The curry takes about 45 minutes to an hour to thicken to the right consistency. Chicken will be done before this, so remove it when perfectly tender and return it later to the completely cooked curry. The potatoes should go in after 15 minutes.

- Taste the finished curry and add salt if needed. Finish with a generous squeeze of lime juice just before serving.

• • •

Green curry is as versatile as it is easy. For any of these four variations, you start by making the curry, leaving out the meat and potatoes and adding about a cup of water along with the coconut milk. When the surface is streaked with oil, it's a sign that the curry is ready for you to go ahead with any of the variations below.

Green Curry with Seafood: Lightly salt about 1 pound of fish chunks or steaks, 1 generous cup of peeled, deveined shrimp, or 1 pound mussels or clams. Add to the curry, bring the heat to a boil, then lower it to a simmer and cook the seafood until it is barely tender, remembering that it will continue to cook in the hot curry even with the heat off. If using mussels or clams, turn off the heat the moment the shells begin to open. Discard any mussels or clams that don't open.

Green Curry with Meatballs: Make 12 small meatballs, about 1½ inches in diameter, from the recipe on page 116. Give them a preliminary shallow-frying or sear them in a heavy skillet with the merest film of oil, just enough to firm them up so they don't fall apart when added to the curry. Gently place the meatballs in the curry when it's completely cooked. Bring the curry to a boil, lower the heat and poach the meatballs for 10 to 15 minutes.

Green Curry with Eggs: Add peeled hard-boiled eggs to the finished curry. Allow 1 or 2 eggs per person, depending on what else you're serving. Let stand for a few minutes before serving.

Green Curry with Vegetables: Vegetable options include chunks of Chinese or Japanese eggplant, or the tiny Indian ones; squashes like zucchini, bottle gourd, snake gourd, ridge gourd, sponge gourd, or tindola; long beans; cauliflower, which is always good with coconut; or string beans. Use 2 to 3 cups of any of these, alone or combined with others. If drumsticks (*Moringa* seedpods, not chicken) are ever an option, they're my absolute favorite in any curry. See the Glossary for how to prepare them.

Savory Braised Chicken with Aromatics | KHARI MARGHI

We are so lucky to be able to get just the parts of chicken that we like most. Growing up, it always seemed to me that everyone wanted the legs and thighs or the wings, with my mother hoping for the neck, my father the gizzard. No one ever seemed to want the breast, which doesn't really fare well in slow-cooked dishes. Now we can design our own chicken. In our house, it's all thighs and legs.

The Parsi approach to cooking chicken is similar to the way we handle meat. Both reflect the ancient Persian tradition of braising the main ingredient with fruits and vegetables. Modern Iranian chicken dishes have a lot in common with ours in their use of fruits and nuts and gentle spicing. Even where chiles are used in these simple braises, they lend flavor without heat.

The recipe instructions give you the traditional procedure, but here's one that works better with the far fattier chickens we get in the United States. Brown the chicken first in a separate dry skillet and then let it sit in the ginger-garlic paste for the requisite hour or so; or if there isn't enough time, add the paste to the softened onions before the chicken goes in. Browning the chicken separately lets you get rid of a lot of the fat, which would otherwise pool on top of the finished dish. *Serves 4 to 6.*

6 to 8 chicken thighs or one cut-up 2 ½- to 3-pound chicken,
    trimmed of excess fat and skin
2 to 3 teaspoons Ginger-Garlic Paste (page 36)
3 tablespoons vegetable oil
1 (2-inch-long) stick cinnamon or cassia
5 whole cloves
3 cardamom pods
2 to 3 dried red chiles
1 large onion or 2 smaller ones, finely chopped
1 to 2 teaspoons (or more) salt

• Rub the pieces of chicken with the paste. Set aside for an hour or so. In a large heavy skillet, heat the oil over medium-high heat. Add the cinnamon, cloves, cardamom, and whole chiles and sizzle for a minute or two. Add the onion and cook, stirring occasionally, until softened. Add the chicken and brown it on all sides. Add 1 to 2 teaspoons salt for a start. Pour in enough water to come up to the top of the chicken without drowning it. Raise the heat to bring the liquid to a boil, then reduce the heat and simmer until the chicken is tender, 35 to 40 minutes. If you need to reduce the cooking liquid, remove the chicken before doing so, but our Parsi meat and chicken stews are supposed to have a fair amount of gravy.

• • •

Chicken with Potatoes (papeta ma marghi): Add potatoes, peeled and quartered, with the chicken and cook them together; or add potatoes that have been peeled, quartered, and fried in the last 15 minutes or so to finish cooking with the chicken. The preliminary frying gives the potato quarters a pleasant texture, but if you're trying to keep fat to a minimum, don't bother. (When made without potatoes, *khari marghi* is often served with a border of *sali,* the angel-hair potato strands on page 200.)

Using milk, half-and-half, or coconut milk for the cooking liquid makes a creamy gravy that goes particularly well with *papeta ma marghi* made with fried potatoes.

If it seems too thin, you can remove the chicken, reduce the liquid, and then return the chicken to the pan.

Note: This is a dish that lends itself well to scaling up. Cook the onions and brown the chicken, increasing the quantities of all ingredients proportionately. Sprinkle the browned and marinated chicken with salt. Set it out in a single layer in a roasting pan. Cover with the softened onion and spice mixture. Add enough water to come up to the top of the chicken without covering it. Put the roasting pan on the stove and bring the liquid to a gentle boil; cover the pan with its lid or with aluminum foil and put it in a 350-degree oven for 35 to 40 minutes or until the chicken is tender but not falling apart.

HAMMERED COPPER
VESSEL WITH LID

Cashew Cream Chicken | KAJU NI GRAVY MA MARGHI

For anyone who thinks chicken is just an everyday thing, wait till you make this fabulous recipe. Parsis love dishes with thick, creamy gravy, especially for festive occasions—a preference we brought with us a thousand years ago from Iran, where chicken is still cooked with ground nuts. Chicken *fesenjan* and Circassian chicken, which use walnuts and almonds, are obvious cousins. Firoza Kanga, my authority on Parsi food, tells me that for a truly extravagant gesture, a Bombay hostess would prefer almonds over cashews, since the imported element always has more cachet. We use cashews here not because they're imported but because they are so very good. The important thing is to find a source of fresh nuts. The rest is easy.

Serve with fried potatoes or a pilaf of quinoa and rice cooked together. A garnish of ruby-red pomegranate seeds would be a lovely Persian touch. *Serves 6 to 8.*

8 to 10 chicken thighs
4 teaspoons Ginger-Garlic Paste (page 36)
3 tablespoons ghee or vegetable oil
3 to 5 dried red chiles
2 (2-inch-long) sticks cinnamon or cassia
6 whole cloves
4 cardamom pods
1 onion, very thinly sliced
2 teaspoons (or more) salt
1 ½ cups freshest raw cashews (they can be broken)
½ cup Yogurt Cheese (page 62) or heavy cream

- Sear the chicken in a heavy dry skillet over high heat until the pieces are browned and have rendered their excess fat. The pan should not be crowded, so you might need to do them in two batches. This won't take long. Rub them with the paste and set aside for half an hour.

- In a Dutch oven, heat the ghee; add the chiles, cinnamon, cloves, and cardamom and let them sizzle. The chiles should start to turn dark, and the cardamom, toasty. Immediately add the sliced onion. Cook, stirring occasionally, until it softens and turns golden brown. Add the chicken and toss it with the aromatics and onion for 3 minutes or so, adding a splash of water if things start to stick. Pour in enough water to barely cover the chicken. Add the salt. Bring to a boil; reduce the heat, cover, and simmer about 20 to 25 minutes. The chicken should be barely tender, not falling off the bones. Remove the chicken from the pan and set aside while you prepare the sauce.

- Put the nuts in a food processor or blender with the yogurt and a cup or so of the cooking liquid. Be sure you leave all the whole spices behind in the pan with the rest of the liquid, but fish out 2 or more chiles and add to the food processor if you want some heat. Process or blend to a creamy consistency. Scrape this mixture into the cooking liquid in the pan and whisk until well combined. The sauce should be fairly thick and will thicken further as it stands.

- Return the chicken to the pan. Taste for salt. Close to serving time, bring the sauce to a simmer, and rewarm the chicken over very low heat so that the sauce doesn't stick to the bottom of the pan and burn. Another way to do this is to finish the cooking in the oven. Put the chicken in a baking dish in a single layer and pour the sauce over it. Cover the dish very loosely with aluminum foil and bake in a 350-degree oven about 30 minutes.

· · ·

Chicken in Almond, Walnut, or Pistachio Gravy: Instead of cashews, try almonds—unblanched for maximum flavor, blanched for creamy whiteness; or try walnuts, either by themselves or combined with almonds, for chicken in the Circassian style; or use raw unsalted pistachios.

Chicken with Apricots | JARDALU MA MARGHI

Jardalu ma marghi is one of those fruit-and-meat dishes that reach far back into ancient Parsi culinary history, long before the migration to India. The starring ingredient in this royal dish is a type of apricot that comes to us from central Asia. Its scientific name is the same as for other apricots, *Prunus armeniaca,* so the only way we can distinguish a *jardalu* from the rest is to call it a Hunza apricot, as they do in Britain, or a *jardalu* in Gujarati. The Hindi/Urdu word, *zardalu,* means "yellow plum." Niggling matters of nomenclature aside, this homely, wrinkled little dried fruit is truly regal in its taste.

Since it belongs to the category of sweet-kernel apricots, it contains a surprise. Crack the pit and you get a tiny nut that's indescribably delicious, well worth the effort to get at it. Carefully remove the pits from the poached *jardalus* when they are cool enough to handle. Abandon the project if you have a batch that refuses to let go of the pits, but even a few for people to taste—my husband's "discovery amount"—can be a revelation. Put the pits in a single layer between two dish towels or double layers of paper towel. Bash them gently with a rubber mallet to break the pits. You'll get the hang of it after the first two or three. Save all the kernels and strew them on the dish before it gets to the table, or if you're serving individual plates, give each person at least one. This is a good project to give to a child because it's a really important contribution.

Madeira or cream sherry adds a wonderful finishing touch right at the end. Serve with fried potatoes or Angel-Hair Potatoes (page 200) or a rice and quinoa pilaf and something green. The variation that follows makes a lovely festive autumn dinner. *Serves 6.*

½ to ¾ pound jardalus (1 ½ to 2 cups)

½ to ¾ cup granulated sugar

6 to 8 chicken thighs

2 teaspoons Ginger-Garlic Paste (page 36)

2 to 3 tablespoons vegetable oil

3 dried red chiles

½ teaspoon cumin seeds

2 (2-inch-long) sticks cinnamon or cassia

5 whole cloves

3 cardamom pods

1 large onion, very thinly sliced

Salt to taste

¼ cup Madeira (Malmsey) or cream sherry

- Rinse the *jardalus*. Combine the sugar with 1 to 1½ cups hot water and stir to dissolve the sugar. Pour this over the *jardalus* and add enough water to come a couple of inches above them. Stir to combine. Let the *jardalus* soak for a few hours or overnight.

- Put the *jardalus* and their liquid in a saucepan and bring to a boil. Lower the heat and cook the *jardalus,* uncovered, until they darken and plump up. Some people just soak the *jardalus,* but I think they need cooking to release their full flavor. Do not pit them yet.

- Sear the chicken in a heavy skillet over high heat until the thighs are browned and have rendered their excess fat. Coat them with the paste and set aside at least 30 minutes.

- Heat the oil in the same skillet. Add the chiles, cumin, cinnamon, cloves, and cardamom and sizzle until the aroma rises and the chiles look toasted. Add the onion and cook, stirring occasionally, until it softens. Add the chicken. Combine well with the onion and spices. Add enough water and *jardalu* poaching liquid to cover. Add salt to taste. Bring to a boil; reduce the heat, cover, and simmer until the chicken is tender, about 30 minutes. Check for salt and sugar. Finish with the Madeira.

- Add the *jardalus* only when you're ready to serve so they don't break up before you present the dish. Pit them and remove the kernels, if you like.

· · ·

Dried-Fruit Variations: Instead of *jardalus,* use 2 to 3 cups dried prunes, peaches, or California or Turkish apricots, singly or in combination. Poach the fruit in 2 to 3 cups of apple juice (enough to cover). Use about 1 cup of the poaching liquid plus 2 cups of water for cooking the chicken. Garnish with toasted sliced almonds.

One Hundred Almond Curry | SAU BADAM NI KARI

In my mother's house and in my grandmother's, One Hundred Almond Curry was always regarded as one of the great festive dishes because of the double extravagance of chicken and almonds. The idea seems quaint now, when chicken is an everyday food both here and in India, and especially in a place like California, where almonds can be used in heedless abundance. Because it's inauspicious to count things out in even numbers, the masala for this curry always has an extra almond added to it, just like the extra rupee added to even-numbered cash presents for weddings and such.

The masala or curry paste is made with spices that are roasted first, to give them a deeper, darker flavor and color than the same ingredients ground without roasting. I like to use chicken thighs because the meat remains succulent and you don't have to worry about breasts drying out before legs are cooked through. Of course, our house is one where a chicken with six legs and no breasts would be the perfect bird.

Serve with Perfect Plain Rice (page 162), toasted or fried Papads (page 162), Simple Onion Kachumbar (page 223), and a raita of cucumbers, spaghetti squash, or bottle gourd. *Serves 6 to 8.*

MASALA

10 dried red chiles

4 teaspoons coriander seeds

3 teaspoons white poppy seeds

2 teaspoons cumin seeds

8 whole cloves

4 cardamom pods

10 black peppercorns

2 (2-inch-long) sticks cinnamon or cassia

½ teaspoon ground turmeric

101 unblanched almonds

8 cloves garlic, peeled

1 (3-inch-long) piece peeled fresh ginger, coarsely chopped

¼ to ½ cup water

CHICKEN

2 pounds chicken thighs, trimmed of excess fat (8 to 10 thighs, depending on size)

3 tablespoons vegetable oil

2 medium onions, thinly sliced

4 cups (about) water

2 teaspoons (or more) salt

Milk of 1 coconut (page 41), or 3 cups canned or frozen coconut milk or reconstituted powdered coconut milk

Juice of 2 Key limes or 2 to 3 tablespoons prepared tamarind pulp (see page 42)

• To make the masala: In a heavy skillet, toast the chiles, coriander, poppy seeds, and cumin over medium heat until the seeds turn brown and the chiles look toasted. Be careful not to char the spices. If you have an Indian wet-dry grinder, all the masala ingredients can now be ground to a fine paste. If you don't, start out by grinding the toasted spices along with the cloves, cardamom, peppercorns, cinnamon, and turmeric into a fine powder in a coffee or spice grinder dedicated to this purpose. Combine this powder with the almonds, garlic, and ginger in a food processor. Pulse until the almonds are finely ground. Add the water, starting with ¼ cup and using more as needed, and process until the mixture is as smooth as you can get it.

· To make the chicken: Heat a heavy skillet, either dry or with the merest film of oil, over high heat. Brown the chicken thighs quickly. Set aside. Discard the chicken fat. Heat 3 tablespoons oil in a deep heavy-bottomed pan over medium heat. Add the onions and brown them, stirring occasionally. Then add the masala paste and stir the mixture for a few minutes over moderate heat until the aroma rises. Keep careful watch because the masala can catch on the bottom of the pan and burn while the surface remains innocently moist. Add the browned chicken, water, and salt. Bring to a boil; reduce the heat and simmer until the chicken is almost tender, adding more water if necessary, about 20 minutes. The gravy should be fairly thick. Add the coconut milk and check for salt. Bring to a boil again and simmer until the chicken is very tender but not falling off the bone, about 15 minutes longer. Add the lime juice and serve.

· · ·

Vegetarian Variation: This curry can be made with eggs instead of chicken. Follow the recipe instructions, simply leaving out the chicken and adding 1 or 2 small hardboiled eggs per person in the last few minutes. For a vegan version, use vegetables like cauliflower, eggplant, and pumpkin, singly or in combination.

Mother's Favorite Chicken | CHICKEN MAIVAHLANS

Chicken maivahlans fits into that category of baked dishes that are offered at nearly every stylish Bombay dinner party: all extravagant things in a cheesy, creamy sauce. (*Maivahlans* means "mother's favorite.") I didn't understand why *chicken maivahlans* was treated with such reverence until I made it myself and realized what an extravagance it must have been in an India where raisins and nuts had become expensive imported luxuries following import restrictions.

This recipe is a distillation of several versions, with our own household's additions and subtractions. The conventional Parsi way of serving *chicken maivahlans* is to break a whole egg for each eater on top of the creamy chicken and then bake it. I don't like this approach for two reasons: You don't really need that extra egg per person, and furthermore, by the time the cream and chicken are baked, rather than simply warmed up in the oven, the eggs are several stages beyond overcooked. A simple egg-and-cream custard topped with sliced almonds is very good, but this version, my favorite, captures the sweet and savory flavors of the chicken cooking liquid in the cream sauce.

The quantities here are for a baking dish large enough to serve eight to ten people, about the size of something you'd make lasagna in. You can assemble the elements ahead of time, leaving the beating of the egg whites and the final baking to the last hour or so before serving dinner. Let the dish stand for ten to fifteen minutes before eating it. As a great lover of room-temperature food, I don't mind letting it stand for an hour.

Chicken maivahlans is very, very rich, so my favorite accompaniment is bitter greens cooked with ginger. Something like lacinato kale (an Italian heirloom kale) gives you the drama of a starkly contrasting color. Lightly dressed watercress or garden cress is a good option. You don't need a starch because of the potatoes in the dish, but offer a crusty baguette for those who like to nibble on something alongside.

Dessert should be something sharp and tart—either a fruit ice such as pomegranate (page 247), which would be very much in the Persian mood, or *oranges glacées*, or just cold mandarins. *Serves 8 to 10.*

CHICKEN

  2 tablespoons vegetable oil
  1 (2-inch-long) stick cinnamon or cassia
  4 whole cloves
  2 cardamom pods
  2 dried red chiles
  1 onion, finely chopped
  2 tablespoons Ginger-Garlic Paste (page 36)
  2 pounds chicken thighs, or 1 (2- to 3-pound) chicken, cut into pieces
  Salt to taste

DEEP-FRIED COMPONENTS

  Peanut or corn oil, for deep-frying
  ¾ cup golden raisins (if possible, soaked in some Madeira or Marsala for a few days)
  ¾ cup sliced pistachios or slivered almonds, plus more for sprinkling on top
  1 pound waxy potatoes (such as Yukon Gold), half-boiled, peeled, and cut into
    ½-inch cubes
  1 onion, very thinly sliced

ASSEMBLY AND TOPPINGS

Ghee or butter, for coating the dish

8 hot green chiles, finely chopped

2 to 3 cups chopped fresh coriander (cilantro) leaves and stems, to taste

Salt to taste

About 2 ½ cups heavy cream or crème fraîche

Madeira or Marsala to taste

4 to 5 large eggs, separated

¾ cup pine nuts or sliced almonds

- To make the chicken: Heat the oil in a large deep skillet over medium heat. Add the cinnamon, cloves, cardamom, and red chiles and sizzle until their aromas are released. Add the onion and paste and sauté until the onions are soft, stirring occasionally. Brown the chicken separately in a cast-iron skillet over medium-high heat in very little oil, to draw off as much of the fat as possible. Add the chicken to the onion. Pour in enough water to cover, salt lightly, and simmer till tender, about 25 minutes. Remove from the heat and adjust the seasonings. When the chicken is cool enough to handle, remove it, reserving the cooking liquid, and pull the flesh away from the bones, dividing it into small morsels (don't worry about unevenness). Set aside.

- For the fried components: While the chicken is cooking and cooling, organize a deep-frying setup. You'll need a baking sheet lined with brown paper or paper towels and a wok, *karhai,* or any pan suitable for deep-frying several ingredients in succession, filled no more than half full with oil. Heat the oil to 375 degrees. Fry the raisins by lowering them into the oil in a wire strainer and removing them the moment they puff up. Drain them on the paper-lined baking sheet; they will deflate as they cool. Fry the nuts for a few seconds and drain. Fry the potatoes to a golden brown. Last, fry the sliced onion; the slices should be allowed to brown to a crisp without burning. Do them in two or three small batches instead of one big one.

- To assemble the dish: Heat the oven to 350 degrees and lightly coat a large ovenproof baking dish with ghee.

- Cover the bottom of the dish with a layer of chicken. Strew the chicken with half the potatoes, onions, raisins, and pistachios. To perk up the taste, sprinkle with half the green chiles and half the fresh coriander. Salt lightly. Cover with the remaining chicken and top with the remaining potatoes, onions, raisins, pistachios, chiles, and coriander. Salt lightly again.

- To make the topping, first fish out the whole spices from the reserved chicken cooking liquid, which should be fairly thick from the onions. If it's not, boil it a little longer to reduce it or thicken it with a little flour (about 1 to 2 tablespoons for 2 cups of liquid). Stir enough cream into this base to make about 3 cups of liquid in all. Salt to taste, add Madeira to taste, and pour this mixture over the chicken, making sure there's enough to barely cover the surface. Whip the egg whites with a good pinch of salt until stiff. Lightly beat the yolks, stir into the whites, and spread over the top of the chicken, going all the way to the edges of the dish. Cover the surface with the pine nuts or sliced almonds.

- Bake until puffed and golden brown, 40 minutes or so. The puffy, browned top will subside into a delicately crunchy crust.

Smoky Masala Grilled Quail

The long-gone Rex Stores on Warden Road in Bombay had a marvelous sign that advertised "all kinds of wild games." Wild games were not part of my family's food scene, but in our San Francisco household, they're welcome in any form. The spices in this masala paste are roasted before grinding, so that they lend a dark, smoky, campfire quality to the quail even if you sear it instead of grilling it.

Quail vary a bit in size. Some people eat less than one, some more than two, so I try to have enough to please everyone, with perhaps a little left over for the next day. I often serve this with polenta or grits or Firoza's Khichri (page 166). *Serves 6.*

12 quail
6 dried red chiles
1 teaspoon black peppercorns
1 teaspoon black cumin seeds
½ teaspoon fennel seeds
2 teaspoons Ginger-Garlic Paste (page 36)
2 tablespoons pomegranate molasses
1 tablespoon vegetable oil
1 ½ to 2 teaspoons salt

- Snip the necks and wingtips off the quail. Butterfly the birds by cutting along the backbone with stout shears and opening them flat.

- In a small heavy skillet over medium-high heat, toast the chiles, peppercorns, black cumin, and fennel seeds, keeping things

GRIPPERS FOR PANS
WITHOUT HANDLES

moving until the spices begin to get dark but not burnt. (If they do burn, start over.) Remove at once and let the spices cool slightly before pulverizing them in a mill. Combine with the paste, pomegranate molasses, oil, and salt.

· About 2 hours before grilling, rub the quail with this mixture. Grill over medium-hot coals for 8 to 10 minutes, until done to your liking.

· · ·

Note: In the absence of a grill, you can cook the quail on one of those stove-top ridged grill pans, or sear them in a heavy cast-iron skillet, in which case you'll probably want to work with two pans side by side. The oven is yet another option. Give the quails a blast at 475 to 500 degrees for about 15 to 20 minutes.

Duck Legs Braised with Little Onions | KANDA MA BATAK

Next to vindaloo, this used to be the most requested duck dish in my mother's house. Sometimes it was made hot, sour, and sweet, but I liked it best as a mild, simple braise with whole onions. In our house, it gets made with onions and little turnips when they're in season. A little Madeira or Amontillado at the end can point up the sweetness of the whole onions.

Serve with plain farro or my husband's three-grain mixture of barley, brown rice, and wild rice all cooked together for 45 minutes. Thanksgiving Brussels Sprouts (page 190; leave out the popped seeds), amaranth, or spinach would all offer a good green counterpoint to the unctuous duck. *Serves 6 to 8.*

6 to 8 duck legs
Salt
2 (2-inch-long) sticks cinnamon or cassia
1 cassia leaf or bay leaf
4 to 6 cardamom pods
3 to 4 dried red chiles
6 whole cloves
1 large yellow onion, finely chopped
3 teaspoons Ginger-Garlic Paste (page 36)
24 (about) boiling onions (1 to 2 inches in diameter)
2 tablespoons vegetable oil, if needed
½ cup (about) Madeira or Amontillado (optional)

- Poke the skin of each duck leg with a fork in several places. Heat 1 or 2 large, heavy skillets, preferably cast iron, over moderately high heat and cook the duck legs 4 at a time until they are browned on both sides and most of their fat is rendered out. Remove from the pan, sprinkle with salt, and set aside. Reserve the duck fat if it hasn't burned.

- Add the cinnamon, cassia leaf, cardamom, chiles, and cloves and cook for a minute or so. Add the chopped onion and cook until softened, stirring occasionally. Then add the paste. Stir for a couple of minutes, adding a splash of water if necessary to prevent sticking and burning. Next add the duck legs, nestling them together in a single layer; don't forget to include any juices they may have exuded. Pour in enough water to barely cover the duck legs. Add a little salt, about 1 teaspoon, raise the heat, and bring to a boil. Reduce the heat, cover the pan, and simmer until the duck legs are tender. Start checking them after 45 minutes.

- While the duck is cooking, peel and trim the boiling onions. In a large heavy skillet, heat the reserved duck fat (or substitute 1 to 2 tablespoons vegetable oil if necessary) over medium-high heat; add the onions and sauté just enough to glaze them. Remove them from the pan and add them to the duck in the last few minutes before serving, so that they can cook through without falling apart. (This preliminary frying of the onions is a Parsi refinement. It's not essential, but it's a nice touch.) Finish the sauce with the Madeira, if you like.

· · ·

Duck with Turnips: Follow the recipe above, but instead of small onions, allow 3 tiny turnips or 3 pieces of larger turnips per person, plus a few more. Peel only if they have thick skins. Sauté them in the reserved duck fat or oil, if you like, and let them cook with the duck in the last few minutes. Like the onions, they should be cooked through but not falling apart.

Grilled Thanksgiving Turkey

It took me at least three years in the United States before I realized that turkey did not have to taste woolly if I made it myself. For years, I played around with various Indian approaches, starting with the Parsi universal meat massage, ginger and garlic. One year, I salted and steamed it Chinese style, which I thought was terrific but which dismayed the traditionalists at the table like my mother-in-law. (This experiment did add something to the technique we now use, however.)

The year we cooked the turkey in a covered Weber grill, having learned how from *The Grilling Book* by A. Cort Sinnes, we knew we had it down. Start with a small bird, anywhere from 8 to 12 pounds. You get excellent flavor with the salting followed by marinating. The turkey can be grilled or roasted—butterflying cuts the cooking time down considerably. With a bird of this size, you might want to ask your butcher to butterfly it for you.

Serve with baked sweet potatoes with chile and lime, Thanksgiving Brussels Sprouts (page 190), a cranberry chutney, and Pumpkin Crescents with Curry Leaves (page 197). Hope for leftover turkey. Follow with pecan pie. I promise you that with this menu, Thanksgiving will never feel like death by food. *Serves up to 10.*

1 (8- to 12-pound) turkey, butterflied
Handful of salt

MASALA
8 to 10 dried red chiles
1 teaspoon cumin seeds
2 teaspoons black cumin seeds, if available
1 (3-inch-long) piece peeled fresh ginger
8 cloves garlic
⅓ cup vegetable oil
2 tablespoons pomegranate molasses
Freshly ground black pepper

- Poke the butterflied turkey all over with a kitchen fork. Rub at least a handful of salt into the top and bottom, especially under the big flap of skin at the breast, gently loosening the skin and massaging salt into the breast meat. Try to do this without tearing the skin. Let the salted turkey sit, covered and refrigerated, at least a few hours or overnight.

- Meanwhile, prepare the masala: In a cast-iron skillet or on a griddle over medium heat, toast the chiles, cumin, and black cumin. Have a window or door open or turn on the hood fan full-blast. When the spices begin to change color and crackle, remove them from the skillet and let them cool. If you're using a wet-dry grinder, the toasted spices, ginger, garlic, oil, and pomegranate molasses can all go in together. Otherwise, pulverize the toasted spices in an electric coffee grinder dedicated to grinding spices. Then put the powder in a food processor along with the ginger, garlic, oil, and pomegranate molasses and turn the ingredients into as thick and smooth a paste as you can with the absolute minimum of added water. Scrape out the bowl thoroughly. You'll have an exciting, dark, smoky paste.

- Rinse the turkey quickly and wipe it dry with paper towels. Poke more holes all over it. Rub it with the paste on both sides and under the flap of skin. You can then either grind a lot of pepper all over the bird or coarsely pound 1 tablespoon or so of peppercorns in a mortar and sprinkle that on. Cover the bird again and leave it to marinate in the refrigerator for 6 to 8 hours.

- Roast the turkey on a Weber or similar covered grill following the manufacturer's instructions. Or heat the oven to 375 degrees and roast the turkey. A 10-pound butterflied bird will take 1½ hours on the Weber and about the same time in an oven. The trick to grilling the turkey so long without burning it is to arrange the coals in a ring around the edge of the grill and to place the turkey right in the middle, so that there are no coals directly under the bird.

- Let stand at least 15 minutes before carving.

Chicken Livers in Green Masala | ALETI PALETI

Anyone who's the slightest bit squeamish about chicken livers will be easily seduced by *aleti paleti*. In the following recipe, timing and technique have been changed to fit our preferences, but the taste is absolutely authentic. *Aleti paleti* is often a combination of hearts, gizzards, and livers, but I prefer the texture of a single-part dish. *Serves 3 to 4.*

1 pound chicken livers or hearts, or a combination

GREEN MASALA
4 green chiles
2 teaspoons Ginger-Garlic Paste (page 36)
2 cups (loosely packed) fresh coriander (cilantro) leaves and stems, coarsely chopped
1 teaspoon cumin seeds, pulverized first if using a food processor

2 tablespoons (or more) oil or ghee
Salt to taste
1 medium onion, chopped
Jaggery or brown sugar

- Prepare the chicken livers by separating the lobes and removing all connective tissue. Cut into 1-inch pieces. (If you're using hearts, trim off any tubes sticking out.) Pat dry with paper towels.

- To make the green masala: Grind together the chiles, paste, fresh coriander, and cumin in a wet-dry grinder or a food processor.

- Heat the oil in a heavy skillet over medium-high heat. Add the chicken livers and brown quickly on all sides. Sprinkle with salt and transfer to a plate. If the pan is full of bits of liver, scrape them out and start with a clean skillet and fresh oil for the next stage. Otherwise, add just a touch more oil and continue. Add the onion and brown, stirring occasionally. Add the green masala and stir for 3 to 5 minutes, adding only enough water to keep the paste from sticking and burning. Add the chicken livers and any juices. Combine gently to avoid turning the livers into mush. Add only enough water to make a thick gravy and bring to a boil; reduce the heat and simmer briefly until the livers are just cooked through. Do not overcook the livers. (Hearts are a little more forgiving.) Finish with a little jaggery, just enough to add a touch of sweetness.

. . .

Aleti Paleti with Potatoes: Some people like to add diced potato to their *aleti paleti*. My mother used to serve it with fried potatoes, a fabulous combination.

Aleti Paleti on Toast: Serve *aleti paleti* hot or at warm room temperature on squares of toast. This recipe will serve about eight to twelve as an appetizer.

Brain Cutlets | BHEJA NA KATLES

On December 31, 1988, we went for a New Year's Eve drive with my parents. My husband, David, knew a lovely spot tucked away in the California coastal redwood forests, Butano State Park. We took a picnic breakfast with us, including some leftovers from the night before, *bheja na katles*—brain cutlets, one of the high points of Parsi cuisine. I'd imagined them impossibly difficult to make, but thanks to my mother's tutorial, I found them quite easy, if a little fiddly. My father pronounced them "correct," and David, suspicious of organ meats, hung back until his first reluctant bite.

These are brains for people who say they don't like brains. At our very first Parsi New Year's dinner at Chez Panisse, we served brain cutlets as part of a first-course plate, calling them brain fritters. No one sent any back.

You can make these cutlets any size you like—six large ones for a main course or sandwiches, or a dozen or so for a first course, or lots of little ones for an hors d'oeuvre. For sandwiches, tuck a room-temperature cutlet into a chapati or whole wheat tortilla heated on a dry griddle. Thin slices of lightly buttered unsweet whole wheat bread are also good. If you're leaving the crusts on, remember to take the butter all the way to the edges, and give anyone who wants it some lettuce, too.

Our local supermarket has calf brains from time to time, and so might yours. Otherwise, ask at markets catering to cuisines that use all parts of the animal—Mexican, Chinese, or halal meat markets, for instance. Both the masala and the brains can be prepared a day ahead, leaving the shaping and frying to the day you want them. They're good reheated, too, but won't keep the texture they have straight from the oil. *Serves 6.*

1 pound lamb, goat, or calf brains
1 pinch ground turmeric
1 teaspoon salt
2 ½ teaspoons Ginger-Garlic Paste (page 36)

GREEN MASALA
2 heaping cups coarsely chopped fresh coriander (cilantro) leaves and stems
½ teaspoon cumin seeds, pulverized first if using a food processor
4 to 6 green chiles

2 to 3 cups fine bread crumbs
2 large eggs, lightly beaten
1 to 1 ½ cups vegetable oil, for shallow-frying
Lime wedges

- Remove any membrane covering the brains. Put them in a saucepan with the turmeric, ½ teaspoon of the salt, and ½ teaspoon of the paste; cover generously with cold water. Bring to a boil; reduce the heat to a gentle simmer and poach the brains for 5 to 10 minutes. They should be barely cooked through. Drain immediately. Refresh with ice water and drain well again. Pick off any membrane you couldn't get on the first round. Leave the brains to cool between two flat plates, placing a 1- to 2-pound weight on top. This makes them uniformly thick and therefore easier to shape and fry.

- In a food processor or a wet-dry grinder, make a green masala from the fresh coriander, the remaining salt, the remaining 2 teaspoons of the paste, the cumin, and the chiles.

- Place the bread crumbs at the ready on a work tray. Divide the brains into six to a dozen or more clumps, depending on how you plan to use them. Working with one clump at a time, cover each clump with a thin coat of green masala. Press each clump down into the crumbs, turn it over, and press again, forming it into a neat, flat oval (the conventional shape, though rounds are fine). You might need to do a little patching and recrumbing. All this can be done hours ahead of time, even the day before. Refrigerate the coated cutlets until you're ready to fry them.

- To fry the cutlets, first organize your operation. You need a skillet, wok, or *karhai* for shallow-frying and a tray lined with paper towels to drain the cutlets, as well as the beaten eggs ready in a shallow dish right next to the stove. Heat the oil until it's hot but not smoking. Slide each cutlet quickly in and out of the eggs and then into the hot oil. Shallow-fry until golden brown on each side. Drain briefly. An alternative frying method is to use a film of clarified butter or oil in a nonstick pan and cook each side until the egg coating is golden brown and omeletlike.

- Serve at once with wedges of lime. This is such a stellar dish that I don't like to put anything else on the plate to share the spotlight.

· · ·

Chutney Fried Fish: Here's a big bonus—you can use this technique for frying fish fillets. Salt them lightly first.

Note: The technique for *bheja na katles* reverses the usual method of dipping something in eggs before it gets rolled in crumbs and fried. It makes a really toothsome skin. Think of it as a transferable technique and try it with slices of a soft, fresh cheese or tofu or even brain dipped in pesto, crumbed and fried in olive oil.

Salted Tongue

Everyone in my mother's house loved beef tongue. A large beef tongue would get covered with coarse salt and some jaggery and a little saltpeter and left to cure in the refrigerator for at least a week. It would then get cooked, trimmed, peeled, and served cold for lunch, usually with Russian Salad (page 213), purplish from the beets and surrounded by shredded romaine.

Ginger and garlic are required for Parsi meat cooking, but you can leave out the chiles. Try at least one for flavor. This tongue is good with Parsi Tomato Chutney (page 231) or the mustardy Parsi Wedding Pickle (page 237), which is my great favorite.

Boiled potatoes and creamed spinach are good accompaniments. Be sure to allow at least a week for the salt-curing, and start the cooking a day before you plan to serve it. *Serves 4 to 6, with leftovers.*

1 beef tongue (3 to 4 pounds)
2 cups (or more) coarse salt
1 onion
4 to 6 slices peeled fresh ginger
3 cloves garlic, smashed in their skins
3 to 4 whole cloves
1 to 3 dried red chiles
1 bay leaf or cassia leaf

- Salting the tongue: If your butcher or market hasn't trimmed the back of the tongue, now's the time to cut away flaps of fat, pipes, and so forth. Using a long-tined fork or skewer, poke the tongue all over. Put the tongue in a deep nonreactive bowl and pack it with the salt, rubbing it in. The tongue should be completely covered with salt, top, bottom, and all the way around. Cover the bowl and refrigerate for at least a week and up to two weeks. Turn the tongue over every couple of days. If you miss a day, don't fret.

- To cook the tongue, start a day ahead of when you want to serve it, allowing you time to chill the tongue and remove the fat on top of the stock in one neat piece. Rinse the salt off the tongue. Bring a large pot of water to a boil along with the onion, ginger, garlic, cloves, chiles, and bay leaf. Add the tongue, making sure it's well covered with water. Bring to a boil again; reduce the heat to a bare simmer and cook the tongue about 1 hour for each pound of its weight. It's done when a thin-bladed knife goes through it with no resistance.

- Remove the tongue from its cooking water. Plunge it into very cold water so that you can handle it. The skin should peel off easily. Trim away any fat, tubes, or sinew remaining. Return the tongue to its cooking liquid. Taste for salt. Let the tongue cool in the cooking liquid. Refrigerate. All the fat will congeal on top, and you'll be able to lift it off easily.

- To serve warm, reheat the tongue in its cooking liquid. Transfer to a platter, slice, and serve.

. . .

Cold Tongue Salad: To serve this tongue cold as a lively first course, cut the meat into fat matchsticks and mix with thinly sliced white onion, chopped green chiles, and fresh coriander (cilantro). Dress with a vinaigrette made partly with lime juice, and serve surrounded by dressed salad greens.

Tongue Sandwiches: Brush slices of buttered white or rustic bread with English mustard or chutney before adding the tongue.

Tongue with Poached Eggs: One of our favorite breakfasts is sliced tongue with poached eggs topped with capers in brown butter and a strewing of fresh tarragon. It's not Parsi, but it's too delicious not to mention.

Note: Calf, lamb, and pork tongues can get the salt treatment, too. They don't need a full week; three or four days is enough. Cook them for a little less time.

Trotters with Black-Eyed Peas | KHARIA

Kharia, a slow-cooked stew of kid's forefeet (trotters) and black-eyed peas, is one of the great dishes of Parsi cuisine. I've been hopelessly and gluttonously fond of it since childhood. Oddly, as much as I love *kharia,* I loathe the other dish made from trotters, a clear, sweet jelly flavored with sherry adored by my mother and many others. Because of the richness of the trotters and the warming properties of the aromatic spices, Parsi cooks tend to serve *kharia* only in the cooler months. Here in San Francisco, that means the summer as well. Gather friends around you when you make *kharia.* It's best enjoyed in the company of robust, uninhibited, slurping eaters.

You need to plan ahead. You can certainly make it the day you want to eat it, but you need to start early. Take your time. The house will smell wonderful. When *kharia* is made at least a day in advance, the flavors get a chance to mature.

No one has yet given me a really good reason why the U.S. Department of Agriculture allows cow's feet and pig's feet to be sold but draws the line at sheep's and goat's feet. I settle for the smallest pig's feet I can find.

Serve *kharia* with rice or crusty bread and Sweet-Sour Kachumbar (page 223). It's best eaten with a spoon and fork in a deep plate. *Kharia* is so rich and intense that the rest of the meal needs to be very fresh and spare. For an appetizer, stick to raw vegetables with a little salt and lime. For dessert, think of the most refreshing fruit in season. Grapes, tangerines, pomelo, or melons would be perfect. *Serves 8 to 10.*

1 ½ to 2 cups black-eyed peas (chaura)
6 pig's forefeet, split lengthwise and cut crosswise, making 4 pieces each
2 teaspoons salt
2 to 3 tablespoons Ginger-Garlic Paste (page 36)

MASALA

10 to 12 dried red chiles
1 teaspoon cumin seeds
1 (2- to 3-inch-long) piece peeled fresh ginger
½ head garlic
2 (2-inch-long) sticks cinnamon or cassia
5 whole cloves
5 cardamom pods

STEW

2 to 3 tablespoons vegetable oil
2 large onions, finely chopped
2 tablespoons Dhana Jiru (page 38)
½ teaspoon ground turmeric
1 to 2 teaspoons cayenne pepper or Indian chilly powder
1 to 2 teaspoons Sambhar Masala (page 37)
1 cup chopped fresh coriander (cilantro) leaves and stems (optional)

- Soak the black-eyed peas in enough cold water to cover them, 6 to 8 hours or overnight. You can hasten the process by bringing them to a boil and letting them cool down.

- In a large stockpot, generously cover the trotters with water (about 3 inches above the trotters). Add the salt and paste. Bring to a boil; reduce the heat and simmer until the trotters are tender, 2 to 3 hours.

- While all this is going on, make the masala paste: If you have a wet-dry grinder, use that to grind together the chiles, cumin, ginger, garlic, cinnamon, cloves, and cardamom. Otherwise, pulverize the dry spices and grind them with the ginger and garlic in a food processor.

- For the stew: When the pig's feet are tender, heat the oil in a large skillet over medium heat. Add the onions and cook until softened, stirring occasionally. Add the masala paste and continue to fry for 3 to 5 minutes, adding a small amount of water if things start to stick. Add this mixture to the pot with the pig's feet. Deglaze the pan with a little water and tip that in as well. Add the black-eyed peas and their liquid along with the *dhana jiru,* turmeric, cayenne, and *sambhar masala.* Bring to a boil, stirring well to combine everything. Reduce the heat and simmer gently until the black-eyed peas are soft and the pig's feet are meltingly tender and falling apart, 2 to 3 hours. Stir from time to time to make sure nothing is sticking to the bottom of the pan, adding water as needed. Oil should float to the top when the gravy is done. Add the chopped coriander toward the end, allowing it to soften. If the gravy seems thin, reduce it a bit over high heat, stirring constantly to avoid scorching.

· · ·

Note: The pig's feet should consist of mostly cartilage, skin, and bone, so ask your butcher for forefeet without a trace of meat attached. Butchers will gladly split and quarter the feet for you.

Parsi Mixed Grill

Parsis and other meat-eating Indian cooks, Muslims and Goans in particular, consider kidney, liver, and other spare parts to be delicacies. Even in the United States, where a lot of people are skittish about them, they are becoming popular again.

Where the French and Chinese do very little to kidneys and liver before cooking them, Parsi and other Indian cooks insist on some preliminary steps. Every liver and kidney dish starts out with a rub of ginger and garlic paste, and in the case of kidneys, a preliminary blanching. For Parsis, the liver and kidneys are usually from a goat. Here in the United States, we can sometimes find goat liver and kidney at halal butchers, but if not, a lamb's will do. If lamb liver is unobtainable, use calf liver.

Liver needs to be sliced about ½ inch thick and have all the skin, tubes, and stringy bits trimmed away. Kidneys, the Parsi way, need a bit more preparation. Take the transparent skin off lamb kidneys, halve them lengthwise, and trim away any tough tissue. You can leave the halves as they are, or cut each in two. My mother's cook used to blanch kidneys either by pouring a lot of boiling water over them in a strainer or by plunging them into boiling water and leaving them for two to three minutes before draining and refreshing them. *Serves 4 to 6.*

½ pound lamb, calf, or goat liver, trimmed and cut into ½-inch-thick slices
6 to 8 lamb kidneys, skinned, trimmed, halved, and blanched
2 teaspoons Ginger-Garlic Paste (page 36)
1 teaspoon Worcestershire sauce

1 tablespoon vegetable oil or bacon fat
Salt to taste
3 tablespoons butter or vegetable oil
1 to 2 onions, thickly sliced
4 firm tomatoes, halved

- Marinate the liver and blanched kidneys in the paste and Worcestershire sauce for at least 1 hour (if longer, cover and refrigerate). Heat the oil in a large heavy skillet over medium-high heat and sear the liver and kidneys until they are browned but not hard. Salt immediately. Both should be barely cooked through, not gray but not pink, either.

- Divide the butter between two skillets, heated to medium-high. Add the onions to one and the tomato halves to the other; soften the onions and pan-fry the tomatoes. Serve the liver, kidneys, onions, and tomatoes together for a Parsi mixed grill.

Masala Grilled Liver and Kidneys | MASALA NA KALEJI BUKKA

In Bombay after nightfall, you'll often see someone on a corner grilling liver, kidneys, and other kebabs on skewers. It's a sign that there's some serious drinking going on in the vicinity. The biggest and best of these stands, Bade Mia behind the Taj Mahal Hotel, now has tables and chairs on the street, a storefront, and a permanent sign. Take your choice of either red or green masala. Or try liver with one masala and kidneys with the other. *Serves 4 to 6 as a main course, or more as an hors d'oeuvre.*

MEAT
1 goat or lamb liver (about 1 pound)
1 pound lamb or goat kidneys, halved, trimmed, and blanched (see page 158)
½ to 1 teaspoon salt
1 tablespoon vegetable oil

GREEN MASALA
4 to 6 green chiles
1 cup (loosely packed) fresh coriander (cilantro) leaves and stems
1 teaspoon cumin seeds, pulverized first if you're using a food processor
2 teaspoons Ginger-Garlic Paste (page 36)

RED MASALA

3 to 6 dried red chiles, soaked in boiling water about ½ hour to soften
2 teaspoons Ginger-Garlic Paste (page 36)
1 teaspoon cumin seeds, pulverized first if you're using a food processor
2 teaspoons coriander seeds, pulverized first if you're using a food processor

2 tablespoons vegetable oil, or as needed
Lime wedges
Very thinly sliced sweet onion

- To prepare the meats: Cut the liver into pieces that can be easily skewered. Kidneys need to be quartered if they're large.
- For the green masala: Combine the chiles, fresh coriander, cumin, and paste in a wet-dry grinder or food processor and grind them, adding a little water as necessary, until a thick paste forms.
- For the red masala: Combine the chiles, paste, cumin, and coriander in a wet-dry grinder or food processor and grind them, adding a little water as necessary, until a thick paste forms.
- Rub the liver or kidneys with either the red or the green masala plus the salt and oil and let marinate for 1 to 2 hours.
- Thread the meats on skewers and grill for just a few minutes over hot coals until browned and barely cooked through.
- Serve hot with the lime and the onion slices.

· · ·

Parsi Anticuchos: You can make a Parsi version of Peruvian *anticuchos*—seasoned, skewered, and grilled cubes of beef heart—by using the masalas above on chicken or turkey hearts, or cubed pork, lamb, goat, or veal hearts, well trimmed to remove all sinew and pipes. Grill until barely cooked through.

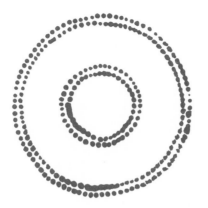

દાલ ચાવલ

RICE AND DAL

Ancient Persia was so well placed along the trade routes between China, India, and the rest of the known world that it had a look at anything interesting moving in either direction. We have evidence of rice cultivation there as early as 1000 B.C.E., most likely as a result of trade with India, and know for certain that rice was part of the diet of the luxury-loving Persians by 400 B.C.E. Wheat was the grain for the general population; rice was for the more affluent, cooked with fruit, orange peel, and saffron, forerunner of the festive *pulaos* and biryanis of today.

Parsis landing on the western coast of India came right into a rice-growing area. While rice, chickpeas, and lentils were already grown in Iran and therefore no novelty, the range and variety of legumes in India made a major contribution to our cuisine. The local diet of Hindu Gujarat was and still is described as *"dal, bhat, shak"*—pulses, rice, and vegetables. Our ancestors took up the first two components with enthusiasm. Lentil and rice dishes now lie at the heart and soul of everyday Parsi fare.

Two dishes stand out for their importance in Parsi life. One is our simple *mori dar* (page 176), plain dal, to be eaten with plain white rice—something that sounds humdrum, yet in Parsi hands turns into one of the most heart- and soul-satisfying things you can put in your mouth. The other is our emblematic lentil potage, *dhansak* (page 178), made with several legumes, several vegetables, and several spices, with or without meat but usually with. This is to be eaten with a really interesting caramelized rice pilaf (page 168). Rice and lentils are sometimes cooked together in a dish known as *pongal* in the south, and as *khichri* or *khichdi* in the north (page 165).

What follows is a lineup of our favorite rice and legume dishes. Most Parsi households I know automatically choose basmati rice even though there are hundreds of other varieties available. There must be something about long, slender, scented grains that strikes a primeval chord. My husband and I love to play with grains in combination with rice, so you have the results of some of these experiments—rice with quinoa or farro (an ancient Italian grain) cooked in the same way as the special rice for *dhansak*. Most of the recipes are really easy, even the *pulaos* and biryanis.

Perfect Plain Rice | BAFELA CHAVAL

Julia Child once told my husband, David, that she thought cooking plain rice for more than two people was one of the hardest things to do. It is and it isn't. Each rice-eating culture has its own unbreakable rules, and within those cultures, cooks have their own magic formulas handed down from generation to generation. To listen to them all can get you very confused. Many rice-consuming families now resort to an electric cooker, but although we have one, we used it only when we had to manage with an electric stove.

There are two basic approaches to cooking plain rice: boiled in lots of water or boiled in just enough water to be completely absorbed by the rice, which is the principle behind electric rice cookers. My mother and her mother used the first method, which resulted in beautifully dry, separate grains, with whatever remained of the nutrition in milled rice going down the drain. In our house, we use the absorption method, which can also result in beautifully dry, separate grains.

Then there's the infinitely variable question of how much rice is enough. There's the timid little quarter cup of suggested American portions, there are the bowls preferred by East Asians, and there are the large mounds you sometimes see in South Asia. An anthropol-

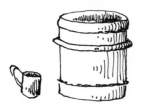

LARGE AND SMALL
GRAIN MEASURES

ogist colleague once invited some Nepali friends to dinner and cooked a box of rice that claimed to serve twelve. The first two Nepali guests in line for the rice helped themselves to most of it.

The kind of rice you choose comes next. There was never any question in my mother's or grandmother's house about the type of rice. There are hundreds of varieties of rice grown in India, but for the Parsis I know, there seems to be only basmati, the very best that the market can provide. "Needle-like grains," my mother used to say, referring to basmati rice's unique ability to expand lengthwise. I like rice from everywhere, although for Parsi cooking, I tend to use basmati or the recently available small, delicate grains of *Surti kolam,* also a long-grain rice in botanical terms. Unlike the Japanese, who prefer young rice, Indians like basmati rice to be old, the older the better. My mother used to say that each batch of rice she bought might mean a small adjustment in cooking time depending on its age; older rice needs more time.

My grandmother used to count out a handful of raw rice per person—with a little extra should unexpected guests show up at the last minute. Like many Indians, my mother used an old cigarette tin for her standard measure, the kind that held fifty cigarettes, and this measure was referred to as a *tipri,* roughly an 8-ounce cup. I remember she also had a smaller tin measure that had contained Vienna sausages in the 1940s. My father stopped smoking in 1956, but constant use kept my mother's *tipris* from rusting. In nonsmoking households, people used condensed or evaporated milk tins.

Wash the rice in several changes of water. Until about twenty to twenty-five years ago, all Indian rice had to be cleaned before cooking. Winnowing trays could be made of basketry materials or metal. Every household had to have one because there was no escaping the task of patiently shaking the rice back and forth, scrutinizing it for chaff and the inevitable pebbles. Modern processing equipment has made the winnowing tray almost obsolete, but it's still a good idea to check the rice before you cook it.

American enriched white rice is supposed to be cooked without washing so that the nutrients added to replace those lost in milling aren't lost all over again. Indian rice must be washed to get rid of the starch or other processing aids such as talc. You can do this in a bowl or in the pan you plan to use for cooking the rice. Pour cold water over the rice, swirling it around, pouring off the water, and repeating the process until the water poured off is almost clear.

Finally, there's the question of whether or not to soak the rice. For

WINNOWING TRAY

biryanis and *pulaos,* yes, for maximum elongation. For plain everyday rice, I don't bother. *Serves 6 generously.*

2 cups basmati or other long-grain rice
Salt to taste
2 teaspoons (about) ghee or butter
A squeeze of lemon or lime juice (optional)

- Wash the rice until the water runs clear. Put it into a straight-sided saucepan with a tight-fitting lid. Cover with enough water to come up to the first joint of your index finger resting on top of the washed rice. (With this method you don't have to measure the water, and it works for any quantity of rice.) Add ½ to 1 teaspoon of salt, or none at all, the ghee, and the optional squeeze of lime juice, which ensures a good white color.

- Bring to a boil; stir once, lower the heat to a bare simmer, cover the pan, and cook for 15 to 20 minutes. (Old rice takes longer. Thai rice will be ready to turn off in about 12 to 13 minutes.) Let the rice sit, covered, at least another 10 minutes. It will stay hot for over half an hour. One visual tip that the rice is perfectly steamed is that individual grains will seem to stand to attention on the top layer and you see little craters. Fluff up gently with a fork or chopstick before serving.

· · ·

Rice with Cumin: Add 1 teaspoon cumin seeds to the rice along with the water, salt, and ghee.

Mixed Rice and Grains: Combine grains like quinoa with basmati. They take the same time to cook, and the contrast in textures is lovely. Another option is to combine basmati with cooked farro. Yet another is to cook black rice separately, and combine with basmati at the last minute for a dramatic effect.

Alternate Cooking Method: My Thai friend Juree Vichitvadakan told me that she adds water up to the second joint of the index finger and lets the rice boil, uncovered, until the water gets below the level of the rice. The cover then gets put on and the heat turned down to almost nothing for 20 to 30 minutes.

Notes: Sometimes things go wrong and the rice is soggy—wet or still hard in the middle. When life sends you lemons like this, make Firoza's Khichri (page 166)!

We're often told by the rice bogeyman that if you lift the lid during the steaming process, it's all over. Not so, as long as you put it right back on.

KHICHRI

Rice and lentils cooked together must be one of the oldest dishes on the subcontinent. Nearly every regional cuisine has its own version: it can be plain or highly spiced; it can be solid or like a soft porridge. Here are two Parsi versions. In the first version, the rice and dal keep their individual character; in the second, they are cooked to a comforting mush.

Mother's Khichri

This *khichri,* the one I grew up with, is a good example of how the food of Gujarat got folded into the Parsi repertoire. In Gujarati vegetarian meals, the *khichri,* like all rice, comes at the very end of the meal. For Parsis, it's the centerpiece. Its usual accompaniments are *patia,* a seafood ragout (page 107); *sahas,* fish or shrimp in a creamy sweet-and-sour sauce (page 103); *khima,* a delicate soupy stew of ground lamb (page 119); or another variant of a popular Hindu Gujarati dish, *dahi ni kaddhi* (page 78), a thick, cumin-flecked yogurt soup.

You can also think of this *khichri* as an Indian risotto and serve it with grilled chicken or seafood. It's a good go-with dish for a menu that's not specifically Parsi. I love *khichri* with a plop of yogurt and Eggplant Pickle (page 235). As the British discovered early on, renaming it kedgeree and putting their own stamp on it, *khichri* makes an excellent breakfast. Try leftover Parsi *khichri* with a poached egg to start the day. *Serves 6 to 8.*

2 cups basmati or other long-grain rice
1 cup red lentils (masur dal) or husked mung beans (mung dal)
1 to 2 tablespoons ghee or vegetable oil
1 (2-inch-long) stick cinnamon or cassia
5 whole cloves
6 black peppercorns
½ teaspoon cumin seeds (or more for cumin lovers)
3 cardamom pods
3 green chiles, slit to the stem
1 small onion, finely chopped
1 ½ teaspoons (or more) salt
½ teaspoon ground turmeric

- Wash the rice and lentils in several changes of water, until the water runs clear. Set aside. Heat the ghee in a medium saucepan over medium-high heat. Toss in the cinnamon, cloves, peppercorns, cumin, cardamom, and chiles; let them sizzle for a minute or so. Add the onion and cook, stirring occasionally, until it browns.

- Now add the rice, lentils, salt, turmeric, and enough water to come up to the first joint of your index finger when resting on the rice and dal. Stir well. Taste and add more salt if you like. Bring to a boil; reduce the heat, cover the pan tightly, and cook for 15 minutes. Turn off the heat and let the *khichri* rest for at least another 10 minutes before fluffing it up gently with a fork or a chopstick.

Firoza's Khichri

This is the ideal food. It makes happy people happier and comforts those who aren't. I've known my friend Firoza Cooper (now Kanga) almost since we were infants. She is my oracle and point of reference regarding Parsi food. Although she gives her cook, Lalji, most of the credit, she herself comes from a line of women known for their good food. In Firoza's house, even the simplest things are perfect, the standard by which all others can be judged. The *rotlis* are so soft that you want a sari made out of them, and this *khichri* of hers is a treasure.

Here is the recipe in Firoza's words: "Equal quantities of *mung dal* and rice soaked together for 10 minutes (half a cup of each is enough for the family). Wash well, add salt and a little *haldi* powder [turmeric], and pressure-cook till soft and mish-mash in texture. In a little *karhai,* heat some good ghee (say, ½ teaspoon), add ½ teaspoon whole *jeera* [cumin], and let it splutter, then immediately add the cooked rice and dal mixture, and cook a little to absorb the flavor—if thick, add water to thin it down, and then eat hot, with *dhai* [plain yogurt, usually made from low-fat or skim milk] to follow."

Precise proportions aren't vital, because *khichri* is a flexible proposition. You can make it as thick or thin as pleases you. Cooked thin, you can serve it as a soup. Cooked thick enough to plop onto a plate, it becomes a Parsi risotto that goes well with grilled or dry-fried *kavabs* (page 116), or fish fried in the Parsi manner (page 96). *Serves 6 to 8.*

1 cup long-grain rice
1 cup husked mung beans (mung dal)
8 cups (about) water
¼ teaspoon ground turmeric

½ to 1 teaspoon (or more) salt
1 tablespoon ghee or butter
1 teaspoon cumin seeds

- Wash the rice and dal in a fine strainer. Soak both together for at least 10 minutes in a deep saucepan. Cover with the water. Add the turmeric and salt. Bring to a boil; reduce the heat and simmer, loosely covered, until the rice and dal become very soft, at least 45 minutes. Stir from time to time and add more water if necessary to prevent burning and sticking.

- When the *khichri* is thick, heat the ghee in a small frying pan over medium-high heat. Add the cumin seeds and when they start to splutter, immediately tip the seeds and ghee into the pot of *khichri* and stir well, letting it simmer for a few minutes more. Adjust the salt to taste.

· · ·

Notes: Alternatively, start with leftover rice, adding a small amount of washed *mung dal* (about a quarter of the volume of the cooked rice).

For a perfect breakfast or light lunch, poach 1 to 2 eggs per person and nestle them on top of each serving of Firoza's *khichri.* If you're serving this for lunch, accompany it with sliced cucumbers or tomatoes or a simple salad.

Simplest Pulao

In Parsi cooking, a *pulao* usually implies rice cooked with meat or fish, but this simple *pulao* is made with meat stock scented with aromatics. It makes a nice accompaniment to the *bhujelu gos* (page 126) or any grilled meat. *Serves 6 to 8.*

1 ½ cups homemade chicken stock or commercial chicken or lamb broth
½ teaspoon Ginger-Garlic Paste (page 36; optional)
1 tablespoon ghee or clarified butter
1 medium onion, finely chopped
6 black peppercorns
1 cassia leaf or bay leaf
2 cups basmati rice, washed
1 ½ teaspoons salt

- Place the stock in a small saucepan over medium heat. Unless your stock is made with ginger and garlic, add the paste to the stock and simmer gently about 15 minutes.

- Heat the ghee over medium heat in a medium saucepan with a tight-fitting lid. Add the onion, peppercorns, and cassia leaf and cook the onions to the verge of browning, stirring occasionally. Add the rice. Give it a quick stir and pour in the stock. Stir in the salt. Bring to a boil; reduce the heat, cover, and simmer over low heat for 15 to 20 minutes. Let stand, covered, at least 10 minutes before gently fluffing up the rice with a fork or chopstick.

Caramelized Fried Rice | VAGHARELA CHAVAL

This is the rice that's the traditional accompaniment to *dhansak,* our emblematic dish. It also goes with *buriyanis* (page 198), vegetable stews made with eggplant or pumpkin. Anyone who eats it plain falls under its spell. This is one of the great rice dishes, and it goes well with non-Parsi food, too. We've served it as an accompaniment to seared duck breast, to grilled pork tenderloin—almost any meat benefits from being next to this gently seductive combination of sweet and savory aromas. You'll probably have leftovers, but the Parsi way is to offer more than your guests can eat. *Serves 6 to 8.*

2 tablespoons ghee, clarified butter, or vegetable oil
1 to 2 teaspoons cumin seeds
4 to 6 whole cloves
2 (2-inch-long) sticks cinnamon or cassia
6 cardamom pods
12 black peppercorns
1 small onion or 2 to 3 small shallots, finely chopped
3 tablespoons granulated sugar
1 to 2 teaspoons (or more) salt
2 to 3 cups basmati rice, washed

- Heat the ghee over medium heat in a heavy-bottomed saucepan with a tight-fitting lid. Add the cumin, cloves, cinnamon, cardamom, and peppercorns and sizzle for a minute to release the aromas. Add the onion and cook, stirring occasionally, until it begins to brown. Add the sugar and keep stirring until it begins to get brown and bubbly. Do not look away or walk off at this point. Add about ½ to 1 teaspoon salt per cup of rice, then add the rice. Add enough water to come up to the first joint of your index finger when resting on the rice. Stir quickly and taste for salt.

Bring to a boil; lower the heat, cover, and cook for 15 to 20 minutes (longer for older rice). Remove from the heat and let the rice rest 10 to 15 minutes before gently fluffing up with a chopstick so as not to break the delicate elongated grains.

• • •

Caramelized Farro: Try cooking farro Parsi style: Wash 2 ½ cups of farro and follow the recipe above, substituting farro for the rice. Increase the cooking time to 35 minutes. Let rest for 10 minutes before serving. Farro is excellent with game birds, venison, and boar.

Tomato Rice

Tomato Rice makes a great accompaniment to meat curries, but it is also good by itself or with meat, poultry, or fish cooked in a simple manner. My mother used to make this with chopped tomatoes cooked into a sauce, but I like the brightness of grated tomatoes. A huge thank-you to Randal Breski for this life-changing approach to tomatoes: until I saw him grate tomatoes into a sauté of rabbit livers and kidneys, I was completely unaware of this easy technique. *Serves 4 to 6.*

1 to 1 ½ cups basmati or Surti kolam rice (or other long-grain rice)
1 to 1 ½ pounds firm ripe tomatoes
8 to 12 black peppercorns
1 cassia leaf or bay leaf (optional)
1 teaspoon cumin (optional)
1 tablespoon ghee or butter
1 teaspoon (or more) salt
1 teaspoon granulated sugar

- Wash the rice in several changes of water in a deep saucepan with a tight-fitting lid, until the water runs nearly clear. Using the large holes of a sharp grater, grate the tomatoes. You'll probably be left with a strip of skin, which you can eat or discard.

- Add the tomatoes to the saucepan. Add the peppercorns, cassia leaf and/or cumin if you like, ghee, salt, and sugar. Slowly add enough water to come up to the first joint of your index finger when resting on the rice. Bring to a boil. Stir well. Lower the heat, cover, and steam for 15 to 20 minutes. Remove from the heat and let stand, covered, for another 10 to 15 minutes. Fluff up gently before serving.

• • •

Mediterranean Variation: Substitute olive oil for the ghee and top the rice with a little torn basil just before serving.

Note: Leftover Tomato Rice makes a good breakfast with sausage and a poached egg.

Grandmother's Pulao | NANA NU PULAO

When my mother got married, Nana, my maternal grandmother, sent her off with some of her favorite recipes, including this one for *pulao,* written out in a clear Gujarati script. The instructions were precise as to ingredients but vague as to quantity. That was for the cook to figure out.

This is a classic gently flavored Parsi *pulao*—festive, extravagant, but actually rather easy to execute. All you have to do is allow enough time for the various steps. You can make the meat and the rice in the morning and put the *pulao* together in the late afternoon. Here, we tend to eat festive rice dishes like this *pulao* for dinner, but in India, it would be as likely to be served at lunch. Earlier generations of Parsi cooks would have given the *pulao* its final cooking over a gentle flame with coals on the lid of the pan, a technique that produces the effect of an oven. Many Parsi eaters would insist on accompanying a mild *pulao* like Nana's with a complex and highly spiced dal as for *dhansak,* which I think tends to elbow out the subtlety of rice, saffron, and aromatics. In our house, we like vegetable accents and a basket of toasted Papads (page 47). This *pulao* is lovely the first day but tastes even better the next; if you make it a day ahead, save the frying for just before you serve the dish. *Serves 8 to 12, with leftovers.*

MEAT

> *2 ½ pounds lean lamb or kid shoulder or shank, boned, carefully trimmed, and*
> *   cut into roughly 2-inch chunks*
> *1 tablespoon Ginger-Garlic Paste (page 36)*
> *3 tablespoons ghee or vegetable oil*
> *3 to 4 dried red chiles*
> *5 cardamom pods*
> *6 whole cloves*
> *2 (2-inch-long) sticks cinnamon or cassia*
> *1 large onion, thinly sliced*

1 quart (about) water

2 teaspoons (or more) salt

RICE

6 cups finest basmati rice

1 teaspoon saffron threads

About ¼ cup lemon or lime juice, or ⅓ cup warm milk

12 whole cloves

10 cardamom pods

4 (2-inch-long) sticks cinnamon or cassia

4 teaspoons (about) salt

1 tablespoon ghee

ASSEMBLY AND FINAL COOKING

½ cup (about) ghee or clarified butter

1 cup whole-milk yogurt

3 boiled unpeeled waxy potatoes (such as Yukon Gold), cut into 1-inch cubes

1 to 2 cups vegetable oil, for deep-frying

½ cup golden raisins

½ to 1 cup slivered almonds

2 large onions, thinly sliced

2 to 4 sheets edible silver leaf (optional)

2 or 3 hard-boiled eggs, quartered (optional)

½ cup shelled peas, parboiled (optional)

- For the meat: Rub the carefully trimmed meat with the ginger-garlic paste and set it aside for at least 2 hours.

- In a large heavy-bottomed pan, heat the ghee over medium-high heat and add the chiles, cardamom, cloves, and cinnamon. Before the chiles turn brown, add the onion and let it soften and turn golden brown, stirring occasionally. Add the meat. Keep things moving over moderately high heat until the meat is lightly browned. Pour in enough water to make a soupy gravy—a quart should do it—and add 2 teaspoons salt to start. Bring the liquid to a boil; lower the heat, cover loosely, and cook until the chunks of meat can be pierced easily with the point of a knife, about 1½ hours. If you test a small piece, it should feel a little resistant to the teeth. Taste the liquid for salt, adding more if necessary. Let the contents of the pan cool down at least to lukewarm.

DEEP STEWING PAN
WITH LID TO HOLD
WATER OR COALS

- To make the rice: Wash the rice in several changes of water in a deep saucepan until the water runs nearly clear. Cover it with fresh water and leave it to soak at least ½ hour to ensure that the grains of rice get as long as they possibly can. In a small bowl, soak the saffron in the lemon juice or warm milk.

- Cover the rice with enough additional water to come up to the first joint of your index finger when resting on the rice. Add the cloves, cardamom, cinnamon, salt, and ghee. Bring to a boil; lower the heat and let the rice cook, uncovered, until the water is absorbed, about 10 minutes. Immediately turn off the heat. The rice should be half cooked, still hard at the center. Carefully tip out the rice onto a large baking sheet or tray and let it cool.

- Remove half the rice to another tray or wide bowl and pour the saffron and its soaking liquid over it, mixing in with a light hand so as not to damage the grains. Keep the other half of the rice plain.

- For the assembly and final cooking: Heat the oven to 300 degrees. Smear the bottom of a wide and deep pan or baking dish (not too heavy, or it will be difficult to turn out the *pulao* when the time comes) with some of the ghee. Lightly spread about ¼ cup of the yogurt over the bottom of the pan, following with a ladleful of the meat gravy. Layer the ingredients in the following order: ½ of the plain rice, ⅓ of the meat, ½ of the cubed potatoes, ½ of the saffron rice, ⅓ of the meat, the other ½ of the potatoes and saffron rice, and the remaining ⅓ of the meat. End with a top layer of plain rice. Dot the top layer with pea-size blobs of ghee. Drizzle it with the meat gravy. Cover the pan with a tightly fitting lid sealed with a paste of flour and water. Of course, you can also seal the pan with a tightly crimped double layer of aluminum foil, but it's not as dramatic.

- Put the pan in the oven and let it cook for 1 hour. Remove from the oven and let it rest, uninspected, for 15 to 30 minutes.

- Meanwhile, heat the oil for deep-frying. Cover a tray with paper towels and have it handy for draining. Start by frying the raisins, removing them with a mesh strainer the moment they swell and letting them drain. Follow with the almonds, removing them the moment they change from ivory to beige; don't let them brown. Next, fry the onions in small batches until brown and crisp. Drain thoroughly. (The raisins, almonds, and onions can be fried earlier in the day and held at room temperature.)

- When you're ready to serve, break the seal and turn the *pulao* out onto a very large platter or tray. You need strong wrists for this, or a little help. One technique is to place the platter on top of the cooking pan, clamp both together, and invert, lifting the pan off the platter so that the *pulao* spills out. You can also rest the rim of the pan on the platter and gently coax out its contents with a wooden spatula. Out of any drafts, carefully place the silver leaf, if you're using it, over the turned-out rice. Strew the dish with the fried onions, almonds, and raisins, placing quarters of hard-boiled egg here and there if you like. I like to add peas, too, at this point.

Nana's Biryani | NANA NI BIRYANI

My grandmother's biryani was so delicious that I started begging for it on my birthday instead of the required plain dal and rice, *dhan dar,* that marks all occasions, happy or sad. My mother yielded, though I could see she felt the finger of tradition wagging at her. This biryani is usually made with kid, though well-trimmed lamb, stewing veal, or boneless chicken thighs work just as well. The masala is made extra-creamy with cashews and white poppy seeds.

Biryani is a rich, decorative meat-and-rice dish from the Mughlai or Muslim tradition. It is food theater at its best. Like the previous *pulao,* it's served on a fine platter and decorated with all the extravagance a household can muster—silver or gold leaf, fried onions, almonds, and raisins, to name just the bare requirements. In many Parsi kitchens, rice dishes like these were finished on a small portable charcoal stove, a *sigri,* with coals on the concave lid of the biryani vessel to provide heat from both directions.

Serve this biryani with a raita (pages 225–26) or Simple Onion Kachumbar (page 223) dressed with yogurt, and toasted Papads (page 47). *Serves 6 to 8, with leftovers.*

MEAT

1 ½ to 2 pounds kid, lamb, stewing veal, or boneless chicken thighs

3 teaspoons Ginger-Garlic Paste (page 36)

8 to 10 dried red chiles

¼ cup white poppy seeds

3 teaspoons coriander seeds

1 ½ teaspoons cumin seeds

2 (2-inch-long) sticks cinnamon or cassia

6 whole cloves

6 cardamom pods

1 teaspoon black peppercorns

½ cup raw cashews (broken ones are all right)

3 tablespoons ghee

4 medium potatoes, peeled and quartered

2 onions, finely chopped

½ teaspoon ground turmeric

2 cups thick yogurt, lightly beaten

1 ½ teaspoons (or more) salt

RICE

3 to 4 cups basmati rice

2 teaspoons saffron threads

⅓ cup warm milk

2 teaspoons salt

1 tablespoon ghee

6 whole cloves

6 cardamom pods

10 black peppercorns

3 (2-inch-long) sticks cinnamon or cassia

ASSEMBLY AND GARNISH

1 to 2 limes

1 to 2 cups vegetable oil, for deep-frying

½ cup golden raisins

½ to 1 cup slivered almonds

1 large onion, thinly sliced

2 to 4 sheets edible silver leaf (optional)

2 or 3 hard-boiled eggs, quartered (optional)

Rose petals from unsprayed bushes (optional)

- Rub the meat with the paste and set it aside while making the masala.

- To make the masala, first toast the chiles, poppy seeds, coriander, cumin, cinnamon, cloves, cardamom, and peppercorns in a heavy skillet over medium heat. The chiles should begin to change color and the cumin, coriander, and poppy seeds should begin to look toasty without burning. Let them cool down before proceeding.

- If you have a wet-dry grinder, grind the masala spices and cashews, adding as little water as possible to make a thick paste. When you remove the paste from the grinder, rinse out the grinder bowl with a little water and save that water to add to the meat later. If you're working with a coffee grinder and food processor, powder the cooled spices in the coffee grinder, then combine them with the cashews in the food processor. Use about ¼ cup water and process the mixture to a smooth paste, adding water in small increments if necessary. Transfer the masala to a bowl. Rinse the processor bowl and save the water.

- Heat the ghee in a big sturdy ovenproof pan over medium-high heat. Lightly brown the potatoes in the ghee. Remove them and set aside. Add the chopped onions to the pan and cook, stirring occasionally, until the onions are softened but not browned. Add the meat and toss it about with the onions until it changes color. Add the masala and the turmeric. Keep turning the mixture over moderately high heat for about 5 minutes, adding small amounts of the saved masala rinse water as necessary to keep things from sticking. Add the yogurt and any remaining rinse water, plus 1 ½ teaspoons salt for a start. The total volume of liquid should barely cover the meat. Bring the mixture to a boil; reduce the heat and cover, leaving a little room for steam to escape. Simmer over low heat until the meat is tender. Boneless lamb and stewing veal take about 45 minutes to 1 hour to get meltingly tender. (If you are using chicken, it will be tender after about 25 minutes, before the gravy's done. In this case, remove the chicken and set it aside until the gravy is reduced and thick, with the ghee floating to the top. Taste for salt and return the chicken to the pan to absorb the flavors of the gravy.) Add the fried potato quarters in the last 15 minutes or so of cooking.

- Wash the rice in several changes of water, until the water runs almost clear. Put it in a large saucepan, add enough water to cover, and soak for 1 to 2 hours. While the rice is soaking, toast the saffron very lightly in a small skillet over a low flame. You want to wake it up without incinerating it. The moment you smell the saffron, stop and tip it into a small bowl. Cover with the milk and let it steep.

- When it's time to cook the rice, pour in enough additional water to reach the first joint of your index finger lightly placed on top of the rice. Add the salt, ghee, cloves, cardamom, peppercorns, and cinnamon. Bring to a boil; reduce the heat to moderate and let the water boil away with the pot uncovered. This will take about 15 minutes. You should not see any water above the top of the rice. Turn the half-cooked rice out onto a baking sheet to cool. Any remaining water evaporates quickly. The rice should be thoroughly cool before you combine it with the meat. Put it outside if it's a cold day and you're in a hurry.

- For the final assembly, cooking, and service: Heat the oven to 300 degrees. Transfer half the meat, potatoes, and gravy

SILVER TRAY

from the pan to a bowl. Carefully pile half the cooled rice onto the meat in the pan, covering it with the other half of the meat and its gravy. The rest of the rice forms the top layer. Poke holes all over the top layer of rice. Dribble the saffron and its soaking liquid into the holes. Squeeze lime juice over the top layer. Seal the lid to the pan with a rope of flour and water turned into a soft, workable dough. Alternatively, seal the pan with a tightly crimped double layer of aluminum foil plus a lid, if there is one.

- Put the sealed pan in the oven and let it cook for 1 hour. Remove from the oven and let it rest for 15 to 30 minutes without breaking the seal.

- Meanwhile, heat the oil for deep-frying. Cover a tray with paper towels and have it handy for draining. Start by frying the raisins, removing them with a mesh strainer the moment they swell and letting them drain. Follow with the almonds, removing them the moment they change from ivory to beige; don't let them brown. Next, fry the onion in small batches until brown and crisp. Drain thoroughly. (The raisins, almonds, and onion can be fried earlier in the day and left at room temperature.)

- When you're ready to serve, break the seal and turn the biryani out onto a very large platter or tray. You need strong wrists for this, or a little help. One technique is to place the platter on top of the cooking pan, clamp both together, and flip them over, lifting the pan off the platter so that the biryani spills out; or rest the rim of the pan on the platter and gently ease out its contents with a wooden spatula.

- Now the theatrical part, if you're using silver leaf. This is a good time to get a child involved. Away from drafts, carefully lay the silver leaf on top of the turned-out biryani. Strew the dish with the fried onions, almonds, and raisins. Place quarters of hard-boiled egg here and there and scatter rose petals over the top, if you like.

Everyday Dal | MORI DAR

This simple dal, when served with rice, becomes *mora dar chaval,* a dish with tremendous significance for Parsis. It may appear anytime, but it has to be eaten on any occasion out of the ordinary. You're supposed to have it for births, birthdays, engagements, wedding days (but not for the wedding feast itself), days of good fortune of any sort, and also, alas, when there has been a death in the household. The underlying lesson is that life cannot be led without experiencing both joy and sorrow in some measure, and we mustn't make too much of either, for both are fleeting. The second lesson is the beauty and value of simplicity. Plain dal sounds as though it might be boring, but it's something that everybody loves, and no one ever seems to get tired of it.

Dal to be served with rice is usually made quite thick, although it can be thinned to a soupy consistency and still taste good. In fact, Gujarati Hindus make a delicious soup called *osaman,* which is nothing more than the water that dal is cooked in, deliciously seasoned.

Mora dar chaval can be accented with seafood, either fried (page 96) or in a ragout known as *patia* (page 108). For vegetarians, *patia* is often made with vegetables like eggplant or pumpkin. *Serves 6.*

1 cup red lentils (masur dal), husked split pigeon peas (tuvar dal),
  or mung beans (mung dal)
½ teaspoon ground turmeric
½ teaspoon (or more) salt
1 onion, quartered (optional)
1 green chile (optional)
4 cups (or more) water
1 to 2 tablespoons ghee or butter
½ teaspoon cumin seeds
2 to 4 cloves garlic, minced
1 to 2 tablespoons finely chopped onion or shallot (optional)

- Pick over the dal to remove stones and chaff. Rinse the dal and transfer to a pot; add the turmeric, ½ teaspoon salt, quartered onion, and chile, if using, along with at least 4 cups water. Bring to a boil; reduce the heat and simmer, partly covered, until the dal is tender. (Masur and mung dals soften in about half the time it takes to cook tuvar dal, which needs a good 45 minutes to 1 hour.) Watch out for overboiling, even with the heat down. It's no big disaster, but it makes an awful-looking mess.

- When the dal is soft and mushy, pass through a sieve or a food mill, or liquefy in a food processor or with an immersion blender, which saves you the trouble of pouring and transferring. The texture of the dal should be thick, smooth, and pourable. Taste for salt.

- To finish, heat the ghee in a small skillet over medium heat. Sizzle the seeds, garlic, and onion, if using, until the garlic begins to brown around the edges and the seeds start to crackle. These sizzling seeds and garlic are known as *vaghar* in Gujarati, *tarka* in Hindi. Tip the *vaghar* into the dal and stir.

• • •

Dal Soup: Dal without the *vaghar* makes an excellent cold soup. I've served it with a blob of yogurt and chive blossoms, or snipped chives or green onion tops.

Note: In my mother's house, it was considered good practice to send dal to the table in a tureen with the *vaghar* floating on top, a last-minute affair, although the flavors have a better chance to combine if you stir in the toasted spices ahead of time. If you're having dal as a first-course soup, you can serve individual portions with a little *vaghar* poured over each one.

Potage of Lentils and Vegetables | DHANSAK NI DAR

Dhansak is our emblematic Parsi dish—the one we're named after by anyone who characterizes people by what they eat. It's a richly spiced puree of several lentils and vegetables, usually cooked with meat or chicken and invariably served with an unusual pilaf of slightly caramelized rice with aromatics (page 168). Sometimes, such as at weddings, this dal is served with *pulao,* in which case it changes its name to *masala ni dar.*

For most Parsis, *dhansak* is equated with Sunday lunch, followed by torpor. I remember that at the end of the siesta, there'd be tea (with cakes and biscuits), and soon after tea the evening excursion, often to the cinema, with tickets bought in advance. Going to the movies wasn't one of those slouch-in, slouch-out occasions. You dressed up. Not full throttle, but not casual. And then you ate again in the interval—ice cream, potato chips, popcorn, samosas, soft drinks. The films were usually English or American, and we went to theaters with names like Regal, Metro, Eros, Strand, Excelsior, and New Empire. The architecture was fanciful art deco (the Eros Cinema is a wedding cake), the interiors what you'd expect of movie palaces from the 1930s. After the film, we returned home for dinner.

The Ripon Club in Bombay, stronghold of Parsi gentlemen, is still famous for its *dhansak* lunches in the middle of the week. Women are allowed in for special meals, but only men seem to be permitted to repair to the large lounge chairs under the larger-than-life portraits of past Parsi worthies to sleep away the rest of the afternoon.

This recipe takes at least two hours to put together, which is why most Parsi cooks resort to a pressure cooker. I find the long, slow cooking both exciting and soothing. The various dals and vegetables look so promising bobbing about in their cooking water and then smell so good as time draws on. My mother's *dhansak* stresses dal; mine puts an emphasis on the vegetables in the interest of a lighter, brighter taste. Begin the *dhansak ni dar* the morning of the day you plan to serve it, although it can be made two to three days ahead.

Half an hour or so before serving, make the obligatory caramelized rice pilaf with aromatics (page 168). Also offer little meatballs (page 116), an onion *kachumbar* (page 223), and Papads, fried or toasted (page 47). Precede *dhansak* with a light hors d'oeuvre, and follow it with fresh fruit or chilled watermelon soup (page 245). *Serves 10 to 12, with leftovers.*

½ to 1 cup split pigeon peas (tuvar dal)

1 ½ to 2 cups of any combination of the following: split chickpeas (channa dal), red lentils (masur dal), or mung beans (mung dal)

1 sweet potato, unpeeled and roughly cut up

1 medium potato, unpeeled and roughly cut up

1 heaping cup peeled cubed pumpkin or bright orange winter squash

2 bunches green onions, tops only

4 cups (loosely packed) spinach or amaranth leaves (about ¼ pound), coarsely chopped

½ cup mint leaves

2 tomatoes, coarsely chopped

1 cup (packed) fresh fenugreek leaves or ¼ cup dried

1 cup (packed) fresh coriander (cilantro) leaves and stems

½ pound eggplant, cubed

6 cloves garlic

2 to 3 green chiles

½ teaspoon ground turmeric

1 to 2 teaspoons (or more) salt

1 tablespoon vegetable oil

1 large onion, finely chopped

3 teaspoons Ginger-Garlic Paste (page 36)

4 teaspoons Dhana Jiru (page 38)

3 teaspoons Sambhar Masala (page 37)

2 teaspoons cayenne pepper or Indian chilly powder

• Wash the dals and pick them over for stones and chaff. Then put them in a large deep pot with the potatoes, pumpkin, green onions, spinach, mint, tomatoes, fenugreek, fresh coriander, eggplant, garlic, chiles, turmeric, salt, and enough water to cover all, 10 to 12 cups. Bring to a boil; reduce the heat and simmer, partly covered, until the dals are soft to the point of becoming mushy, about 1 hour. Let the mixture cool a little, and then puree until smooth. (Traditionally, *dhansak* was put through a colander with a wooden masher and returned to the pot. You can do the same, or puree it in batches in a blender or food processor, or leave it in the pan and puree it with an immersion blender.)

- To finish the *dhansak,* heat the oil in a small pan over medium-high heat. Add the chopped onion and let it soften, stirring occasionally. Add the paste, *dhana jiru, sambhar masala,* and cayenne. Stir for 3 to 5 minutes, adding a teaspoon or so of water if things start to stick. Transfer the contents of the pan to the puree. Give things a good stir to combine thoroughly. Bring to a boil; lower the heat and simmer over low heat, stirring from time to time so that the dal doesn't stick to the bottom of the pan. When the oil floats to the top, after about 45 minutes, it's a sign that the *dhansak* is done. Taste for salt. *Dhansak ni dar* should be thick but pourable.

COLANDER AND
DAL MASHER

• • •

Dhansak with Meat or Chicken: Simmer 2 pounds of shoulder of kid or lamb, kid or lamb riblets, stewing veal, or chicken thighs with 2 teaspoons ginger-garlic paste, in enough water to cover, until barely tender. Use the resulting stock to make the dal-vegetable puree. Put the meat back into the *dhansak* in its final stages of cooking, during the last 15 minutes.

Note: If you can't find pigeon peas, make up the quantity with whatever you can find.

Lentils and Lamb Tongue | MASUR MA JIB

Masur is the word for unhusked brown lentils (husked, they are known as red lentils and called *masur dal*) as well as the name for this dish, which is the very heart and soul of everyday Parsi cooking. There are Parsi households where some member of the family insists on *masur* for dinner every single evening, month after month, year after year. Although my favorite *masur* in my mother's house was usually cooked with goat tongues, meatless *masur* is every bit as satisfying and delicious. The recipe is easily adaptable to either approach.

There are times when even markets you count on for lamb tongues won't have them. In that case, calf or pork tongue works very well. As for the lentils, you can make *masur* with the regular supermarket variety, but the smaller, darker varieties imported from India or France or grown in the United States, such as Beluga, give the dish a better taste and texture, though they take a little longer to cook.

Masur can be made days in advance. Serve with crusty bread and, if you like, a sweet red onion, coarsely chopped just before serving and sprinkled with coarse salt. I like some greens with *masur,* or a bowl of cucumbers dressed with lime and salt, or some raita-type thing. Many Parsis like creamy scrambled eggs with *masur,* which may sound weird but works suprisingly well. *Serves 6, with leftovers.*

MEAT

6 to 8 lamb tongues (1 ½ to 2 pounds), trimmed of all fat and gristle

3 teaspoons Ginger-Garlic Paste (page 36)

2 teaspoons salt

MASUR

2 cups brown lentils (masur)

2 tablespoons vegetable oil

2 medium onions, finely chopped

2 teaspoons Ginger-Garlic Paste (page 36)

2 teaspoons Dhana Jiru (page 38)

1 teaspoon Sambhar Masala (page 37)

1 teaspoon cayenne pepper or Indian chilly powder

½ teaspoon ground turmeric

1 teaspoon (or more) salt

1 to 2 green chiles, slit to the stem

2 tomatoes, coarsely chopped or grated

2 to 4 medium potatoes, quartered (peeling optional)

1 cup chopped fresh coriander (cilantro) leaves and stems

1 walnut-size lump of jaggery or 2 tablespoons brown sugar (optional)

1 to 2 tablespoons prepared tamarind pulp (see page 42) or cane vinegar (optional)

- To prepare the meat: In a large deep pot, cover the trimmed tongues generously with cold water. Add the paste and salt and bring to a boil. Lower the heat and simmer the tongues until they can be pierced easily with a thin knife, about 45 minutes, more for larger tongues. Remove them and plunge them into cold water, reserving the tongue broth. Peel the tongues while they're still warm. I know that some cuisines leave tongue skin on, but for Parsi cooks it has to go. Cut the tongues in half lengthwise, and if they're big, cut them into quarters or thick slices. Set aside.

- To make the *masur:* Inspect the lentils for gravel and wash thoroughly in a bowl to float off the chaff. In a deep, heavy pan or Dutch oven (I like enameled cast iron because it can go straight to the table), heat the oil over medium heat. Add the onions and cook, stirring occasionally, until softened. Add the paste, *dhana jiru, sambhar masala,* cayenne, turmeric, 1 teaspoon salt, and green chiles; cook over moderate heat for 3 to 5 minutes, stirring constantly to avoid sticking or burning, and adding a splash of water if necessary. Now add the tomatoes, potatoes, lentils, and reserved tongue broth (or about 6 cups of water), and bring to a boil. Lower the heat and simmer about 15 minutes. Add the tongue and continue simmering, covered, until the oil floats to the top and the lentils are completely soft, adding a little extra water if you need to. This will take from 40 minutes to an hour over low heat. The consistency you want is slack but not soupy (you should be able to eat it with a fork). Add the fresh coriander and simmer a few minutes more.

· If you want a sweet-and-sour taste, add the jaggery and the tamarind. Otherwise, stop here, after checking the salt.

. . .

Notes: If you've got a table of both meat eaters and vegetarians (even vegans) and don't want to make two separate meals, a meatless *masur* is a good thing to serve. The vegans are happy with lentils; ovo-lactos can add something yogurty; and meat eaters can be appeased with any of the following: ham, grilled sausages, a boiled salted tongue, grilled chicken, or Parsiburgers (page 118).

If you can't find the spice compounds and haven't made them yourself, you can make *masur* with cayenne pepper, cumin seeds (1 teaspoon, crushed), and turmeric. In this case, do make it sweet-and-sour, with brown sugar and tamarind or lime juice.

Leftover *masur* makes excellent fool-around food: serve it with bits of warm Chapatis (page 44), pita, or whole wheat tortillas, along with some Yogurt Cheese (page 62) or Creamy Panir (page 63) or any soft fresh cheese, plus some sliced cucumbers and mint leaves.

Split Chickpea Stew | CHANNA NI DAR

Channa, easier to say than "split chickpea," is one of India's most common and democratic foods. A smaller variety of what we know as chickpeas or garbanzos, roasted *channa* is sold by street vendors all over the country and relished by rich and poor alike as a good "time-pass item" (as someone on a train described it—a very endearing way of thinking about munch). Parsis use ground roasted *channa* in curries to give them richness and body. Husked and split, *channa* turns into a really tasty legume used as part of the dal lineup for *dhansak,* our big Parsi dish; and on its own, it makes this delicious stew.

Serve with crusty bread or Chapatis (page 44), a cabbage or cucumber and onion salad, and a bowl of yogurt. This makes a perfect dinner for fall through early spring. Like its sister dish, *masur, channa* is very good at room temperature, served as part of an hors d'oeuvre or snack with soft cheese, cucumbers, and flat bread. You can find fabulous flat breads at Middle Eastern groceries. Some look like bath mats, others like hallway runners. They're all good. Warm them in the oven, then wrap them in a thick napkin and let people break pieces off to use as scoops or platforms. *Serves 6 to 8.*

2 cups split chickpeas (channa dal)
2 medium onions, chopped
2 green chiles, slit to the stem
2 tomatoes, chopped or grated
½ teaspoon ground turmeric
1 teaspoon (or more) salt
2 to 3 medium potatoes, peeled and cubed
2 tablespoons vegetable oil
2 teaspoons Ginger-Garlic Paste (page 36)
1 teaspoon Sambhar Masala (page 37)
½ teaspoon Dhana Jiru (page 38)
½ teaspoon cayenne pepper or Indian chilly powder
½ cup chopped fresh coriander (cilantro) leaves and stems, plus extra for garnish

- Inspect the chickpeas for gravel and wash thoroughly to get rid of chaff. Put them in a saucepan and add enough water to cover generously. Let them soak at least 4 hours or overnight.

- Drain the *channa* and put it back in the pan with half the chopped onions, reserving the rest for finishing the dish. Add the chiles, tomatoes, turmeric, and salt. Cover with water. Bring to a boil; lower the heat, cover loosely, and simmer about 45 minutes to 1 hour, until the *channa* is tender. Halfway through, add the potatoes. They are supposed to be a bit mushy, so don't fret about precise timing.

- When the *channa* is cooked, heat the oil in a medium skillet. Add the rest of the onions and cook until lightly browned, stirring occasionally. Add the paste, *sambhar masala, dhana jiru,* and cayenne and stir the mixture over moderate heat for a few minutes, adding small splashes of water to prevent sticking. Tip the contents of the skillet into the *channa.* Deglaze the pan with half a cup of water; add that as well, along with the fresh coriander.

- Bring the legumes to a boil again; reduce the heat and simmer gently until the oil floats to the top, about 30 to 40 minutes. The consistency should be something like baked beans. Add water as necessary. Adjust the salt. When you're ready to serve, sprinkle the top with coarsely chopped fresh coriander.

• • •

Black-Eyed Pea Stew (chaura): Black-eyed peas are equally delicious prepared this way. With regular dried black-eyed peas, you can make a Parsi hoppin' John and serve it on New Year's Day with rice and a platter of sausages.

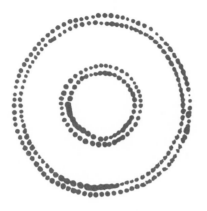

તરકારી

VEGETABLES

I'm always fascinated to see what's considered exotic in a market. Bombay markets are rich with choice. There's a special section of vegetable stalls reserved for things like red cabbage, baby corn, sweet red peppers, asparagus, mushrooms, avocados, basil, and boutique lettuce. When my parents lived in Cochin in the fifties, the local bazaars were crammed with snake gourd, eggplants, long beans, pumpkins, plantains, and a variety of greens, but all the same my aunt in Ootacamund used to send them a weekly basket of what were called "English vegetables"—cauliflower, cabbage, carrots, string beans, and occasionally chayote, known in India as chow chow.

Here in the United States, we seem to have the very best of all possible vegetable worlds, and in San Francisco, we're especially lucky. Whatever anyone considers exotic or familiar, we seem to have it. There are two or three items that are a treat to find even in the San Francisco Bay area. I'm including them because it's better to have the information at hand when drumsticks, tindola, guar beans, and field (hyacinth) beans appear in the market than to have people wondering what to do with these fabulous vegetables.

Many Parsis of my parents' generation and earlier, men particularly, made a fetish out of hating vegetables in any recognizable form. In my mother's house, vegetables were always cooked thoroughly and then a little more to be sure. In our house we do things a different way. If we're serving a Parsi fish or meat dish, we keep the vegetable accompaniments very clear, recognizable, and lightly seasoned. Since many of the vegetable dishes in this chapter are complex enough to stand on their own, we generally serve these as an accompaniment to plainly cooked meat or fish, or as a base for the ever-popular "eggs on something."

Allium Confit | TARELA KANDA

The inspiration for this confit is a seasonal delicacy in Bombay—young garlic shoots, *lilu lasan,* the cloves tiny and the greens as fine as chives. We buy bunches of them and soften them in ghee or oil with nothing else except a little ginger-garlic paste and perhaps a green chile.

In the spring, when farmers' markets are filled with young onions, red and white, leeks, and garlic (all members of the genus *Allium*), I love to make a Parsi-style stew with a combination of as many allium varieties as there are to play with. You'll need a large sauté pan or wok. Don't fret about proportions or quantities. Just have fun and feel virtuous, too, because you're practicing the kind of cooking the world needs now, *poubelle cuisine,* in which you make delicious use of things that most people mistakenly throw out, such as the green tops of any members of the onion family. *Serves 6 to 8 (makes about 2 cups).*

> *4 to 5 bunches green onions, young onions, skinny leeks, or young garlic with tops, any or all*
> *2 to 3 tablespoons ghee or unsalted butter*
> *1 tablespoon Ginger-Garlic Paste (page 36)*
> *2 to 3 fresh green chiles, finely chopped (optional)*
> *Salt to taste*

- Prepare the alliums: Wash and trim off the roots and old-looking outer leaves. Slice the alliums crosswise, including the green parts.

- Heat the ghee in a large sauté pan or wok over medium-high heat. Add the paste and let it sizzle for a minute along with the green chiles, if you want a bit of heat.

Add the mixed alliums and keep turning them over and over in the pan until they begin to collapse. Lower the heat and let them stew gently until they're almost jammy in consistency, adding water only if necessary to keep things from sticking and burning. Add salt to taste.

. . .

Note: This is a good base for Eggs on Anything (page 89) and an excellent topping for pizza or a savory tart.

Kenya Masala Butter for Corn on the Cob

After the crescendo of heat and humidity, the monsoon comes to Bombay with a drum-roll of thunder and a downpour that makes people shout and cheer in the streets. The monsoon also brings its own smells—wet earth, wildly happy plants, and everywhere in the air, the smell of corn on the cob roasting over portable charcoal stoves. As in Mexico, the usual accompaniments are salt, powdered chile, and lime.

Good corn in season needs very little embellishment, but when embellishment is called for, try this compound butter. It was inspired by one served at the Aberdare Country Club in the Kenyan highlands as an accompaniment to a curry at the club's traditional Sunday lunch. Never, before or since, have I seen a compound butter served as an adjunct to something already so complex in flavor. I was more enchanted with this butter than anything else in the meal and try to make it at least once every corn season. The corn can be boiled, steamed, or grilled. *Makes enough for 8 to 12 ears of corn.*

2 or 3 dried red chiles
2 cloves garlic
½ teaspoon cumin seeds
¼ pound (1 stick) butter, room temperature
Salt to taste

- In a small saucepan, cover the dried chiles (one of them a chipotle if you want a smoky taste) with water. Bring to a boil; reduce the heat, simmer for 5 minutes, and leave the chiles to soak until they are thoroughly softened. Drain. Puree the chiles in a food processor, in a mortar, or, even better, with the Sumeet Multi-grinder. You can puree the chiles and garlic together if you're sure of the degree of heat you want. Otherwise, puree the garlic separately.

- Bruise the cumin seeds in a mortar. Put the butter into a bowl and whisk it until it looks creamy. Add the cumin seeds and garlic. Add the chile paste a bit at a time, tasting as you go. Start with half and add the rest only if you enjoy it. Add salt to taste. Let the butter stand at cool room temperature or refrigerate it up to a week or so, until you're ready to serve the corn.

- There's also a food processor method: Bruise the cumin seeds with a pulse or two of the food processor, then add the butter, garlic, and softened chiles in stages or all at once. Process to a creamy consistency, and salt to taste.

· · ·

Note: This butter is also excellent with baked potatoes or grilled fish or chicken. Try it as an hors d'oeuvre with little boiled potatoes or shrimp grilled or seared in a nearly dry skillet. Lime wedges as an accompaniment, of course.

Stir-Fried Long Beans | CHAURA

Long beans may look like extra-long string beans, but they're a totally different vegetable with a distinct taste and texture. One variety of long bean gives us black-eyed peas (also called *chaura;* see the Glossary). Many Parsis I know group them with tindola (ivy gourd) in the category of unglamorous vegetables, but I love them, however they're cooked. They're sometimes turned into a soft-textured bean stew with onions, ginger, garlic, and tomato (see the recipe for ridge gourd, page 193). But my favorite thing to do with them is to cut them into pea-size pieces, which has a marvelous effect on their texture; give them a quick parboil, which further enhances their texture; and rapidly stir-fry them with cucumbers. This approach is drawn from Gujarati cooking, and I learned it from Madhur Jaffrey at the Great Chefs cooking school in Napa Valley. *Serves 4 to 6.*

> *½ pound young long beans, cut crosswise into pea-size pieces*
> *1 tablespoon vegetable oil*
> *4 coin-size slices peeled fresh ginger, julienned*
> *2 green chiles or 1 to 2 dried red chiles*
> *10 to 12 curry leaves*
> *½ teaspoon brown mustard seeds*
> *2 medium-size firm cucumbers (about 1 pound), seeded and diced into pea-size pieces*
> *½ teaspoon (or more) salt*
> *¼ cup chopped fresh coriander (cilantro) stems and leaves*

- Bring a saucepan of water to a rapid boil. Add the long beans and parboil for no more than a minute. Remove and drain.

- Heat the oil in a large skillet or wok over medium-high heat. Add the ginger, chiles, and curry leaves. When the ginger looks toasted, add the mustard seeds; the moment they begin to pop, add the long beans, cucumbers, and salt, stir-frying until the vegetables are barely tender. Quickly stir in the fresh coriander and check the salt before serving.

· · ·

Long Beans with Coconut: Add ½ to 1 cup freshly grated coconut to the pan along with the coriander.

Long Beans with Yogurt: You can also combine the stir-fried vegetables with about 1 ½ cups lightly beaten yogurt. Taste for salt. Sprinkle with more coriander before serving.

Mother's Wobbly Cauliflower Custard

My mother used to be such a self-deprecating cook, yet she managed to come up with the most perfect things of their kind. She never rushed and never used the high flames we like to cook with. Her baked cauliflower is a perfect expression of her patience and delicacy in cooking, and years later she is still renowned for it. Baked cauliflower is a standard in many Parsi households, but nowhere does it have the trembling delicacy of my mother's. The key to success with this recipe is to keep a light hand throughout.

This is the recipe in her words: "Boil a small cauliflower. Warm some milk. Add eggs, salt, grated cheese, and chilly powder or chopped green chillies. Pour over drained cauliflower. More grated cheese on top. Bake in hot water in a moderate oven until set."

Mother would have used the processed cheddar cheese that's the standard in India. In our house we use more interesting ones (or we use up leftover nubs), such as fontina, Parmesan, aged Monterey Jack, or cheddar, alone or in combination.

Serve with something crisp and a little salad for a perfect light lunch. I'm always hoping for cold leftovers, but it isn't often that we get any. *Serves 4 to 6.*

1 small cauliflower (about 1 pound) or part of a larger one
Salt to taste
4 large eggs

3 cups warm milk or half-and-half
1 cup (or more) grated cheese
Chopped fresh green or red chiles (optional)

· Heat the oven to 350 degrees and lightly butter a 1 ½- to 2-quart baking dish.

· Boil the cauliflower in lightly salted water until tender. Or steam the cauliflower until thoroughly tender. Break it into small florets, chop the stem into small bits, salt the cauliflower lightly, if necessary, and crowd into the prepared baking dish.

· Beat the eggs lightly with the warm milk. Add about ¾ cup of the grated cheese and, if using, the chiles to taste. Pour the egg mixture over the cauliflower, which should be covered thoroughly but not drowned. Strew the rest of the grated cheese over the top.

· Put the baking dish in a larger pan containing enough hot water to come 2 inches up the sides of the dish and bake about 30 minutes. The custard should be very wobbly, and the top should be set and golden but not at all brown.

· Remove the pan from the oven and let it stand at room temperature for 5 to 10 minutes before serving.

· · ·

Cauliflower Gratin: For a more robust version, make 2 to 3 cups of thin béchamel, using part cauliflower cooking liquid and part milk. Let it cool slightly before adding the eggs, cheese, chiles, and salt. Pour over the cauliflower. Sprinkle with more grated cheese, dot with butter and fine bread crumbs, and bake at 350 degrees in a pan of hot water until the top is golden brown, about 35 to 40 minutes. Let rest for a few minutes before serving. I love this cold for breakfast the next day. Steamed chayote can be turned into an excellent gratin using the same method.

Thanksgiving Brussels Sprouts

Pulling Brussels sprouts apart is well worth the effort, but I go to the trouble only once a year, to go with our masala-grilled Parsi turkey (page 149). I owe this idea completely to David Tanis and Alan Tangren, café chefs at Chez Panisse in the 1980s. There they were one fall afternoon, patiently turning a case of Brussels sprouts into a fluffy mound, pulling them apart leaf by leaf. *Serves 6 to 10.*

1 ½ pounds Brussels sprouts
2 tablespoons vegetable oil

¾ teaspoon brown mustard seeds or fennel seeds
1 tablespoon shredded peeled fresh ginger
1 dried red chile
2 to 3 pinches (or more) of salt

- Using a sharp paring knife, cut out the core of each sprout and tease the leaves apart. This can be done a day ahead. Put the leaves in a tightly sealed plastic bag and refrigerate.

- Heat the oil in a large skillet or wok. Add the mustard seeds. When the mustard seeds begin to pop (or the fennel seeds to crackle), throw in the ginger, the chile, and 2 to 3 good pinches of salt. The moment the ginger starts to brown, add the sprout leaves and stir-fry until they are barely tender. Check for salt.

. . .

Thanksgiving Leafy Greens: A bunch or two of collard greens and lacinato kale (sometimes called dinosaur kale), tough stems and ribs trimmed off, then blanched and cut into ribbons, makes a good alternative to Brussels sprouts.

Note: If pulling the leaves apart sounds too tedious, you can slice the sprouts thinly on a mandoline or by hand.

Braised Greens | BHAJI

Try this way of cooking greens with whatever's in season. If you have a garden or access to a farmers' market with vendors from Asia, you'll have an infinite variety of greens to choose from, even some you thought were not possible to eat, like squash or bean greens. In India, Parsis usually go for amaranth, spinach, or fenugreek greens, or sometimes dill greens in combination with spinach. It's difficult to be precise about the quantity because some greens lose more water than others. Always get more than you think you need, because the leftovers, should there be any, are such a nice bonus.

This way of cooking greens is also the foundation of a popular egg dish, *bhaji par ida* (see Eggs on Anything, page 89). *Serves 4 to 6.*

1 to 2 pounds greens (enough to give you about 2 to 3 cups cooked)
1 tablespoon vegetable oil
1 to 2 green chiles, slit to the stem
1 small onion, chopped
1 teaspoon Ginger-Garlic Paste (page 36)
¼ teaspoon ground turmeric

½ teaspoon cayenne pepper or Indian chilly powder
½ teaspoon (or more) salt
1 tomato, chopped with skin and seeds (optional)

• Remove any tough stems and wash the greens. With mature fenugreek, you often need to go further and strip the leaves off the stems. Steam the greens until just wilted, or put them in a pan over medium heat with no more than the water adhering to the leaves and let the greens collapse. You should have about 2 to 3 cups. Drain. Chop the greens if you like, or turn them into a rough-textured puree in a food processor.

• Heat the oil in a sauté pan over medium heat. Add the green chiles and let them sizzle for a moment before adding the onion. When the onion softens, add the paste, stirring to keep the contents from sticking. Add the turmeric, cayenne, and about ½ teaspoon salt for a start, and stir for a few moments before you add the chopped tomato, if using. Let the tomato cook down a little.

• Add the greens, combine well, and braise over low heat, partly covered, until the greens are tender and well flavored with the other ingredients. This should take about 30 minutes. The consistency should be fairly dry, not swimming.

• • •

Bhaji with Peas: If you have a handful of shelled peas, you can add them to the greens in the last few minutes of cooking. Sometimes potatoes, boiled and cubed, are cooked together with amaranth and fenugreek greens.

Note: Bitter greens like fenugreek call out for a touch of sweetness. Add about 1 tablespoon of crushed jaggery or light brown sugar, or to taste. For other greens, such as amaranth, add that touch of sweetness only if it appeals to you.

Quick-Cooked Greens | "EXPRESS" BHAJI

I learned this approach in the Seychelles in 1984 from the family on the other side of the hedge. In both Mauritius and the Seychelles they like their greens, *brèdes,* cooked this way. So does everyone else who ever encounters this method, which works with greens of any sort. If the greens are tough or leathery, blanch them briefly. Otherwise, they're in and out of the pan before you know it.

Amaranth is one of those neglected food plants you see all over the world, more often growing in driveways and parking lots than for sale in markets. In California, we find it at farmers' markets and Chinese and Southeast Asian groceries. There are

many varieties of amaranth, leaves large and small, plain green or tinged with ma-
roon. All are delicious. Some require stripping off tough stems; others have tender,
succulent stems. *Serves 4 to 6.*

> *1 to 2 pounds greens (amaranth, spinach, watercress, green onion or*
> *other onion greens, snow pea shoots, bean greens, chard, lacinato kale,*
> *collards, chile greens) or cabbage, plain or Savoy*
> *1 ½ to 2 tablespoons oil*
> *Salt to taste*
> *1 fresh green or red chile, or 1 (or more) dried red chile*
> *4 to 6 coin-size slices peeled fresh ginger, julienned*

- Wash the greens and trim away any tough stems. If using lacinato kale, older chard,
older amaranth, chile greens, or bean greens, blanch them very briefly (about a
minute) in boiling water. Drain, rinse with cold water if not using them immediately,
and set aside. Some greens need chopping. I slice the stems finely and the leaves in
broader ribbons so that everything gets done at the same time. Cabbage needs to
be shredded.

- Heat the oil in a wok over highish heat. Throw in some salt, the chile, and the
ginger. When the ginger starts to sear, immediately add the washed or blanched
greens. Use tongs to keep the greens moving so that the bottom layer doesn't get
charred while the top stays uncooked. Quick-cooking greens like watercress or young
pea shoots need no more than a minute or two. Longer-cooking greens need to be
covered and the heat reduced for just a few minutes.

- Turn out and serve.

· · ·

Note: If you're cooking greens for more than three to four people, it's easier to do
successive small batches of greens than one giant, billowing heap.

Ragout of Ridge Gourd or Snake Gourd | TURIA ATTVA PARVAL NU SAKH

I wonder how many people are aware that the loofahs they scrub themselves with are
the fibrous skeleton of a really delicious vegetable, the sponge gourd that Parsis know
as *turia.* And I wonder how many people who eat it as a vegetable know that it is the
same plant they scrub themselves with. *Turia* is a Parsi favorite. Thanks to the pan-
Asian markets all over the United States, sponge gourd is easy to find. The scientific
name for *turia* is *Luffa,* and it comes in two guises: *Luffa cylindrica,* which is what

loofahs are made from; and *Luffa acutangula,* the ridge gourd, sometimes called Chinese okra, though I don't know why. Both can be cooked without peeling.

Every year brings something new to the Alemany farmers' market where we go every single week. There's always something to surprise or thrill. One of my big thrills came a few years ago when snake gourd, *Trichosanthes cucumerina,* made its appearance. In Bombay markets, snake gourds *(parval)* stretch on and on, sometimes curling in on themselves, and no vendor expects you to buy more than a foot or so, which will be obligingly cut off and weighed. Our local snake gourds come in well-behaved lengths, but they're just as delicious.

The following recipe is a versatile one because it adapts itself well to either of these gourds, or to any other summer squash. You can serve it as it is, steam eggs on top of it to make *turia par ida* (see Eggs on Anything, page 89), or add small shrimp to the mixture (see the variations). *Serves 6.*

2 tablespoons vegetable oil
2 green chiles, slit to the stem (optional)
1 to 2 large onions, chopped
3 teaspoons Ginger-Garlic Paste (page 36)
½ to 1 teaspoon cayenne pepper or Indian chilly powder
¼ teaspoon ground turmeric
2 to 3 tomatoes, coarsely chopped
2 tablespoons jaggery or brown sugar
¾ teaspoon (or more) salt
1 ½ to 2 pounds ridge gourd, snake gourd, or sponge gourd
Chopped fresh coriander (cilantro) leaves and stems, for garnish

- Heat the oil in a roomy skillet or wok over medium heat. If you're adding green chiles, let them sizzle first before the onions go in to soften and turn golden. Add the paste, cayenne, and turmeric, stirring them together for a minute or two. The chopped tomatoes go in next, along with the jaggery. Let the mixture cook down until the tomatoes no longer seem watery. Add the salt, about ¾ teaspoon to start. Taste the mixture. It should be sweet, tart, and hot.

- While the tomato base is cooking down, prepare the gourds. Young ridge gourds may not need peeling—just a gentle scraping, if that. Lightly peel the ribs off more mature specimens. Snake gourd and young sponge gourd do not need peeling. Cut gourds into ½-inch cubes and combine well with the tomato base. Pour in a splash of water to generate steam.

- Raise the heat to boiling; reduce the heat, cover the pan, and leave to simmer until the gourd is cooked through and tender, about 10 minutes. Uncover for the last few minutes to let excess water evaporate.
- Check the seasoning, adding more salt or sugar as needed. Serve sprinkled with the fresh coriander.

• • •

Ridge Gourd Ragout with Shrimp: Sometimes tiny shrimp, fresh or dried, are added to the tomatoey *turia* mixture (but not the *parval,* for some reason, although it would be equally good). Use the smallest shrimp you can find. Half a pound or a cup of fresh peeled and deveined shrimp should do it. Lightly rub the shrimp with the dry rub on page 97 and fry them very quickly in little or no oil before adding them to the *turia* in the last couple of minutes.

Guar Bean Ragout: Guar, or cluster, beans can be cooked following this recipe. They need to be checked for stringiness, even if they look young and tender. Unlike regular green beans or long beans, guar beans have to be cooked until soft, or they aren't pleasant to eat.

Bitter Gourd (Bitter Melon) Ragout: This vegetable is a big Indian favorite, though it will be an acquired taste for anyone unprepared for its aggressive bitterness. Cut a medium (6 to 8 inches long) bitter gourd into ½-inch cubes. Sprinkle with at least 2 tablespoons salt and rub it in well. Set aside for an hour or so. Some but not all of the bitterness will be leached out. Drain the cubed bitter gourd and rinse off the salt. Go ahead with the recipe above. Bitter gourd must be thoroughly cooked. Increasing the amount of sugar will offset the bitterness, although bitterness is one of the desirable qualities of this vegetable. Made a day ahead, a bitter gourd dish calms down.

Ivy Gourd | TINDOLA

The only time my mother ever came to the Alemany farmers' market with us, in 1986, she went into shock when she found out what we were prepared to pay for what in Bombay is regarded as the lowliest green vegetable, the tindola (accent on the first syllable). It's true, the price was very high—four dollars a pound, versus twenty cents in India—and it changed hands like some rare or illegal substance, hidden from general view in the back of the stall, sometimes requiring just eye contact to ascertain if there was any to be had. When I told a visitor about tindola and how it was a vegetable without honor in its own country but exceedingly valuable here, she asked the vendor why. He grinned broadly and replied, "Monopoly!"

No more monopoly now. Tindola, *Coccinia grandis,* appears at a number of stands at our farmers' market, and you can generally buy it from Indian groceries that have a produce section. Tindola resembles a gherkin in size and color. It should be firm and bright green. The taste and texture are so distinctive that it's well worth the pursuit.

Tindola was one of my favorite vegetables at home in Bombay. My mother usually served it whole with meat in a stew, or cut into rounds as a base for an egg dish. This vegetable manages to taste different every way you cut it. Left whole, in a stew like *kharu gos* (page 112), it soaks up cooking juices and releases them in a burst of flavor as you bite into it. As tempting as it is to eat all vegetables raw or barely cooked, tindola must be well cooked, not necessarily to squishy tenderness but beyond the stage where it makes your mouth pucker. *Serves 6.*

1 tablespoon vegetable oil
3 coin-size slices peeled fresh ginger, julienned
1 to 2 fresh red or green chiles, slit to the stem
½ teaspoon (or more) salt
1 pound tindola, sliced vertically or horizontally

- Heat the oil in a heavy skillet or wok over medium-high heat. Add the ginger and chiles and sizzle until the ginger starts to turn golden brown. Add about ½ teaspoon salt and follow with the tindola. Stir-fry until the slices are fully cooked but still crisp, testing as you go. If some slices char a little around the edges, don't worry. That lends flavor. Tindola's ready to eat just after it loses that bright green quality we prize so much in other stir-fried vegetables. Check for salt and serve at once.

• • •

Tindola Raita: Make a delicious tindola raita by tipping the stir-fried tindola into 1 to 2 cups lightly salted yogurt. Garnish with chopped fresh coriander.

Tindola Ragout: For another way of cooking tindola, see the ridge gourd ragout (page 193).

Eggs on Tindola (tindola par ida): Tindola sliced into ¼-inch rounds and cooked as here makes a delicious base for egg (see Eggs on Anything, page 89).

Pumpkin Crescents with Curry Leaves

I've been there only once but haven't ever forgotten the excitement both David and I felt when we went to the River Café in London over fifteen years ago. Since then, the owners have come out with several books, each packed with ideas that have now become old friends. One of my favorite River Café recipes is the wood-roasted pumpkin. Being a good Parsi magpie, I've taken the idea and given it a twist that's sure to convert anyone who thinks pumpkin is good only for carving or pie. Anything I've said about olive oil not figuring in Parsi food can be ignored here. Olive oil is essential to the success of this recipe. The quantities are suggested, and it can be scaled up or down without any trouble at all. This side dish is still excellent days later, eaten cold right out of the fridge. *Serves 6.*

> *1 medium pumpkin (about 2 to 3 pounds), pared and cut into*
>   *½- to ¾-inch-thick crescents*
> *¼ cup (or more) olive oil*
> *4 to 6 cloves garlic, finely chopped*
> *Maldon salt or some other coarse flaky salt to taste*
> *2 to 3 fresh or dried red chiles*
> *1 cup (loosely packed) fresh curry leaves or ½ cup home-dried ones*

- Heat the oven to 400 degrees.
- In a bowl, mix the pumpkin crescents with the oil, garlic, and salt. Using sharp kitchen scissors, snip tiny bits of chile, seeds and all, into the bowl. Turn out the mixture onto a shallow roasting pan or baking sheet. Strew curry leaves over the surface. Roast for 45 minutes to 1 hour, until the pumpkin is tender. Serve hot or warm.

. . .

Notes: The oven temperature is something you can fiddle with. Should you have something else going at 350 degrees, the pumpkin will accommodate itself to a lower temperature, but you might have to give it a bit longer.

No curry leaves? Never mind. The chiles and garlic are completely satisfying. Not many curry leaves? Use what you've got and tear them up to get more mileage out of them.

Eggplant Stew | VENGNA NI BURIYANI

Buriyani, though eaten with rice, isn't to be confused with biryani, an elaborate rice dish. *Buriyanis* made with eggplant or pumpkin are perfect to serve a mixed group of meat eaters and vegetarians without making anyone feel obviously singled out. *Kavabs* made of meat (page 116) or shrimp (page 99) can be served separately to make everyone happy.

Serve with Caramelized Fried Rice (page 168), its traditional accompaniment, or a pilaf made from rice and quinoa. A bowl of yogurt or a cucumber-and-yogurt salad would be a good counterpoint. *Serves 4 to 6.*

3 tablespoons vegetable oil
1 teaspoon cumin seeds
1 to 2 green chiles, slit to the stem
1 large onion, finely chopped
2 teaspoons Ginger-Garlic Paste (page 36)
½ teaspoon ground turmeric
½ teaspoon (or more) cayenne pepper or Indian chilly powder
1 teaspoon Dhana Jiru (page 38; optional)
1 teaspoon (or more) salt
2 pounds eggplants, cut into 1-inch cubes
½ to 1 cup coarsely chopped fresh coriander (cilantro) stems and leaves

• Heat the oil in a large saucepan with a lid over medium-high heat. Add the cumin seeds and sizzle without browning them. Follow with the green chiles and toss them about until they blister. Add the onion and let it soften and start to brown, stirring occasionally. Add the paste, turmeric, cayenne, and *dhana jiru,* if you like, and stir about 3 minutes, adding a tablespoon of water or so if the mixture seems to be burning and sticking. You want to add just enough water to keep things moving; you don't want a puddle. Add the salt. The eggplant goes in next, and everything gets tossed together. Now pour in about 2 cups water and bring to a boil; stir, reduce the heat, cover, and stew until the eggplant is very soft and turns into a savory mass when stirred. This should take about half an hour. Eggplants vary in how much water they give off as they cook, so check in fifteen minutes to see if you need to add a little more. If in half an hour the eggplant still seems very soupy, uncover the pot and turn up the heat to allow the excess water to evaporate. Adjust the salt and *dhana jiru,* if you're using it for that authentic Parsi taste (it's good without it, too). Stir in the fresh coriander or save it for sprinkling over the top just before serving.

. . .

Pumpkin or Bottle Gourd Buriyani: You can substitute peeled, cubed pumpkin or bottle gourd for the eggplant. Some people like a touch of sweetness. If you do, add a small amount of jaggery or brown sugar at the end.

Note: The common Indian English word for eggplant or aubergine is *brinjal,* probably derived from the Portuguese *berenjena.*

Sautéed Okra | TARELA BHIDA

Okra cooked this way is often used as a foundation for eggs (page 89), but we like it just by itself or as an accompaniment to simply cooked meat or fish. My grandmother used to deep-fry the okra before adding it to the sautéed onions, which gives the dish an unctuous texture. Do not be alarmed if the okra turns gummy in the early stages of cooking; it doesn't last. This way of cooking okra makes converts of those who claim they loathe it. *Serves 4 to 6.*

> *2 tablespoons ghee or vegetable oil*
> *1 large onion, finely chopped*
> *2 teaspoons Ginger-Garlic Paste (page 36)*
> *½ teaspoon salt*
> *1 pound okra, cut crosswise into ¼-inch-thick slices*
> *2 to 3 green chiles, finely chopped*
> *½ cup chopped fresh coriander (cilantro) stems and leaves*

Heat the ghee in a 10-inch skillet over medium heat. Add the onion and let it soften, stirring occasionally. Add the paste and fry for 2 to 3 minutes, taking care that it doesn't stick or burn. Add the salt, okra, and chiles and continue stir-frying until the okra is completely tender, about 10 minutes. Add the fresh coriander and combine well. Taste again for salt and serve hot or at room temperature.

Sweet-Sour Tomatoes | KHATTA-MITTHA TAMOTA

When tomatoes are tasty, plentiful, and too soft to be used in a salad, make this dish instead. They don't all have to be the same color. Parsis usually serve these tomatoes with an egg topping (page 89). Cooked down a bit, they also make a fabulous barbecue sauce, especially if you increase the cayenne. Try parboiled baby back pork ribs blanketed with this tomato mixture and cooked in a low oven until they're tender. *Serves 4 to 6.*

2 to 3 tablespoons vegetable oil
2 green chiles, slit to the stem
1 medium onion, finely chopped
1 to 2 teaspoons Ginger-Garlic Paste (page 36)
½ teaspoon (or more) cayenne pepper or Indian chilly powder
2 to 3 pounds ripe tomatoes, coarsely chopped with skin and seeds (4 to 6 cups)
1 ½ tablespoons brown sugar or jaggery
Salt to taste
Small handful of chopped fresh coriander (cilantro) stems and leaves

- Heat the oil in a heavy wide pan or skillet over medium-high heat. Add the chiles and sizzle briefly, following them with the onion and paste. Let the onions soften and brown around the edges. Then add the cayenne, stirring for a minute or so before adding the tomatoes and brown sugar. Cook the mixture over high heat for a minute or so, then reduce the heat and let the tomatoes cook down to the consistency of a loose jam, about 10 to 15 minutes. Stir from time to time to keep the bottom from caramelizing. Add salt to taste and the fresh coriander. Add more sugar if you like. The effect should be sweet-tart without being sugary.

Angel-Hair Potatoes | SALI

First, a note on pronunciation. *Sali* here is pronounced with a short *a*. With a drawn-out vowel, "saali," it means something completely different. The surface meaning of *sala*, "brother-in-law," and *sali*, "sister-in-law," are innocent enough, but in vernacular use they're epithets, not always jocular.

I don't know any other Indian cuisine that features straw potatoes quite the way we do. Ours are finer than fine, deep-fried but not allowed to color beyond blond. *Sali* is often used as a contrasting component with unctuous meat dishes such as Chicken with Apricots (page 141) or *khima* (page 119). I like it strewn over any festive rice dish for a fabulous contrast in texture.

My mother says that her cooks and her mother's cooks used to hand-cut the *sali*. She and I tried several approaches—the mandoline, a Japanese box grater, or hand-cutting all the way. The best result came from stacking even, thin slices made on the mandoline or box grater and then hand-cutting them into the finest julienne. The art is to get *sali* fine enough, but not too fine, because then it clumps when fried. It's not quite as absurdly laborious as it would seem. One large russet potato yields quite a mound of *sali* (about two cups), enough for a small handful each for six people.

Although it's always much better made close to the time of serving, *sali* can be made earlier in the day, or even earlier, and hidden from wandering hands in an airtight tin. You can reheat it in an oven at about 300 degrees. *Serves 6 to 8.*

2 russet potatoes
1 teaspoon salt
Vegetable oil, for deep-frying

· Peel the potatoes. If cutting by hand, slice them as thinly as you can short of transparency. Stack the slices and julienne them as finely as you can to make about 4 cups potatoes. Soak the potatoes in cold water with the salt for at least an hour. Drain.

· Spread the potatoes out on a towel and blot them dry with another towel. Some people like to use a salad spinner lined with a kitchen towel or sturdy paper towel to keep the potato strands from escaping through the slots.

· Pour oil to a depth of at least 3 inches into a wok or a saucepan that gives you maximum depth and heat to 375 degrees. Deep-fry the potatoes no longer than it takes to cook the strands through, doing small amounts at a time. It doesn't save time to do larger handfuls, and you risk grease-sodden clumps. The potatoes should be pale straw-colored when they come out of the oil. This is a good time to remember my grandmother's dictum that things always look paler in the frying oil than out of it. Drain the *sali* on paper towels or brown paper bags.

Potato Wafers | PAPETA NA WAFER

If I had to draw a Parsi food pyramid, it would rise out of a plinth of potato chips. In Bombay a potato chip, usually described as a finger chip, is what Americans know as a French fry. American potato chips are known as wafers in Bombay, in both English and Gujarati. Parsis take wafers seriously. They're the first thing put onto the banana leaf for wedding and initiation banquets. There are several businesses dedicated to nothing but wafer production, where a vat of hot oil never sleeps. The proprietor sits near the vat, an enormous woklike affair, turning and draining and chatting, while minions in the back madly slice potatoes to keep up with an endless stream of customers.

This is the way it used to be, anyway. The same companies, Victory and OK, and probably others, now make wafers in fac-

garlic
ginger
potato
chips

DAVID KING'S VISION OF THE
PARSI FOOD PYRAMID

tories or large sheds, not at the point of sale. They're still superlative, but nothing can beat walking away with a warm and slightly greasy brown paper bag that smells headily of newly fried potatoes.

Use any suitable potato. Kennebecs or Idaho russets are the usual recommendation, but skinny fingerling potatoes make ethereal miniature chips. Allow the equivalent of one full-size potato per person, plus an extra. A mandoline or Japanese Benriner slicer or box grater is the best way of getting uniformly thin slices. For easy slicing, choose potatoes you can hold comfortably.

Potato wafers can be made ahead of time and reheated, but nothing's as good as getting them straight out of the pan. If you have any left over, now's the time to make Eggs on Potato Chips (page 90). *Serves 4 to 6.*

About 1 ½ pounds potatoes (4 to 6 medium)
3 to 4 cups vegetable oil, for deep-frying
Salt to taste

· Using a mandoline or box grater, thinly slice peeled or unpeeled potatoes. The slices should be floppy and translucent. Soak in a bowl of water at least 1 to 2 hours to get rid of excess starch. Change the water if you need to. Some Parsi cooks add salt to the soaking water.

· Dry the potatoes well, first in a salad spinner and then between towels.

· Organize your frying station. Line at least 2 trays with a base of plain brown paper bags, laying paper towels over them. Heat the oil slowly in a wok or deep-fryer to about 370 degrees.

· Use a frying basket if you have one. Drop the chips into the oil one by one so that they don't clump together. Fry to a pale gold, keeping two things in mind—first, that successive small batches always work better than overcrowding the chips; and second, my grandmother's dictum, that everything looks lighter-colored in the oil than out of it. Be prepared for a few initial mistakes.

· Drain the wafers on the paper towel–lined sheets and sprinkle lightly with salt.

Parsi Hash Yellow Potatoes | PAPETA NU SAKH

Indian regional cuisines nearly all have a recipe for cooking potatoes and onions together. This Parsi version is adopted from the Hindu vegetarian cooking of Gujarat. The recipe is rather loose; the amounts of potato and onion can be pushed this way or that depending on the effect you want. In fact, you can leave out the potatoes altogether and have an onion dish.

Serve with freshly fried Puris (page 45) for a popular Parsi combination known as *puri bhaji.* Whole wheat tortillas or Chapatis (page 44) are equally good. With some yogurt and sliced tomatoes and cucumbers, you'll have an excellent light lunch. These potatoes also make a good accompaniment to meat and chicken. Try Parsiburgers (page 118) with them. Slightly altered, this recipe forms the base for the classic Parsi egg dish *papeta par ida* (see the variation at the end of this recipe). *Serves 8.*

> *2 pounds Yellow Finn, Yukon Gold, Bintje, or plain red-skinned potatoes*
> *2 tablespoons vegetable oil*
> *1 teaspoon brown mustard seeds*
> *1 teaspoon cumin seeds*
> *3 to 4 green chiles (or dried red chiles), slit to the stem*
> *20 to 30 curry leaves*
> *1 pound onions, very thinly sliced*
> *½ teaspoon ground turmeric*
> *1 ½ teaspoons (or more) salt*
> *1 cup (or more) coarsely chopped fresh coriander (cilantro) stems and leaves*
> *Lime wedges*
> *½ cup roasted or fried cashews (optional)*

- Parboil the potatoes in a pot of boiling salted water until half-cooked, about 8 minutes. Cool them slightly, then peel, quarter, and slice them about ½ inch thick, or cook them through and crush them with your hands for an appealing rough texture.

- Heat the oil in a large skillet, and when it's very hot add the mustard and cumin seeds. As soon as the mustard seeds begin to fly about, add the green chiles and curry leaves. Let them sizzle a few moments and then add the onions. Stir-fry the onions with the aromatics until they are soft and translucent. Stir in the turmeric and at least 1 ½ teaspoons salt. Add the potatoes and toss over low heat until everything is well blended and the potatoes are completely cooked, about 10 minutes. Taste again for salt. Add lots of fresh coriander. Serve hot or at room temperature, garnished with more fresh coriander and wedges of lime. If you have roasted or fried cashews around, they make a particularly good topping, coarsely chopped and strewn liberally over the potatoes.

• • •

Eggs on Potatoes (papeta par ida): To use as the foundation for Eggs on Anything (page 89), parboil the potatoes, peel and quarter them, and cut them into ¼-inch-thick slices. Follow the recipe above, omitting the mustard seeds. When the potatoes are barely done, top with the eggs.

Fried Plantains | TARELA KERA

In Parsi Gujarati, bananas and plantains are both called *kera.* What we know here as plantains are described as *tarvana kera* (bananas to be fried). *Tarvana kera* become *tarela kera* (fried plantains), which are served as part of the middle of the meal rather than at its end, just as they are in Latin American cuisines. This recipe serves four, but it's no problem to adjust it for any number; just make one plantain per person.

My husband thinks that there's no meal under the sun that couldn't be adorned by fried ultraripe plantains. That gives you an idea of how often we have them. In a Parsi meal, *tarela kera* are often served with *kharu gos* (page 112), the basic Parsi meat stew. Fry them at the last minute and garnish the stew with them just before serving.

More and more mainstream markets now carry plantains, although the best places to find the soft, black ones, the sweetest, are markets catering to Central American and Caribbean cooks, who know them as *maduros.* For Parsi purposes, look for uniformly black fruit, jelly-soft to the touch, what my cousin Lyla would describe as ready to give to the cow. *Serves 4.*

4 soft ripe plantains
1 cup (about) vegetable oil, for shallow-frying

- Peel the plantains and slice in two lengthwise. If they're very long, also divide each piece into two horizontally. Alternatively, cut them into 2- to 3-inch lengths without splitting them lengthwise. Heat the oil in a large heavy skillet over medium heat. Add the plantain pieces and shallow-fry till they turn a deep golden brown. Drain on paper towels and serve immediately.

· · ·

Eggs on Plantains (kera par ida): When sautéed with onions, chiles, and fresh coriander (cilantro), fried plantains take on an unusually exotic taste. Parsis love to poach eggs on a base of plantains cooked this way (see Eggs on Anything, page 89). Served with simply cooked meat or chicken, the plantains taste almost like a chutney. I have to thank my old school friend Amy Nicholls for demonstrating how delicious such a sauté can be when made with regular bananas instead of plantains and no preliminary frying.

Baked Plantains: If frying is anathema, bake the plantains in their skins for about 30 minutes at 350 degrees until they split open. We do them in a toaster oven.

Wedding Stew | LAGAN NU ISTU

This stew is often found on festive menus, served as a course on its own, or as the vegetable component of an everyday meal. The vegetables traditionally used are potatoes, sweet potatoes, elephant's foot yams, carrots, peas, and sometimes cherry tomatoes in a sweet-and-sour base of melted onions and tomato, like a Latin American *sofrito.* Some versions include a banana, but not my mother's. She stresses that the vegetables should be cut into cubes the size of a child's fingernail.

The traditional method for making this stew is to fry the vegetables separately, but I prefer to roast them. Use a combination of any root vegetables you like, leave out the Parsi spicing, use olive oil, and take the dish into that vague Mediterranean category. Should you ever find an elephant's foot yam (*Amorphophallus* spp.) at an Indian shop, it's worth a try, especially if you don't have to buy the whole elephant-foot-size article. (In India, vegetable sellers cut off just as much as you need.) In a Parsi meal, serve *lagan nu istu* with *katles* or *kavabs* (page 116); in a non-Parsi meal, with grilled or roasted chicken, along with an assertive green vegetable such as amaranth greens or kale. For a very simple lunch, just *lagan nu istu* with Chapatis (page 44) and a little yogurt or Creamy Panir (page 63) would be perfect. Or eat it with Everyday Dal (page 176) with rice. *Serves 6 to 8.*

2 cups peeled and cubed sweet potatoes

2 cups peeled and cubed waxy potatoes (such as Yukon Golds)

2 cups peeled and cubed carrots

1 ½ teaspoons (about) salt

4 tablespoons (about) vegetable oil

2 (or more) green chiles, slit to the stem

1 teaspoon cumin seeds, pounded

3 medium onions, finely chopped

2 teaspoons Ginger-Garlic Paste (page 36)

½ to 1 teaspoon cayenne pepper or Indian chilly powder

½ teaspoon ground turmeric
2 to 3 ripe tomatoes, finely chopped or grated
½ cup cane vinegar
1 tablespoon or more jaggery or brown sugar
1 to 2 cups young peas (frozen peas are all right in a pinch)

• Heat the oven to 450 degrees. Lay the sweet potatoes, waxy potatoes, and carrots out on a baking sheet. Salt them lightly and drizzle them with about 2 tablespoons of the oil, or mix them in a bowl with 2 tablespoons oil and about 1 teaspoon of the salt. Roast until golden, about 25 minutes.

• While the vegetables are roasting, heat the remaining 2 tablespoons oil (or the same amount of ghee) in a large skillet over medium heat. Add the chiles and cumin and sizzle for a couple of minutes. Add the onions and let them soften over moderately low heat, stirring occasionally. Add the paste, cayenne, and turmeric and stir for about a minute. Add the tomatoes and let things stew until you get a thickish sauce; a few minutes should do it. Add the vinegar and jaggery and about ½ teaspoon of the salt. Taste. It should be hot, sweet, and sour.

• Now add the roasted root vegetables, combine everything gently, and let the mixture stew, covered, until the potatoes and sweet potatoes are cooked through, about 15 minutes. Add the peas at the very last moment. Check the balance of seasonings again before you serve the dish.

Parsi Ratatouille

Some summers ago, we were fooling around with farmers' market trophies—ridge gourds, yellow squash, small eggplants with tight, bright purple skins, peppers and tomatoes in a range of colors. My chef friend David Tanis walked in on the scene of a large wok full of simmering vegetables and said, "Oh, *ratatouille Parsoise!*"

The idea is to combine the ingredients for a conventional ratatouille but to use Indian or pan-Asian squash and eggplants, though anything good and in season will work. Quantities are approximate. Make more than you think you'll need, because leftovers get better with standing; use them as a base for Eggs on Anything (page 89).

This can be cooked a little ahead and left to stand while other dishes are prepared. It can be served warm or at room temperature. *Serves 6 to 8.*

3 to 4 tablespoons light olive oil or peanut oil

2 to 3 fresh green or red chiles, slit to the stem

½ teaspoon (or more) cumin seeds

2 large onions, sliced

1 to 2 tablespoons Ginger-Garlic Paste (page 36)

1 teaspoon cayenne pepper or Indian chilly powder

3 to 4 large ripe tomatoes, coarsely chopped

4 tablespoons jaggery or brown sugar

1 teaspoon (or more) salt

1 pound eggplant, cut into small cubes

2 to 3 bell peppers (any color), cut into strips

1 pound Asian squash (ridge, sponge, snake gourd) or summer squash,
*   cut into small cubes*

- Heat the oil in a large skillet or wok. Add the chiles and sizzle for a moment until the skins blister. Add the cumin seeds and let them crackle. Add the onions and let them soften, stirring occasionally. Stir in the paste and the cayenne. After a few moments, add the tomatoes and jaggery and let the mixture cook down for a few minutes to a sauce consistency. Add the salt. Eggplant, peppers, and gourds or squash go in next, all tumbled together with the sauce. Add enough water to generate some steam and increase the heat to boil the sauce. Reduce the heat, cover the pan, and let the vegetables cook gently until they're completely tender, bathed in a thick, rich tomato sauce.

- Let the ratatouille stand if you have the time.

· · ·

Parsi Caponata: Follow the general idea of the ratatouille but leave out the squash and peppers. Cut the eggplant into small dice, and include 2 to 3 stalks of celery, chopped; a splash of wine vinegar; ½ cup golden raisins, if you like; and, at the end, a handful of rinsed capers. This is one of the few recipes in which I would use olive oil. Serve warm or at room temperature as a side dish, or put it on toast as a canapé.

Papri Claypot Stew | UMBARYU

Papri—hyacinth, or field, beans *(Dolichos lablab)*—appear at farmers' markets in the late summer. The first arrivals are small, celadon-colored crescent beans edged in bright purple. Filipino vendors are the usual growers. At least once a year, I make *umbaryu, papri* with other vegetables and *kavabs* cooked in a claypot to be opened at the table. The pungent and slightly bitter quality of *papri* is offset by the other ingredients. In rural Gujarat, *umbaryu* is made in the cooler months in a clay water pot, mango leaves stuffed into the opening, sealed with straw and cooked outdoors in embers in an earth oven. The everyday Parsi treatment of *papri* is to cook it with meat (it can be added to *kharu gos,* for example), an average weekday dinner dish; but since we don't have it that often, I like to do it up, adding everything but the mango leaves and straw. *Umbaryu* originates from the Surat region, where Hindu cooks know it as *undhyu,* meaning "upside down," referring to the need to turn the disinterred claypot upside down to serve its contents. The Parsi version, *umbaryu,* refers to the threshold, *umbar,* beyond which the pit was dug in the kitchen yard. Except for the added meat, the Parsi version differs little from the Hindu.

If you can't get hyacinth beans, you can substitute Romano (runner) beans. Serve with thick yogurt, Chapatis (page 44), and, as we do, some sliced cucumbers with lime and salt. *Serves 8.*

> *12 to 16 (about) meatballs (page 116; optional)*
> *1 pound tender field beans (papri), the edges destrung on both sides,*
>   *or Romano beans, destrung if necessary*
> *1 (6-inch-long) unpeeled sweet potato, cut into ½-inch-thick rounds*
> *2 to 3 small Chinese or Japanese eggplants, cut crosswise into 1-inch-thick rounds*
> *6 to 8 tiny potatoes*
> *3 to 4 small heads of garlic, left whole*
> *1 bunch of green onions, tops and all, cut into 2-inch segments*
> *2 organic bananas, peel and all, cut into 1-inch segments*
> *2 teaspoons Sambhar Masala (page 37)*
> *2 teaspoons Dhana Jiru (page 38)*
> *1 teaspoon ajwain seeds*
> *4 to 6 green chiles*
> *1 teaspoon ground turmeric*
> *2 to 3 tablespoons vegetable oil*
> *2 teaspoons (or more) salt*

- If you're making *umbaryu* for meat eaters and including the meatballs *(kavabs),* make them small and brown them without cooking them through.

- Heat the oven to 350 degrees.

- In a large bowl, mix together the field beans, sweet potatoes, eggplants, tiny potatoes, garlic, green onions, bananas, *sambhar masala, dhana jiru, ajwain* seeds, chiles, turmeric, oil, and salt. Add the *kavabs* last and mix them in very gently so as not to break them. (If you have vegetarian eaters, cook and serve the *kavabs* separately.) Pile everything into a clay casserole with a tight-fitting lid. We use the kind you roast chicken in or a French bean pot.

- Cover and bake for about 1 hour. The beans must be cooked to sepia-colored softness. Resist the temptation to undercook them. If you do, they will taste nasty, but all you need to do to correct that is to cook them longer. You know the beans are done when they are completely soft.

- Bring to the table in the claypot. Remove the lid at the very last moment.

• • •

Note: Umbaryu is good theater when opened at the table right after it comes out of the oven, but like many things, it's really better the next day, after the flavors have coalesced.

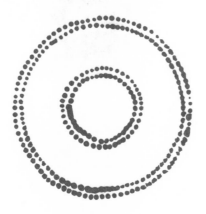

સેલડ

———◆———

SALADS

Nearly every vegetable stall in Bombay has a small section devoted to lettuce, or *salit*. It's usually a delicate leaf lettuce and, as often as not, it sits neglected and wilting through the heat of the day. In my childhood, *salit* appeared as a restrained border for sliced beets, tomatoes, cucumbers, and onions—the green salad of so many Bombay restaurant menus—or as a surrounding garnish for mounds of mayonnaise-dressed meat, fish, or vegetables; either way, perfunctory appearances. I knew only one public place that served just lettuce, freshly picked, with oil and vinegar. This was my parents' club, which ran a magnificently polyglot kitchen.

Salads by that name entered Parsi cuisine in the nineteenth century, which saw a shift in our general domestic style from Hindu-influenced to European. It's not as though Parsi cooking shunned raw vegetables entirely, but they appeared in small amounts as accents to the main event. As Parsi menus began to expand to allow in the food of anywhere at all, salads became more popular, though lettuce as the central theme was slow in coming. But now it's here. Vegetable stalls in Bombay now sell rocket (arugula) and radicchio and carefully grown boutique greens. In return for all the questions I ask about Parsi food, one of the things I'm most asked for in Bombay is advice about green salad. This should be neither surprising nor anomalous. Mainstream American cooks saw salad in terms of gelatin and mayonnaise, with lettuce as a plate liner, until after World War II. Other cuisines, too, have become salad conscious, eating it for pleasure and excitement, not just to appease the Goddess of Roughage. One generation's eccentricities become another generation's traditions. If a Parsi serves salad, eventually it becomes Parsi food.

All through my childhood, I loved salad and felt there was never enough of it, at home or at school. One of the great joys of setting up my own kitchen many years ago in Baltimore was the ability to indulge in green salad—just lettuce, oil, and vinegar— a pleasure that has intensified over the years with the immense variety of greens, oils, and vinegars now available even in supermarkets all over the United States. This chapter offers the merest sampling of some salads from the Parsi cuisine of my childhood, but we'll begin with a discussion of my household favorite, a green salad, offering not a recipe but loose directions.

Green Salad

Nowadays, every well-stocked grocery in Bombay carries extra-virgin olive oil, but in my childhood, olive oil—French—came in small bottles from the chemist (drugstore in the United States), where it was sold for cosmetic or medicinal use. Cosmopolitan Parsi households kept it on hand for mayonnaise or vinaigrettes. The olive-oil belt ends in Iran, where other vegetable oils and clarified butter take over, so it isn't surprising that the use of olive oil isn't an intrinsic part of Parsi cuisine. There's a general supposition that olive oil doesn't go with Indian food, and that therefore a salad dressed with it would add a jarring note. Possibly. With many dishes, it might be dissonant. But after thinking about Mediterranean cuisines and their many once-Persian meat and vegetable dishes made with olive oil, I've changed my mind. Now I use olive oil freely in salads and some vegetable dishes.

In our house, salad is a part of nearly every lunch and dinner. Because we eat salad as a separate course, we don't worry about any clash of cuisines. Moreover, we are lucky to be able to play with endless combinations of oils and vinegars to strike just the right note. Where olive oil might not work with a particular Parsi dish, I use avocado or rice bran oil, or various nut oils—such as walnut, pistachio, or macadamia—

and I've recently started experimenting with argan oil from Morocco (pressed from the nuts of the argan tree, *Argania spinosa*), which seems particularly successful with watercress. My favorite vinegars for a salad in an otherwise purely Parsi sequence of courses are based on rice, coconut, or cane—or I use one of the slightly sweet Austrian vinegars or a good balsamic. Korean vinegars made with apples and pears are a fairly recent addition to the already overloaded oil-and-vinegar division of our kitchen. Try citrus and other fruit juices, such as passion fruit—or even the extracted pulp from fresh tamarind (page 42)—as the acid component in your vinaigrette.

Russian Salad

Like Italian eggs and Irish stew, Russian salad has become a Parsi standard. It also appears in modern Persian cooking as Salade Olivier. This is about as close to salad as Parsis of the previous generation ever wanted to come. It's a delicious combination of cubed potatoes, beets, carrots, peas, and green beans coated in a mustardy mayonnaise, always homemade. In my aunt Mani's house in Ootacamund, Russian salad would inevitably accompany a salted cut of meat known as "hump," which resembled corned beef and which I've never seen anywhere else in the world; in my mother's house, Russian salad usually accompanied ox tongue, also salted.

Ingredient quantities are elastic and can be increased or decreased without dire consequences. Beets have a way of taking over the color of the dish, so if bright pink bothers you, try Russian salad with Chioggia or golden beets, or even white ones if you can find them. Make your own mayonnaise if you can. It's easy, and tastes leagues better than anything in a jar.

Serve Russian Salad with tongue, ham, or cold chicken, or with fish, lobster, or shrimp. *Serves 6 to 8.*

2 to 3 medium potatoes

1 to 2 carrots

2 medium beets

1 cup tiny peas, the smaller the better

¼ pound green beans, cut into ¼-inch lengths

1 to 2 cups mayonnaise

½ to 1 teaspoon Colman's dry mustard

Chopped green chile, or cayenne pepper or Indian chilly powder (optional)

- Boil each vegetable separately in salted water until tender (peas should be barely blanched). Peel and cube the potatoes, carrots, and beets. Combine the mustard and mayonnaise and toss with the vegetables just before serving so that the mixture doesn't get lurid-looking too soon. Be sure that the mayonnaise is as you want it before you mix it with the vegetables. Add enough chile to give it that Parsi punch.

Beet Salad | BEETROOT NU SALAD

The secret to this Parsi beet salad is one of our hidden favorite seasonings, Worcestershire sauce—often overused, but in this salad, a lively addition of pungency and sweetness. The beets can be boiled, steamed, or baked. Served in my mother's house, this salad had a ring of Romaine-type lettuce standing all round it. You can lightly dress greens of your choice and mound the dressed beets in the middle. *Serves 4 to 6.*

> *3 to 4 cups cubed or sliced cooked beets*
> *½ to 1 cup paper-thin slices of sweet onion, red or white*
> *2 tablespoons olive oil*
> *Splash of cane, malt, or sherry vinegar*
> *Few shakes of Worcestershire sauce*
> *Salt to taste*
> *Lightly dressed salad greens, for garnish*

- Combine the beets and onion, saving a few onion rings for the top. Dress to taste with the oil, vinegar, Worcestershire sauce, and salt. This can be done several hours ahead. Serve surrounded with dressed salad greens and garnished with the reserved onion rings.

Cabbage Salad with Lime and Mint

Cabbage is a great boon in hot climates, where lettuces wilt if they make it to a market at all. Cabbage salad was one of my early favorites. The version I had at boarding school was something akin to coleslaw, with a cooked flour-and-vinegar dressing. At home, it was usually dressed with lime, salt, and chiles. Here, we often add a little olive oil. *Serves 6.*

> *1 sweet red or white onion, sliced paper-thin*
> *1 pound green cabbage, finely shredded*
> *2 to 3 fresh red or green chiles, finely chopped*

½ cup shredded fresh mint leaves
1 cup chopped fresh coriander (cilantro) stems and leaves
3 tablespoons (about) olive oil (optional)
Juice of 2 (or more) limes
Salt to taste
Granulated sugar to taste (optional)

- If the onion is at all acrid, sprinkle the slices with salt and let them sit for at least half an hour before rinsing them and going on with the recipe.

- Combine the onion with the cabbage, chiles, mint, and fresh coriander. Add the olive oil, if you like. Generously squeeze lime juice over the salad, adding salt, and sugar to taste if you want it. Serve right away so that the cabbage keeps its crunch and the coriander doesn't turn olive-green from the acid. It'll still taste fine after a while, but will have turned into a pickle of sorts.

TWO WATERCRESS SALADS

We know it's spring when our favorite watercress vendor comes to the Alemany market. She tucks herself into a corner where her regulars are sure to find her, and we buy at least two beautifully groomed bunches a week until her season ends, which she kindly announces a week ahead.

The first salad here is an unusual watercress and raw turnip combination; the second is a more tropical treatment.

Watercress and Turnip Salad

Serves 4.

1 bunch of infant turnips (about 10) or radishes, finely sliced, skin and all; or 1
*   heaping cup peeled and sliced or chopped fresh water chestnuts*
1 bunch watercress
1 to 2 green chiles, finely chopped
½ young red onion, finely chopped
½ cup fresh coriander (cilantro) leaves
3 tablespoons olive oil
1 tablespoon (or more) lime juice to taste
Salt to taste

· Combine the turnips, watercress, green chiles, onion, and fresh coriander. Dress with the olive oil, lime juice, and salt. That's all.

Chopped Watercress Salad with Ginger Vinaigrette

The vinaigrette for this salad uses rice bran or avocado oil for an interesting change. *Serves 4 to 6.*

1 small shallot, minced
2 teaspoons minced peeled fresh ginger
2 tablespoons rice vinegar or light cane vinegar
Pinch (or more) of salt
1 to 2 bunches watercress
1 firm ripe avocado
4 tablespoons rice bran oil or avocado oil
½ cup diced hard ripe mango
½ cup diced cucumber

· Let the shallot and ginger macerate in the vinegar while you go about preparing the salad ingredients. Add a pinch of salt.

· Chop the watercress coarsely, stems and all. Peel and cube the avocado.

· Combine the oil with the vinegar, shallot, and ginger mixture. Taste for salt. Toss the watercress, mango, and cucumber together with the dressing, leaving the avocado for the last so that it doesn't get mashed up and nasty-looking. Using your fingers, mix the avocado very lightly into the topmost layer of the salad after you've checked the salt and acid balance.

· Serve at once.

Carrot and Raisin Salad | GAJAR NU SALAD

My mother used honey to great advantage in two things: this carrot salad and her famous "Italian" eggs (page 58). You can leave out the extra sweetness if the carrots and raisins together seem sweet enough to you. The Hindu Gujarati version of this salad might add a teaspoon or so of popped mustard seeds. Adjust the quantities of chile and lime juice to suit your palate. *Serves 4 to 6.*

1 pound carrots, grated
1 cup freshly grated coconut (see page 40; optional)

1 (or more) finely chopped green chile
½ cup raisins
½ cup (or more) chopped fresh coriander (cilantro) stems and leaves
Juice of 3 (or more) limes
Salt to taste
1 to 2 tablespoons honey

- Toss the carrots and the coconut, if using, with the green chile, raisins, fresh coriander, lime juice, salt, and—because it's my mother's way—the honey.

- To keep the texture lively, make this salad fairly close to the time you serve it. Leftovers are good but not as bright.

Corn, Green Mango, and Coconut Salad

Home from boarding school, I would go around "spending the day" with friends and relatives. Spending the day involved showing up before lunch, which one expected to be extra-good, lolling about in the afternoon in the fashion of the house, then tea, either at home or out somewhere, or a matinee, or a swim before we were returned to our parents. My mother's older sister, Perviz, would sometimes take me to Elephanta Caves, where I put her on the spot by asking her to explain to an eleven-year-old what a lingam was. The most memorable of her lunches featured a corn salad. The corn we get in the United States is a lot more tender and sweet than the Indian and Mexican types, which are as chewy as they are flavorful.

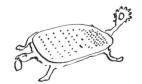

"TORTOISE" GRATER
FOR VEGETABLES, WITH
A COCONUT GRATER
AT THE END

Corn salad is a particularly good accompaniment for crab or lobster, or for grilled or fried fish, shrimp, or squid. *Serves 4.*

3 ears cooked corn
1 small hard green mango
1 cup freshly grated coconut (see page 40)
½ cup finely chopped fresh coriander (cilantro) leaves and stems
1 to 2 fresh green or red chiles, very finely chopped
Juice of 1 to 2 limes
Salt to taste

- Cut the kernels off the cobs. Peel the mango and dice it into cubes the same size as the corn kernels. Measure out about ½ cup and save the rest for another use.

Combine the corn and mango with the coconut, fresh coriander, and chiles, and add lime juice and salt to taste. Serve the salad soon after it is made.

. . .

Note: Only fresh coconut will do. No substitutions. If you cannot find a sound coconut that tastes sweet when you open it, leave it out of the recipe and add about ½ cup finely chopped sweet red onion.

Cucumber and Ginger Salad

Nothing could be simpler than this cucumber salad, or a more perfect accompaniment for so many of the dishes in this book. The addition of a little finely minced ginger emphasizes the fresh clarity of salt and lime, that magic combination. *Serves 6.*

2 cucumbers (about 2 pounds)
Juice of 1 to 2 limes
Salt to taste
2 to 3 teaspoons finely chopped peeled fresh ginger
¼ cup shredded fresh mint leaves (optional)

- If the cucumbers are coated with wax, peel them. Halve the cucumbers lengthwise and remove the seeds if you don't like them. Cut the cucumbers into thin slices. Dress the slices with lime juice and salt. Add the ginger in small increments to taste; it doesn't take much to make an effect. Add mint just before serving, if you like. You might even want to add a drizzle of olive oil.

Smoky Eggplant Salad | VENGNA NU BHARAT

This eggplant salad can be found all the way across the Middle East to India. The seasonings might be different, but the idea is the same. The Parsi version, in keeping with our love for sweet things in savory guises, uses sugar, which I consider optional.

About ten years ago, when I was at lunch at an old friend's house in Bombay, she introduced me to this dazzling technique of smoking the salad after it was fully assembled, rather than roasting the eggplants over coals to char the skin. With or without this extra touch, *vengna nu bharat* can be offered with bits of flat bread or lettuce scoops before a meal, along with Creamy Panir (page 63) or a fresh goat cheese, or as a great adjunct to grilled fish or shrimp, Parsi style (page 96) or plain. *Serves 4 to 6, more as a first course.*

1 large ripe eggplant (1 ½ to 2 pounds)
1 sweet onion, red or white
2 firm ripe tomatoes, peeled and chopped (optional)
2 to 3 cloves garlic, finely chopped (optional)
1 to 3 green chiles, finely chopped
1 cup coarsely chopped fresh coriander (cilantro) leaves and stems
Salt to taste
Juice of 2 or 3 limes
2 teaspoons (or more) granulated sugar (optional)
1 to 2 teaspoons ghee or olive oil

- Heat the oven to 375 degrees.
- Prick the eggplant in a couple of places with a fork so that it doesn't explode in the oven. Roast it on a baking sheet until it's soft and collapsed, about 40 minutes.
- Halve the eggplant. Scrape the pulp into a bowl. Halve the onion, trim off the top and bottom, and peel off the skin. Then peel off the outside layer of one onion half. This layer forms an onion cup that will be used later in the recipe. Set it aside and chop the rest of the onion.
- To the eggplant, add the chopped onion, optional tomato and garlic, chiles, and fresh coriander. Season to taste with salt and lime juice, as well as sugar, if you like.
- Place the onion cup on top of the eggplant mixture. Put a lump of live charcoal in the onion cup (see the note) and drizzle the ghee over it to generate lots of smoke. Cover the bowl tightly with a pot lid or a plate and leave undisturbed for at least 15 minutes. Remove the spent coal and the onion cup before serving at room temperature. This is one of the most dazzling easy effects you can imagine.

• • •

Note: Do not use instant-lighting charcoal, or charcoal lit with lighter fluid, for this recipe.

Pomelo and Coconut Salad

I first tasted this combination at my friend Gool's house, where her mother served it to us for lunch when we came back from college. It is a salad you can make only in winter, when pomelos come into season. Grapefruit would seem to be the logical substitute, but it doesn't work as well. Pomelos (accent on the first syllable) look exactly like giant grapefruit, but they have a character and internal structure all their own, not at all uniform. They may seem dry while you're working on them, but within the segments, each little capsule is bursting with juice. See the note for tips on sectioning pomelos. *Serves 4 to 6.*

> *1 large pink or white pomelo, sectioned*
> *1 cup (or more) freshly grated mature coconut, cut into long shreds, or*
>   *a julienne of young coconut (see page 40)*
> *½ cup chopped fresh coriander (cilantro) leaves*
> *2 to 3 green chiles, finely chopped*

- Set out the pomelo sections in a single layer on a platter. Sprinkle with the coconut. Strew with the fresh coriander and green chiles. No need for anything else. If the pieces of pomelo tend to untidiness, some large, some small, some crumbly, forget the decorative layout and lightly toss everything together.

· · ·

Pomelo Salad with Avocado: When avocado joins the picture, the combination of textures is sublime. Add avocado in pieces compatible with the pomelo—slices if you have sections, cubes if you're working with random chunks. If you add avocado, you'll need to add a little salt, too.

Pomelo Salad with Greens: You can use this salad as the topping for a bed of watercress, curly endive, or escarole lightly dressed with a vinaigrette of rice-bran oil and rice vinegar.

Pomelo and Crab Salad: For a princely meal, serve with a generous mound of freshly picked crabmeat. Accompany with warm boiled or roasted potatoes.

Note: There are several approaches to sectioning pomelos. The restaurant way, which ensures tidy even sections, results in more wastage than a home kitchen needs. My way is to peel off the pomelo skin in quarters, pull apart the sections, cut off the top edge with a sharp knife, and then peel the membrane off. If you're lucky, you'll get perfect sections free of pith and membrane. I've found that a pomelo that has been sitting around for a week or two as a splendid, golden object of contemplation is much easier to work with than one fresh off the tree. To make things even easier, if you have the time, peel the entire fruit and let it sit in its membrane underwear for a few hours or overnight, so that it's dry before pulling apart.

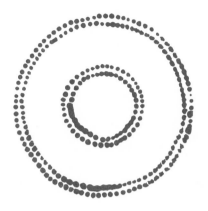

અચાર

CHUTNEYS, PICKLES, AND RELISHES

There are two schools of thought on pickles and chutneys. My mother thought that a well-seasoned dish didn't need to be embellished. My father was in the other camp. He loved having at least three different pickles and chutneys on hand at all times because every dish, however well seasoned, could be made even more exciting. I'm somewhere in the middle. To me, chutneys and pickles are like jewelry for food. Sometimes you want to make a strong statement, sometimes a restrained one.

Kachumbars and raitas are another matter. Where a pickle or chutney is an optional adjunct to a meal, a well-chosen *kachumbar* or raita can be an essential accessory, just the thing needed to balance taste and texture. As with a salsa, there are dishes you wouldn't dream of eating without a *kachumbar*. Parsis have two basic ones—a plain onion relish, and one made sweet and sour with jaggery and tamarind. Raitas, or *raitus* in Gujarati, offer balance and contrast in taste and temperature. You'll find four of my favorites, all easy to make.

Chutney and *pickle* are almost interchangeable terms, covering a wide territory. In India, the word *pickle* generally implies the use of oil as a preservative, while *chutney* generally, but not always, implies the use of acid. Both chutneys and pickles can be quickly made or extremely labor-intensive. Some are made to be eaten at once, like the quick lime juice pickles (see Parsi Crudités, page 53). Others keep for a few days or a week—the Date and Tamarind Chutney (page 230) and the Fresh Turmeric and Ginger Pickle (page 234), for example. Some, like the Eggplant Pickle

(page 235), go on for a year; and some, like the fruit-crammed Parsi Wedding Pickle (page 237), actually a chutney, last for years. The best thing to do is to explore these recipes throughout the year. Make the tomato chutney and eggplant pickle in summer, the wedding pickle in the fall and winter, and delicious Parsi Green Chutney (page 227) any time at all.

CLAY JAR, USED FOR
STORING PICKLES

The chapter ends with a recipe for an unusual jam, made with bottle gourd, which Parsis eat as an accent for savory dishes, as well as on toast.

TWO KACHUMBARS

In my mother's house, and probably her mother's, whenever rice was served, there would always be a little bowl of *kachumbar,* sometimes known as *kachubar.* Parsi cooking lays no claim to this. By this or any other name, we share it with several other Indian cuisines.

Kachumbar immediately makes us aware of how much Indian and Mexican food have in common. What is *kachumbar* if not a *salsa cruda* composed of onions, tomatoes, fresh coriander (cilantro), and chiles, all as finely chopped as the cook desires? Parsis have another type of *kachumbar,* as well, in which onions, green chiles, and fresh coriander are bathed in a sweet-sour dressing made of tamarind and jaggery. *Kachumbar* and raitas aren't really supposed to be eaten as salads, so in India, they're served in far smaller quantities than the average Californian would be happy with. The size of the dish and spoon tip you off to how much you're supposed to take (very little).

Simple Onion Kachumbar

This recipe is put together in less than five minutes. It's the usual accompaniment to curry and rice, *pulaos* and biryanis all over India. It also makes a first-rate quasi-mignonette sauce for raw oysters or clams. Any *kachumbar* is best eaten within an hour or two of making it. No need to throw out leftovers, though; just realize that they won't taste as vivid. *Serves 4 to 6.*

> *1 large sweet red or white onion*
> *Salt*
> *1 to 2 firm ripe seeded tomatoes, chopped (optional)*
> *½ cucumber, seeded and finely chopped (optional)*
> *2 to 4 green chiles, very finely chopped*
> *½ cup chopped fresh coriander (cilantro) leaves and stems*
> *Lime juice, vinegar, yogurt, or coconut milk (optional)*

- If you're making a *kachumbar* with nothing more than onion, slice it finely. If you're using tomatoes and cucumbers, chop the onion. If the onion seems strong, sprinkle it with salt and let it stand for at least half an hour before proceeding with the recipe.

- Squeeze and strain the salty liquid out of the onion by pressing against the bottom of a strainer. Taste a bit. You might need to rinse off the salt. Mix the onion, tomatoes and cucumber if using, chiles, and fresh coriander together close to serving time. Serve as is or dressed with lime juice, vinegar, yogurt, or coconut milk. If you use coconut milk, you'll need a little squeeze of lime with it. Taste for salt and add if necessary.

Sweet-Sour Kachumbar | GOR AMLI NU KACHUMBAR

This *kachumbar* brilliantly offsets anything with lentils. Serve with *dhansak* (page 178), *masur* (page 180), or *channa ni dar* (page 182)—the traditional partners—or as a sauce for grilled pork, chicken, fish, or shrimp. One person I know likes it as a dip for potato or corn chips.

You can make it a couple of hours or more ahead of time, but in that case, leave the fresh coriander to the last so that it doesn't get sodden. *Serves 6.*

> *1 large sweet red onion, finely chopped*
> *Salt (optional)*
> *1 walnut-size ball (or more) jaggery or 2 to 4 tablespoons (or more) dark brown sugar*
> *1 walnut-size ball compressed tamarind (see page 42)*

1 medium cucumber, seeded and finely chopped
½ to 1 cup coarsely chopped fresh coriander (cilantro) leaves and stems, to taste
2 to 4 green chiles, very finely chopped

- Taste the onion after you chop it. If it is at all strong, let it sit in a hefty sprinkle of salt for at least half an hour. Press out the salty liquid before proceeding, rinsing the onion if necessary.

- Jaggery is sometimes very soft, sometimes rock-hard. If it's hard, crush it with a rolling pin or rubber mallet and soften just as much as you're going to need in a bowl with a little boiling water.

- In a small bowl, cover the tamarind with ½ to ¾ cup boiling water and let it sit at least 30 minutes. Stir the mixture well and push it through a stainless steel mesh strainer. Return the residue to the bowl, barely cover it with hot water, and push it through the strainer again. Be sure you get all the tamarind off the bottom of the strainer.

- In a medium bowl, combine the onion, jaggery, tamarind, cucumber, fresh coriander, and chiles. Taste for salt, sweetness, acid, and heat. This isn't a salad, so you should feel a distinct kick. The consistency is slightly soupy.

. . .

Kachumbar with Green Mango: In season, add ½ to 1 cup peeled hard green mango in fine dice.

Note: Two shortcuts for a sweet-sour *kachumbar:* one is to use commercial tamarind pulp, the Thai brands being superior; the other one is to use balsamic vinegar instead of tamarind and omit the sugar.

FOUR RAITAS

A raita is a boldly flavored mixture of yogurt and vegetables or sometimes fruit, served with other dishes for contrast and emphasis. With raita (*raitu* in Gujarati, *raita* in Hindi) we see the links between Parsi and Mughlai, or courtly northern Indian, food. Raitas are often served with *pulaos* or biryanis as an accent rather than as a salad, to cool rather than to provoke. Raitas in India are a teaspoon item. In keeping with our California love for vegetable matter in larger amounts, we serve all raitas in larger bowls with bigger spoons, with some exceptions noted below.

Here are four favorites. The number of people served depends on what else is going on in the meal.

Banana Raita | KERA NU RAITU

This was my mother's favorite raita. The combination of bananas and mustard sounds odd, but it really works. This is a small-spoon raita for *pulaos* and biryanis. *Serves 4 to 6.*

> *1 to 2 teaspoons Colman's dry mustard*
> *1 cup plain yogurt*
> *1 to 2 firm ripe bananas (no green on the skin)*
> *Salt to taste (optional)*

- Starting with 1 teaspoon, whisk Colman's powdered mustard into the yogurt until you get that wasabi feeling in the back of your head. The yogurt will taste a bit bitter. Don't worry; just let it sit for 2 hours or so. Close to serving time, slice the bananas into the yogurt-mustard mixture. Taste. You might want to add a tiny bit of salt.

Cucumber Raita | KAKRI NU RAITU

Cucumber raita needs no introduction. Is there anyone who doesn't love it? *Serves 4 to 6.*

> *1 large cucumber (about 1 pound)*
> *Salt*
> *2 cups plain yogurt, lightly whisked*
> *½ sweet red onion, finely chopped (optional)*
> *1 to 2 green chiles, finely chopped (optional)*
> *½ cup shredded mint leaves (optional)*
> *½ cup chopped fresh coriander (cilantro) stems and leaves (optional)*
> *Cayenne pepper or Indian chilly powder and pounded toasted cumin seeds,*
>   *for garnish (optional)*

- Peel and seed the cucumber. Grate or slice it and sprinkle it with salt. Let it sit for half an hour before tipping it into a colander or strainer and pressing all the water out. Taste a piece of cucumber. If it's unbearably salty, give the cucumber a quick rinse and press out all the water again. Stir the cucumber into the yogurt. Now is the time to add onion and chiles, if you're using them. Taste for salt after the cucumber and yogurt have sat together for at least half an hour. Mint and/or fresh coriander may be added just before serving. The classic garnish is a dusting of cayenne or Indian chilly powder and some pounded toasted cumin.

Onion Raita | KANDA NU RAITU

Onion raita has the perfect punch to serve with *pulaos* and biryanis. It's good with any grilled meat or fish, too. Make it with a red onion for more color. *Serves 4 to 6.*

> *1 large sweet red or white onion*
> *Salt*
> *1 to 2 fresh red or green chiles (optional)*
> *½ cup chopped fresh coriander (cilantro) stems and leaves (optional)*
> *1 ½ cups (about) plain yogurt, lightly whisked*

- Chop or slice the onion finely. Sprinkle the onion with salt and let it stand for half an hour. Squeeze out the brine. Taste. Rinse off excess salt if necessary.

- Chop in a green or red chile or two and some coriander leaves, if you like, and combine everything with plain yogurt, going for a fairly slack consistency.

Seared Ginger Raita | ADU NU RAITU

This is a raita I love. It has different personalities depending on whether you make it with raw ginger, seared ginger, or a combination of both, which I like best. This is one you can play with.

Ginger raita is wonderful with plain rice or *pulaos* and biryanis, or with any simply grilled fish or fried shrimp. *Serves 2 to 8.*

> *1 ½ cups plain yogurt, lightly whisked*
> *¼ cup very finely chopped peeled fresh ginger*
> *Salt to taste*
> *1 tablespoon peanut oil or sesame oil (not toasted sesame oil)*
> *1 to 2 fresh red or green chiles, slit to the stem, or dried chiles, left whole or seeded*
> *1 branch curry leaves (about 6 to 10)*
> *¼ cup finely julienned peeled fresh ginger*
> *½ teaspoon brown mustard seeds*
> *Chopped fresh coriander (cilantro) leaves, for garnish*

- Spoon the yogurt into a 3- to 4-cup mixing or serving bowl. Add the chopped ginger and salt to taste.

- Heat the oil in a small pan over medium-high heat. Add the chiles and let them sizzle for a minute. Follow with the curry leaves and when they begin to change color, add the julienned ginger and toss it about on high heat until it begins to brown and caramelize. Quickly throw in the mustard seeds. The moment they begin to pop and fly about, tip the entire contents of the pan into the yogurt. Stir well. Let rest for half an hour or so before serving. Check for salt again. Garnish with fresh coriander. This can be made some hours ahead and kept cool until serving time. It will keep well for a couple of days.

Parsi Green Chutney | LILI CHATNI

In some lucky houses, *lili chatni* appears on the table at every meal. It's that addictive, like salt and lime. Nearly every community in India has some kind of green chutney made with fresh coriander, mint, green chiles, and lime, but we think ours is best, as do many non-Parsis. I use my mother's formula, but she likes things sweet rather than sour, so I adjust away from sugar toward acid. Green chutney is one of those things you want to have left over. It keeps for at least a week refrigerated and can be successfully thawed. (Note, I didn't say "frozen." Anything can be successfully frozen.) In my mother's house *lili chatni* was ground on a masala stone, the scent of the bruised ingredients so sharp and strong that they made you giddy with anticipation. Next to a stone, a wet-dry grinder gives the best results (see page 30).

This recipe makes about a cup of *lili chatni,* enough to serve with *khara ras chaval* (page 114), mild and savory soupy meat over fluffy white rice. For Fish in Banana-Leaf Parcels (page 100) and for Shirin Sabavala's fabulous Green Chutney Soufflé (page 88), you will need to double the recipe. If you're using a Multigrinder, the junior Sumeet so practical for everyday use, successive small batches are unbelievably quick and easy to put together. I can't recommend this tool enough.

We love green chutney with Creamy Panir (page 63), Bellwether Farms ricotta, or Manouri cheese from Greece and just-warmed whole wheat tortillas or Chapatis (page 44). *Serves 6 to 12.*

½ cup grated fresh or frozen coconut (see page 40)
1 cup fresh coriander (cilantro) leaves and stems
¼ teaspoon cumin seeds, pounded
12 fresh mint leaves
3 green chiles
2 cloves garlic, coarsely chopped
1 teaspoon (or more) salt
Juice of ½ lime (or more)
1½ teaspoons granulated sugar

- If you're starting with fresh coconut, remove the tough brown rind using a heavy-duty peeler or a short, sharp knife. Grate it manually or cut it up into small pieces and throw it into a food processor or wet-dry grinder with the fresh coriander, cumin, mint, chiles, and garlic. Add salt, starting with 1 teaspoon, lime juice to taste, and sugar. If you're using a food processor, add just enough water to keep the blades moving. Ideally, the chutney should be smooth, thick, and solid enough to stand on a plate. Although the taste won't be any different, the chutney you get with a food processor will be thinner and coarser in texture. Taste the chutney. You want it to be hot, sour, sweet, and salty.

• • •

Green Chutney Sandwiches: My all-time-favorite snacky thing is a sandwich of green chutney enclosed in two thin buttered slices of good firm white bread. Trim off the crusts, if you like. This is guaranteed to make any Indian person very happy.

TWO GREEN MANGO CHUTNEYS

Make these chutneys when you can find hard green mangoes. These mangoes should be white inside, distinguishing them from the mangoes picked to ripen over time, which are yellow, regardless of how hard they are in the bin. In Bombay, young green mangoes signal a change in season from the cooler winter months to the seemingly endless hot months before the monsoon. When they appear on trees or at markets, it's pickle- and chutney-making time. My mother with her tiny household didn't do much pickle making, but with my father's family full of ardent chutney and pickle makers, she didn't have to, since my grandmother and aunts kept us generously supplied with his favorites. What they couldn't make, we bought from Poonjiaji's, Parsi makers and exporters of the famous Major Grey's mango chutney.

The first chutney here is fresh, to be eaten immediately as a dip or a sauce; the other is the mango chutney many non-Indians think of as an integral part of an Indian meal. For both of them, you need hard, green mangoes picked with no intention of their ever ripening.

Markets in the United States don't yet sell embryonic green mangoes, their seeds barely formed, but in markets where there are enough buyers we are now seeing larger immature specimens with seeds. Look in Indian, Southeast Asian, and Latin American shopping areas.

Fresh Green Mango Chutney | KACHI KERI NI CHATNI

The idea for this fresh green mango chutney came from a cooking class my mother took in June 1941. Her notes refer to this stunning thing as simply "Chutney." I've substituted ginger for garlic and jaggery for granulated sugar and added some fresh coriander.

This chutney makes an exciting dip for *bhajjias,* fried morsels of vegetables or cheese (page 57); or try it as a sauce for grilled fish or shrimp, served as an hors d'oeuvre or a main course. *Makes about 1 ½ cups.*

1 ½ cups peeled and roughly cut-up hard green mango
1 to 2 green chiles, coarsely chopped
2 teaspoons chopped peeled fresh ginger
½ teaspoon cumin seeds, pounded
¼ cup coarsely chopped fresh coriander (cilantro) leaves and stems
A few fresh mint leaves
2 to 3 teaspoons jaggery or brown sugar
Salt to taste
Lime juice (optional)

- Combine the mango, chiles, ginger, cumin, fresh coriander, mint, and jaggery in a food processor or wet-dry grinder. Pulse until you get a smooth sauce. Adjust seasoning with salt and lime juice.

Major Ordle's Green Mango Chutney | KERI NI CHATNI

Over the years, so many people have wailed about trying to make mango chutneys that don't turn out anything like Major Grey's. Ripe mangoes will never give you the correct texture. This recipe produces superior mango chutney, but you have to start with fruit that's unambiguously white when you cut it open. Mangoes and vinegars can vary in acidity, so start with 2 cups of sugar but have more handy for adjustments. *Makes about 1 ½ quarts.*

3 to 4 large hard green mangoes (about 4 pounds)
2 ½ cups (or more) raw, unwashed sugar or turbinado sugar (or half light brown,
 half granulated)
2 teaspoons (or more) salt
2 cups cane, coconut, or malt vinegar

2 (or more) teaspoons cayenne pepper or Indian chilly powder
¼ cup very thinly sliced peeled fresh ginger
¼ cup very thinly sliced garlic
2 (2-inch-long) sticks cinnamon or cassia
4 whole cloves

- Peel a mango. Cut it into 3 pieces (consult the diagram on page 243 for the easiest way): the 2 "cheeks" and the central part containing the seed. Put the cheeks flat side down on a cutting board and cut them into roughly ¼-inch-thick slices. Cut around the seed. Slice those pieces, too. Keep going, peeling and slicing the mangoes, until you have about 6 cups. If you have a kitchen scale, weigh them. You should have about 2 pounds.

- Put the sugar, salt, vinegar, cayenne, ginger, garlic, cinnamon, and cloves in a heavy nonreactive pan. Bring to a boil; reduce the heat and stir until the sugar has dissolved. Cook about 5 minutes more, then add the sliced mangoes. Combine well. Bring to a boil again; reduce the heat to very low and simmer, uncovered, until the mangoes are translucent and the chutney looks like a thin jam. This should take 45 minutes to an hour. Stir gently from time to time to keep things from sticking, but not so much that the slices of mango get massacred. Some will turn mushy, but you'll still have some texture in the chutney from the ones that don't. Remove from the stove to cool.

- After the chutney has cooled down enough that it doesn't burn your mouth, taste it. You might want to add more salt, vinegar, sugar, or cayenne. Adjust the taste to suit you, then bring the chutney to a boil again; cook it for 2 to 3 minutes more and let it cool again.

- Bottle when cool, or pour the hot chutney into sterilized jars and cap when cool.

Date and Tamarind Chutney | KHAJUR NI CHATNI

The word we know as *tamarind* came from the Arabic *tamar-i-hind,* the "date of India." Date of India or date of California, or anywhere, makes a perfect chutney. Versions of date and tamarind chutney appear in several South Asian cuisines, all the way down to Sri Lanka. It's not necessary to use Medjools for this chutney, though of course they'd do very well.

Fried cubes of Creamy Panir (page 63) or any soft cheese are heavenly with date chutney. *Makes about 2 cups.*

1 cup pitted dates
1 cup thick prepared tamarind pulp (see page 42)
¼ cup (or more) jaggery or brown sugar
Salt to taste
½ teaspoon cayenne pepper or Indian chilly powder
½ teaspoon (or more) cumin seeds, pounded

- If the dates seem hard and chewy, soften them by covering with boiling water and soaking until soft, at least an hour.

- When the dates are soft, drain and combine with the tamarind pulp, jaggery, salt, and cayenne in a food processor bowl. Pulse until smooth, adding just enough water to keep the blades moving. The chutney should be thick and spoonable, though you can thin it out to use as a dipping sauce. Strain if you want to remove any gritty bits of date skin. Then add the pounded cumin. Taste for salt and sugar. Let stand for a few hours to allow the flavors to blend before serving.

- Since this is an uncooked, water-based chutney, it should be refrigerated. I find it keeps well for up to a week.

Parsi Tomato Chutney | TAMOTA NI CHATNI

I've been making this chutney every summer for more than forty years. It's an easy recipe that lends itself to other fruit, like plums or peaches (see the variations). You'll find that it's ready to eat soon after you make it and equally good months later, though its character changes into something like a vintage marmalade. Unless you go through a lot of chutney or have a horde of chutney-loving friends, try to make no more than you can use in a year. The recipe quantities are only a guideline; exact amounts are less important than the total effect.

Serve this chutney with grilled meat or chicken, with salted ox tongue or ham, along with boiled potatoes and greens. I sneak it into sandwiches, too: Parsi omelets folded into chapatis spread with tomato chutney; little crustless tea sandwiches made with Creamy Panir (page 63) and chutney, either spread in bands or mixed together; or a grown-up version of the American peanut butter and jelly—peanut, almond, or cashew butter and tomato chutney on whole wheat bread. *Makes about 3 quarts.*

6 pounds ripe tomatoes, any color
1 cup finely julienned peeled fresh ginger
1 cup very thinly sliced garlic

3 cups (or more) cane, malt, or cider vinegar

1 to 2 cups raisins (optional)

4 cups (or more) turbinado sugar, or half light brown and half granulated sugar

3 tablespoons (or more) cayenne pepper or Indian chilly powder

1 (2-inch-long) stick cinnamon or cassia

8 whole cloves

1 tablespoon (or more) salt

Julienned or grated peel of 1 to 2 unsprayed oranges or tangerines (optional)

- Coarsely chop the tomatoes. Put them in a heavy nonreactive pan with the ginger, garlic, vinegar, raisins if you like, sugar, cayenne, cinnamon, cloves, and salt. Bring to a boil, stirring so that everything gets well combined; lower the heat and simmer, uncovered, stirring every now and then, until the chutney reaches the consistency of a soft jam. This may take up to 4 hours over very low heat, less if you're prepared to baby-sit the chutney with the heat turned up for quicker cooking. I've found that patience and the lowest heat leave you with a chutney that holds on to its tomatoey brightness.

- Adjust the balance of sugar, salt, and vinegar while the chutney is still warm, and add more cayenne if you want the chutney hotter. If you like, add the orange peel toward the end.

- You will need to fine-tune the balance, so let the chutney sit for a day before you bottle it, to allow the flavors to settle. Remember that this is a chutney—it should be forceful, declamatory. You want a chutney to light up your mouth, to have some punch. Sweet! Sour! Salty! Hot! The biggest mistake with chutney is to think of it as a spiced jam. Never leave out the salt or undersalt in the name of some diet deity. I tend to give the chutney away as soon as I make it, so I don't go to great lengths with the bottling process. I just put the jars and tops through the dishwasher and give them an extra jolt of boiling water before I fill them.

· · ·

Fruit Chutneys: Substitute tart plums or peaches for the tomatoes. In the fall and winter, try using apples, or Asian pears and cranberries, or just Asian pears. If you're using cranberries, you may want to leave out the raisins. In small quantities, say two or three cups of fruit, you can make this chutney in a flash, about half an hour.

Homemade Tomato Ketchup: Commercial ketchup is so reviled that we forget it started out as a delicious, exciting accent to many foods. In my childhood, we loved "tomato sauce," as we called it, in any form, commercial or homemade, and to this day, I have an unabashed yen for ketchup and French fries, a favorite Indian snack. The ingredients for the tomato chutney above also make a superlative ketchup, and nothing could be simpler. To make about 3 cups, start with about a quart of pureed tomatoes, leaving the seeds in for extra texture. Add about ⅓ cup sugar, white or light brown; ½ cup vinegar of your choice; 2 teaspoons ginger-garlic paste (or 3 cloves garlic and 1 finger-joint-size piece of ginger, chopped very finely); ¼ to ½ teaspoon Indian chilly powder (or cayenne pepper); a 2-inch stick of cinnamon or cassia; and 4 cloves. Combine well, bring the mixture to a boil, reduce the heat to very low, and let the mixture cook down slowly until it's the consistency of ketchup—very thick—stirring from time to time to keep it from sticking to the bottom. This should take at least 1½ to 2 hours. Add salt to taste when the ketchup is as thick as you want it. Pour into jars and store in the refrigerator.

Rhubarb Chutney | RHUBARB NI CHATNI

Persians in antiquity believed that the first man and woman sprang out of a rhubarb plant. Paula Wolfert asked me about this, and I had to look it up to find out more, just the way a Toda informant in Ootacamund had to page through W. H. R. Rivers's 1906 monograph on his people to answer my questions. Modern Persian cooking features rhubarb cooked with lamb, clearly a dish of ancient origin; but among Parsis in India, at least a thousand years removed from our homeland, rhubarb has not survived in either popular myth or cuisine, appearing instead in dishes of the Raj like rhubarb and custard.

Make this chutney with the spring's first rhubarb, slender green stalks barely tinged with pink, or with the skinniest stalks you can find, so that its texture stays rough. For our Chez Panisse New Year's dinner on March 21, 2005, we served it on squab liver toasts. *Makes about 2 cups.*

½ pound jaggery or 1 cup light brown sugar
½ cup granulated sugar
½ cup cider, white wine, or rice vinegar
1 teaspoon cayenne pepper or Indian chilly powder
2 (2-inch-long) sticks cinnamon or cassia
4 whole cloves
2 tablespoons finely julienned peeled fresh ginger
1 teaspoon (or more) salt
1 pound rhubarb

- Measure the sugars, vinegar, cayenne, cinnamon, cloves, and ginger into a non-reactive pan. Add 1 teaspoon of salt for now. Bring to a boil; reduce the heat and simmer while you prepare the rhubarb.

- Trim the leafy tops off the rhubarb stalks and cut the stalks into ¼-inch dice. Stir the rhubarb into the simmering syrup. Bring the mixture to a boil and cook over medium-high heat until the rhubarb is barely tender, a few minutes. If you want a rough-textured chutney, transfer the cooked rhubarb to a bowl and boil down the syrup until it starts to thicken—at about 220 degrees—before returning the rhubarb to the pan for a final minute or two. If you don't mind a jammy consistency, skip this step and cook the rhubarb in the syrup until it softens and thickens.

- If the chutney seems at all watery, let the fruit and syrup cook together again until the chutney thickens, but keep it on the slack side: It will thicken as it cools. Check for salt. The chutney should be emphatically sweet, hot, and tart. You might need to adjust the salt again after the chutney is thoroughly cool.

- Bottle and store in the refrigerator for short-term use. Serve at room temperature.

Fresh Turmeric and Ginger Pickle | ARADH NU ACHAR

Fresh turmeric rhizome looks like a cousin of ginger, which it is. The inside is usually a bright carroty orange. Modern Western medicine is now beginning to realize the enormous pharmaceutical value of turmeric. Indeed, some enterprising American thought it would be a good idea to apply for a patent—never mind that turmeric has been grown in India for thousands of years and spread from there in both directions, adopted wherever it went as a plant of nearly infinite medicinal properties. It is anti-inflammatory, antiseptic, and good for a list of ailments internal and external, including high blood pressure and pimples. I first knew fresh turmeric infused in hot, sweet milk as the traditional Parsi home remedy for bronchitis. (Dried and in smaller, less startling amounts, it appeared in almost every savory Parsi dish.)

One of my life's heroes, Usha Desai, was admired not only for the exquisite subtlety of her food but for her consideration of the minute details of everyday living. It was at her Juhu Beach house in Bombay that I learned to like taro, and it was at that same meal, monsoon waves crashing, palm trees rattling in the wind, that I tasted fresh turmeric with ginger and lime, a smell and taste so sharp I can still remember it vividly. It was served in a tiny amount right at twelve noon on each person's silver *thali*. At another lunch, there was yet a different taste, *amba aradh,* "mango ginger," similar to turmeric in appearance but paler, with the taste and scent of green mangoes. I was dazzled.

Ten years after that, fresh turmeric began to appear at our Indian grocery in Berkeley and, next to it, the thinner, paler rhizomes of what is commonly known as mango ginger. It was finding out about mango ginger and turmeric that kindled my passion for studying food plants of the tropics. As often as I could, I re-created Usha's turmeric pickle, sometimes solo, sometimes in combination with *amba aradh* and regular ginger. I used to eat it with rice and yogurt, until Krishna Riboud put together her breakfast of turmeric pickle with fresh cheese and whole wheat tortillas.

Unless you're sure of how hot you like things, add the chiles in small increments, or leave them out altogether in favor of a little extra ginger. This recipe makes about ¾ cup. *Serves 15 to 30.*

2 to 3 ounces fresh turmeric rhizomes, mango ginger, or a combination
1 to 2 tablespoons very finely chopped peeled fresh ginger
1 to 3 fresh green or red chiles, finely chopped (optional)
Juice of at least 3 Key or Mexican limes or 1 Persian lime
Salt to taste

- Peel the turmeric and cut into very thin slices. If the turmeric rhizomes are as thick as a carrot, quarter them lengthwise first. If you're worried about yellow stains on your hands, wear rubber gloves.

- Mix the turmeric slices in a small nonreactive bowl with the ginger, the chiles if you like, and lime juice and salt to taste. You will probably need the juice of at least 3 Key limes or 1 Persian lime. Remember, this is a pickle, and it is supposed to taste bold.

- Let stand a good hour before serving. Stir the turmeric in the salt and lime brine from time to time, so that it pickles evenly. This pickle keeps well for more than a week, refrigerated in a glass jar.

Eggplant Pickle | VENGNA NU ACHAR

This eggplant pickle is as easy to make as it is addictive. Use any eggplant you like except the tiny bitter Thai ones. My favorite is the bright purple-skinned Japanese variety because there's never a chance of bitterness, but some people like the stronger taste of the Indian and Italian types.

This is a great adjunct to grilled fish or meat, or to plain roast chicken. I love it with plain yogurt and rice. (Add a simple dal for a perfectly satisfying vegetarian main course.) When I'm having a skinny lunch, a small amount of pickle makes cottage cheese something quite wonderful. *Makes about 2 quarts.*

2 cups mustard, peanut, or sesame oil (not toasted sesame oil)
2 teaspoons fenugreek seeds
2 teaspoons cumin seeds
2 teaspoons fennel seeds
¾ cup very thinly sliced garlic
¾ cup finely julienned peeled fresh ginger
2 tablespoons cayenne pepper or Indian chilly powder
2 teaspoons ground turmeric
5 pounds eggplant, cut into 1-inch cubes
1 cup fresh green or red chiles, halved or cut into thirds
2 ½ cups (or more) cane or malt vinegar
¾ cup (or more) granulated or light brown sugar or light-colored jaggery
2 tablespoons (or more) salt

- In a deep nonreactive pan, heat the oil until it's very hot. Splutter the fenugreek, cumin, and fennel seeds in it, watching carefully that they don't burn. If they do, fish them out with a strainer and start again. Immediately add the garlic and ginger and let them sizzle until the edges get golden. Lower the heat and add the cayenne and turmeric, stirring well for a minute or two. The eggplant and chiles go into the pan next, followed by the vinegar, sugar, and salt. Stir well to combine and bring to a boil; reduce the heat and simmer, uncovered, until the eggplant softens completely and the oil floats to the top, 45 minutes to 1 hour. Do not add water under any circumstances. If things look as though they are going to stick, add small amounts of vinegar. While the pickle is still warm, adjust the balance of sweet, salt, sour.

- Bottle when cool, stirring first to incorporate the oil. It doesn't hurt to float a little film of oil on top before screwing the cap down.

· · ·

Chile Pickle: If you ever get a crop of chiles of any type that you need to use up, dispense with the eggplant and make this pickle using about 4 pounds of just chiles—all green, all red, or a mixture of both. Add 1 to 2 tablespoons crushed brown mustard seeds when you throw in the cayenne and turmeric, and decrease the sugar. This is one pickle that must be left alone for at least a week. As it mellows, it loses the sting of fresh chiles without losing the excitement.

Notes: Some people grind the ginger, garlic, and other spices to a paste, but I like the texture this way.

Your choice of vinegar depends on what you like and what's available. If you can, use cane or malt vinegar or even white wine or rice vinegar. Cider vinegar is all right. The distilled white stuff is not.

Parsi Wedding Pickle | LAGAN NU ACHAR

If we were Chinese, we'd call this Eight Treasure Pickle or something equally poetic. It's the first thing served at a Parsi wedding, or for a Navjot. You sit before a pair of overlapping banana leaves while servers file by with the first offerings—a dollop of this hot, sweet, mustardy "pickle" (technically a chutney) accompanied by a pile of potato wafers and a *rotli*. The banquet of ten courses, all rich, all delicious, all offered twice, has officially begun. Like any of the other banquet dishes, wedding pickle can be eaten or made at any time of the year. It's crammed with expensive and luxurious dried fruits over a base of coarsely grated carrots. Sometimes there's more carrot than fruit, but it's no less appealing.

My mother didn't go in much for pickle making, although her mother and my aunt Mani both did, as did my paternal grandmother, who was considered an expert. They had store cupboards lined with big earthenware jars, white on the bottom, brown on top. The moment the door to the cupboard was opened, there'd be a lingering smell of vinegar and spice. When David and I got married in 1987, I made a large batch of wedding pickle to give away to friends and continue to do so every few years, enjoying every part of the process, from shopping to bottling to giving it away. California is the perfect place for making *lagan nu achar*. Luxurious dried fruits are available in abundance, and even the elusive jujube is to be found at several farmers' markets in late summer and into autumn, and other times at Chinese medicine markets. For everyone else, several growers ship all over the country. (See Sources.)

Here's a formula that'll produce a *lagan nu achar* of a very high order. Remember, though, you have to taste it and be sure it pleases you, and you have to know that precise proportions are not all that important. I've cut back considerably on the traditional amount of mustard, but you can increase it, bearing in mind that its bite mellows over time, as we all should. One rule, though: No water at all. At any stage.

This pickle is lots of fun to make, especially when you've got some weddings to celebrate. Serve at room temperature as the opening course of a Parsi wedding feast. Or try it with a good ham or corned beef or tongue (page 154), or with a roast chicken. Or try it as a sandwich filling, mixed with cream cheese and rolled up in a whole wheat tortilla or chapati. *Makes about 8 quarts.*

2 cups whole dried jardalus, pits left in, or dried apricots

4 to 6 cups (or more) cane or apple cider vinegar

2 cups pitted prunes (optional)

1 (2-inch-long) stick cinnamon or cassia

4 teaspoons cumin seeds

1 teaspoon cardamom seeds

1 teaspoon whole cloves

¼ cup Colman's dry mustard

3 cups (or more) jaggery or brown sugar

5 tablespoons cayenne pepper or Indian chilly powder

4 to 6 tablespoons sea salt

8 cups coarsely grated mature carrots

2 to 3 cups ripe fruit pulp (mango, apricot, unsweetened applesauce, or persimmon)

2 cups dark raisins

2 cups dates (the drier kind), cut lengthwise into eighths

2 cups dried jujubes, cut lengthwise into eighths

2 cups dried figs (Mission or Kadota), cut into eighths

- In a bowl, set the *jardalus* to soak in enough vinegar to cover, along with prunes if you've decided to use them. Bash the cinnamon into smaller pieces. Bruise the cumin, cardamom, and cloves in a mortar. Wet the mustard with vinegar. Stir vigorously and set aside.

- Put 4 cups of the vinegar in a large stainless steel or enameled pot. Add the jaggery, the bruised spices, the cayenne, and 2 to 3 tablespoons of the salt. Stir over moderate heat until the sugar melts thoroughly. Add the carrots, fruit pulp, *jardalus,* raisins, dates, jujubes, figs, and prunes if you like, plus a little extra vinegar if the contents of the pan seem too dry. Bring the mixture to a boil over moderately high heat; reduce the heat and simmer at least 45 minutes to 1 hour, stirring every now and then, until the dried fruits are tender and the carrot shreds are perfectly cooked through. You may need to add ¼ cup vinegar from time to time to keep things from getting too dry. Taste for salt and sugar. Add more of each if the pickle is too vinegary. Add the reserved mustard paste and combine thoroughly. Bottle when cool.

· This pickle keeps well for 1 to 2 years at room temperature and longer in the refrigerator, although 5 years is too long because you end up with a dark brown, musty mixture of no particular character.

• • •

Carrot and Raisin Pickle: To make this a carrot and raisin pickle, double the quantity of carrots and raisins and leave out the other dried fruits.

Note: Feel free to experiment with other dried fruits, including peaches, pears, cherries, cranberries, and dried plums.

Bottle Gourd Jam | DODHI NO MORAMBO

The word *morambo* in Gujarati comes from the Persian *murabba,* a sweet, spiced jam made of fruits, vegetables, or flowers. I've never been able to understand why so many Parsi households insist on rather horrid commercial Indian versions of temperate-climate fruit jams, when minimal effort and locally available materials provide such luscious options. For Parsis, a *morambo* can be served in either the savory or the sweet part of the meal, which is why we've included it on the border between pickles and desserts. My father, for instance, liked to have it with *dhansak,* which I thought was like having jam with beef stew.

Travelers to Sicily may have encountered the bottle gourd as *cucuzza,* which is now its fashionable marketing name in the United States. Sicilians use it for making sweets not too different from this *morambo*—a clear link with the Arab and therefore ancient Persian influence on their culture and cuisine. We see bottle gourd *(dodhi, dudhi,* or *lauki)* at farmers' markets around the country and at Chinese or Philippine groceries, where it is known as *upo.* It's hard to think of a more versatile or useful vegetable.

Choose a firm, young, tender, and slender specimen that's not too bulbous at the bottom. Serve this jam for breakfast with toast, muffins, brioche, Chapatis (page 44), or whole wheat tortillas. A soft, fresh cheese is the perfect link between the sweetness of the *morambo* and the bread. Try our Creamy Panir (page 63). Serve strong coffee or a pot of strong black tea with mint and lemongrass. That's a good breakfast.

Refrigerated, *morambo* keeps for weeks. *Makes 3 to 4 cups.*

2 to 3 pounds bottle gourd or, in a pinch, large zucchini
2 cups (more or less) turbinado or light brown sugar
4 whole cardamom pods, bruised
1 or 2 (2-inch-long) sticks cinnamon or cassia
4 whole cloves
Pinch of salt
Lime juice and rose water to finish (optional)

· Peel the gourd and grate it coarsely so that the cooked strands will have some texture. If it's grated too finely, you end up with mush. Using your hands, squeeze out any accumulated liquid. Measure the grated gourd (you should have 4 to 5 cups). Put it into a pan with half its volume in sugar. Add the cardamom, cinnamon, cloves, and salt. Bring to a boil; reduce the heat and cook over moderate heat until the syrup cooks down to a jammy consistency and feels tacky between your fingers. Remove from the stove and let cool. When the *morambo* is lukewarm, if you like, finish it with a squeeze of lime and a splash of rose water for authenticity.

· · ·

Green Mango Morambo: If you can get hold of really hard green mangoes, still white inside, they make a very interesting *morambo.* Grate coarsely and proceed as for bottle gourd. Squeezing water out of them is not necessary. They need ¾ their volume in raw, unwashed sugar. No rose water necessary here.

Pineapple Morambo: Coarsely chop the flesh of a just-ripe pineapple. Measure it, along with any juice squeezed out of the skin, and put it in a pan with ⅔ its volume in raw, unwashed sugar and the same spices as above. Bring to a boil; reduce the heat and cook until the *morambo* is dark amber and sticky. No rose water here, either.

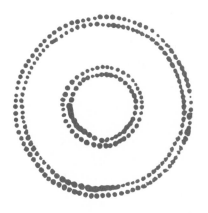

મીઠાઈ

---◦◇◦---

SWEETS AND DESSERTS

Sweets are a regular punctuation mark in every Parsi life. Auspicious days, whether personal or religious, are usually celebrated with the distribution of sweets, and all the days in between are improved by their consumption. On birthdays, it gets even better. Breakfast consists of one of the required sweets, such as *sev* (page 257) or *rava* (page 259), with sweet yogurt. Lunch will probably involve a special "pudding," as we still call desserts, following the English pattern. Teatime brings a birthday party and a birthday cake. More sweet treats such as chocolates end a birthday dinner party. Seven months into a pregnancy? You send around a conical sweet called a *ladva* to friends and family. If there's an unmarried girl in the house, she gets to pick off the tip. (A friend's permanently unmarried state was once attributed to her father's picking off the *ladva* point before she got to it.) Pass an exam? Parents send around sweets. Move into a new place? More sweets to be sent around. The festivals of other religious communities in Bombay are also occasions for sending and receiving sweets, which often arrive still warm at breakfast time. Sweet making and sending are among the perfect expressions of Bombay's nondenominational food culture. Each community has special sweets prized by all the others. Hindu sweet makers are known for their halvahs, *barfis, jalebis,* and *gulab jamuns* (*golab jam* in Gujarati); Muslims for luscious cream pastries called *malai na khaja,* and other extraordinary things called *aga hi dahri* ("holy man's beard") or *bagalyu* ("little stork"), feathery and flaky; Parsis for *ladva* and *penda;* Goan and Irani bakeries for fruitcakes.

The fruits of the Iranian plateau are still Parsi favorites for ending a meal—pomegranates, melons, watermelons, grapes, and oranges, joined by the universal Indian passion, mangoes. My grandmother and mother followed similar patterns for ending meals. Lunch usually ended with fruit—fresh, dried, or a combination—and whatever confection happened to be in the house, Indian sweets or chocolates or both. Cakes and biscuits (cookies) were generally relegated to teatime, and dinner ended with something wet like a cold soufflé or mousse, a jelly, a custard, trifle, bread-and-butter pudding, blancmange, some milky Parsi pudding, or—for a special treat—ice cream or *kulfi* (ice cream made with boiled-down milk), or whatever fantasy the family cook could devise for dinner parties. In my grandmother's household, ice cream and *kulfi* were laboriously churned in an American device. My mother used her freezer trays to make a refreshing ice milk, usually made of custard apple to please my father.

ROCK SUGAR
CONTAINER

In our house, everyday meals end with fruit, but if there are guests, even one, there's always a dessert, even if it's nothing more than a small glass of freshly squeezed orange juice and a cookie, or yogurt and honey with fruit, or an assemblage of whatever little morsels we can lay our hands on—dried fruit, nuts or marzipan, dark chocolate, candied peel, and such—with a glass of dessert wine. I have to restrain myself here because I really love making desserts of all types, especially birthday cakes, and had we included every single family favorite over three generations, this chapter would have occupied more than half the allotted pages of the book.

Mangoes

One of the greatest rewards of Bombay's hot months is the mango season. It starts with little green mangoes, which go straight into pickles; and before long the madness is upon us, heat and mangoes. There are hundreds of varieties of mangoes in India, but only western India has the Alphonso. In Bombay, procuring, securing, and ensuring a household's continuing supply of good Alphonsos becomes a preoccupation that lasts until there are no more to be had, just around the time the monsoon begins. In a lively history of the making of Bombay, P. M. Malabari reports on particular mango trees with such a reputation for the quality of their fruit that Mughal emperors sent for them all the way from Delhi. Not far from where my parents once lived, there was supposed to be a tree that bore mangoes all year round. Sad to say, it got cut down more than a hundred years ago.

When there are Alphonsos or any good mangoes around, the Parsi dessert question is solved. Why bother with anything else?

There used to be a definite mango season, but we're now beginning to get them almost all year round from one tropical country or another. In the United States, mangoes grow abundantly in Florida and Hawaii. In recent years, California has begun to grow astonishingly luscious mangoes—Manilas in the summer and brilliant green Keitts, with no fibrous strings, in the autumn.

Americans are often told to buy mangoes when they're soft. Please don't do this. If a mango is soft, it's on its way out and will taste that way, flat and turpentiney instead of sweet and tart. Buy only firm and unbruised mangoes on the underripe side. Color is not a reliable indication of ripeness; a red blush is a characteristic of some varieties, but others are green even when fully ripe. Be sure that the mangoes don't go home next to anything that might bruise or dent them. To hasten ripening, wrap mangoes in newspaper.

It isn't necessary to eat mangoes standing over a washbasin, as some claim is the only way to deal with them. All you do is stand a mango up on its pointed end and cut it on either side of the stem. You'll end up with two cheeks and the center with the seed. If the mangoes are big, as many American varieties are, serve each person a cheek on a plate with a spoon. Serve mangoes at room temperature, or cool but not refrigerator-cold.

You can also slice mangoes easily this way: Cut them into three. Cut each cheek in half. Using a sharp paring knife, run it between the pulp and the seed. Cut the mango into slices down to the skin, then cut them loose. There will be two good slices on either side of the seed. What happens to the seed is a household affair. There's usually someone who loves it.

Sometimes mangoes can be stringy. As children, we amused ourselves making mango bunnies from sucked-dry, shampooed seeds. Or you can make *am ras,* as Gujarati cooks do: strain

ONE WAY TO CUT A MANGO

the pulp through a sieve and dilute it with water to a drinkable consistency, sweetened just a little. Serve cold but not icy. You can also make a ripe mango fool by sweetening the pulp with plain granulated sugar and combining it with lightly whipped cream or with part cream, part yogurt. Best served cool with a cake or cookie counterfoil.

Fruit Juice Jelly

Years ago, when I visited my aunt in Ootacamund in the mid-seventies, my eye fell on a five-sided aluminum Mickey Mouse mold with Mickey on top, and Minnie, Goofy, Donald Duck, Pluto, and Mickey again on the sides. Unbelievable. I asked Mani Masi if she would consider parting with it. It was the jelly mold of my happy early childhood and is still in use here in San Francisco.

Molded desserts are old-fashioned, certainly, but so much fun. The Mickey Mouse mold probably held many jellies made with crystals in the usual colors; it probably saw pink and white blancmanges, or even jellied port in the pre-Prohibition days. In this house, I use it for jellied fruit juice and a delicate jellied yogurt.

For methods of squeezing pomegranate juice, see page 274. *Serves 4 to 6.*

¾ cup water
1 packet (½ ounce) powdered gelatin
1 ¼ cups unsweetened pomegranate juice, or blood orange or tangerine juice
½ cup granulated sugar
Lemon juice (optional)

- Put ¼ cup of the water in a small saucepan. Add the gelatin to it and let it soften and swell. This should take a few minutes. Over very low heat, melt the gelatin. Add a little of the fruit juice to the gelatin and then pour the mixture back into the bowl or pitcher containing the rest of the juice. Combine the remaining ½ cup of water with the sugar and bring to a boil to make a simple syrup. Let cool. The pomegranate mixture should be a bit sweeter than you would want it as a drink, so add the syrup to the juice bit by bit until it reaches that stage. You may need to add a squeeze of lemon juice to spark it up.

- Pour the mixture into a mold dipped in water or simply into a serving bowl and refrigerate a few hours until set.

- Turn it out to serve by dipping the mold briefly in hot water, holding a serving dish over it, and then quickly turning it over. Give it a sharp tap if the jelly doesn't fall onto the dish at once.

Jellied Pineau des Charentes

Here's a twist on an old Parsi favorite of jellied port or sherry with stewed prunes. Pineau des Charentes is a little extravagant, but you can serve only a little bit of it with a compote of fresh fruit. It's like having your dessert wine and fruit all at once. You could even throw some grapes into the mold or dish. Any sweet dessert wine will do, not just Pineau des Charentes.

Serve with a delicate cookie like the Crisp Cashew Wafers (page 260), made with walnuts or almonds, and a garnish of summer fruit. *Serves 6.*

1 ½ cups Pineau des Charentes
1 cup water
1 packet (½ ounce) powdered gelatin
½ cup granulated sugar
Lemon juice (optional)

- Pour the wine into a bowl. Put ¼ cup of the water in a small saucepan. Add the gelatin to it and let it soften and swell for a few minutes. Add another ¼ cup of the water and melt the gelatin over very low heat. Add a little of the wine to the gelatin mixture and add this to the bowl containing the rest of the wine. Combine the remaining ½ cup of water with the sugar and bring to a boil to make a simple syrup. Let cool and pour the syrup in small amounts into the wine mixture until it seems definitely sweet. Add a squeeze of lemon juice if you like.

- Pour into a mold rinsed out in water, or into a serving bowl. Refrigerate until the jelly sets. If you like, add grapes, halved if very big, when the jelly is partly set.

- Turn out the jelly by dipping the bottom of the mold briefly in hot water, holding a serving dish over it, and quickly turning it over. Tap if the jelly doesn't fall into the dish at once.

Summer Melon and Rose Water Dessert Soup

On December 22, the pre-Islamic Zoroastrian Yalda festival, modern Iranians celebrate the turning of the solar year by holding an all-night vigil, chattering and munching on good things in order to chase away evil. The most important good thing is an out-of-season watermelon, thought to be not only auspicious but good for the health in winter. Mehdi Shirvani, whose company, Mashti Malone's, makes Persian ice cream in Los Angeles, tells me that his mother had a special room for storing melons harvested in summer; others had to count on mediocre cold-storage fruit. "Not like America," he says, "where you just go to the market." In India, Parsis have forgotten this ancient festival, but the watermelon remains a favorite fruit, taking the edge off the ferocious heat that precedes the monsoon.

In those hot months between April and June, my mother cubed watermelon, sugared it heavily, and scented it with rose water, serving it at the end of lunch. While I love most food at room temperature, iced watermelon makes one of the most refreshing warm-weather desserts imaginable, and it is the perfect light, bright ending to a meal with an intense main course. In our house, we often puree watermelon and serve it with melon balls of contrasting colors floating about in it. Pure Omar Khayyam. Nothing can beat the gorgeous familiar pinkish-red of watermelons, but now that we have orange and yellow ones to play with, plus cantaloupes and honeydews and many other melons, the temptation to go color crazy can't be resisted. *Serves 6 to 8.*

1 (or more) melon, such as cantaloupe or honeydew
6 cups (or more) cubed and seeded watermelon
Superfine sugar
Rose water
Lime juice (optional)
White rum (optional)

- Prepare melon balls, preferably of contrasting colors, allowing about 5 per person. Cover and put them in the refrigerator to chill.

- Puree the cubed watermelon. Sweeten it by adding small amounts of sugar at a time. Chill the puree.

- Taste for sweetness again after it's thoroughly cold. Add a small amount of rose water by the half teaspoon. You want the scent to be almost subliminal, not like hand lotion. Add a squeeze of lime if you want a touch of tartness and the white rum for a little extra kick. Add the melon balls and serve in small chilled bowls.

· · ·

Reverse Variation: Make your puree out of one of the other melons and use watermelon as an accent.

Note: The best way to choose a watermelon is to look for one that seems heavy for its size and has a patch of yellow where it rested on the ground ripening.

ROSE WATER
SPRINKLER

THREE WATER ICES

There are times when a meal can lead up to a voluptuous cymbal-crashing finale of a dessert; but when the savory courses are complex and ornate, nothing follows them as dramatically as the sharp exclamation of a fruit ice.

In Bombay's hot months—that is, most of the time—street vendors sell ice *golas*—balls of shaved ice with brightly colored syrups poured over them. It's an old, old tradition, pouring syrup over snow, one that Parsis probably enjoyed in Iran, which gave us the word *sharbat* and all its variants, *sherbet, sorbet, sorbetto, sorbete,* and so forth.

Conventional American fruit sherbets are made with egg whites and gelatin for volume and stability. I prefer the clarity of nothing but fruit, water, sugar, and citrus for balance. Unlike with ice cream, undersweetening a fruit ice in the interest of subtlety does not make it taste better. Flavors become dimmer in the course of freezing, so keep that in mind when you're adjusting the sugar and acid balance.

Pomegranate Ice

Pomegranates and Parsis go back a few millennia. Like the fish, the pomegranate is one of our central symbols: its color, its seeds, its shape and structure all suggest fertility, joy, and abundance. Ritual trays of fruit for religious ceremonies require a pomegranate. Getting the juice out of pomegranates can be a challenge, with juice flying all over, but a large Mexican-style hinged juicer for squeezing citrus halves works nicely. This is Chez Panisse's formula for a superlative pomegranate ice. *Serves 6 to 8.*

¾ cup granulated sugar
¾ cup water
1 ½ cups unsweetened pomegranate juice
Lime or lemon juice
Rose water (optional)

- Combine the sugar and water in a small saucepan over moderate heat. When the sugar dissolves completely, stir the syrup into the pomegranate juice. Taste and adjust the acidity with the lemon or lime juice. A Parsi cook might shake in some rose water at this point.

- Freeze for an hour. Stir midway through to be sure it doesn't separate. When it's frozen solid, you can serve it by scraping away at it to make pomegranate snow, or give it a quick run through a food processor to smooth out the texture. Put it into a smaller container until you're ready to serve it. If you like ices on the slushy side, let the container sit at room temperature for a few minutes to soften.

- Alternatively, freeze the mixture in an ice cream maker following the manufacturer's instructions.

Citrus Ice

Citrus ices are knockouts for color and flavor. Don't even think of making them with anything but freshly squeezed juice. It takes less time than mixing up a concentrate.

If you have the time, serve citrus ices with segments of the fruit they're made from. For even finer embroidery, use a little tangle of strands of citrus peel poached in heavy syrup. *Serves 6 to 8.*

1 ½ to 2 cups freshly squeezed grapefruit, tangerine, or blood orange juice
1 cup granulated sugar
1 cup water
Salt
Lime juice (optional)
Angostura bitters or Campari (optional)

- Skim off any floating seeds but do not strain the juice. Make a simple syrup by stirring together the sugar and the water over moderate heat until the sugar has dissolved. Cool the syrup. Add a cup of cooled syrup to the juice. Taste. Add a speck of salt. Add the rest of the syrup in increments (you may not need all of it). With tangerine or blood orange, you may need a squeeze of lime for balance.

- Freeze in an ice cream maker, or pour the juice into a shallow container and let it freeze solid, scraping off crystals to serve. With grapefruit ice, coarse crystals are particularly appealing to the eye. Serve a grapefruit ice with a dash of bitters or ½ teaspoon or so of Campari for a gaudier effect.

Melon Ice

Especially with a hint of rose water, melon ice conjures up Arabian nights, court-yards, fountains. Not bad for something that takes minutes to put together. All else being equal, choose a melon of a color that fits in with the rest of the meal. *Serves 6 to 8.*

1 cup water

1 cup granulated sugar

3 to 4 cups melon puree (from 2 to 3 pounds melon)

Lime or lemon juice to taste

Rose water

Unsprayed rose petals (optional)

- Make a simple syrup by stirring together the water and sugar over moderate heat until the sugar has dissolved. Pour half the syrup into the melon puree, adding the remainder bit by bit until the mixture is sweet enough, which means a touch too sweet to eat at room temperature. Add the lime or lemon juice to taste.

- Freeze in an ice cream maker, or in a shallow container in the freezer, putting it through a food processor once the ice has frozen solid.

- Just before serving, spray rose water lightly over the bowls. You want just a breath of it. Small rose petals make a lovely garnish.

FOUR JARDALU DESSERTS

Jardalus, known in Britain as Hunza apricots, come from Afghanistan, or the part of Pakistan that borders it. This is perhaps the Shangri-La of *Lost Horizon* fame, where the people claim they owe their longevity to a diet rich in these unusual apricots and their kernels. Their scientific name is the same as that of any other apricot, *Prunus armeniaca,* but they're a variety known in Gujarati as *jardalu,* which means "yellow plum." *Jardalus* are like no other dried apricot on the market, but you have to cook them to unlock their full flavor, and taste them to realize this.

Hunt for *jardalus* at Indian, Pakistani, or Afghan markets or get them via the Internet (see Sources), which is convenient but doesn't allow you a close-up look at what you're buying. *Jardalus* come in several shades of brown, from beige to chestnut. The light ones are considered the choicest, but the dark ones also have great depth of flavor. Occasionally a batch will turn out fibrous, not perfect for serving whole but perfectly suitable in recipes where the *jardalus* are to be strained.

Parsis exploit the rich taste of *jardalus* in savory dishes as well as sweet. Our chicken or lamb with *jardalus* is nothing short of seductive (page 141), but I think that *jardalus* really come into their own in desserts. We'll start here with simple poached *jardalus,* go on to a fool and an ice cream, and end up with a very grand finale, my mother's trifle.

GRANDMOTHER'S
SUGAR CANNISTER

Poached Jardalus

The other recipes in this section start with a foundation of these poached *jardalus*. Although they're so sweet that you'd think they wouldn't need any added sugar, the soaking and plumping process leaves them in need of a sweet boost. This makes all the difference in the eventual taste of the poached fruit.

Serve poached *jardalus* with crème caramel, crème anglaise, or sabayon, or try them with vanilla ice cream or yogurt and a wafer cookie. *Serves 6.*

½ pound jardalus (about 1 ½ cups)
½ cup granulated sugar
Pinch of salt
Port or Madeira (optional)

- Rinse the *jardalus* and soak them in a quart of water for at least 6 hours or overnight. Put them in a pan with their soaking water, the sugar, and the salt. Bring to a boil; reduce the heat and cook the *jardalus,* uncovered, until they have plumped up and darkened considerably, about 20 minutes. If the syrup is thin, remove the *jardalus* with a slotted spoon and reduce the cooking liquid over higher heat. Return the *jardalus* to the syrup and let them cool.

- I like to pour some port or Madeira into the lukewarm syrup. You can remove the pits before serving, or let people fend for themselves. (The pits can be cracked open and the edible kernels removed: see page 141.)

Jardalu Fool

If you've ended up with poached *jardalus* that are fibrous, put them through a strainer, reserving the pits for their kernels (see page 141). Measure the puree. For every cup of puree, whip 1 cup of heavy cream. Fold the two together. Nothing could be easier. If you want to cut back on the calories, make it a combination of vanilla yogurt and whipped cream. Lighten vanilla yogurt with whipped cream; then fold in the *jardalu* puree. Serve with Ragnhild's Cardamom Cake (page 266).

An alternative approach is simply to stir half-and-half into *jardalu* puree and turn it into a dessert drink. I remember being served tiny glasses of this as a child when visiting friends of my parents and longing to have it again. Try some Armagnac or cognac in this *jardalu* "shake."

Jardalu Ice Cream

Most of the time, I think that the best flavor of ice cream is vanilla because it's the perfect foil for so many fruits—fresh, in a compote, or poached. One of the few exceptions is *jardalu* ice cream. If you have a favorite custard-based recipe for ice cream, use it, halving the sugar and adding a cup or more of sweetened *jardalu* puree to the mixture before freezing it. Otherwise, simply follow these instructions for a voluptuous iced dessert with a truer fruit taste.

Serve drizzled with a little Armagnac and sprinkled with *jardalu* kernels if you have the time to get at them. Otherwise, strew with some lightly toasted sliced almonds. *Serves 6 to 8.*

3 cups heavy cream, or 2 cups whole milk and 1 cup cream
¼ cup granulated sugar
Salt
1 to 2 cups Poached Jardalus (page 250), pitted and pureed

- Heat the cream along with the sugar and a speck of salt. Add the *jardalu* puree, stirring it in gradually and tasting as you go. Use your taste to tell you when to stop. Remember that the mixture has to be able to stand up to being frozen, so make it taste more vivid than if you were simply eating it at room temperature. Let it chill before freezing according to the instructions that come with your ice cream maker.

Mother's Famous Jardalu Trifle

My mother was famous for this trifle. She would dismiss her efforts with a wave of her well-manicured hand: "It's nothing. So easy." What she didn't tell most people was her special trick, in post-Independence, Prohibition-era Bombay, of using Drakshasava, a herbal fortified wine sold at the chemist's as an Ayurvedic remedy, which made it all right in the eyes of the booze police. Now, decades later, you can buy fortified wines in Bombay, but I recently took great glee in making Ma's trifle with Drakshasava for friends there; they couldn't begin to guess the mystery ingredient.

This is a dessert that requires assembly rather than cooking. For a start, you need a good sponge cake, homemade or bought from a bakery that uses vanilla, not vanillin. Then you need a bottle of the fortified wine of your choice, and some cream for the topping. The only exotic ingredient is the pound of *jardalus*. Quantities are elastic. Since this is a party dessert, the quantities here are for a group. You should make this trifle at least a day before the event. *Serves 12.*

1 pound Poached Jardalus (page 250; double the recipe)
2 cups (or more) port, Madeira, or cream sherry
2 (9-inch-diameter) round sponge cakes, split horizontally
1 cup whipping cream
Sliced almonds, if not using the jardalu kernels
Silver leaf (optional)

- Let the poached *jardalus* cool in their syrup. Drain, reserving the syrup. Pour at least 2 cups of the booze of your choice into the syrup and set it aside. Split the *jardalus* in half, reserving the pits. Crack open the pits, remove the kernels (see page 141), and set aside.

- To assemble the trifle: Set the first layer of sponge cake in a deep serving bowl, glass or ceramic, and drench it with the syrup mixture. Cover the surface with a third of the *jardalu* halves, saving the best-looking ones for garnish. Then repeat with two more layers of cake, syrup mixture, and *jardalus.* Thoroughly wet the top layer with any remaining syrup, stretching it with more booze if you need to. Cover tightly and refrigerate.

- Close to serving time, take the trifle out of the refrigerator. Whip the cream—barely sweetened, if at all—spread it over the trifle, and decorate with the reserved choice pieces of *jardalu* and the reserved kernels strewn over the top. If you haven't got *jardalu* kernels, scatter sliced almonds on top. Silver leaf adds an extra-festive touch.

· · ·

Trifle Cake: If you want to turn the trifle into a cake, assemble it in a bowl or a soufflé dish, cover with plastic wrap, and put a plate with a 1-pound weight on it over the plastic wrap. Close to serving time, turn out the trifle onto a deep serving dish and decorate it with 1 to 1 ½ cups heavy cream, whipped into soft peaks. Sweeten the whipping cream if you like, or flavor it with an orange liqueur. Decorate with *jardalu* kernels or sliced almonds. Serve cool. If there's any left over, it will keep, refrigerated, for several days. My friend Mehlli Gobhai froze his leftovers and gave rise to a new variant. It was absolutely delicious straight out of the freezer.

Prune Trifle: There are no substitutes for *jardalus,* but you can make Ma's trifle with pitted prunes instead. So underrated here, prunes are a great treat in Bombay. My mother thought that using prunes was far more luxurious than our readily avail-able *jardalus.* You'll need to soak and poach the prunes with some added sugar first, about ½ cup for 1 pound pitted prunes. For the rest of it, proceed as with *jardalus,* substituting sliced unblanched almonds for the scattering of kernels on top of the dessert.

Cardamom Caramel Custard | ELCHI CUSTARD

We've all heard of fruit ices used as palate cleansers in a long dinner, but Parsis have an even more novel punctuation mark in the middle of a wedding banquet. After the wafers comes the fish; after the fish comes the egg dish; after the egg dish comes chicken; then a dense, rich custard followed by meat, *pulao* and dal, and the sweet course, usually *kulfi* (rich Indian ice cream). The custard is *lagan nu kastar,* wedding custard, made of many eggs and boiled-down milk, studded with *charoli* (*chironji* nuts) and perhaps raisins, heavily flavored with cardamom, nutmeg, and vanilla and then baked. *Lagan nu kastar* appeared in my mother's house only if someone sent it over. She preferred a lighter caramel custard such as this one, also a Parsi standby, and would sometimes flavor it with cardamom and nutmeg.

CUSTARD PAN

Serve with a blood orange compote, or one made with Poached Jardalus (page 250) or prunes, or with a medley of winter fruit—quinces and prunes, with peeled Fuyu persimmons sliced in just before serving. *Serves 6.*

⅓ cup plus ½ cup sugar
2 cups half-and-half
1 ½ teaspoons cardamom seeds, pounded
4 large eggs
Pinch of salt

· Combine ⅓ cup of the sugar, the half-and-half, and the cardamom in a saucepan. Bring to a boil; remove from the heat and set aside to let the cardamom flavor develop. One hour should do it; more won't hurt.

· To make the caramel: Over moderate heat, stir the remaining ½ cup sugar in a small heavy saucepan with 2 tablespoons water until it melts. Keep stirring until it changes color to a dark brown. Things move very quickly at this point. Add a splash of water and quickly pour into a 4-cup baking dish, ceramic, glass, or metal, tilting the dish this way and that until the caramel coats the bottom. Set the dish aside until you're ready to make the custard.

· Heat the oven to 350 degrees.

- Lightly beat the eggs with the salt. Pour in a small amount of the cardamom-infused half-and-half. Whisk the egg and half-and-half mixture into the rest of the half-and-half. Strain it into the caramel-lined dish.

- Set the dish in a large baking pan. Pour in enough hot water to come halfway up the sides of the dish. Bake in the middle of the oven about 35 minutes, until a knife slid into the custard an inch away from the center still looks wet. Don't worry; the custard will thicken and firm up as it cools. Remove the custard from the water bath.

- Cool to room temperature and then chill thoroughly, several hours or overnight, before turning out onto a deep dish, allowing the melted caramel to drip over the sides of the custard.

. . .

Notes: Should you ever end up with an overcooked custard, weeping and full of holes, don't despair. Tip the whole custard, caramel and all, into a blender or food processor, buzz it till it's smooth again, and freeze it as an ice cream. It makes you want to overcook a custard in order to do it again.

If you're in a shop that sells Indian utensils, or if you're at a market in India, look for a pan like the one shown on the previous page. It's the perfect thing for making the caramel and baking the custard. I've had mine now for thirty years, and the crown in the bottom shows that it was made before Independence in 1947.

Milk Pudding | KHIR

Khir isn't a Parsi proprietary dessert. Many Indian regional cuisines have versions of this luscious pudding made of milk boiled down till it's like heavy cream. The *khir* in my mother's household was made with rice or with *sev:* not the *sev* you see sold in the snack foods section of an Indian market—the bright yellow threads and squiggles made out of *besan,* chickpea flour—but an ultrafine pasta far, far thinner than capellini. Parsis use it for sweets like this milky pudding and for *sev dahi,* the birthday pudding in this chapter. It's sold toasted or untoasted. Buy the untoasted variety. The Elephant brand is reliable. As the box claims, "It does not form clump."

Khir has always been one of my favorite Parsi sweets, both comforting and festive, garnished with chopped nuts, sometimes raisins, and finished with a dusting of freshly grated nutmeg. *Serves 6 to 8.*

1 cup untoasted sev, or 1 ½ cups cooked basmati rice
6 cups whole milk
1 (2-inch-long) stick cinnamon or cassia
3 tablespoons (or more) granulated sugar
Pinch of salt
1 teaspoon (about) rose water (optional)
Freshly grated nutmeg, sliced almonds or pistachios, and unsprayed rose petals,
  for garnish (optional)

- If you're using *sev,* break it up into a 1-cup measure. Empty the cup into a strainer and pour boiling water over the *sev,* or cover it with boiling water and quickly strain it. Set aside while the milk cooks down.

- In a large saucepan, bring the milk and cinnamon to a boil. Reduce the heat as much as you can and let the milk cook down, about 20 minutes. Add the sugar, salt, and *sev* and let the mixture thicken over low heat. *Khir* should be the consistency of a thick pouring custard, something you serve in a bowl rather than on a plate.

- Pour it into a serving bowl. When it's cool, add the rose water, if you like. Refrigerate several hours, until chilled. Serve garnished, if you like, with a dusting of freshly grated nutmeg and a scattering of nuts and rose petals.

· · ·

Khir with Fruit: To introduce a refreshing fruity note, you could serve *khir* as a topping over little green grapes, sliced strawberries, blackberries, sliced peaches, or orange segments.

Note: I like to serve intense milky desserts at the end of a meal that has no other dairy products playing a significant part.

Sweet Milk with Semolina Puris | DUDH PAK PURI

Dudh pak puri is one of my very favorite Parsi desserts. To eat it was always an act of gluttony following an act of extreme patience, because *dudh pak* needs to be carefully boiled down until the milk is the consistency of a thin white sauce. Do not wander too far away from the pan. Thank technology for cordless telephones.

Serve with crisp globular puris (the kind made with semolina, not the whole wheat flour puris on page 45), which you can often buy at Indian groceries if you don't want to make them yourself. No Indian cook would criticize you for buying a good-quality commercial puri. The important thing is to have something slightly salty and crisp along with the cool sweetness of the *dudh pak*. The semolina called for here is known as *suji* at Indian groceries; do not buy semolina flour. *Serves 6.*

2 quarts rich whole milk
½ to 1 cup granulated sugar
1 cup all purpose flour
1 cup fine semolina (suji, not semolina flour)
½ teaspoon salt
½ cup (or more) water
Vegetable oil, for deep-frying
Finely chopped blanched almonds (optional)
Freshly grated nutmeg, crushed cardamom, or unsprayed rose petals,
   for garnish (optional)

· To make the *dudh pak:* Bring the milk to a boil in a large pan with a heavy bottom. Reduce the heat to a bare simmer and let the milk cook down, stirring occasionally in the beginning and constantly at the end, until it's the consistency of a thin béchamel, but still white. This can take up to 30 minutes. Sweeten to taste with the sugar, starting with ½ cup, and simmer for a few more minutes. This is where Parsi and Occidental cooks might differ—the Parsi cook would add a lot more sugar. Let chill thoroughly before serving.

· To make the puris: Mix the flour, semolina, and salt, by hand or in a food processor, adding enough water, starting with ½ cup, to make a stiff dough that can be kneaded and rolled. Give the dough a few turns under the palm of your hand after you've taken it out of the work bowl. Cover and let it rest for 1 hour or more at room temperature.

· Roll out the dough as thin as you can, about ⅛ inch thick, and cut it into small rounds no more than 1½ inches in diameter. Use a glass or a cookie cutter, anything with the right diameter.

· Pour the oil to a depth of 2 to 3 inches into a wok and heat over medium-high heat until hot but not smoking, about 360 to 370 degrees. Drop the dough rounds into the hot oil in batches and fry until the puris swell and get crisp, pushing them down into the oil in order to make them puff up. Remove at once and drain on paper towels. (They can be made days ahead and stored in an airtight tin after they've cooled.) If they don't puff and swell, don't be upset; eat them anyway. They're really quite hard to make, and some things need to be repeated until they're perfect.

- Some cooks like to put finely chopped blanched almonds in *dudh pak,* which I might do depending on the rest of the meal. You can grate nutmeg over the top or sprinkle the *dudh pak* with pounded cardamom seeds. Or strew the top with little rose petals, my favorite; or all of the above.

- To serve, ladle out small portions of *dudh pak* into small bowls and pass around the puris. To eat, puncture a hole in a puri, spoon in the *dudh pak,* and pop the whole thing into your mouth.

Vermicelli and Sweet Yogurt Birthday Breakfast | SEV DAHI

Our Iranian forebears celebrated birthdays with the roasting of a whole sheep, ox, or camel. Birthday celebrations are a lot tamer now, but auspicious days, birthdays in particular, require special breakfast foods: this dish of warm, sweet vermicelli *(sev)* and sweetened yogurt *(mitthu dahi),* and the following recipe for creamy semolina pudding called *rava.*

Sev dahi is one of those fundamentally Parsi things all of us need to know how to make. My mother's *sev* always turned out perfectly, and never in clumps, but her method never worked for me. I like the clarity of this alternative version, which requires just *sev,* ghee, sugar, and water.

Mitthu dahi is usually homemade—slightly boiled-down sweetened milk with a spoonful of starter from the household's current batch. A thermometer is handy unless you're a practiced yogurt maker. My mother would make it from time to time with a particularly delicate touch, using an improbably small amount of starter. When she felt lazy, she'd buy *mitthu dahi* from the Parsi Dairy Farm or the Ratan Tata Industrial, where busy Parsi women spend all day making and selling the things that people seldom make anymore. Hers was always better. Here in the United States there's much more good sweetened yogurt than there is time to make your own. It's all right to go out and buy it and use it in place of the *mitthu dahi.* Look for brands without additives and synthetic flavoring. *Serves 6 to 8.*

MITTHU DAHI
5 cups whole milk
2 scant tablespoons (or more) sugar
2 teaspoons tart plain yogurt

SEV

¼ pound untoasted sev

3 to 4 tablespoons ghee

¼ cup golden raisins

¼ cup slivered almonds

¾ cup (or more) sugar

Pinch of salt

¾ cup water

½ teaspoon crushed cardamom seeds

1 to 3 hard-boiled eggs in their shells

• To make the *mitthu dahi:* Combine the milk and sugar and bring to a boil. Immediately turn the heat down as low as you can and let the milk reduce for 15 to 20 minutes. It doesn't have to get thick, just a little concentrated. Let it cool to just above body temperature.

• Using your fingers, smear the plain yogurt on the inside of the bowl in which you want to serve the *mitthu dahi.* When the milk has cooled down enough, pour it into the bowl. Put this bowl in a warm place where it won't get disturbed. A laundry room or near a water heater might be just right. Cover it with a towel and let it be until the yogurt is set. In a warm climate, this can happen in hours. In a cooler place, it might take up to a day. Don't be tempted to keep visiting it and jiggling it. (If you have a yogurt maker, use it. We don't. I rather enjoy the challenge of finding the right spot in the house.) When the yogurt's firmly set, refrigerate it until well chilled.

• To prepare the *sev:* First break it up into smaller lengths. If you bought the *sev* in a 1-pound box, empty a quarter of it into a deep bowl and break it up carefully; it has a way of flying all over the place if you don't keep it contained. If it's in a ¼-pound plastic bag, break up the *sev* before you open the bag. Empty that into a bowl, too.

• In a deep skillet or wok, heat the ghee over medium heat. Quickly pass the raisins through the hot ghee, just long enough to make them swell. Scoop them out and set aside. Fry the almonds to a pale toasty color, remove, and set aside. Add the *sev* to the skillet and fry until it's light brown. Some bits will be darker than others. The important thing is to keep shaking the pan, turning over the *sev* gently.

- Make a simple syrup by stirring together the sugar, salt, and water over moderate heat until the sugar and salt have dissolved. Add the *sev.* Cover the pan and continue cooking about 3 minutes. The *sev* should be soft but not soggy. Turn up the heat if the syrup has not been absorbed, shaking the pan to keep the contents moving.

- Turn out onto a serving dish. Sprinkle with the crushed cardamom and the reserved almonds and raisins. Nest the hard-boiled eggs in the *sev.* These are for auspiciousness and don't need to be eaten at the same time. Serve warm with the chilled *mitthu dahi.*

Semolina Birthday Breakfast Pudding | RAVA

Semolina spells comfort and sustenance to some and the horrors of enforced childhood eating to others. To Parsis the word *rava* means both this rich pudding garnished with nuts and raisins and the semolina from which it's made. I sometimes lighten it with whipped cream for a festive dessert, to be served with a fruit compote befitting the season: strawberries in spring, mangoes or peaches in summer, apples and prunes in the fall, and grapes and grappa-soaked raisins in winter.

You can buy *rava* or *suji* at Indian groceries, or if you can't, use farina or Cream of Wheat (but not the instant kind). *Serves 6.*

2 tablespoons ghee or unsalted butter
2 tablespoons semolina (rava or suji)
1 pint whole milk
2 pinches of salt
3 tablespoons (or more) granulated sugar
½ teaspoon crushed cardamom seeds
Rose water and/or vanilla extract (optional)
About ⅓ cup toasted sliced almonds (optional)
About ¼ cup raisins plumped in grappa, or in butter or ghee (optional)
Freshly grated nutmeg (optional)

- Melt the ghee in a heavy-bottomed saucepan. Add the semolina and stir for a moment. Whisk in the milk and a pinch of salt. Stirring constantly, bring the mixture to a boil; immediately reduce the heat and stir or whisk while the *rava* thickens. Stir in the sugar, sweetening to taste. (Parsis tend to like their *rava* very sweet.) Add another pinch of salt and the cardamom. Keep stirring until the *rava* is the consistency you want; some like a fairly slack *rava,* and others like it to set like polenta. Some people add a touch of vanilla and a couple of teaspoons of rose water. Serve with a strewing of sliced almonds and raisins, if you like, and an optional grating of nutmeg.

• • •

Creamy Rava: After the *rava* has thickened to the point at which you would pour it into a bowl or a dish to set, scoop it into a food processor with ½ cup whole almonds. Give the machine a few pulses until the mixture is creamy-smooth and the nuts are thoroughly chopped. Turn the *rava* into a bowl and let it cool. Whip ½ cup cream to soft peaks. Fold into the cooled *rava.* The consistency should be thick and light. Add crushed cardamom, vanilla, or rose water, and pour into a decorative serving bowl. Strew with sliced almonds or pistachios. Lay as much edible silver or gold leaf over the surface as you like. Refrigerate until time to serve, up to a day ahead. Before serving, sprinkle with rose petals, or violets if your garden is full of them.

Crisp Cashew Wafers | KAJU MAKRUM

Every luxury hotel in Bombay seems to have a patisserie turning out éclairs and such, but the great pastry treasures of Bombay come from tucked-away places like the Paris Bakery on Dookar Galli (Pork Alley). Legend says that the present owner's grandfather, an Irani, thought he was opening the Parsi Bakery, but the sign painter got it wrong and it came out as Paris. Not so, says the owner; it was the Paris Bakery from the start. One of my favorites there is the *kaju makrum,* cashew macaroon, a flat cashew wafer scented with cardamom. For anyone who loves easy effects, this is the cookie for you. It's easy to make and easier to gobble up. I owe the inspiration for these cookies to Sylvia Vaughan Thompson.

If you want a thinner cookie, leave out the flour. You can substitute walnuts, pecans, almonds, or hazelnuts for the cashews. *Makes about 30.*

1 cup raw cashews
¾ cup granulated sugar
1 large egg
2 tablespoons all purpose flour
½ teaspoon cardamom seeds, bruised
¼ teaspoon vanilla extract
Pinch of salt

- Heat oven to 375 degrees. Prepare 2 baking sheets, by lining them with either aluminum foil or parchment paper, by buttering them and dredging them with flour, or by lining them with silicone rubber sheets like Silpat.

- Place the cashews on another baking sheet and dry them in the oven for 5 to 10 minutes as it heats. Watch them, as they shouldn't even begin to brown. (This step is not necessary for other nuts.)

- Throw the cashews, sugar, egg, flour, cardamom, vanilla, and salt into a food processor and pulse it a few times until the nuts are ground to a paste and the dough is fairly stiff. Alternatively, chop the nuts very finely and mix the dough by hand.

- Drop the dough in small spoonfuls—½ to 1 teaspoon is big enough— onto the prepared baking sheets, spacing at least 2 inches apart. Wetting the spoon or miniature scoop first helps a lot. Bake for 12 to 15 minutes. The cookies will be a pale toasty beige. They are soft when they come out of the oven, but turn crisp as they cool. Let stand for a few minutes before transferring them from the baking sheet to a tray or rack. You will need a skinny but sturdy metal spatula or pancake turner to do this. Let the cookies cool.

SILVER
STORAGE BOX

• • •

Note: It's best to bake these cookies one sheet at a time in the center of the oven, but you can have two sheets going if you're vigilant. To ensure that the cookies bake evenly, switch the baking sheets from top to bottom and front to back halfway through. No long phone calls in another room.

Cardamom Shortbread | NANKHATAI

These cookies originated in Gujarat, where they are especially popular with Parsis and Muslims. *Nankhatai* weren't ever made in my mother's house but they appeared fairly often, brought back as a food souvenir by travelers to Surat and Navsari, strongholds of traditional Parsi culture, or bought from local sweetmeat shops. During times of Muslim festivals like Ramzan (Ramadan), the street stalls in Muslim areas of Bombay are piled high with tissue-wrapped *nankhatai,* wrapped back-to-back just like amaretti. The best *nankhatai* are made with pure ghee, but most of the commercial, cheaper versions settle for a Crisco-like shortening, which is fine for texture but not for taste.

In western India—Bombay, Poona, parts of Gujarat—festive processions will often be accompanied by musicians known popularly as *nankhatai* bands, possibly because some of the bands may have originally been made up of moonlighting bakers and vendors of *nankhatai*. The tunes they played were "It's a Long Way to Tipperary," "Marching through Georgia," "My Bonnie Lies over the Ocean," "Pistol-Packing Mama," "Swanee River," and, in the 1960s, the immensely popular theme from the film *Come September,* all slightly off-key with lots of percussion and brass and comic opera uniforms. Nowadays, although the instruments and costumes are the same, the tunes are all drawn from current Hindi film hits.

If you're making the usual two-inch cookies, this recipe will yield about twenty; or you can make lots of smaller ones. They should be made a day or more ahead, to let the cardamom flavor permeate. *Makes about 20.*

½ cup ghee
½ cup superfine sugar
1 teaspoon yogurt
⅔ cup all purpose flour
⅔ cup fine semolina (suji or rava)
¼ to ½ teaspoon cardamom seeds, pounded
⅛ teaspoon cream of tartar
⅛ teaspoon baking soda
Chironji nuts (charoli), slivered almonds, or cardamom seeds, for decoration

- Using a mixer or food processor, cream the ghee with the sugar and yogurt until pale and fluffy. (If you don't have superfine sugar, sometimes sold as baker's sugar, use regular granulated sugar and give it a few pulses in the food processor before adding to the ghee.) Add the flour, semolina, cardamom, cream of tartar, and baking soda and mix or process until the mixture resembles fine meal. It will not be a dough, nor should it be.

- Heat the oven to 250 degrees.

- Gently press a heaping teaspoon in your palm until it forms a ball, or use a miniature ice cream scoop. Compress the ball slightly by squeezing it between your palms. What you want to end up with is a flattened round. Top with 1 or more *charoli.* Try putting the nuts in your right palm before plopping in the mixture to be shaped. That way, the mixture shapes itself around the nuts, which are then securely embedded. Any other way of getting them on and stuck in place is just fine. Place on an ungreased baking sheet and repeat with more dough and nuts.

- Bake for 30 to 40 minutes. *Nankhatai* should cook through without browning at all. Let cool on the sheet until hard enough to handle. When they have completely cooled, store in an airtight container at room temperature.

• • •

Note: Charoli (accent on the first syllable) is a "nut" the size and shape of a large brown lentil, often used in sweets. It's the seed of *Buchanania latifolia,* commonly called *chironji* in India, from the family Anacardiaceae, which means it's related to mangoes and cashews. You can find it at Indian groceries. Don't buy very much at a time, and store what you don't use in the freezer.

Giant Cookie

This is a Parsified version of the Italian *torta sbrisolona* first brought to our house by Margaret Fabrizio. It has all the buttery richness of *nankhatai* and takes less than five minutes to put together; and the idea of demolishing a giant cookie never fails to delight and entertain. For a celebration, decorate the cookie with a sheet of silver leaf and strew with rose petals. This cookie is best eaten the day it's made. Note that the recipe calls for semolina flour, the durum wheat flour used for making pasta, but you can substitute fine *suji* or *rava. Serves 2 to 6.*

¼ cup (½ stick) butter, room temperature, plus more for the pan
¼ cup ghee
½ cup granulated sugar
¾ cup all purpose flour
¾ cup semolina flour, or fine suji or rava
Pinch of salt
1 teaspoon cardamom seeds, bruised
½ cup whole almonds

- Lightly butter a 9-inch-diameter pie dish or cake pan. Heat the oven to 350 degrees.
- Cream the butter, ghee, and sugar in a food processor. Add the flour, semolina flour, salt, cardamom, and almonds. Pulse until the mixture turns into fine crumbs.
- Tip into the prepared pan. Smooth the surface by pressing lightly with your fingers. Bake for 25 to 30 minutes until pale gold. Let it cool thoroughly in the pan before turning out and serving.

Date Pastries | KHAJUR NI GHARI

Any Parsi reader will want to know why there's a recipe for date pastries, *khajur ni ghari,* and none for *dar ni pori* (a similar fried pastry with a mashed lentil filling), since both are hot teatime favorites. Pure bias. *Khajur ni ghari* is not only one of the best Parsi pastries, it's also one that conveys a sense of the ancient food connections stretching from India across the Middle East to Turkey and North Africa.

Gharis are usually fried, preferably in ghee. When my mother and I were cooking together, we made the traditional pastry using rice flour and rose water and then fried it, but for the sake of experiment we also enclosed some of the filling in flaky pie pastry and baked the *gharis* as little turnovers. The results were the *ghari* of angels, and now I prefer them baked. The pastry recipe comes from Alan Tangren, former head of the Chez Panisse pastry department, and is reproduced here with his consent. It makes about twenty ounces of dough. If you have a favorite flaky pastry formula, feel free to use your own. To combine the old and the new, use a generous splash of rose water as part of the liquid used in making the pastry.

Serve *khajur ni ghari* with tea or as a dessert. It is good with a small scoop of ice cream, Persian clotted cream from a Middle Eastern grocery, or yogurt and whipping cream mixed with perhaps a splash of rose water. Turkish coffee or espresso to follow would be the perfect finale. *Serves 6 to 10.*

FILLING

1 tablespoon ghee or butter
1 cup finely chopped soft pitted dates
1 tablespoon (or more) honey or sugar
½ teaspoon grated orange peel
½ teaspoon cardamom seeds, pounded
¼ cup chopped walnuts
Pinch of salt
Rose water

PASTRY

2 cups all purpose flour
¾ teaspoon granulated sugar, plus more for sprinkling
¼ teaspoon salt

12 tablespoons (1 ½ sticks) chilled butter, cut into ½-inch pieces
  (or half butter, half ghee)
½ cup ice water

2 tablespoons melted butter or ghee

- To make the filling: Heat the ghee in a small, heavy pan over medium heat. Add the dates and sauté them, mashing them as you stir, for a minute or two. Add the honey and taste to see if you need to add more, because dates can vary in sweetness. Stir in the orange peel, cardamom, walnuts, and salt. If the mixture seizes up, add a splash of water or orange juice and it will relax. The filling should be a thick paste. Remove from the heat and let cool a bit. Add a small splash of rose water, just enough to scent it subtly.

- To make the pastry: Combine the flour, ¾ teaspoon sugar, and salt in a mixing bowl. Add the chilled butter, squeezing and breaking up the pieces with your fingertips until they're no larger than lima beans. Toss the flour mixture with one hand while dribbling in ¼ cup of the water. Squeeze any remaining large pieces of butter into smaller ones while mixing and tossing. Continue adding water and tossing until the dough clings together and there are no dry particles at the bottom of the bowl. Divide the dough in half, press each half into a ball, and wrap tightly in plastic wrap. Press down to flatten each ball into a disk. Refrigerate at least an hour before rolling.

- Heat the oven to 375 degrees. Line two baking sheets with parchment paper or Silpat.

- On a lightly floured surface, roll out one of the disks into a 12- by 16-inch rectangle less than ⅛ inch thick. Cut out six 5-inch-diameter circles. Place the circles on the prepared baking sheets. Repeat with the remaining disk. To make two larger pastries, simply divide the dough into four portions, rolling each out into a 9- to 10-inch-diameter circle. You can be as neat or free-form as you like.

- To assemble the *gharis,* spread the filling onto 6 of the circles to within ½ inch of the edge. Brush the edges of the dough with water and top with the other 6 dough circles. Press the edges together and crimp with a fork. Poke 3 or 4 holes in the top of each, brush with melted butter, and sprinkle with sugar. This last step gives the top crust a brilliant crunch. Bake in the middle of the oven for 25 to 30 minutes, or until well browned.

- Cut into wedges and serve warm or at room temperature.

Cardamom Cake

The recipe for this cake, one of the most precious gifts I've ever received in my life, comes from a generous Swedish friend, Ragnhild Langlet, a textile artist of extraordinary talent. The cake became an immediate favorite in our household, an honorary Parsi dessert and our most requested birthday cake.

We met Ragnhild Langlet in a Berkeley garden in the early summer of 1987 at a potluck wedding celebration to which she brought an unassuming cake baked in an unassuming pan. That unassuming little cake was one of the most powerful things I've ever tasted. It was suffused with the scent of cardamom, crunchy whole seeds throughout, sweet enough, rich enough, light enough. Cake perfection. The taste is so exotic, so tropical, yet so adaptable to any cuisine that it's a surprise to know that it comes from Sweden, which turns out to be the world's second-largest market for cardamom, India being number one.

This cake is excellent the first day, even better the next and the next and the next, if it lasts that long. Serve with fruit or a custard or ice cream. There's nothing that it doesn't complement. *Serves 6 to 10.*

2 to 3 tablespoons sugar, for the pan
Sliced unblanched almonds, for topping (optional)
4 large eggs
1 ⅓ cups granulated sugar
1 ⅓ sticks unsalted butter
1 tablespoon cardamom seeds
1 ⅓ cups all purpose flour
Pinch of salt

- Heat the oven to 350 degrees. Prepare a 9-inch-diameter springform pan by buttering it liberally, sprinkling in 2 to 3 tablespoons sugar, and shaking the pan until the bottom and sides are coated with sugar. Don't worry about extra sugar on the bottom. Cover the bottom with sliced almonds if you want a particularly crunchy topping. Ragnhild also suggested ground almonds or bread crumbs. If you want to be absolutely sure that the topping won't stick, use a parchment paper disk to line the bottom of the pan before buttering and sugaring it.

- Using a stand mixer if you have one, a handheld beater, or a powerful and patient arm, cream the eggs and sugar until thick and pale and tripled in volume, about 5 minutes. Melt the butter in a little saucepan. Bruise the cardamom seeds in a mortar.

Quickly fold the flour and salt into the egg and sugar mixture, followed by the butter and the cardamom. Give the batter a thorough stir before tipping it into the prepared pan. Thump the pan on the counter to settle the batter.

- Bake the cake for 30 to 35 minutes. The top should feel dry and spring back when lightly pressed, and a skewer or knife inserted into the center should come out dry. Remove from the oven and leave in the pan about 5 minutes. Run a knife around the sides of the pan before inverting the cake onto a rack to cool. Remove the bottom of the pan carefully while the cake is still very warm. Let cool before serving.

. . .

Rose Geranium Cardamom Cake: For our dear friend Catherine's birthday in 1987, I embedded rose geranium leaves in the top of the cake (actually the bottom of the springform pan) along with the almonds, and served it with a winter fruit compote also lightly scented with rose geranium. If you can ever get near a cardamom plant, which is a member of the ginger family, try a leaf from it, too.

WOODEN FLOUR SIFTER

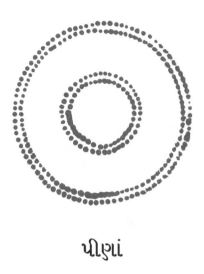

પીણાં

———— ◆ ————

DRINKS

Parsis are no strangers to wine. Legend says that wine was discovered long ago, during the reign of Jamshed, the mythical philosopher-king of Persia. He was so fond of grapes that one day he decided to preserve them in jars. Sampling his experiment, he thought they tasted odd. Instead of throwing them out, he put the jars aside, marked as poison. A woman in Jamshed's household had such a bad headache that she wanted to die. Spying one of the marked jars, she drank its contents down and fell into a swoon from which she recovered happily. From that day on, the now-renamed jars contained *zehr-i-khoosh,* "poison of delight."

This charming tale arguing for a Persian origin for wine is backed up by archaeological evidence: a pottery jar dating to about 5000 B.C.E. Chemical analysis of residue in it has identified wine with an additive from the terebinth tree as a preservative, resulting in something like Greek retsina. We know that by the time the Persian Empire held sway over large parts of the known world, wine was widely drunk, served, and stored in vessels of great imagination, artistry, and whimsy. The Arab conquest of Persia brought this happy boozing to a halt. From that time on, any winemaking or distillation of spirits was solely in the hands of the oppressed Zoroastrian minority. Those who left took their knowledge and their thirst with them to India. Until wine-bibbing Europeans arrived centuries later, our Parsi forebears evidently made do with fermented palm sap and other local brews.

The most common drink with everyday Parsi meals in India is iced tap water, first conscientiously boiled, of course, sometimes with a squeeze of lime in it. Water goes with everything and no one is ever apologetic about offering it or asking for it, except in public places, where it's still regarded with some mistrust. (India now has a vigorous bottled water industry, with its attendant garbage problem.) Every house used to have an unglazed earthenware vessel, a *matla,* for keeping boiled drinking water pleasantly cool, and most still do. For breakfast and at teatime, it was and is strong black tea offered with milk and sugar. Coffee used to be a random idiosyncrasy (in my parents' house I was the only one who took it seriously), enjoyed more often as a sweet, iced between-meal drink. Nowadays, espresso bars are a popular aspect of the restaurant scene. In my mother's and her mother's time, visitors would be offered *sharbat,* rose- or fruit-flavored syrups diluted with cold water, or perhaps a fizzy soft drink made by one or the other Parsi manufacturer, Roger's or Duke's. On festive occasions in my mother's youth, men would drink whisky (scotch) and soda while women would be offered port mixed with lemonade, the equivalent of 7Up. For ceremonial feasts, servers still circulate with the same brightly colored sweet fizzy drinks popular in my mother's youth: raspberry, orange, and purplish Vimto, though, sad to say, Coke, Pepsi, and Indian colas have made these seem hopelessly old-fashioned and therefore unpopular in everyday life.

Until the post-Independence Prohibition Act of 1949 lowered the boom on the sale and public consumption of alcohol, wine and spirits flowed freely in Bombay. After that, everyone, little old ladies and all, had to get a doctor's certificate saying they were addicted to alcohol in order to apply for modest monthly allotments known as permits. Bars became known as permit rooms, where you had to show your card and get whatever you ordered marked off against your allotment. Liquor could be served in private houses, but the choices were limited. Now that Prohibition's gone, a thriving Indian wine industry produces some admirable bottlings, and Bombay restaurants actually have wine lists again. In keeping with a growing worldwide wine consciousness, many Bombay hosts now offer it with meals, though it's still a special-occasion thing rather than the everyday drink it is for many in the United States and Europe.

DRINKING VESSEL

You will note that I haven't said anything about beer. Neither David nor I like it. In my parents' house, there was always beer around, though I remember it being drunk only in the afternoons before or with lunch, especially if there were guests. You shouldn't on any account feel obliged to drink beer with Parsi or any other Indian food. The old refrains "Hot food kills wine!" and "Wine doesn't go with Indian food!" are nonsense. Drink beer if you like, but not because you think you have to when you'd rather have a glass of wine.

Here in our house, we favor intense, fruity reds that aren't too tannic: varietals from Portugal, Spain, Sicily, and the south of France, or old-style Australian Shiraz and New Zealand Pinot Noir. For whites, we gravitate toward heavier white Burgundies; Alsatian, Austrian, and German wines; and Spanish Albariño and Italian Arneis. There's also nothing wrong with champagne or Prosecco or *cava* throughout the meal, and some dishes respond well to fermented ciders, which I particularly like at lunchtime. With dessert, we offer luscious sweet wines—Sauterne, Muscat, Riesling, Eiswein.

This chapter includes some of my favorite drinks sympathetic to Parsi food, apart from wine. Some don't need a recipe at all. Scotch-and-soda continues to be a favorite in today's Bombay, sometimes drunk throughout the meal. (Let's leave port and fizzy lemon in the past.) One of the very best tropical nonalcoholic drinks, *nariyal pani,* coconut water, is getting easier to find as young coconuts make their way into our markets here. Don't bother with the packaged coconut water from Southeast Asia or the Philippines; hold out for the fresh. It's work to get at the water, but worth it. *Nariyal pani,* like the tomato, lime, or watermelon drinks below, can be spiked with light rum or vodka. These are just suggestions to give you an idea of the vast range of possibilities in front of you. Your best course is to follow the advice of our Parsi sage, Meher Baba, whose words of wisdom, seldom more apt, were: "Don't worry, be happy."

Mani Masi's Tomato and Orange Drink

You'll recognize this as a cousin of *sangrita,* the Mexican tomato and orange juice combo warmed with red chile powder. My aunt Mani was always looking for something new and probably came across this in her magazine travels. The success of this drink depends on freshly made tomato juice. Although my aunt served it as a nonalcoholic alternative for her guests, it makes a fabulous base for a Bloody Mary (or Bloody Mehra), garnished with a stick of cucumber along with the lime (see the variation). *Serves 6.*

2 pounds ripe tomatoes
6 to 10 oranges, tangerines, or mandarins
Salt to taste
2 teaspoons (or more) freshly ground black pepper
6 lime wedges

- Cut up the tomatoes and put them in a nonreactive pan. Add a splash of water. Bring to a boil; lower the heat, cover, and allow to cook until soft. Blend and strain, or put through a food mill, wetting the residue and sending it through a second time. If necessary, dilute with water to a tomato-juice consistency. Squeeze the oranges until you get an equal amount of juice, more or less. Combine the juices. Add salt to taste and grind in what you think is an insane amount of pepper. You'll need 2 teaspoonfuls at least. Serve in small glasses over ice with a wedge of lime.

· · ·

Bloody Mehra: Add vodka or tequila to taste and garnish with cucumber sticks.

Tomato-Orange Ice: You can also turn this tomato drink into a savory ice. Be sure the mixture is highly seasoned. If you have an ice cream maker, follow the instructions that come with it. If not, pour the juice mixture into a shallow tray. Freeze till almost solid. Whomp it up in a blender or food processor and refreeze to a slush. Or scrape it into bowls or glasses like a granita. Serve with wedges of lime.

Fresh Limeade | LIMBU PANI

Wherever you go in India, you'll find *limbu pani,* a freshly made drink of limes and water. In the north, they often drink *limbu pani* unsweetened, with salt, but in Bombay it's usually sweetened with sugar or syrup. There's nothing particularly Parsi about either this drink or the next, except that they go so well with or before our food. Limes vary so much in size, acidity, and juiciness that it's simply not possible to be precise about quantities. You have to taste. Mexican hinged lime squeezers make short work of what can otherwise be a tedious job. They're easy to find, not only at Mexican markets but at mainstream kitchen supply stores. Wooden citrus reamers also work, but they're often too big for a small Key lime. *Serves 1.*

1 (or more) lime
Salt to taste
1 teaspoon (or more) superfine sugar
¾ cup to 1 cup water
1 lime slice

- Squeeze the lime. Add a speck of salt and the sugar. Stir until dissolved. Add water, 6 to 8 ounces per serving, depending on whether you're adding ice. Float a thin slice of lime in the glass for its visual appeal.

Fresh Lime Soda

Fresh lime soda, like *limbu pani,* is found all over India, but the traveler can order it with impunity, unlike *limbu pani,* since the bottle of soda is generally opened in front of you. *Serves 1.*

1 (or more) lime
Superfine sugar or simple syrup
Ice cubes
Club soda or fizzy mineral water

- Squeeze the lime. Add sugar or simple syrup to taste. Add the ice cubes and club soda. Stir.

. . .

Note: Either *limbu pani* or fresh lime soda can be turned into an alcoholic drink. Gin, vodka, or rum is the customary choice.

Watermelon Drink

Watermelons come into season exactly when you need them the most in Bombay. Just to look at one is refreshing. When it's so hot that eating anything, even a piece of watermelon, is too hard to think about, this drink comes to the rescue. It's perfect for a crowd because it pleases all ages and all preferences. Tipplers add liquor; the abstemious refrain. Try *charanda* from Mexico, *cachaça* from Brazil, or any white rum.

The brilliant pinkish-red of a standard watermelon is hard to improve on, but some of the other colors we now get can look pretty spectacular. If you have a choice, let the rest of what you serve determine the color of your watermelon drink. *Makes about 2 gallons.*

4 to 5 pounds watermelon
1 to 2 cups superfine sugar
6 to 10 limes (Key limes if possible)
Ice

• Cut up the watermelon and puree the pulp. Tip it into a large container, straining out the seeds if you need to. Taste for sweetness and then add the sugar gradually. Halve or quarter the limes, depending on their size. Squeeze them into the drink and throw in the spent rinds. Add water to taste: You're aiming for something that tastes of the fruit but doesn't give you the sense that you're making a meal of it. Adjust the sweetness and acidity with sugar and lime. Pour over ice in the serving container of your choice. If you're using lots and lots of ice, hold back on the water because the ice will melt soon enough.

THREE POMEGRANATE DRINKS

However it's done, getting the juice out of pomegranates is fiddly work because the delicious light pink to deep ruby seeds are tightly enclosed in astringent membrane and pith. First put on an apron or an old shirt. According to *Chez Panisse Fruits,* the way to get the sweetest juice is to split or quarter the fruit with a sharp knife and submerge the pieces in a bowl of cold water, using your hands to separate the seeds from the membrane and pith. The seeds will settle to the bottom and bits of membrane will float to the top, where you scoop them away. Drain the seeds and buzz them briefly in a blender or food processor. Press the pulp through a stainless steel or nylon strainer.

An easier way to juice pomegranates is to ream them as you would orange or grapefruit, using some kind of juicer-squeezer. This can be messy, especially if you use an electric juicer, and it can sometimes make the juice taste too astringent. I find the fastest, neatest method is to use a large cast-metal Mexican-style hinged citrus juicer. These are now easy to find at kitchen stores and in catalogs.

Easier still, settle for commercial pomegranate juice. Its recent popularity as an antioxidant now means we can get good-quality juice all year round. Pomi, Knudsen's, and Trader Joe's are reliable brands, and farmers' markets sometimes have a pomegranate vendor who sells juice as well.

Pomegranate Spritzer

Our first pomegranate drink is such an easy one. I particularly like it because it gives guests who aren't drinking alcohol something interesting and refreshing. *Serves 1.*

⅓ cup (about) pomegranate juice
Ice cubes (optional)

½ cup (about) sparkling water
Sprig of mint or twist of orange or tangerine peel, for garnish

- Fill a glass a third of the way up with the pomegranate juice. Add some ice cubes if you like, then top off with fizzy water. Garnish with the mint or citrus peel.

Pomegranate Kir Royale

Here's an idea for an aperitif to serve before a Parsi meal. You don't need much of a recipe, just a bottle of the sparkling wine you like to drink, plus some pomegranate syrup. The size and the strength of the mixture are up to you. *Serves 1.*

Sparkling wine
Pomegranate syrup to taste

- Pour the sparkling wine into a glass of your choice, big or small. Pour in a small amount of the syrup. You'll have to do a taste test yourself to determine how much. However you serve the drink, mixed by you or stirred up by your guest, the effect is beautiful, the taste refreshing.

• • •

Plain Pomegranate Kir: You can use a still white wine, too, for a plain pomegranate Kir. I just love the bubbly kind.

Note: If you can't find pomegranate syrup (not to be confused with pomegranate molasses), here's how to make it. Combine 2 cups pomegranate juice and 1 cup sugar in a nonreactive pan. Bring to a boil; reduce the heat and simmer 10 to 15 minutes. Let cool. You'll end up with a thin syrup.

Pomegranate and White Rum Cocktail

Make an easy sneaky cocktail: Mix white rum or *aguardiente* and pomegranate juice in a proportion that suits you. For a longer drink, add a splash or two of fizzy water. You can also make this drink in a cocktail shaker, pour it into martini glasses, and garnish with lime slices just before serving. *Serves 1.*

Ice cubes
1 to 2 ounces rum
4 to 6 ounces pomegranate juice
Lime juice to taste

- Fill a glass about halfway with ice cubes. Pour in the rum and pomegranate juice. Add a squeeze of lime juice and stir.

Parsi Tea with Mint and Lemongrass

In my mother's house, and all the other houses I knew, the day began with strong, black tea served with milk and sugar. Some people even liked to have tea brought to them in bed. Later in the day, there'd be more tea, again served with milk and sugar. My mother still gets restive if there's no tea in sight by four in the afternoon, and she still sees it as one of the day's official mealtimes. I love the idea of pausing in the middle of the afternoon, but when dinner is around seven-thirty, tea can't be an official meal as it is in India, where dinner doesn't get served until nine o'clock.

The hills around the school I went to in South India were covered with lemongrass—introduced, like lantana, but aggressively naturalized over time. In those days, we didn't have much use for the leaves because the flower stalks were what we needed for building things or for playing fiddlesticks, known in the United States as pickup sticks. At home it was a different story. Parsis use the upper leafy portion, calling it green tea, *lili chai,* in combination with fresh mint and black tea. In fact, Bombay vegetable stalls often sell lemongrass and mint either bundled together or sold right next to each other. Here, we wait for the occasional farmers' market vendor to bring in sheaves of fresh lemongrass with its leaves. Dried leaves make acceptable tea, but handling a hank of fresh leaves is more fun.

The standard way to make this tea is to add a few long leaves of lemongrass, about six, twisted up into a knot, and a handful of mint to the black tea you like—Assam, Darjeeling, Ceylon, Nilgiri—in a warmed teapot. The rule of thumb is a teaspoon of tea per cup and an extra one for the pot. Pour boiling water over the leaves, let steep for at least 5 minutes, and serve with milk and sugar. You can also drink it as it is or with lemon, but I have never known any Parsis in India to do so.

Some households mix the tea, lemongrass, mint, milk, and sometimes sugar all together with the required amount of water in a saucepan, bring it to a boil, and simmer it for a few minutes. If you're making the tea for a crowd, you can increase the quantities, brewing everything up in a giant pot, but in this case, let people add their own sugar because there are some of us who cannot stand sweet tea.

Here in San Francisco, we often leave out the black tea and make a simple infusion or tisane out of just the lemongrass and the mint.

Hot Weather Yogurt Drink | CHHAS

Starting in April, Bombay gets hotter and more humid every day until, two months later, the monsoon clouds gather and finally drench and quench the parched city. It's a time of low energy, flagging appetites, and the constant need for something cool and restoring. *Chhas* is considered a sovereign remedy for wilted bodies, especially in the middle of the day. Strictly speaking, *chhas* is the whey of churned butter—true buttermilk—though nowadays it refers to a mixture of yogurt and water, seasoned with cumin. *Chhas* is made salty and just this side of being watery so that it refreshes and restores electrolyte imbalances without filling you up. Look for a tart yogurt. It makes all the difference. *Serves 2 to 4.*

1 pint tart plain yogurt
½ to 1 teaspoon cumin seeds, freshly ground or pounded
1 ½ cups (about) water
Salt to taste
Ice (optional)

· Whisk the yogurt and ground cumin seeds with the water or buzz together in a blender. Salt to taste. Serve cool or chilled, with or without ice.

Indio Date Shake

Date shakes are one of the glories of American street food. The street in this case is the highway running through Indio, California, the date capital of the United States. As you approach from either direction, stands proclaim the local offering. Driving through the desert might make anything cool and wet seem appealing, but date shakes exceed all expectations. Unless you have a bottomless capacity for rich, thick, sweet milk shakes, one of the enormous glasses you're handed will serve four easily.

Any Parsi who has passed through Indio and stopped for a date shake must feel a compulsion to go straight home and make one without delay. That's what I wanted to do in 1971, watching very carefully as our two enormous shakes were blended. I couldn't wait. Here's an excellent honorary Parsi dessert drink, combining something we've have been eating for millennia—dates—with ice cream. Unlike the Indio vendors, I serve it in small glasses as a liquid dessert. This recipe is a reconstruction based on memory. Feel free to tinker with the proportions. Serve with a crisp cookie. *Serves 6 to 8.*

1 ½ cups soft pitted dates
1 cup (or more) milk or half-and-half
1 pint ice cream (undersweet homemade the best)

- If the dates have loose, tough skin, peel it off, or push the dates through a strainer. Sometimes the skin never gets blended enough and makes for a gritty texture.
- Put the dates in a blender with the milk and ice cream. Pulse until smooth.
- Serve in a small 4-ounce glass with a teaspoon.

· · ·

Date-Walnut Shake: Try adding a handful of walnuts to the blender.

New Year's Milk Shake | FALUDA

Faludeh in Iran is a frozen dessert of wheat-starch noodles in a rose-scented syrup. *Faluda* in northern India is a dish of *kulfi* (rich ice cream) and wheat-starch noodles. *Faluda* in Bombay is a glorious milk-shakey affair in a tall glass. At the bottom, there's a layer of soaked basil *(Ocimum basilicum)* seeds, *tukhmuriya ni biya,* with a slippery-crunchy texture that's like nothing else. On top of the *tukhmuriya ni biya* is a layer of translucent noodles made of wheat starch. Both of these layers are seen through intense pink rose syrup, although amber-colored saffron syrup is an option. Milk appears to float over this foundation without disturbing it. For extra luxury, there might be a scoop of vanilla ice cream or *kulfi.* To eat the *faluda,* you stir everything up with a long spoon.

Faluda is supposed to be eaten on March 21, Navroz, the old Persian New Year's Day, but that doesn't mean you can't find it or eat it for the remaining 364 days. The best places to find *faluda* outside someone's house is in Bombay's beloved Irani-run restaurants, often named after British or Iranian royals. (Iranis are Zoroastrians who left Persia for India in the late nineteenth century, many of them starting up restaurants and bakeries that are still flourishing concerns run by the descendants of the founders.) Rustom Jeejeebhoy, fountainhead of Parsi lore, used to tantalize me by describing the delights of his favorite Irani restaurant, the King Victoria, hidden away on the edges of the mill district, but he never found himself able to take me there or even come up with the address. "Look, dear, I just haven't got the time now. We'll go, we'll go . . ."

To make *faluda* worthy of the King Victoria in the United States you need two common things, milk and ice cream, and two slightly more esoteric items, rose syrup and basil seeds. I leave out the wheat-starch noodles because it's more fun to crunch seeds. Rose syrup can be found in Indian or Middle Eastern groceries. I suggest the Middle Eastern brands, for a truer rose flavor. For total extravagance, look for exquisite organic rose syrup from Italy. Read the labels to make sure you're not getting an entirely synthetic product. The basil seeds come from Indian or Southeast Asian markets. Buy the Southeast Asian ones; the Indian basil seeds are often sandy. For more information, see the Glossary.

At the Chez Panisse March 21 dinners, we serve *faluda* in small glasses as a dessert drink. Instead of ice cream we use ice milk, which keeps things refreshing. *Serves 6.*

1 tablespoon basil seeds
2 cups (or more) water
3 cups (about) chilled whole milk or half-and-half
½ cup (about) rose syrup
½ cup (about) vanilla ice cream or ice milk

- Soak the seeds in the water for 1 to 3 hours. A tablespoon doesn't seem like much, but the seeds swell up enormously.

- Line up your glasses, tall or short. First put a spoonful of soaked seeds in the bottom of each glass, 2 teaspoons or so for small glasses, 1 to 2 tablespoons for tall glasses. Then pour in the milk to within an inch of the top of the glass. Follow that with 2 teaspoons to 2 tablespoons of rose syrup, depending on the sweetness of the rose syrup, the size of the glass, and your taste. It doesn't seem likely, but specific gravity will cause the syrup to sink below the milk in a neat band. If you do it the other way around, the syrup and milk get mixed and the dramatic banded effect is lost. Last, put a little ice cream in every glass.

MENUS

In any cuisine, familiar or new, there are the perennial questions of what to have and how to put it all together. The menus shown here are divided into two sections—the way my mother and grandmother organized their meals, and the way we do now in San Francisco. My grandmother's and mother's menus were more elaborate than ours today, especially when they entertained. Traditional Parsi hospitality requires a lavish succession of extravagant dishes, most vividly demonstrated by the ceremonial banquets served at Navjots and weddings. The wedding dinner menu below is more for historical interest than a suggestion.

One of the comfortable things about Parsi food is that you already have everything you need to serve it. Parsis use knives, forks, and spoons—knives and forks for things that need cutting; spoons and forks for dishes like rice and curry, which are more sensibly eaten with a spoon anyway. We eat with our hands (using the tips of the fingers of the right hand) at ceremonial feasts served off banana leaves, although spoons and forks are offered to those who don't want to get their fingers messy. Meals can be served in courses or not, according to the customs of a household.

Traditional Parsi hospitality also has its own etiquette. Guests are always warmly welcomed even if they arrive without notice, and if invited, they are neither required nor expected to bring anything. Hosts press food and drink on them, and it's not polite to sit without accepting something, if only a glass of water. If a guest praises the food, the host must say "But it's nothing like your house!"—even if everyone knows it's a lot better—and chide the guest for not eating enough. When visitors leave, the host's parting words are *Jarur aojo!* "You must come back!"

Recipes marked with an asterisk are found in this book.

Traditional Menus

EVERYDAY BREAKFAST

Eggs any way

Bread or toast

Butter and jam

Tea

EVERYDAY LUNCH

Fried fish and tartar sauce

Bombay Curry*

Perfect Plain Rice*

Cold soufflé or fruit

Tea, alone or with cake, biscuits, and sandwiches (any or all)

SUNDAY LUNCH

Potage of Lentils and Vegetables, made with chicken or lamb*

Caramelized Fried Rice*

Shrimp, Squid, or Fish Balls*

Simple Onion Kachumbar*

Mangoes or tangerines and torpor

EVERYDAY DINNER

Eggs on Anything, served over Sautéed Okra*

Cutlets, served with Parsi Tomato Gravy*

Lentils and Lamb Tongue*

Chocolate pudding

WEDDING DINNER | LAGAN NU BHONU

A wedding menu is served on banana leaves, with all dishes offered a second time except panir and sweets. The panir here is the floating kind, hard to make, hard to find. Served along with the nuts, *pan,* the universal Indian digestive, consists of a betel leaf *(Piper betle)* wrapped around shaved betel nut *(sopari, Areca catechu),* and flavorings, fastened with a clove.

Chapatis, Potato Wafers, and Parsi Wedding Pickle (lagan nu achar)*

Basket panir (topli nu panir)

Wedding-Style Fish (lagan no sahas)*
Eggs on Anything, served over onions (kanda par ida)*
Kid Stewed with Potatoes (kid papeta ma gos) or masala chicken*
Wedding custard (lagan nu kastar)
Grandmother's Pulao, made with kid, served with masala ni dar*
Kulfi
Nuts and pan
Fizzy soft drinks

Modern Menus

BREAKFAST AFTER THE FARMERS' MARKET
Blood orange juice or melon, depending on the season
Parsi Scrambled Eggs*
Whole wheat Chapatis with butter*
More of same with jam or honey
Parsi Tea with Lemongrass and Mint*

BREAKFAST PICNIC AT THE BEACH OR ON A JOURNEY
Orange juice or Mimosas
Parsi Omelet sandwiched in lightly buttered Chapatis or good rustic bread,
    with avocado slices and a brush of Parsi Tomato Chutney*
Grapes and Date Pastries*
Coffee or tea

IN-NEED-OF-COMFORT BREAKFAST
A bowl of Firoza's Khichri with one or two poached eggs on it*
Darjeeling or Nilgiri tea

AN EASY CRUMBLESS LAZY MORNING PICNIC IN BED
Figs and cherries
Creamy Panir, with walnuts and mint leaves*
Warmed Chapatis*
Homemade apricot jam or Bottle Gourd Jam*
Coffee, tea, champagne, or Navarro Gewürztraminer grape juice and fizzy water

A LIGHT SPRING LUNCH

*Eggs on Anything, served over Allium Confit**

*Smoked Fish Spread on toasted thin baguette slices**

Young greens dressed with avocado oil and rice vinegar

Strawberries

*New Year's Milk Shake**

A LIGHT SUMMER LUNCH

*Eggs on Anything, served over Sweet-Sour Tomatoes**

*Toasted Papads**

Sunflower sprouts with a dressing of rice bran oil and lemon juice

Fruit

FESTIVE CASUAL INDOOR-OUTDOOR SUMMER LUNCH

*Roasted Cashews with Ajwain**

*Potato Wafers**

*Mother's "Italian" Eggs**

*Masala Seafood with shrimp and squid on skewers**

*Parsiburgers—spicy for adults, gingery and garlicky for kids**

Rice and corn salad with flecks of avocado, green chiles, and fresh coriander

*Parsi Ratatouille**

Green salad with a fruity vinaigrette

Watermelon

*Giant Cookie**

BIRTHDAY LUNCH

*Everyday Dal**

*Perfect Plain Rice**

*Pomelo and Coconut Salad with crab, on a bed of greens**

*Toasted Papads**

*Semolina Birthday Breakfast Pudding with a fruit compote**

TEA PARTY

*Parsi Green Chutney on crustless sandwiches**

*Smoked Fish Spread on crustless sandwiches**

*Cardamom Cake**

*Date Pastries**

*Darjeeling or Nilgiri tea, plain, or Parsi Tea with Mint and Lemongrass, milk and sugar**

SPRING DINNER

*Carrot and Raisin Salad**

*Fish in Banana-Leaf Parcels**

*Parsi Hash Yellow Potatoes**

*Quick-Cooked Greens**

*Milk Pudding**

VALENTINE'S DAY LATE SUPPER

*Chicken Livers in Green Masala, made with chicken hearts**

Salad of hearts of romaine and fresh hearts of palm

*Jellied Pineau des Charentes in a heart-shaped mold, with blood orange segments**

OUR OWN MARCH 21 DINNER

Lots of fried things—sliced sweet potato, eggplant, lotus root, taro stem, fenugreek greens,
*   spinach leaves, and a big bowl of Date and Tamarind Chutney**

*Nana's Biryani with Angel-Hair Potatoes, garnished with pistachios and silver leaf **

*Seared Ginger Raita**

*Braised Greens (use flowering mustard greens)**

*Toasted Papads**

Clementines

*New Year's Milk Shake**

SUMMER MAJOR BIRTHDAY DINNER

*Masala Seafood made with shrimp**

*Everyday Dal served as a chilled soup with chives and chive blossoms**

*Twice-Cooked Grilled Kid**

*Simplest Pulao**

*Smoky Eggplant Salad (use a coal from the grill)**

Amaranth wilted with seared ginger and tomato

*Cardamom Cake served with sweet yogurt and a plum compote**

ANY-SEASON FAMILY DINNER

*Parsiburgers with mint**

Avocado slices with a squeeze of lime juice

Baked or boiled new potatoes

Steamed seasonal vegetables

Green salad

Fruit

SUMMER DINNER FOR A GRADUATE

*Roasted Cashews with Ajwain**

*Taro-Leaf Rolls**

*Fish in Coconut Milk**

*Perfect Plain Rice**

*Chopped Watercress Salad with Ginger Vinaigrette**

*Jardalu Ice Cream**

RUSTIC FALL DINNER

*Miniature Irene's Fabulous Fish Cakes**

*Lentils and Lamb Tongue**

Crusty baguette

*Cabbage Salad with Lime and Mint**

Sweet onions, coarsely chopped, with coarse salt

Yogurt, grapes, and honey

FALL BIRTHDAY DINNER

*Roasted Cashews with Ajwain and watermelon radish pickles**

*Everyday Dal**

*Perfect Plain Rice**

*Seafood Ragout**

*Mother's Favorite Chicken**

Lacinato kale stir-fried with ginger

Curly endive salad

*Pomegranate Ice and Cardamom Shortbread**

THANKSGIVING DINNER

Grilled Thanksgiving Turkey with a watercress garnish*

Stuffing with wild mushrooms and Parsi Garam Masala*

Thanksgiving Brussels Sprouts*

Quick cranberry and Asian pear chutney

Pumpkin Crescents with Curry Leaves*

Cardamom-crusted pecan pie

FESTIVE WINTER BIRTHDAY DINNER

Roasted Cashews with Ajwain*

Everyday Dal*

Crab Gratin*

Chicken with Apricots braised with dried prunes and cherries and garnished with
   Angel-Hair Potatoes*

Farro and wild rice pilaf

Salad of bitter greens

Semolina Birthday Breakfast Pudding with raisins in grappa, Fuyu persimmons,
   and blood oranges*

CHRISTMAS DINNER

Parsi Pâté on toast*

Oysters with Simple Onion Kachumbar "mignonette"*

Smoky Masala Grilled Quail*

Firoza's Khichri*

Turnips and their greens

Watercress dressed with argan oil and lemon juice

Mother's Famous Jardalu Trifle*

RECOVERY DINNER AFTER NEW YEAR'S

Quick-pickled lotus root

Mulligatawny with Perfect Plain Rice*

Chayote crescents with lime and salt

Green salad with pomelo

Raisins on their stems, walnuts, and dried figs

FESTIVE COCKTAIL PARTY

Pomegranate and White Rum Cocktail or Pomegranate Kir Royale*
Scotch and soda
Fresh Limeade or Fresh Lime Soda for nondrinkers*
Roasted Cashews with Ajwain*
Toasted Papads*
Cheese and Almond Crisps*
Mother's "Italian" Eggs, made with extra-small eggs*
Miniature Parsiburgers in soft rolls or focaccia*
Masala Seafood (use shrimp) with lime*
Smoky Eggplant Salad, with romaine scoops*
Yogurt Cheese, with toasted Chapati triangles*
Smoked Fish Spread on toast*
Tangerines, grapes, dates, dried figs, and walnuts

GLOSSARY

The ingredients below are listed according to their common names in English, followed by their name in Parsi Gujarati. To help you shop for them at stores or farmers' markets, their Hindi name may also appear.

AJWAIN OR AJOWAN SEED | AJMO

Ajwain (Trachyspermum ammi or *Carum copticum)* is used all over the subcontinent for food and medicine. Its culinary and medicinal use extends to the Middle East and Africa. Parsis add it to bean dishes and flavor savory snacks with it. Because they have aromatic constituents in common, *ajwain* is often confused with thyme or oregano seed. All three are high in thymol, a powerful antiseptic and anti-inflammatory. *Ajwain* is actually an umbelliferous plant (in the same family as carrots and parsley) related to cumin, caraway, dill, and anise; like them, it is thought to have powerful medicinal properties as a digestive. Sometimes it's bundled into a cloth, warmed, and used as a poultice for chest complaints.

"AJWAIN" LEAF | AJMO NA PATRA

This is another botanical mix-up. These big, fleshy, thyme-flavored leaves with scalloped edges belong to a botanically unrelated plant, *Coleus* or *Plectranthus amboinicus,* sometimes known as Cuban oregano, an easy grower in warm climates or seasons. *"Ajwain"* leaves are perfect for batter-frying and cooking as a vegetable. Several cultures use them as a remedy for chest troubles, especially coughs. Look for them at Southeast Asian or Latin American groceries or farmers' market stalls, or try to grow some yourself. Plants root easily from cuttings.

ALMOND | BADAM

Almonds *(Prunus amygdalus)* are native to central and western Asia and most certainly were a part of the cooking of ancient Persia. For Parsis, they are the most highly prized nut, a sign of bounty and prosperity, and a properly outfitted ritual tray, a *ses,* will usually have a few almonds on it for their symbolic value. They are also prized for their contribution to savory meat and chicken dishes and are a popular garnish or main ingredient in sweetmaking.

AMARANTH | CHOLAI BHAJI

In any of its varieties, red, green, or bicolored, amaranth (*Amaranthus* spp.) is one of the most popular greens with Parsis, who usually cook it with onions and tomatoes, sometimes with meat or under eggs, or serve it deep-fried as a garnish. There's

hardly a food plant in the world as widely distributed. Here in the Bay Area, it grows neglected and unharvested in driveways and parking lots. Look for it at Chinese or Southeast Asian markets or specialty produce stores.

ASAFETIDA | HING

Asafetida isn't really a part of Parsi cooking, except in one instance: our spice mixture known as Sambhar Masala (page 37). A resin collected from the roots of a fennel-like plant, *Ferula assafoetida,* native to central Asia, asafetida, whose name translates as "stinking resin," is valued as a digestive and a flavor booster in many Indian cuisines. It's most commonly found powdered, greatly diluted if not altogether adulterated with wheat flour. Look for it in resinous form, and do not be put off by its sulfurous smell.

BASIL SEED | TUKHMURIYA NI BIYA

Tiny, black seeds of a type of basil, *Ocimum basilicum,* found in central Asia as well as South and Southeast Asia, *tukhmuriya* is valued for its cooling and soothing properties. Basil seeds are an indispensable part of a sweet milky drink, *faluda* (page 278), that Parsis are supposed to drink on March 21 but can enjoy all year round. When soaked, the seeds expand quickly and dramatically into black specks with a translucent, jelly-like coating. You can find them in Indian shops, sometimes sold as *takmaria,* or at Thai or Southeast Asian markets as *med maeng lak.* The Thai product often has less sand and chaff than what we get from India.

BITTER GOURD | KARELA

Also known as bitter melon or bitter cucumber, bitter gourd (*Momordica charantia*) comes in several varieties. Most commonly found in U.S. markets is an unevenly ridged spindle-shaped variety that is 4 to 12 inches long, along with one that's similarly shaped

but smaller and covered with little bumps. What they have in common is an intense bitterness that can be only partly leached out with salt. Chinese cooks use salty black beans to balance the bitterness; Parsi cooks use sweetness, usually jaggery, and cook the vegetable until it is almost meltingly soft. Bitter gourd does not need to be peeled. To prepare it, cut it into slices or cubes, sprinkle heavily with salt, and let it rest for about 2 hours. Squeeze out the accumulated water and rinse the bitter gourd before cooking. In Indian and other traditional medical systems, bitter gourd juice (from either the gourd or the even more bitter leaves) is the sovereign remedy for liver problems and diabetes.

BLACK-EYED PEAS | CHAURA

Parsis love dried black-eyed peas *(Vigna unguiculata)* in a richly flavored stew with goat trotters, or cooked by themselves. In the late summer, we buy them fresh at the farmers' markets. As with favas, their preparation entails some patient shelling, but they are delicious when young and green and take no time to cook.

BOTTLE GOURD | DODHI

The bottle gourd *(Lagenaria siceraria)* is a vegetable with a long history, dispersed in both directions from its tropical African origins. Dried, it's used to make water bottles, cups, and mu-  sical instruments. Young and tender bottle gourds are a favorite Parsi vegetable, with a gentle, neutral quality that lends itself to savory as well as sweet treatments. Besides being available at farmers' markets, they're increasingly sold at mainstream markets, not just those catering to Indian and other Asian clients. Look for bottle gourd sold as *upo* (Tagalog) or *cucuzza* (Italian).

CARAWAY | SHAH JIRA

Caraway seeds *(Carum carvi)* go into the making of Dhana Jiru (page 38; also called *dhansak masala*), a compound powdered spice. Otherwise, they don't appear much in Parsi cooking except in cakes, biscuits, and *vasanu,* a wintertime fortifier made with seeds and spices.

CARDAMOM | ELCHI

Before Parsis even came to India, it is likely that our ancestors were using Indian cardamom, which must have come to Persia along the ancient spice routes. Cardamom is the fruit or seedpod of a member of the ginger family, *Elettaria cardamomum,* native to India. Parsis use cardamom liberally in savory and sweet dishes. At the end of a meal, its properties as a digestive are particularly welcome. There's some confusion about green versus white cardamom. The white ones are bleached, but they are otherwise the same. Buy cardamom pods whole in small quantities from places that are likely to have a quick turnover. I keep a jar of already husked cardamom seeds for lazy moments, but buy these in even smaller quantities. Many Parsi women carry cloves and cardamom in their handbags as an emergency munch or mouth refresher. I do, too.

CARDAMOM, BLACK | ELCHO

The large, dark, rough-skinned seedpod of black cardamom *(Amomum subulatum),* another member of the ginger family, is a variety of cardamom not used a great deal in Parsi cooking, except as an ingredient in a complex spice blend of many aromatics known as *dhansak masala* or Dhana Jiru (page 38). Occasionally, it finds its way into *pulaos* or biryanis.

CASHEW | KAJU

Imagine the jubilation when the Portuguese brought cashews *(Anacardium occidentale)* to India from Brazil. India is now one of the world's major exporters of this beloved, wickedly addictive nut. Buy cashews raw and unsalted, and select for taste, not size. It's so easy to roast them yourself. Commercially "roasted" cashews are usually fried, which means they're likely to go stale sooner. For thickening gravies and curries, there's no need to buy whole cashews—broken ones will do. Some organic farms on the west coast of India have started exporting cashews to the United States, and they're excellent.

CASSIA | TAJ

This is what Parsis often use as cinnamon. It's a little different from the smooth, tightly furled quills of true cinnamon. Cassia *(Cinnamomum cassia)* looks like flat bits of dark, rough, brownish-gray bark lined in russet; it has a pronounced robust cinnamon scent and a sweet flavor. Look for it at Indian or Southeast Asian groceries. If you can't find it, use cinnamon, *Cinnamomum zeylanicum.*

CASSIA LEAF | TEJ, TAJ, OR TAMAL PATTA

The leaves of cassia (see above) are often referred to by Indian writers as bay leaves.

They are not. Look for dried cassia leaves at Indian and Southeast Asian groceries. Parsis use cassia leaves in *pulaos* and as an ingredient in Dhana Jiru (page 38), a complex spice blend. Bay leaves can be substituted, but use half the quantity.

CHICKPEAS | CHANNA

Channa can refer to the whole chickpea *(Cicer arietinum),* one of India's favorite munch foods, sold everywhere to everyone. *Channa dal* refers to the husked and split version, a particularly tasty legume. Whole roasted *channa* is used in Parsi cooking as a thickener for curries. The dal is turned into a warmly spiced stew on its own or a part of *dhansak* (page 178). Chickpea flour *(besan)* is used in *patrel* (page 54) and as a thickener for Yogurt Soup (page 78). It's also a good facial scrub, often mixed with rose water, cleaning without drying out the skin.

CHILES, DRIED RED | MARCHA

Chiles *(Capsicum annuum* v. *annuum)* came to India with the Portuguese, though I have heard people arguing about which way the exchange really went. A note on orthography here: in Indian and British English, it's a chilly; more than one and you have chillies. In Bombay, most Parsi households use two kinds of dried red chiles—the Kashmiri, for its brilliant color when ground; and the Goa, for its heat. Outside India, we have to make do with what is exported and imported. Most commonly available at Indian and other Asian markets is the cayenne variety. Buy it in small amounts and store it out of the light. If it gets so old that the color fades, start over with a new batch. Parsis use whole dried red chiles to flavor dishes without making them hot. They are not intended to be eaten except by someone who takes delight in doing so. If you're particularly sensitive to capsaicin, shake the seeds out; otherwise, leave them in. See also Chilly Powder, Indian, below.

CHILES, FRESH GREEN AND RED | LILA MARCHA

For many years, anyone in need of fresh green chiles *(Capsicum annuum* v. *annuum)* had to be content with whatever was available, mostly jalapeños and serranos. Now we can find the particular chiles we need for most cuisines. For Parsi food, the fresh chile of choice is again the cayenne variety, commonly sold as *chile de árbol* or labeled as a Thai chile. Even the tiny, hot Vietnamese chiles will do in a pinch. Serranos and jalapeños, however delicious, don't have the "correct" taste or texture. Look for long, hot green chiles at farmers' markets and groceries catering to Indians and Southeast Asians. Fresh red *chiles de árbol* are more mature versions of the same chile.

I find that using scissors to snip chiles instead of chopping them keeps capsaicin off my fingers. Leave the seeds in unless you are nervous about the heat. You have to taste each batch ôf chiles, and even within one handful there can be some variation, just like people. Fresh green chiles are often used whole in Parsi food. Depending on the amount of heat you want them to deliver, you can slit them or leave them whole. Whoever gets a whole chile can either enjoy it or ignore it. It usually gets pushed to the side of the plate.

CHILLY POWDER, INDIAN | MARCHA NI BHUKHI

This is the same as cayenne pepper, and is not to be confused with paprika or Tex-Mex chili powder. Chilly powders vary in color, heat, and fineness of grind. For Parsi purposes, we need one with good color, a fine grind, and moderate heat. It's tempting to buy gorgeous large packets of the stuff, but unless you go through a lot of it, buy in modest amounts more often. Korean groceries sell excellent chilly powder, bright and fragrant. Ground chile, like ground anything, loses its spark and flavor more rapidly. Store it in a jar out of the light.

CHIRONJI NUT | CHAROLI

About the size and color of lentils, *chironji* nuts are the small seeds of a tree *(Buchanania latifolia)* grown for its timber and other economic purposes. Colonel Heber Drury, writing in the late nineteenth century, says the "natives" prized them as a substitute for almonds. Nowadays, it would be quite the opposite. Parsis use *charoli* in sweets, embedded in the top of cakes and biscuits, or as a garnish for milky puddings. Should you not be able to find them at an Indian grocery, use chopped pistachios or almonds. *Charoli* is both scarce and expensive; store it in the freezer to keep it sweet.

CINNAMON | TAJ

This is the true cinnamon, *Cinnamomum zeylanicum,* that comes in highly aromatic, tightly furled quills from Sri Lanka or Southeast Asia. Where cassia (see above) has a sweet intensity of flavor, true cinnamon has a headier scent and for centuries has been regarded as the superior spice. Parsis don't make a distinction between the two.

CLOVES | LAVANG

In Parsi food taxonomy, cloves *(Syzygium aromaticum)* and cinnamon are spoken of in the same breath. When one is used, the other generally is, too. Pounded cloves, along with cinnamon, cardamom, and other aromatics, go into Dhana Jiru (page 38) and Parsi Garam Masala (page 37). They are used whole in meat dishes, in cooking rice, and in making chutneys. Parsi women sometimes carry a box of cloves and cardamom around as a mouth refresher.

COCONUT | NARIYAL, KOPRU

Nariyal refers to the whole coconut, and *kopru,* to the flesh. Coconut palms *(Cocos nucifera)* fringe the length of India's western coast, where Parsis landed after the long flight from Persia. Dairy-loving Parsis found in coconut milk the smooth, creamy qualities they must have cherished in the food of their abandoned homeland. It's hard to imagine Parsi food without coconut. We love coconut in all its stages. Young and tender, the shell barely formed, it makes one of the most refreshing drinks on earth; in its leathery state, the flesh is delicious eaten with unrefined sugar; mature coconuts are used for their grated flesh or for extracting milk. The liquid in the coconut is known as coconut water. What you get from squeezing the grated flesh is coconut milk; and if that milk stands, cream rises to the top.

Alternatives to cracking open a coconut are to buy frozen, unsweetened grated coconut or coconut milk; unsweetened canned coconut milk; or dried, powdered coconut milk. Compared to these options, desiccated coconut often smells and tastes stale. Please see page 41 for a detailed discussion of making coconut milk. A favorite childhood treat was coconut eaten with jaggery. Try it.

CORIANDER LEAF (CILANTRO) | KOTHMIR

At its best, fresh coriander *(Coriandrum sativum)* has a green pungency that you can smell as you approach it. You'll find it in any well-run Parsi kitchen along with its companions, green chiles, curry leaves, and limes. In varying amounts, it goes into so many dishes that you'd think everything would taste the same; it doesn't. I buy close-to-blooming *kothmir* at farmers' markets, where it's sold in feathery-leafed bunches bursting with flavor. See also Coriander Seed, below.

CORIANDER SEED | DHANA

Coriander seed is as intrinsic to the taste of Parsi cooking as its leaf is. The seed is ground into powdered and paste masalas, usually with its companion spice, cumin, both members of the parsley or carrot family, the Umbelliferae. Coriander seed is often said to have a citrus quality. See also Coriander Leaf, above.

CUMIN, BLACK | KALA JIRA

Related to ordinary cumin in that it's also umbelliferous, black cumin *(Bunium bulbocastanum* or *B. persicum)* has slender elongated seeds that lend a dusty, smoky, intriguing quality to anything that's cooked with them. It's also vastly more expensive than conventional cumin. *Kala jira* is not used a great deal in Parsi food except in elaborate *pulaos* and biryanis. I like it in marinades and rubs as well. Ask for it at Indian groceries (as *kala zira* or *kala jira*) because it's sometimes tucked away. Do not be misled by mail-order sources into ordering *Nigella sativa* seeds, which are often erroneously called black cumin.

CUMIN SEED | JIRU

If it's possible to have a favorite spice, cumin *(Cuminum cyminum)* is for me a top contender, earthy, pungent, savory. When combining it with coriander, Parsi cooks usually use half as much cumin. It seasons snack foods, rice, and all manner of savory dishes, and is one of the principal ingredients of Dhana Jiru (page 38), one of our characteristic spice mixes. The Oxford English Dictionary, the American Spice Association, and Webster's tell us to call this spice "cum-min," not "kew-min," so please don't correct anyone who says it this way.

CURRY LEAF | KARI PATTA

Related to citrus, curry-leaf plants *(Murraya koenigii)* grow freely in many parts of India. The name derives from the Tamil names, *kara pincha* and *kara veppala,* rather than through any link with curry. In Bombay, vegetable sellers give them away with a purchase. They're a major contributor to the authentic taste and mood of Indian cooking, tasting and smelling of nothing but themselves. Parsis use *kari patta* in curries, dals, vegetable dishes, and snack foods, where they join other aromatics in starting or finishing a dish. Curry-leaf plants can be grown where it is warm but need to be brought indoors in winter. Several nurseries sell plants (see Sources).

Store curry leaves in the refrigerator or in a cool larder in a loose plastic or paper bag so that they dry rather than rot. Dry and curled up, they're still usable. The leaves can be frozen. In general, a leaf that dries around your house can still lend scent and flavor to a cooked dish, but never, ever bother to buy dried leaves from a shop. The same goes for dried coriander and parsley. I think it's wrong to sell them.

DAL | DAR

Dal is the common Indian term for the many varieties of dried and split legumes. Both words, *dar* and *dal,* are used in Parsi food terminology.

DATES | KHAJUR

Parsis love all dried fruits and nuts, a category known as *meva,* but we have a particularly long connection with the date *(Phoenix dactylifera).* Hard, dry dates, *kharak,* are used in making wedding pickle; softer ones, for my favorite Parsi pastry, *khajur ni ghari* (page 264).

DHANA JIRU

Dhana jiru literally means "coriander and cumin [ground together]," but for Parsis, it's the name for a complex spice mixture containing about a dozen aromatic and flavoring spices in addition to the two that give it its name. See page 38 for a recipe, and Sources for commercial alternatives.

DHANSAK MASALA

This is the compound powdered spice used in seasoning not only *dhansak,* the emblematic Parsi dish, but many others. It can be left out, but the taste of the finished dish will not be traditionally correct. The term *dhana jiru* (see above) is often used interchangeably with *dhansak masala.*

DILL | SUVA

Dill, *Anethum graveolens,* is a popular digestive in its seed form and is used in Parsi cooking in special fortifying sweets. Leaves are used more often as a vegetable than as an herb, usually in combination with spinach. Big bunches of fresh dill greens can be found at farmers' markets wherever there are Southeast Asian vendors. Dill greens cooked as a vegetable are surprisingly delicious.

DRUMSTICKS | SEKTA NI SINGH

Drumsticks are the dangling seedpods of the
Moringa oleifera tree, and they do indeed resemble drumsticks. Oil extracted from the seeds, *ben* seed oil, was once used in watchmaking and repair. Native to India, *Moringa* is now a common tree in the New World tropics, though sadly underused as a food source. Leaves, flowers, and seedpods can all be eaten. Philippine vendors sell bunches of leaves as *malungay,* but the seedpods are the real treat. Indian groceries and other specialty produce markets sometimes sell them. Though widely available at Indian markets, canned or frozen drumsticks can give you only a faint impression of the real thing.

To prepare drumsticks for stews or curries, trim off the tops and bottoms and pare or scrape off the tough, ridged, dull green outer skin. Cut into finger-length segments and bundle them together in threes or fours tied with a strip of pared-off skin or kitchen string. This may seem unduly fiddly, but it keeps the drumstick segments from breaking apart in stews.

EGGPLANT | VENGNA

Brinjal is the common Indian English word for the familiar purple vegetable also known as eggplant or aubergine, the latter word derived from Arabic, not French. From its ancient origins in India, eggplant *(Solanum melongena)* spread in both directions, brought to the New World by the Spanish, who got it from the Arabs, who got it from the Persians. Eggplant comes in a bewildering array of shapes, sizes, and colors. Parsi cooks select the size and shape with a particular dish in mind. Large, fat, and full of seeds; long and slender; small and egg-shaped—each has its place. For the

Smoky Eggplant Salad (page 218), seeds are desirable; for eggplant steamed whole, the slender Chinese or Japanese varieties are best; for stuffing or as part of a stew or a curry, use the little eggy ones.

ELEPHANT'S FOOT YAM | SURAN

The large, bulbous tuber of *Amorphophallus campanulatus,* known as *suran* in Gujarati and *zimikand* in Hindi, is aptly named, for its size and shape resemble nothing so much as an elephant's foot. It's a popular starchy root vegetable in Bombay, where vegetable sellers will cut off just as much as the buyer needs. Every now and then, it appears in Indian shops in the United States, and if you're not required to buy the whole thing at vast cost, it's well worth trying. It needs to be peeled before cooking.

FENNEL SEED | VARIALI

Another umbelliferous relative of cumin, caraway, anise, *ajwain,* and dill, fennel *(Foeniculum vulgare)* isn't used a great deal in Parsi cooking, though it's considered a salutary thing to chew after a meal, sometimes lightly toasted and mixed with crystals of rock sugar. Its stomach-settling properties are put to use with an infusion for colicky babies called Woodward's Gripe Water, a nineteenth-century patent medicine that's still sold in India today

FENUGREEK LEAF | METHI BHAJI

Fenugreek *(Trigonella foenum-graecum)* is a generally popular green leafy vegetable, prized for its tonic effect on the system. It is sold in bunches with fully formed trifoliate leaves, but Parsis like to eat them in their sand-grown sprout stage, threadlike white stalks and leaf tips barely formed but full of flavor. *Methi* is required in *dhansak;* cooked with onions and fresh coriander leaves (cilantro), it's a favorite substrate for eggs. Fully grown *methi* may require a preliminary blanching. If you are unfamiliar with *methi,* try it first in combination with potatoes or another green (page 191). See also Fenugreek Seed, below.

FENUGREEK SEED | METHI

Anyone who has tasted artificial maple flavoring knows the assertive flavor of *methi* seed. It is also one of the characteristic ingredients in commercial curry powders for export and figures in the frequently used Parsi spice mixes *sambhar masala* and *dhana jiru.* It has a powerful, lingering quality some people find disturbing, others exciting and comforting. One of the most popular Parsi pickles made with small green mangoes is known as *methia nu achar,* or fenugreek pickle, after its dominant flavoring ingredient.

FIELD BEANS OR HYACINTH BEANS | PAPRI

Long cultivated in India, this flat bean, *Dolichos lablab,* with purple-tinged edges is now an entrenched part of Parsi cuisine. Cooked with or without meat in stews, *papri* has a flavor particularly well set off by *ajwain* seed. It appears at farmers' markets in the summer, sold by Philippine vendors, and can also be found at Indian markets occasionally. Unlike ordinary green beans, which can be delicious when crisp, *papri* has to be cooked thoroughly to be fully appreciated. The slightly bitter mature dried beans within the pod *(valpapri)* are sold and cooked as a dal in India. Parsis know *valpapri* as *titori.*

GARLIC | LASAN

There is only one kind of garlic *(Allium sativum)* to use in Parsi cooking—fresh heads. If you're ever using cookbooks written for the Indian public, keep in mind that garlic cloves in the United States are much bigger than Indian ones. The recipes in this book assume the U.S. variety. Garlic—with its partner, ginger—is the foundation of all Parsi savory dishes.

GHEE

Ghee is often described as clarified butter. It is, but cooked further, so that the milk solids become toasty and granular before the liquid is poured off (see the recipe on page 35). While regular or clarified butter can be used as a substitute, the taste will definitely not be the same. In bygone days, lavish, visible use of ghee was the mark of a good host. The miraculous thing about ghee is that even a little bit makes a huge difference to the results of a dish. Please try scrambling eggs with ghee (page 84)—it's the perfect way of understanding this wonderful food. Among Parsis, melted ghee is used in votive oil lamps, where it makes the flame burn true, bright, and relatively smokeless.

GINGER | ADU

Ginger *(Zingiber officinale),* along with garlic, is one of the mainstays of Parsi cooking. It's used in its fresh form, the rhizome, in any number of dishes, mostly savory. Dried, it's part of *vasanu,* a Parsi wintertime mixture of seeds, dried fruits, and spices, eaten to fortify mind and body, almost like the Italian *panforte.* There was a time when fresh ginger was difficult to find. Now we can be happy that fresh ginger is a supermarket item. Whether to peel ginger is up to you. Sometimes the skin is so thin that it can be easily scraped off.

GINGER-GARLIC PASTE | ADU LASAN

This finely ground paste of roughly equal parts fresh ginger and garlic (page 36) is essential to Parsi cooking. *Adu lasan* is rubbed on meat and poultry before cooking, and most savory dishes start with a small amount of it sizzled in oil along with softened onions.

GUAR BEANS | GUARPHALLI

A particular favorite in Hindu Gujarati cuisine, these slender green beans appear at farmers' markets and Indian markets from time to time, sold as expensive exotics, which makes Indians chuckle. This is the plant *(Cyamopsis tetragonoloba)* that yields what chemists call gum guar (commonly known as guar gum), with its many uses in food technology. The young and tender beans have a slightly bitter edge that is tempered by cooking with tomatoes or a touch of sweetness. Parsis cook *guarphalli* with braised meat—definitely a dish in the family-night category, but absolutely delicious. Seen out of that particular context, it's a vegetable well worth exploring. Make Guar Bean Ragout (page 195), or add the beans to Savory Braised Lamb (page 112). Larger beans need to be strung.

HONEY | MADH

Every household has to have its bottle of honey. In Bombay, this might be the intriguing dark, thin forest honey from the hills near Poona. Honey is seen more in medicinal than in gastronomic terms. The sovereign remedy for colds and sore throats is a soothing hot toddy of honey, lime juice, and brandy.

JAGGERY | GOR

The word *jaggery* comes to us from the Tamil *chakri*. It refers to solid, unrefined cane or palm sugar sold in blocks or cones; it is made by boiling down cane or palm syrup and pouring it into forms. Jaggery is always available in Indian markets, sold in conical blocks or broken up in packets. Sometimes it's soft and pale, sometimes darker, variability being a characteristic of artisanal products. If you can't find it, use palm sugar from Thailand, Malaysia, Indonesia, or Sri Lanka. If none of those comes to hand, use brown sugar or sorghum. The consistency of jaggery available in American markets can vary from fudge-soft to rock-hard, and there may not be a choice. Sometimes you might need the blunt side of a sturdy cleaver to hack pieces of jaggery off the block; at other times, the kind of knife you see in the illustration will do quite well.

JARDALU

These sweet-kernel dried apricots *(Prunus armeniaca* 'Hunza') come from Afghanistan or Pakistan, where they're grown in high valleys from six thousand to eight thousand feet above sea level. The "almonds" of sweet-kernel apricots contain little or none of the prussic acid found in conventional varieties. The Gujarati name *jardalu* comes from the Persian *zard-alu,* "yellow plum." Kid or chicken dishes cooked with *jardalus* are among the best known and most loved in the Parsi repertoire. Look for *jardalus* at Indian, Pakistani, or Afghani groceries, checking them carefully through the plastic bag to be sure they look sound and aren't riddled with holes. Color is less important. *Jardalus* as we buy them in the United States are too hard to be eaten as is; they need to be soaked and poached (see page 250). Be sure to take the time to crack open the pits to get to the kernels, which are like the best almond you've ever tasted.

JUJUBE | BOR

Grown across Asia from China to Iran, this fruit *(Zizyphus jujuba),* sometimes known as a Chinese date, appears at California farmers' markets at the end of the summer.

 Unlike the name of the popular candy, the name of the fruit is pronounced *joojoob.* The fruit is sweet, but not much else. It is one of the components of a correctly made *lagan nu achar,* the traditional Parsi Wedding Pickle (page 237). The size of small plums, fresh jujubes start out lemon yellow, turning a reddish brown as they ripen and wrinkle. Look for dried jujubes in Chinese medicine shops. They look like dark reddish-brown wrinkly dates.

KOKAM

A fruit native to the western coast of India, *kokam (Garcinia indica)* has a luscious relative, the mangosteen. *Kokam* lends a subtle acidity to stews and curries. Parsis slip several sections of purple-black *kokam* rinds into curries as an alternative to tamarind. Buy it at Indian groceries, looking for *kokam* that feels leathery-soft. The hard variety is not bad, but it has a less-delicate taste. *Kokam* needs no preparation except a quick rinse.

LEMONGRASS | LILI CHAI

Lemongrass *(Cymbopogon citratus)* for Parsis means the long, citrus-scented, blade-like leaves, not the woody, bulbous stem end used in Southeast Asian cooking. The leaves are bundled into a teapot or saucepan along with mint and black tea to make a characteristically Parsi brew drunk with milk and sugar. Most markets sell only the stems, but perhaps market pressure will persuade them to offer the leaves as well. Lemongrass is not hard to grow, though it is hard to keep it contained.

LENTILS, BROWN | MASUR

The word *masur* describes the whole lentil *(Lens culinaris)*, smaller and darker than the common American variety. In its husked form it's known as *masur dal* (see Lentils, Red, below). For Parsis, protein-rich *masur* is one of the core dishes of our kitchen repertoire. Regular supermarket lentils will work perfectly well in making *masur* (page 180), but there's something extra-good about making it with smaller, darker lentils such as those from France, or with one of the various American boutique varieties, such as Beluga.

LENTILS, RED | MASUR NI DAR OR MASUR DAL

Husked brown lentils give us dark orange *masur dal,* the familiar "red" lentil. This is one of the quicker-cooking legumes, ready to eat in less than half an hour. Brown and red lentils can be bought at Indian groceries, certainly, but also at natural food stores in bulk bins. Keep them in a tightly closed container and they last for a long time.

LIME | LIMBU

When Parsis talk of limes, we think of what are known as Mexican or Key limes *(Citrus aurantifolia).* Yes, you can use Persian or Bearss or Silver or Rangpur limes, but the taste will not be that elusive thing, "correct." Lemons are to be used only as a last resort.

LONG BEANS | CHAURA

The word *chaura* refers to both the black-eyed pea and the whole tender green pod of *Vigna unguiculata* v. *sesquipedalis.* The closest thing we have in the United States to the tender green-bean stage of black-eyed peas is the long bean. These may look like long string beans, but they are definitely different. Parsis have several ways of enjoying them (see page 188). They can be cooked with meat or by themselves.

LOTUS ROOT | KAMAL KAKRI

This is the underwater rhizome of the lotus plant, *Nelumbium nelumbo* or *N. nucifera.* Fresh lotus root is sold either wrapped in individual segments, or as it grows, like salamis linked together, sometimes encrusted in mud. Lotus root doesn't figure

in Parsi cooking except idiosyncratically. Buy only fresh, sound-looking segments. Don't bother with canned or bottled lotus root.

MACE | JAVINTRI

The yellow, peachlike fruit of the nutmeg tree *(Myristica fragrans)* contains an ovoid, glossy brown seed wrapped in a web of brilliant red that fades to a quiet orange. This web is mace, with a lighter, more floral character than nutmeg, the spice within the seed. Parsis use it in making spice mixtures and in flavoring sweets. I can still remember my aunt showing me a fresh nutmeg fruit when I was five and splitting it open to show me what was inside. Be sure to store mace out of the light and buy it in strands, not powders.

MANGO | KERI

Native to India, where there are hundreds of varieties, but now pantropical, mangoes *(Mangifera indica)* are at the very top of many people's list of favorite fruits. The west coast of India is home to one of the most prized varieties, the Alphonso, which sometimes blinds Bombay people to the many other varieties on the market. Parsi cooking uses mangoes at all stages of ripeness. Green—meaning unripe—mangoes and middling-ripe ones are pickled in brine or oil, made into chutneys or jams, added to *dhansak* and other lentil dishes, and turned into drinks. Ripe mangoes are best eaten just as they are, though they lend themselves to lush ice creams, *kulfis,* and other desserts. Alphonso mangoes haven't been permitted into the United States yet, but there are successive waves of good to excellent mangoes of other varieties all year round, it seems, because somewhere in the world it's mango season. Buy mangoes that are firm, not soft. A red blush is not an indicator or a guarantee of ripeness, but a characteristic of certain varieties. Several Southern California growers have had great success with mangoes. These are generally green-skinned, full of flavor, and not at all fibrous.

MANGO GINGER | AMBA ARADH

Cousin to turmeric, mango ginger *(Curcuma amada)* is also a member of the ginger family. Its growing habit resembles that of turmeric, with shorter sections branching off longer, thicker ones. Green (unripe) mango and mango ginger smell so much alike that it's obvious how the plant got its popular name. Parsis view this as a medicinal plant with powerful anti-inflammatory properties, both internally and externally. I've even seen some European homeopathic arthritis remedies featuring extract of *Curcuma amada.*

It sometimes appears as a pickle, which is a good way to enjoy its piquant taste. Indian markets selling fresh turmeric may also have a bin of mango ginger nearby, called *am haldi.*

MASALA

Three syllables to describe what would otherwise take sentences. Masala is a broad category that refers to spices in general. It also refers to a single spice, or to several spices whole or ground that go into a specific dish. Masalas can be pounded dry or ground wet into a paste. In the ideal Parsi house, masala pastes are ground on a stone slab with a stone roller every morning for the day's use. From time to time, an itinerant craftswoman called a *tankiwali* will come to the door and painstakingly hammer new depressions into both slab and roller so that they keep their grip. In the pragmatic Parsi house of today, our handsome masala stones have become objects of contemplation, and what we use for powdering and grinding masalas is the indispensable wet-dry grinder (see page 30).

Many Parsi dishes start with *sabut masala,* whole spices cooked in ghee or oil to release their flavor. These are to be pushed to the side of the plate.

MINT | FUDINA

In Bombay, common mint *(Mentha spicata)* is often sold next to its tea partner, lemongrass leaves. Apart from being included in *dhansak,* its other culinary uses in a Parsi kitchen are idiosyncratic. We use it a lot; my mother did not.

MUNG BEANS | MAG

Whole green mung dal *(Vigna radiata)* is not as frequently used in Parsi cooking as the husked, split variety, which goes into *dhansak* and *khichri.* Not only does it cook quickly, but it's supposed to be easier to digest than the more robust *arhar* and *channa* dals. Look for it at Indian and Southeast Asian groceries.

MUSTARD POWDER | RAI

Parsis use mustard *(Brassica nigra)* in two forms. Mustard seeds (see below) are used as a finishing spice, heated in oil until they pop and release a toasty, mellow flavor. Crushed or ground to a powder, mustard becomes pungent and a little bitter. It goes into pickles and chutneys, such as our fruity wedding pickle, *lagan nu achar* (page 237), as well as into Banana Raita (page 225). It's also used mixed with vinegar or water into a paste as an accent in non-Parsi "English" food. Buy mustard at Indian groceries. You're sure, then, of getting the right kind (Colman's is also good).

MUSTARD SEED | RAI NA DANA

Parsis use whole mustard seeds in a *vaghar* (see page 32), where they are popped in hot oil along with other seasonings as a finishing touch to a dish. Mustard seeds (*Brassica* spp.) come in three colors: dark ivory (often called yellow), brown, and black. For Parsi food, stick with the brown. Mustard seeds need preliminary popping in hot oil to release their nutty flavor; otherwise, they float around doing not much of anything. I've seen recipes in which some innovative cook throws unpopped mustard seeds into a dish, but the results are not happy.

NUTMEG | JAIPHAL

Sailors approaching the Spice Islands of Indonesia could smell nutmeg *(Myristica fragrans)* on the breezes wafting offshore. Grate nutmeg in your kitchen and the scent reaches the next room. Parsis use nutmeg in dry spice mixes for its sweet warmth, and we grate it into or over sweets, especially those with milk. In Parsi food taxonomy, nutmeg is associated with cardamom. Please buy nutmeg whole and grate or powder it as needed. It keeps for a long time, especially when it's still in its outer shell. A little nutmeg grated on warm sweetened milk is a household remedy for insomnia; a lot of nutmeg is considered narcotic.

OKRA | BHIDA

In Indian English, we call these pods ladies' fingers. Okra *(Abelmoschus esculentus)* came to both India and the New World from Africa. Parsis love okra cooked with eggs or with braised meat, a dish probably of Persian origin that is found all over the Arab world. Okra is now a supermarket vegetable. Commonsense rules of selection apply: Whether it's ridged or smooth, green or dark pink, buy okra when it's young, firm, tender, and not streaked with black.

ONION | KANDO

Indian onions *(Allium cepa)* have a smell, taste, color, and texture of their own. The skins are rosy, the flesh is pink-purple, and their taste is so sweet and pungent that they're delicious even eaten raw. They are different from American yellow onions and even from sweet red ones, more closely resembling large shallots. Not quite as juicy when cut, they brown more easily, like shallots. Until someone starts to grow them in the United States, we have to settle for the onions available. Unless otherwise specified, use yellow onions. From time to time, we can buy large shallots that look and behave like Indian onions. Should you ever find them, buy them. In South India, shallotlike small onions are liberally used in cooking, but Parsis tend to stick with the larger variety sometimes called Bombay onion. For recipes using raw onions, look for Vidalia, Maui, or other sweet varieties.

PEPPERCORNS, BLACK | MARI NA DANA

Indian cooking could be divided into B.C. and A.C.—before and after chiles. In the B.C. period, black pepper, *Piper nigrum*—indigenous to the western coast of India— was the sole spice with fiery heat. Black peppercorns are a seasoning staple in Parsi kitchens, and were used in pre-Islamic Iran, where there was already a flourishing spice trade moving across Asian land and sea routes. Peppercorns are used whole, by themselves or along with other aromatics, in scenting and flavoring rice and meat dishes. Where cuisines of Western countries use pepper automatically as a seasoning, Parsis use it purposefully when its particular effect is wanted.

PIGEON PEAS | ARHAR DAL OR TUVAR DAL

Arhar and *tuvar* are both Gujarati words for the husked, split pigeon pea *(Cajanus cajan)* so popular in Latin America and the West Indies. Pigeon pea is the most widely used dal in India and certainly the most important one for Parsis, who see it as the dal of choice for *mori dar* (page 176) and the principal dal for *dhansak* (page 178). Look for it at Indian groceries; it's sold coated in oil and uncoated—the choice is yours. It takes a good 45 minutes to an hour to soften.

PLANTAIN | TARVANA KERA

Although they belong to the same genus as bananas, plantains *(Musa sapientum* or *M. paradisiaca)* are different in that they need to be cooked before eating. They can be cooked in their hard green stage, in their softer yellow stage, or when the skins turn completely black and the insides get really soft. Parsis cook plantains in their ripe stage, usually frying them as an accompaniment to braised meat, under eggs, or in a sweet. The best place to look for plantains is at markets geared to Central American and Caribbean customers. Ask for *maduros,* ripe ones.

POMEGRANATE | DARAM

Like fish and coconut, the pomegranate *(Punica granatum)* plays a dual role in Parsi life for its symbolic value and for its use in food, and goes far back into pre-Islamic Zoroastrian culture. To open a pomegranate tells you what it represents—abundance, fruitfulness, prosperity—and its ruby color is considered auspicious. How fortunate we are, then, that it tastes so good, sweet and tart. And now we are told that it is laden with antioxidants—the ideal food in form and function. Parsis eat the fruit fresh and drink the juice (for how to juice pomegranates, see page 274). Pomegranates have a relatively short season in the fall, but specialty produce stores and better supermarkets sell them into the winter months and even into early spring. Although by then they have begun to look tired and battered, they can be sound and juicy inside.

POMEGRANATE MOLASSES

Molasseslike only in appearance, pomegranate molasses is simply the boiled-down juice. Parsis in India generally don't use it, although it does play a part in modern Zoroastrian cooking in Iran. In our house, we always have it on hand for marinades. Middle Eastern markets sell pomegranate molasses in several brands. My favorites are Sadaf, more fruity, and Cortas. You can make your own by boiling pomegranate juice until it's dark and thick.

POMELO OR PUMMELO | PAPENAS

Also known as shaddocks, pomelos *(Citrus maxima)* are botanical ancestors of grapefruit. Their origin is South or Southeast Asia, but their distribution is worldwide. In appearance, they look like enormous grapefruit, but their rind has a characteristic and distinct smell. Inside, they're pithy, and either pink or white. The fruit itself is eaten for its flesh rather than its juice. For juice, go to grapefruit; for saladworthy sections of citrus with little capsules bursting with flavor, stick with pomelos and buy specimens that seem heavy for their size. Look for them at Chinese and Southeast Asian markets, farmers' markets, and specialty produce stores. The season begins in early winter and goes on for three months or so. The peel can be candied or turned into a delicious chutney.

POPPY SEED | KHASKHAS

Indian cooks use only the white seeds of a white variety of the opium poppy *(Papaver somniferum),* rather than the more familiar slate-colored seeds sprinkled on bagels. White poppy seeds have a creamy flavor accented by toasting. Alas, they don't have any of the narcotic properties of the juices from unripe seedpods. Parsis use *khaskhas* in thickening and enriching sauces or gravies. Stirred into melted and thickened jaggery, *khaskhas* makes a really interesting chewy candy, wonderful for children but disastrous for fillings and other dental fittings. Buy only white seeds for use in Indian cooking. Look for them at Indian markets. They smell stale when stored too long, so buy only enough to ensure a short-term supply.

POTATO | PAPETO, PAPETA

Parsi food taxonomy pairs onions with potatoes *(Solanum tuberosum),* a New World introduction, courtesy of the Portuguese. Onions and potatoes are invariably sold next to each other at Bombay markets and keep on meeting in any number of dishes. Potatoes are always on hand in a Parsi household. They're usually medium-size, yellowish-brown-skinned, and of the waxy rather than the mealy type. Yellow Finns and Yukon Golds are good equivalents. Certain dishes call for tiny potatoes, which are usually bought as needed. Rare, antique black silk saris embroidered in China with coin-size yellow and white dots are described as *kanda-papeta,* onions and potatoes.

RAISINS | DARAKH

Grapes (*Vitis* spp.) were grown in ancient Persia, so we may assume that raisins were there, too. Raisins are partnered with almonds in Parsi food categories. They appear on the ritual tray, the *ses,* as symbols of prosperity, and they're used as lavishly as circumstances allow in garnishing sweet and savory dishes. We have so many types of raisins to choose from. Parsis go for the golden ones over the dark. Recently, we've been seeing brilliant pink raisins from Flame grapes. These are spectacular, and I buy them whenever they're available.

RICE, BASMATI

India has hundreds of varieties of rice *(Oryza sativa),* but for many Parsis there's only one, basmati, which means "fragrant." Basmati is an extra-long-grain rice grown in the foothills of the Himalayas in both India and Pakistan. Its two main characteristics are its lovely scent and the grains' ability to expand lengthwise while they're cooking. Some California- or Texas-grown rice is now called basmati, but this is a misleading marketing term. It may be good rice, but basmati it's not. You can now find basmati rice in supermarkets, but I always buy it in ten-pound cloth bags at Indian or Pakistani groceries. Agricultural technology has done basmati rice both a service and a disservice: You no longer have to spend hours winnowing out chaff and pebbles, but monkeying about with fertilizers and high-yield seeds has resulted in rice that is no longer as fragrant as people remember it.

RICE, PRESSED | POHUA

This looks like rice that has been run over with a steam roller. *Pohua,* or *poha* in Hindi, is rice that has been soaked, parched, and then flattened. In preindustrial days, the flattening was done by hand in a mortar. Rice in this form is the foundation for a type of fried snack food popular all over India and for various quick-cooked savory or sweet dishes. Parsis cook pressed rice in the Hindu style, with potatoes and popped mustard seeds, or make a milky dessert out of it. Look for it as *poha* in Indian markets, where it comes in a finer and a coarser flake. Buy the finer of the two.

RICE, SURTI KOLAM | SURTI KOLAM

This fragrant, small-grained variety of rice comes from the area surrounding Surat in the state of Gujarat, where Parsis settled on arriving in India. Many people from the region prefer it to longer-grained basmati. I like having it on hand but do not see it as a substitute for basmati.

RIDGE GOURD | TURIA

Also known as Chinese okra, perhaps because of the ridges, the ridge gourd, *Luffa acutangula,* is a spectacular-looking vegetable that deserves wider use outside of the Asian cuisines that know and love it. *Turia* has a marvelous ability to soak up the flavors of whatever it's cooked in, yet keep its shape and texture. Young specimens don't need to be peeled or have their ridges pared off. (And see Sponge Gourd, below, also known as *turia.*)

ROSE SYRUP

For Parsis, rose syrup falls into the category of a *sharbat,* a syrup to be diluted with water to make a refreshing drink. The commercial Indian brands are alarmingly pink and synthetic; Middle Eastern, French, and Italian brands are a little closer to the flower, and some Italian and French rose syrups are delightful. Rose syrup is essential for *faluda,* the milky, festive New Year's drink (page 278).

ROSE WATER

Rose water is the by-product of steam-distilling rose petals. The essential oil of roses floats to the top, and what remains is rose water. For Parsis, rose water has eons of ritual, symbolic, and culinary importance behind it. A rose water sprinkler, a *golabaz,* is part of the assembly of objects on the ceremonial tray, the *ses.* In former days, arriving guests were sprinkled with rose water. Very few sweet dishes, especially those made with milk, are not scented with rose water. Good rose water can be delicate, exquisite, transporting. It's also hard to find. Indian rose water can seem unpleasant to some noses. Middle Eastern brands seem to have a truer flower note. The best I've found so far comes from Iran. To have an authentic taste, certain sweets need a touch or breath of rose water, so I always have it on hand, not just for the *golabaz.* A household remedy now almost extinct because of the ever-soaring price of sandalwood is the mixture of sandalwood powder and rose water as a complexion aid (see Sources).

SAFFRON | KESAR

It takes seventy thousand *Crocus sativus* flowers to produce one pound of saffron. Each one of those flowers has to have its stigmas carefully removed, so it isn't a surprise that saffron is the world's most expensive spice. Saffron originated in western Asia but spread in both directions. It has been grown in Kashmir for almost two millennia. We can be fairly sure that saffron was part of the diets of luxury-loving Persians in pre-Islamic times. Luxury-loving Parsis enjoy it to this day in *pulaos,* biryanis, and sweet dishes, especially nut halvas and *kulfi,* a rich ice cream. In the United States, we get excellent saffron from Spain, and also from Iran. Buy saffron from stores where there's likely to be brisk turnover.

SAMBHAR MASALA

Sambhar masala is one of the key spice mixtures in Parsi cooking. It is important to distinguish here between two similar-sounding items. There's the *sambhar* of South Indian cooking, a lentil and vegetable soup, and there's *sambhar masala* as used by Parsis. The masala sold to make the South Indian *sambhar* is different from the Parsi formulation. To make certain Parsi dishes taste both correct and delicious, *sambhar masala* is necessary, though it certainly isn't used in every single savory thing. Making your own (page 37) isn't difficult with a coffee mill reserved for grinding spices, or see Sources for commercial alternatives.

SEMOLINA | RAVA

Known all over the United States as the familiar Cream of Wheat, *rava,* or *suji* in Hindi, hardly needs an introduction. *Rava* is made from hard durum wheat, which is also commonly used in making pasta. Modern milling techniques have supplanted the ancient Indian method of dampening grain for some hours before grinding, then sifting the solids twice. In Parsi cooking, *rava* gives its name to one of the two required auspicious-day sweets. Look for it at Indian groceries, where it comes either fine or coarse (buy the fine), or get it off the supermarket shelf. Durum flour, even finer than semolina, isn't part of the Indian kitchen, but it's perfect for making the Giant Cookie (page 263).

SESAME OIL | TIL NU TEL

The seeds may not be used much in Parsi cooking, but the pale gold oil is very popular for cooking and pickle making. This type of sesame oil is not to be confused with the toasted seasoning oil sold at East Asian markets. Sesame oil from South India is sold as gingelly oil. Cold-pressed sesame oil can be found at natural food stores or Indian groceries. Like any oil, it should be bought only where there is quick turnover.

SESAME SEED | TIL

A seed of ancient cultivation, sesame *(Sesamum orientale* or *S. indicum)* is an important part of Indian cuisine—though less so for Parsis, where its use seems limited to
sweets, for instance a chewy candy made with jaggery. I have all three colors on hand,
the black, the brown, and the white, but use them mostly in other cuisines.

SEV

Sev can be either of two things in Parsi cuisine, an ingredient or a finished snack food.
As an ingredient, it is a fine threadlike pasta made from wheat flour and used mostly
for making sweets. The word *sev* also means an extruded seasoned chickpea-flour paste
fried and eaten as a snack.

SILVER LEAF | VARAK

All over India, the ultimately extravagant touch in finishing sweets or festive *pulaos*
and biryanis is to lay sheets of beaten silver on top of them. This is pure silver beaten
to flyaway fineness between leather pads. In India, it's sold in bundles, each leaf separated from the other with tissue. Here, you can buy edible silver and gold leaf from
framers and gilders. When you're working with silver, stay out of any current of air—
a fan, an open window, a heat register—or it will fly out of control. Silver is lovely;
gold is even more festive. You may have to reassure guests unfamiliar with edible silver that it isn't tinfoil and that it won't damage their fillings.

SNAKE GOURD | PARVAL

There are three vegetables known as *parval* or *padval.* Besides the snake gourd *(Trichosanthes cucumerina),* there is a *parval* that looks like a green tomato and a small,
spindle-shaped one. The snake gourd is named for its length and its eccentric habit
of growth. Some specimens look like fantastic
wind instruments. I don't know many Parsis
who cook *parval,* a vegetable regarded as tedious
or unstylish in Bombay, but I love it. For the past few years, we've been getting it
at our local farmers' market, sold by Southeast Asian vendors. The specimens we
see are baggable, not yards long, but their taste is similar. Even when it's young, *parval* is hollow inside. *Parval* is an obliging vegetable that stands up to brief or long
cooking.

SPONGE GOURD | TURIA

This is the gourd, *Luffa cylindrica,* that turns into a loofah in its maturity. While it's
still in its youth, it makes a delectable vegetable with the same properties as its cousin

the ridge gourd (see above)—good texture and an ability to absorb surrounding flavors. Parsi cooks use both types of *turia* interchangeably.

STAR ANISE | BADIAN

The dried seedpods of star anise *(Illicium verum)* figure in Parsi cooking mostly in compound masalas like *dhana jiru* and occasionally get put into the caramelized rice for *dhansak,* although this is a matter of family tradition and preference.

SUGAR | SAKAR, KHAN

One of the distinguishing characteristics of Parsi food is the touch of sweetness in many savory dishes. Sometimes the sweetness comes from aromatic spices like cinnamon or cardamom, at other times from the addition of sugar. Parsi households always have three kinds of sweetener, white sugar, jaggery, and honey, the last used more as a medicine than as a food for pleasure.

SWEET POTATO | RATALU

Of New World origin, the sweet potato *(Ipomoea batatas)* must have become an instant success with sweet-loving Parsis, who take it even further by steeping cooked sweet potatoes in heavy, cardamom-scented syrup. Sweet potatoes in the Wedding Stew (page 205), for instance, can be any type of sweet potato you like, including the orange-fleshed ones mislabeled yams.

TAMARIND | AMLI

Tamarind comes from the seedpod of a leguminous tree *(Tamarindus indica)* native to Africa but has been used so long in India that the Arabs called it "date of India," *tamar-i-hind.* Now found and used in both Old World and New World tropics, tamarind is indispensable to the Parsi kitchen as a souring agent in curries and fresh chutneys. The pulp surrounding the seeds is sold worldwide in compressed blocks or in gunnysacks at Bombay's traditional grocers. Compressed tamarind pulp needs to be soaked and strained before use (see page 42). Markets in the United States often sell whole brittle-shelled tamarind seedpods. The strained pulp of these is paler and fresher-tasting than what you get from darker, riper, compressed block tamarind. I sometimes use it in dressings for green salads.

TARO | ARVI

One of many plants with South and Southeast Asian origins but pantropical distribution, taro *(Colocasia esculenta)* has been used in India for a long time both for its arrow-shaped leaves and for its corms or tubers, which can be the size of marbles or melons. Taro leaves can be found at West Indian or Philippine markets, Indian markets occasionally, or farmers' markets, sold by Philippine and Southeast Asian vendors, who also sell taro stem for slicing and stir-frying. Corms can be found at Chinese, Philippine, and Southeast Asian markets.

TINDOLA OR IVY GOURD

Known more commonly in U.S. markets by its Indian name—tindola or tindora—ivy gourd *(Coccinia grandis)* is one of the most common vegetables at any Bombay stall. Tindolas look like little gherkins, but unlike cucumbers, they must be cooked

through to be enjoyed and for any residual astringency to disappear. They are one of my favorite vegetables, and I will go to any lengths to secure a supply when they are available. Canned and frozen tindola can be found at Indian markets. Ignore the canned ones. In times of tindola deprivation I've bought the frozen variety, but I've decided it's better to wait for the fresh ones.

TURMERIC | ARADH

Wherever it has traveled from its South Asian origins, turmeric *(Curcuma longa)* has become an invaluable plant. It is used as a seasoning, a food color, a dye plant, a cosmetic, and a medicine, with a long list

of healing properties both internal and external. As with many other members of the ginger family, the most useful part of the plant is the rhizome. The fresh rhizome is used in Parsi household medicine and is sometimes turned into a lime- and salt-cured pickle (page 234). Dried rhizomes, whole or ground, are used to give food a yellowish color as well as a flavor. Parsi households often have both forms. Turmeric dries almost rock hard, so pounding it by hand can be quite a venture. While it lasts indefinitely as a color, turmeric kept too long loses its distinct scent. If you don't get a strong smell when you open a jar, you need to get some more.

VEGETABLE OIL | TEL

In the old days, ghee was used as a cooking fat for most Parsi dishes. Then came health consciousness and the increasing use of oil, often hydrogenated to look like ghee. In time, hydrogenated oil was found to be even worse for the health than ghee, and we then started using unhydrogenated oils. Because we seem to want to live in a state of perpetual anxiety about what we eat or cook with, one vegetable oil after another gets put on trial and condemned. My recommendations for Parsi cooking are to use peanut or grapeseed oil for deep-frying; to use sesame, grapeseed, or sunflower oil the rest of the time; and to be unafraid of ghee where its taste makes a difference.

VINEGAR | SARKO

Bombay Parsi households invariably have a bottle of strong cane vinegar for general use in cooking and pickling. In the United States, we can buy cane vinegar from Louisiana, the Philippines, Martinique, and India. In fact, you can now buy the very brand Parsis cherish, Kolah's from Navsari, the stronghold of Parsi religion and traditional culture (see Sources). A good alternative is coconut vinegar from Sri Lanka or the Philippines. I always love the gentle sweetness of Japanese rice vinegar for Parsi food in instances where a darker product would affect the color.

WORCESTERSHIRE SAUCE

Every Parsi pantry I know has a bottle of "Worcester sauce," as we call it in Bombay. It might seem odd, but less so when you learn the nineteenth-century Indian origins of this English seasoning staple. Lea & Perrins, grocers and chemists in the town of Worcester, were asked to make up a recipe brought back from Bengal. It contained tamarind, molasses, soy sauce, anchovies, vinegar, chiles, cloves, and cinnamon, the ingredients for a liquid chutney. Worcester sauce entered Parsi cuisine through the British connection and never left.

YOGURT | DAHI

In many Parsi houses, yogurt is made every day using starter from the previous batch. Following custom, milk is boiled when it comes into the house and the cream that rises to the top gets skimmed off. Family yogurt is therefore usually made from low-fat or nonfat milk, and its texture is thinner than that of commercial yogurt in the United States. Whether whole milk or nonfat, look for yogurt that doesn't have stabilizers and thickeners added. My favorite brands have the slightly sour tang of homemade Bombay yogurt. Yogurt to be used in cooking can be dripped through cheesecloth or a fine sieve to get the excess moisture out of it.

SOURCES

Ingredients

All of the ingredients in this book can be found at supermarkets or specialty groceries in the United States. For a state-by-state directory of Indian groceries: www.thokalath .com. This has proved reliable when checked against known Bay Area resources.

For general Indian supplies (rice, dals, spices, jaggery, etc.), try the following: Sinha Trading, 121 Lexington Avenue, New York, NY 10016. No Web site, but a good, well-stocked shop and courteous mail-order service. Telephone 212-683-4419, fax 212-251-0946. Kalustyan at www.kalustyans.com. (Note that kalustyan.com gets you the parent corporation in New Jersey.) Telephone 800-352-3451. The shop at 123 Lexington Avenue, New York, NY 10016 is well worth a stop for its wide range of products. Namaste at www.namaste.com. 695 Lunt Avenue, Elk Grove Village, IL 60007. Telephone 312-373-1777.

For Parsi spice mixtures like *sambhar masala* and *dhansak masala,* Sydney-based Manny's (Mehernosh Seervai) will ship anywhere in the world: www.mannyspices .com.au. Excellent, prompt customer service by e-mail or telephone, (02) 9808-1403.

For an excellent, well-priced, nicely balanced American cane vinegar, head to www.steensyrup.com in Abbeville, Louisiana. This company also makes a good dark cane syrup. Telephone 800-725-1654. There is a small retail outlet at 119 Main Street, Abbeville, LA 70510.

For high-quality spices: www.penzeys.com of Brookfield, Illinois, with retail stores in the Midwest and on the East Coast. Telephone 800-741-7781.

For a wide range of coconut products and paraphernalia, try Wilderness Family Naturals in Minnesota: www.wildernessfamilynaturals.com. Telephone 866-936-6457.

For superlative Indo-Persian ice creams, delicate rose water, and excellent saffron from Iran, Mashti Malone's in Los Angeles, which will ship nationwide: www.mashti malone.com. For the nearest retailer, call 866-767-3423 (866-ROSEICE).

Rose syrup can be ordered from Purely Organic, which offers a delicate, hand-crafted Italian product: www.purelyorganic.com. Telephone 877-201-0710. A beautiful French rose syrup is made by Monin: www.monin.com. The Web site leads you to a distributor in your area. These are the two best rose syrups I've been able to find so far.

For edible silver and gold leaf, www.goldleafcompany.com. Telephone 718-815-8802.

For curry leaf plants, try Bhatia Nurseries, www.bhatia-nurseries.com, telephone 212-221-7040; Alan's Tropical Fruit Trees, www.troptrees.com, telephone 727-686-3110; or the California Tropical Fruit Tree Nursery, www.tropicalfruittrees.com, telephone 760-434-5085.

Look for fresh curry leaves and other things such as various greens and gourds at Indian, Chinese, and Southeast Asian markets, and at local farmers' markets. Buy mangoes, green or ripe, from Latin American markets or from places where Indians shop. Indians have an unfailing nose for excellent mangoes, and where you find good ripe ones, you're also likely to find the right sort of hard green ones for making chutney.

Mail order is wonderful if there's no alternative, but nothing beats the glee of rummaging around in person. For a national directory of farmers' markets: www.ams.usda .gov/farmersmarkets/ and www.fruitstands.com. Seeds for many Indian vegetables can be found at www.seedsofindia.com.

Equipment

Sumeet Asia Grinder or Multigrinder: www.sumeet.net. Telephone 800-268-1530 to speak to Arti or Mihir Premji. They will look after you and your machine forever. Similar machines can be found at Dual Electronics, www.appliances.safeshopper.com, telephone 713-784-3825, or Chennai Imports, www.chennaiimports.com, telephone 647-438-7677.

Other kitchen equipment, such as coconut grating stools, rotary coconut graters, and inexpensive, heavy-duty stone mortars and pestles can be hunted down at Indian and Southeast Asian markets and on the Internet.

FURTHER READING

This is a cookbook. It follows that my compressed account of the rise and fall of three Persian empires, the history of Parsis in India, and the intertwined growth of Bombay and the Parsi community must be laughably superficial. Readers interested in Zoroastrianism and Parsis are urged to explore the references listed below and to browse the Internet, which offers perspectives ranging from scholarly detachment to an ardent zealotry easily spotted by its quarrelsome tone and the universal rhetoric of religious fundamentalism. The following four Web sites are a mere starting point: www.avesta.org, www.zoroastrianism.com, www.parsicommunity.com, and www.TheParsi Chronicle.com for a vivid glimpse into contemporary concerns. Columbia University's www.iranica.com is an encyclopedic resource for questions on Iranian history and culture, topics you can also pursue at sasanika.com and iranian.com, both of which have links to many other sites. UNESCO's Parsi Zoroastrian Project seeks to salvage what remains of Parsi material and expressive culture. Its Web site, www.unescoparzor.com, has an interesting image gallery. Sue Darlow's sympathetic and evocative photographs of contemporary Parsi life can be seen at www.anothersubcontinent.com/contemporaryparsis.html. For an affectionate, nostalgic first-person account of vanishing Parsi household customs, especially as they relate to food, Bhicoo Manekshaw's *Parsi Food and Customs,* listed below, remains unequaled. Contemporary Parsi fiction offers rich ethnographic detail in the work of Boman Desai, Farrokh Dhondy, Firdaus Kanga, Rohinton Mistry, Bapsy Sidhwa, Thrity Umrigar, and Ardeshir Vakil, among others.

Persia, Parsis, and Bombay

Boyce, Mary. *Zoroastrians, Their Religious Beliefs and Practices.* London: Routledge & Kegan Paul, 1979, repr. 2001.

Conlon, Frank F. "Dining Out in Bombay," in *Consuming Modernity: Public,* Carol A. Breckenridge, ed., pp. 90–127. Minneapolis: University of Minnesota Press, 1995.

Curtis, John E., and Nigel Tallis, eds. *Forgotten Empire: The World of Ancient Persia.* Berkeley: University of California Press, 2005.

Daryaee, Touraj. "The Cheese and the Lizards: Zoroastrian Cuisine and Propaganda in Late Antiquity." *Society for the Study of Zoroastrianism* 2 (forthcoming, 2007).

Davies, Philip. *The Splendours of the Raj: British Architecture in India, 1660–1947.* London: Penguin, 1987.

Dhalla, Maneckji Nusservanji. *Zoroastrian Civilization.* New York: Oxford University Press, 1922.

Dwivedi, Sharada, and Rahul Mehrotra. *Bombay: The Cities Within.* Bombay: India Book House, 1995.

Godrej, Pheroza J., and Firoza Punthakey Mistree, eds. *A Zoroastrian Tapestry: Art, Religion & Culture.* Ahmedabad: Mapin Publishing, 2002.

Herodotus. *The Histories.* Translated by Aubrey de Sélincourt. London: Penguin, 1972.

Hinnells, John. *Zoroastrian and Parsi Studies: Selected Works of John R. Hinnells.* Williston, Vt.: Ashgate Publishing, 2000.

Johnson, Paul. *Fish Forever.* New York: Wiley, forthcoming.

Kamerkar, Mani, and Soonu Dhunjisha. *From the Iranian Plateau to the Shores of Gujarat: The Story of Parsi Settlements and Absorption in India.* Mumbai: Allied Publishers, 2002.

Kanga, Kavasji Edalji. *Extracts from the Narrative of Mons. Anquetil du Perron's Travels in India.* Bombay: Commercial Press, 1876.

Karaka, Dosabhai Framji. *History of the Parsis.* London: Macmillan, 1884.

Kulke, Eckehard. *The Parsees in India.* Delhi: Vikas, 1974.

Luhrmann, T. M. *The Good Parsi: The Fate of a Colonial Elite in a Postcolonial Society.* Delhi: Oxford University Press, 1996.

Malabari, Phiroze B. M. *Bombay in the Making.* London: T. Fisher Unwin, 1910.

Mehta, Suketu. *Maximum City: Bombay Lost and Found.* New York: Alfred A. Knopf, 2004.

Menant, Delphine. *Les Parsis.* Translated by Ratanbai Ardeshir Vakil. London: privately printed, 1902.

Modi, Jamshedji Jivanji. *The Religious Ceremonies and Customs of the Parsees.* Bombay: British India Press, 1922.

Mody, Nawaz, ed. *The Parsis in Western India: 1818 to 1920.* Bombay: Allied Publishers, 1998.

Mookerji, Radha Kumud. *Indian Shipping: A History of the Sea-Borne Trade and Maritime Activity of the Indians from the Earliest Times.* New Delhi: Munshiram Manoharlal, 1912, repr. 1999.

Motafram, Ervad Ratanshah R. *History of Ancient Iran.* Bombay: Society for the Promotion of Zoroastrian Religious Knowledge and Education, 1993.

Moulton, James H. *The Treasure of the Magi: A Study of Modern Zoroastrianism.* Oxford: Oxford University Press, 1917.

Palsetia, Jesse. *Parsis of India: Preservation of Identity in Bombay City.* Leiden: Brill, 2001.

Patel, Sujata, and Alice Thorner, eds. *Bombay: Mosaic of Modern Culture.* New Delhi: Oxford University Press, 1995.

Randeria, Jer. *Parsi Mind.* Delhi: Munshiram Manoharlal, 1993.

Schafer, Edward. *The Golden Peaches of Samarkand: A Study of T'ang Exotics.* Berkeley: University of California Press, 1963.

Taraporevala, Sooni. *Parsis: The Zoroastrians of India. A Photographic Journey 1980–2004.* New York: Penguin, 2004.

Tindall, Gillian. *City of Gold: The Biography of Bombay.* London: Penguin, 1982, repr. 1992.

Unvala, Jamshedji Maneckji. *The Pahlavi Text "King Husrav and His Boy."* Paris: Paul Geuthner, 1921.

Zubaida, Sami, and Richard Tapper, eds. *A Taste of Thyme: Culinary Cultures of the Middle East.* London: Tauris Parke, 1994, repr. 2000.

Food, Food Plants, and Food History

Achaya, K. T. *A Historical Dictionary of Indian Food.* New Delhi: Oxford University Press, 1998.

———. *Indian Food: A Historical Companion.* New Delhi: Oxford University Press, 1994.

Andrews, Jean. *Peppers: The Domesticated Capsicums.* Austin: University of Texas Press, 1984.

Billing, Jennifer, and Paul W. Sherman. "Antimicrobial Functions of Spices: Why Some Like It Hot." *Quarterly Review of Biology* 73 (1998): 3–49.

Burkill, I. H. *A Dictionary of the Economic Products of the Malay Peninsula,* 2 vols. Kuala Lumpur: Ministry of Agriculture and Co-operatives, 1966.

Collingham, Lizzie. *Curry: A Tale of Cooks and Conquerors.* Oxford: Oxford University Press, 2006.

Dalby, Andrew. *Dangerous Tastes: The Story of Spices*. Berkeley: University of California Press, 2000.

Daryaee, Touraj. "What Fruits and Nuts to Eat in Ancient Persia?" www.iranian.com/Daryaee/2005/November/wine (accessed December 8, 2005).

———. "Wine Good and Fine: The Art of Wine in Ancient Persia." www.iranian.com/Daryaee/2005/November/wine (accessed December 8, 2005).

Davidson, Alan. *The Oxford Companion to Food*. Oxford: Oxford University Press, 1999.

Drury, Colonel Heber. *The Useful Plants of India: With Notices of Their Chief Value in Commerce, Medicine and the Arts*. Madras: Higginbotham, 1873.

Flandrin, Jean-Louis, and Massimo Montanari. *Food: A Culinary History from Antiquity to the Present*. New York: Penguin, 2000.

Gopalan, C., B. V. Ramastri, and S. C. Balasubramanian. *Nutritive Value of Indian Foods*. Hyderabad: National Institute of Nutrition, Indian Council of Medical Research, 1981.

Herklots, G. A. C. *Vegetables in South-East Asia*. London: George Allen & Unwin, 1972.

Keay, John. *The Spice Route: A History*. Berkeley: University of California Press, 2006.

Kiple, Kenneth, and Kriemhild Coneè Ornelas, eds. *The Cambridge World History of Food*. Cambridge: Cambridge University Press, 2000.

Laufer, Bertold. *Sino-Iranica: Chinese Contributions to the History of Civilization in Ancient Iran*. Chicago: Field Museum of Natural History, 1919. Repr. Taipei: Ch'eng Wen Publishing, 1978.

Martin, Franklin W., Ruth M. Ruberté, and Laura S. Meitzner. *Edible Leaves of the Tropics*. North Fort Myers, Fla.: ECHO, 1998.

McGovern, Patrick E. *Ancient Wine: The Search for the Origins of Viniculture*. Princeton, N.J., and Oxford: Princeton University Press, 2003.

Nadkarni, K. M. *Indian Materia Medica*. Bombay: Popular Prakashan, 1976.

Parry, John W. *Spices*. 2 vols. New York: Chemical Publishing Company, 1969.

Pruthi, J. S. *Spices*. New Delhi: National Book Trust, India, 1976.

Purseglove, J. W. *Tropical Crops: Dicotyledons*. Harlow, Essex: Longman, 1981.

———. *Tropical Crops: Monocotyledons*. Harlow, Essex: Longman, 1981.

Purseglove, J. W., et al. *Spices*. Tropical Agriculture Series. London: Longman, 1981.

Rosengarten, F. *The Book of Spices*. Wynnewood: Livingston Publishing, 1969.

Siemonsma, J. M., and Kasem Piluek, eds. *Vegetables: Plant Resources of South-East Asia*. Bogor, Indonesia: PROSEA, 1994.

Staples, George, and Derral Herbst. *A Tropical Garden Flora: Plants Cultivated in the Hawaiian Islands and Other Tropical Places.* Honolulu: Bishop Museum Press, 2005.

Thompson, Sylvia Vaughan. *Economy Gastronomy.* New York, Atheneum, 1963.

Tindall, H. D. *Vegetables in the Tropics.* Basingstoke, Hants.: Macmillan, 1993.

Turner, Jack. *Spice: The History of a Temptation.* New York: Alfred A. Knopf, 2004.

Uphof, J. C. T. *Dictionary of Economic Plants.* 2nd ed. Wurzburg: J. Cramer, 1968.

Van Wyk, Ben-Erik. *Food Plants of the World: An Illustrated Guide.* Portland, Ore.: Timber Press, 2005.

———. *Medicinal Plants of the World: An Illustrated Scientific Guide to Important Medicinal Plants and Their Uses.* Portland, Ore.: Timber Press, 2004.

Vaughan, J. G., and C. Geissler. *The New Oxford Book of Food Plants.* Oxford: Oxford University Press, 1997.

Watt, Sir George. *A Dictionary of the Economic Products of India*, 10 vols., 1893. Repr. Delhi: Periodical Experts, 1972.

Cookbooks

Albless, Sheroo. *My Favourite Recipes.* Pondicherry: Sri Aurobindo Ashram Press, 1956.

Arberry, A. J., ed. *Royal Dishes of Baghdad: 157 Selected Recipes of High Nutritional Value and Delight.* New Delhi: Global Vision, 2003.

Batmanglij, Najmieh Khalili. *New Food of Life: Ancient Persian and Modern Iranian Cooking and Ceremonies.* Washington, D.C.: Mage, 1994.

Bhaisa, Sylla J. *Party Recipes: Over 350 Recipes for Special Occasions.* Bombay: Jaico Publishing, 1978.

Dalal, Katy. *Jamva Chaloji: Parsi Delicacies for All Occasions.* Mumbai: Vakils, Feffer and Simons, 1998.

Dubash, Dinbai Pestonjee. *Svadisht Vani Sangraha: Part 2.* Bombay: Shri Art Printers, 1315 (1915).

———. *Svadisht Vani Sangraha: Part 6.* Bombay: Suresh Printery, 1948.

Gray, Rose, and Ruth Rogers. *The Café Cook Book: Italian Recipes from London's River Café.* New York: Broadway Books, 1998.

Hambro, Nathalie. *Particular Delights.* London: Jill Norman & Hobhouse, 1981.

Hekmat, Forough. *The Art of Persian Cooking.* New York: Doubleday, 1961.

Hopkinson, Simon. *Roast Chicken and Other Stories: A Recipe Book.* London: Ebury Press, 1996.

Manekshaw, Bhicoo J. *Parsi Food and Customs.* New Delhi: Penguin, 1996.

————. *Regional Recipes of India.* Bombay: Nachiketa Publications, 1974.

Mathilde, Da. *325 Recettes de Cuisine Créole.* Paris: Jacques Grancher, 1975.

Mehta, Jeroo. *101 Parsi Recipes.* Bombay: Jeroo Mehta, 1979.

————. *Enjoyable Parsi Recipes.* Bombay: Vakils, Feffer and Simons, 1992.

Nariman, Bapsi. *A Gourmet's Handbook of Parsi Cuisine.* Bombay: Tarang, 1987.

Nasrallah, Nawal. *Delights from the Garden of Eden: A Cookbook and a History of the Iraqi Cuisine.* Bloomington, Ind.: Authorhouse, 2003.

Shaida, Margaret. *The Legendary Cuisine of Persia.* New York: Interlink Books, 2002.

Sinnes, A. Cort, and Jay Harlow. *The Grilling Book: The Techniques, Tools, and Tastes of the New American Grill.* Berkeley, Calif.: Aris Books, 1985.

Thompson, Sylvia Vaughan. *Economy Gastronomy.* New York: Atheneum, 1963.

Time and Talents Club, ed. *Recipes.* Bombay: Time and Talents Club, 1959.

————. *Recipes.* Bombay: Time and Talents Club, 1975.

Vahadia, Meherbai Jamshedji Nasserwanji. *Vividh Vani: Part 1.* Bombay: Jam-e-Jamshed Printing Works, 1915.

————. *Vividh Vani: Part 2.* Bombay: Jam-e-Jamshed Printing Works, 1915.

Vicaji, Gulbai Bapuji, and Freny Kaikushroo Sanga. *Manpasand Mishtaan: Part 5. Svadisht ane decorated vaniyo nu pusthak.* Bombay: Solan Printing Press, 1958.

Waters, Alice, with Fritz Streiff and Alan Tangren. *Chez Panisse Fruit.* New York: HarperCollins, 2002.

Waters, Alice, with David Tanis and Fritz Streiff. *Chez Panisse Café Cookbook.* New York: HarperCollins, 1999.

Yasmin. *Favourite Parsi Recipes.* Bombay: Yasmin Sibal, 1975.

INDEX

A

Abelmoschus esculentus, 305.
    See also okra
adu. See ginger
adu lasan (ginger-garlic paste),
    36, 112, 300
adu nu raitu, 226–27
ajmo. See ajwain
ajmo na patra. See Cuban
    oregano
ajowan. See *ajwain*
ajwain, 289
    butter, for corn on the cob, 51
    roasted cashews with, 50–51
"ajwain" leaf. See Cuban oregano
akuri, 85–86
    pattis stuffed with, 123
Albless, Sehra, 64
aleti paleti, 151–52
Allium cepa, 305. *See also*
    onion(s)
allium confit, 186–87
    eggs on onions, 90
Allium sativum, 299. *See also*
    garlic
almonds, 289–90
    almond gravy, chicken in, 140
    cheese and almond crisps,
      51–52
    crisp almond wafers
      (variation), 260–61
    giant cookie, 263
    one hundred almond curry,
      142–44
am haldi, 304
am ras, 243–44
amaranth, 192–93, 290
    amaranth leaf fritters, 57

braised greens, 191–92
    meat cooked with greens,
      114–15
    potage of lentils and
      vegetables *(dhansak),* 162,
      178–80
Amaranthus. See amaranth
amba aradh. See mango ginger
amli. See tamarind
Amomum subulatum, 292
Amorphophallus campanulatus,
    205, 298
Anacardium occidentale, 292.
    See also cashews
Andrew's Goa curry, 106–8
Anethum graveolens, 297. *See also*
    dill
angel-hair potatoes, 200–201
anticuchos, Parsi, 160
appalams. See papads
appetizers. *See* beginnings
apples
    fruit chutney, 232
apricot kernels, 141, 301
apricots *(jardalu),* 141, 249, 301
    chicken with, 141–42
    jardalu fool, 250
    jardalu ice cream, 251
    jardalu shake, 251
    Mother's famous *jardalu* trifle,
      251–52
    Parsi wedding pickle, 237–39
    poached *jardalu*s, 250
aradh. See turmeric
aradh nu achar, 234–35
argan oil, 213
Argania spinosa, 213
arhar dal. See pigeon peas

arvi. See taro
asafetida, 37, 290
Asian pears
    fruit chutney, 232
Asian squash. *See* gourds
aspic, tomato, 76
avocado, pomelo salad with, 220

B

badam. See almonds
badian (star anise), 312
bafela chaval, 162–64
baffat, 129–31
Bana, Dhun, 63
banana leaves, 100–101, 102
    fish in banana-leaf parcels,
      100–102
bananas, 204. *See also* plantains
    banana raita, 225
    papri claypot stew, 208–9
basic equipment, 30, 33
    sources, 316
basic ingredients, 34–48
    glossary, 289–314
    sources, 315–16
basic techniques, 32–33
basil seeds, 278, 290
    New Year's milk shake,
      278–79
basmati rice, 162, 163, 308.
    See also rice
bay leaves, 292
bean greens
    quick-cooked greens, 192–93
beans. *See also* long beans; mung
    beans
    field or hyacinth beans, 208,
      299; *papri* claypot

TEXT: 11/14.75 Adobe Garamond
DISPLAY: Deepdene and Adobe Garamond
DESIGNER: Nola Burger
COMPOSITOR: Integrated Composition Systems
ILLUSTRATOR: David Shaw King
INDEXER: Thérèse Shere
PRINTER AND BINDER: STI Certified, Fremont CA